MENTORING AND SUPERVISION FOR TEACHER DEVELOPMENT

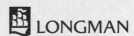

Alan J. Reiman

North Carolina State University

Lois Thies-Sprinthall

North Carolina State University

LONGMAN

An imprint of Addison Wesley Longman, Inc.

New York • Reading, Massachusetts • Menlo Park, California • Harlow, England
Don Mills, Ontario • Sydney • Mexico City • Madrid • Amsterdam

Acquisitions Editor: Virginia L. Blanford
Sponsoring Editor: Art Pompinio
Associate Editor: Arianne J. Weber
Project Coordination and Text Design: Ruttle, Shaw & Wetherill, Inc.
Cover Design: Chris Hiebert
Electronic Production Manager: Christine Pearson
Manufacturing Manager: Willie Lane
Electronic Page Makeup: Ruttle, Shaw & Wetherill, Inc.
Printer and Binder: Maple-Vail Book Manufacturing Group
Cover Printer: Coral Graphic Services, Inc.

For permission to use copyrighted material, grateful acknowledgment is made to the copyright holders on p. 370, which is hereby made part of this copyright page.

Library of Congress Cataloging-in-Publication Data
Reiman, Alan.
    Mentoring and supervision for teacher development / Alan J. Reiman,
  Lois Thies-Sprinthall.
      p.   cm.
  Includes bibliographical references and index.
  ISBN 0-8013-1539-5
    1. Teachers—Training of.   2. Mentoring in education.
  3. Teachers—In-service training.   4. Student teachers—Supervision
  of.   I. Thies-Sprinthall, Lois.   II. Title.
LB1707.R45   1997
370'.711—DC21   97-21568
                                                 CIP

ISBN 0-8013-1539-5

12345678910—MA—00999897

BRIEF
C·O·N·T·E·N·T·S

PART IV

CURRENT ISSUES AND FUTURE TRENDS 311

DETAILED C·O·N·T·E·N·T·S

CHAPTER 2

PART II
THREE DIMENSIONS OF TEACHER DEVELOPMENT 37

CHAPTER 3

CHAPTER 4

PROMOTING DEVELOPMENT: *A Framework for Action*   66

CHAPTER 5

CONCERNS AND CAREER PHASES: *Dimensions of Teacher Change*   83

PART III
DEVELOPMENTAL SUPERVISION AND COACHING FOR TEACHER DEVELOPMENT   107

CHAPTER 6

THE PERSONAL DOMAIN   109

CHAPTER 7

THE INTERPERSONAL DIMENSION   126

CHAPTER 8

IDENTIFYING MODELS AND METHODS OF INSTRUCTION 144

CHAPTER 9

PROMOTING GROWTH THROUGH CYCLES OF ASSISTANCE 176

CHAPTER 10

DATA COLLECTION 195

CHAPTER 11

SUPERVISION AND POST-CONFERENCES 218

CHAPTER 12

SUPERVISION AND THE COACHING PROCESS 240

CHAPTER 13

GUIDED REFLECTION: *An Emerging Construct* 262

CHAPTER 16

TEACHER DEVELOPMENT RESEARCH ISSUES AND METHODS   333

CHAPTER 17

TEACHER DEVELOPMENT AND REVITALIZATION ACROSS THE CAREER SPAN   348

SPECIAL F·E·A·T·U·R·E·S

BIOGRAPHIES

CONTEMPORARY ISSUES

SPOTLIGHT ON EDUCATIONAL LEADERS

P·R·E·F·A·C·E

Mentoring and Supervision for Teacher Development is a text that synthesizes the fields of instructional supervision, adult development, teacher education and mentoring, and ongoing professional development. As such, it forges links between preservice teacher education, induction and mentoring, and school-based supervision. You will find a hopeful and empowering *teaching/learning framework* for educators who wish to engage colleagues in active, sustained, reflective, and progressively collaborative learning, teaching, and growth experiences.

This book supplements the emerging developmental supervision and coaching literature. Our goal is to identify emerging trends across a number of educational disciplines. Thus, the arenas of teaching and educational leadership are spanned in the text with particular attention given to teaching. Practical examples and case studies are drawn from our extensive work with urban, suburban, and rural school systems in North Carolina as well as a number of state, national, and international public school/university consortia. The text also links preservice education, induction literature, and ongoing professional development (inservice education). We incorporate examples and research on school renewal, supervision, professional development schools, laboratory and field experiences, adult development, peer coaching and staff development, as well as our experiences as teachers, administrators, staff developers, teacher educators, and professors of supervision. Further we have drawn insights from teachers, counselors, principals, directors of staff development, mentors, and clinical educators as we have field-tested the principles and practices described in the text.

The term *supervision*, as used in this book, refers to a school-based or school- and college-based activity that improves instruction through guided assistance and discourse between educators. The audience for this book includes all educators who are engaged in supervision, mentoring, or collaborative inquiry from preschool through college. The book is intended for graduate students in educational supervision or teacher education. Instructors of courses such as "Instructional Supervision," "Supervision in Teacher Education," "Introduction to Supervision and Coaching," and "Supervision and Mentoring of the Novice Teacher," will find this book valuable. The text also could be used by practicing teacher educators, clinical educators, and staff developers who are planning and implementing clinical education, mentoring, supervision, peer coaching programs, or professional development schools. Some of the more traditional content found in supervision textbooks has been compressed in order for us to comprehensively cover supervision, coaching, and mentoring as they relate to the teacher and to adult development.

Although supervision has traditionally been caught in the apparent dilemma of evaluation versus support and assistance, our experiences with literally thousands of teachers and principals indicate that teacher development and supervision for evaluation can be joined. However, we believe that the major emphasis of supervision for development must be given to support. Because our overall goal is promoting the learning and development of all persons to their fullest potential so they may be active participants in a democratic society, we believe the cornerstone of effective supervision is caring and thoughtful assistance for and between educators as developing adults. The raison d'être of mentoring for teacher development is "progressively collaborative teaching" (Tomlinson, 1996)* that is principled, flexible, student-centered, and empathic.

At the end of each chapter, you will find a section entitled Supervision for Teacher Development Activities. Typically there are three sections: Applied, Portfolio Development, and Suggested Readings. The Applied activities may be used as in-class activities with graduate students or as outside class assignments. The Portfolio Development activities are designed to be completed in sequence. The goal is for the graduate student, prospective mentor or coach, or prospective teacher educator to build a performance-based portfolio that demonstrates supervisory competencies.

The *Instructor's Manual* includes instructional aids for in-class discussion and practice, test items that could be introduced to graduate students as out-of-class activities and self-evaluations, and a sampler of transparency masters. The activities at the end of each chapter forge new ground by providing theory and research-based activities that promote learning of supervisory skills and growth and development. For example, coaching principles are built into many of the activities, allowing for introduction of theory and rationales, demonstrations, and practice activities. Further, there are numerous activities that promote deeper reflection on the part of the graduate student. The exercises are numerous. We encourage you as the instructor to make choices based on your expertise and experience and to join us in our vision to promote a democratic ideal. We also strongly recommend that you dialogue in writing with students' journals based on the format introduced in Chapter 13. When we provide optimum environments for developing students and teachers to their fullest potential, the American dream of free people in a free country is realized.

---

*Tomlinson, P. (1996). *Understanding mentoring*. Buckingham: Open University Press.

ACKNOWLEDGEMENTS

There is an African proverb which states that it takes a whole village to raise a child. It also takes the community to support teacher development across the career span. Certainly that has been the case as we have developed this text while teaching classes to prospective mentors. In fact, it is impossible to acknowledge all the professionals who contributed to the development of this book. Many public and private school clinical mentor teachers, staff developers, principals, clinical instructors, school-based teacher educators, university teacher education faculty, and counselors from North Carolina and Minnesota have helped us refine the ideas in this book through their work in classrooms.

We are most appreciative of the unique work and contributions of mentor educators who have implemented the ideas presented in this book as these teacher leaders have prepared ever-expanding cadres of clinical mentor teachers for their respective school systems. Thank you for making theory visible in practice and practice visible in theory, and for modeling effective instruction, caring and empathy, and support and challenge as you participated in "real" school reculturing.

The folks at Addison Wesley Longman have been most helpful. Ginny Blanford guided us in the early stages of writing and Arianne Weber provided valuable support in the later stages of writing. And we are most fortunate to have had Janet Nuciforo's editorial expertise "down the stretch." Closer to home we need to recognize both the professional and moral support and challenge of our spouses. Norman Sprinthall has provided invaluable assistance to us and is responsible for numerous clarifications of how cognitive developmental theory connects to supervision and mentoring. His scholarship in adolescent and adult development offers continuous insight. And Evelyn Reiman, an experienced university administrator, continues to extend our thinking on how the college experience encourages "growth" opportunities.

We would also like to thank the following reviewers who provided us with helpful suggestions for improvement, enabling us to write a better book:

Janet Elaine Alleman, Michigan State University

Daisy E. Arredondo, West Virginia University

Gary Breegle, David Lipscomb University

R. Mason Bunker, University of Massachusetts, Amherst

Vivienne Collinson, University of Maryland, College Park

Joe L. Cornelius, Tennessee State University, Nashville

John C. Daresh, Illinois State University

Patricia E. Holland, University of Houston

Helen M. Marks, Ohio State University

Sharon Oja, University of New Hampshire
Jerry L. Pulley, University of Texas, Pan American
L. Nan Restine, Oklahoma State University
Martin W. Schoppmeyer, University of Arkansas
Marilyn Tallerico, Syracuse University

Alan J. Reiman
Lois Thies-Sprinthall

P·A·R·T
I

INTRODUCTION
AND HISTORY

. . . . . .

*I*n Part I we introduce you to supervision, in particular, developmental supervision and mentoring, and its origins. Further, the need for a guiding theoretical framework is recommended. Otherwise, practice wanders between fads without recognizing which interventions truly make a difference.

In Chapter 1 we discuss who is responsible for supervision and mentoring, and review some of the issues associated with various definitions of supervision. The challenge of identifying a guiding theory is explored and recommendations are made vis-à-vis the "Goldilocks Principle." Chapter 2 shifts to the historical origins of clinical supervision at Harvard University, and then reviews supporting research on the content of supervision and the effectiveness of supervisory techniques.

C·H·A·P·T·E·R
1

Supervision: An Overview

• • • • • •

 INTRODUCTION

The purpose of developmental supervision and mentoring, like that of teacher education and other professional development experiences, should be to promote the learning and growth of teachers as persons and as professionals. Teachers who are *learning* are becoming more adept in a broad range of instructional strategies including building positive relationships with students and parents, assessment, lesson planning, classroom management and discipline, and instructional presentation and evaluation. Teachers who are *growing* are becoming more tolerant of ambiguity; more humane in their interactions with students, parents, and professional colleagues; more principled when facing ethical dilemmas; and more capable and flexible in their capacity to solve complex human-helping problems. Because our overall goal is promoting the learning and development of all persons to their fullest potential so they may be active participants in a democratic society, we believe the cornerstone of effective supervision is caring and *progressively collaborative teaching* between educators as developing adults.

In this book we describe instructional supervision research, theories of the adult learner, and coaching, supervising, and mentoring skills that can facilitate learning and development. Further, we give significant attention to the developing novice teacher in preservice teacher education and the beginning teacher in the initial two years of teaching (induction phase). This book is intended for graduate students in educational supervision or teacher education. However, the text also could be used by practicing teacher educators, supervisors, mentors, and staff developers who are planning and implementing clinical education, mentoring programs, instructional supervision and/or peer coaching programs, or professional development schools.

WHO IS RESPONSIBLE FOR SUPERVISING AND MENTORING?

During the last 15 years it has been our experience that a variety of persons may be involved in improving classroom and school instruction and could be referred to as supervisors or peer coaches. Among them are school principals, assistant principals, instructional specialists, mentor teachers, instructional lead teachers, teacher study groups, counselors, clinical teachers, college faculty, program directors, college/school collaborative inquiry teams, and central office personnel. When any of these persons commit time to developing knowledge and a repertoire of applied skills in developmental instructional supervision and coaching, we would call them supervisors or peer coaches.

Thus, the term *supervisor* connotes the process of instructional supervision and coaching, rather than one's title. And as some of our colleagues have submitted, "behind every successful school is an effective supervision program" (Glickman, Gordon, & Ross-Gordon, 1995, p. 7). This book, then, provides an overview of knowledge and theory, interpersonal skills, and applied skills that are employed by persons with supervisory or coaching responsibilities.

However, the role of assistance rather than assessment is emphasized, although both processes are described and both play a role in the teaching profession. The type of supervision described in this text can best be summarized as a process of direct, differentiated, and sustained assistance. In fact, developmental supervision, as we characterize the process, extensively draws from such educational superstars as John Dewey, who emphasized that teacher learning and growth do not magically and spontaneously unfold. Instead, they depend on appropriate interaction between the teacher and his or her colleagues. His ideas have had a great influence on the evolution of supervision (Glanz, 1992). In Dewey's mind, we all are responsible for supervision.

WHAT IS CLINICAL INSTRUCTIONAL SUPERVISION?

Morris Cogan, who originated clinical supervision as a discipline in the 1950s, emphasized that instructional supervision, to be successful, must not be delivered through scattershot methods that are not framed by theory and that amount to little more than "sporadic visits" followed by general comments. In fact, he believed that casual supervision did more harm than good,

Educational leaders give time and commitment to developing and applying mentoring or supervisory skills.

which is why he stated that, "Teachers are better left alone than merely tampered with" (Cogan, 1973). For Cogan, supervision plays a major role in the health of a school and in the growth of teachers. His research and the system he developed, called clinical supervision, acknowledged that, too often, supervision is employed halfheartedly. Supervision must operate within the school and depends on direct observation. Its objective is to encourage genuine collaboration in which there is no superior-subordinate relationship, no assumption of the supervisor "teaching the teacher."

Before Cogan, we might have concluded that the pedagogical requirements for supervision were simple rather than complex and involved little time or thought. Cogan, however, changed all that. His efforts also began to account for a most important yet neglected part of the supervision equation, namely, teaching from the protégé's point of view, by reminding us that :

> Clinical supervision is conceptualized insofar as possible from within the teacher's viewpoint. That is, it is principally shaped to be congruent with the teacher's universe, with his internal landscape, rather than with that of the supervisor (Cogan, preface, 1973).

Thus supervision, like other forms of human interaction, only seems easy. In fact, as we shall point out in this text, developmental supervision is another form of teaching and is one of the most complex activities a person can undertake. As we progress through the text we hope to peel away some of the layers of this complexity. This chapter takes a first step. You will be introduced to some of the broader issues related to supervision, mentoring, and teacher growth and development.

Perhaps the only certainty is that supervision and mentoring will become more complex in the upcoming years. Our society has begun to acknowledge the importance of educating all its citizenry. Yet attaining that vision requires increased dialogue at all levels in society. Recent national trends such as the increase in single-parent families, a renewed call for early education, a shift toward critical thinking skills, the adoption of new learning technologies, growing violence in schools and communities, the increased disparity between social classes, and continued efforts to mainstream students (Goodlad, 1990) will bring more pressures to the educational system. Further, there has been a broadening definition of the role of supervisor. Increasingly, teachers are assuming supervisory and mentoring roles with student teachers, beginning teachers, and even experienced teachers (Houston, 1990). Professional development is a lifelong enterprise and each phase in a teacher's career brings its own unique challenges and rewards. Faced with these complexities, supervision will need to prepare skilled teachers who can think critically about these complex societal and educational issues. A democracy needs teachers who can prepare students to participate thoughtfully and compassionately at local and national levels (Dewey, 1974). Developmental supervision can promote this vision. Yet a third of our children are undereducated (Kozol, 1992). We cannot afford to let such trends continue.

As we review the broader issues of developmental supervision you may want to answer the following questions:

- How is C. P. Snow's metaphor of two cultures related to supervision?
- Can formative and summative supervision coexist?
- Who participates in developmental instructional supervision?

 ## THE PROBLEM OF DEFINITION

How two educators work together to improve interactions one educator has with children, parents, and/or colleagues is at the heart of supervision. Only in the last 20 years, however, has research been more systematically conducted on how supervision with educators increases student learning, novice educator learning, and/or school climate. To further complicate matters, the field of supervision is an emergent one that draws on an immense growing knowledge base on how humans learn (Furth & Pajak, 1997). This knowledge base includes research in psychology, sociology, education, and philosophy. Very recently, the discipline has recognized that teachers must play a more central role in supervision (Glickman, Gordon, & Ross-Gordon, 1995; Sergiovanni, 1990), and researchers have begun to investigate how teacher supervision occurs across the series of career phases: (1) preservice, before full-time teaching; (2) induction, the first year to three years of teaching; and (3) inservice, the career teacher (Burden, 1990; Fessler & Christensen, 1992). And supervision includes a variety of educators: teachers at various grade levels and instructing different subjects, principals, central office personnel, and college faculty.

Perhaps it is no surprise then that the discipline of supervision has struggled with an identity problem as it has worked to integrate knowledge from the larger fields of psychology, education, sociology, and philosophy. Sometimes the struggle has felt like pushing a rope. On one hand the psychologists and sociologists are pressing for discovery of basic laws of human behavior through experimental and phenomenological inquiry. Progress is slow, and at best, the development of basic theory proceeds more at the speed of a glacier than that of a late afternoon summer shower. There are no quick returns. These traditions of science are married to the view that without basic theory, practice wanders aimlessly.

On the other hand is the profession of education. Like law and business, educators concern themselves with practice. To those in the education profession, theory seems like "another case of excessive navel contemplation." Clearly such conclusions are to be expected. After all, the teacher, counselor, and school principal cannot quietly withdraw from the daily demands of their work to ponder the latest psychological theory or research finding. Parents would be pretty unhappy if they heard some teacher saying, "We will be postponing classes for the next three weeks while I learn about new research findings on how to effectively question." Instead, educators must face the daily complexities and challenges of their profession by employing some theory and research and a lot of practical knowledge and wisdom. It is not uncommon to hear a teacher proclaiming, "Look, I don't have time for all that theoretical gobbledygook, there are papers to grade and kids to teach." Yet despite the unique attributes of each tradition, there are certain essential processes and issues that are common to supervision.

SUPERVISION DEFINED

This text focuses on developmental instructional supervision, which can be defined as an in-class and in-school process for refining and expanding instructional repertoire that accounts for and differentiates between support and challenge according to the teachers' individual learning and developmental needs. Such a process promotes both individual and schoolwide change, learning, and growth. Schools that link instruction, classroom management, discipline, and student- and family-centered efforts with staff development, formal and informal developmental instructional supervision and coaching between teachers, collaborative inquiry, and direct assessment between the principal and teacher, tend to be schools that are collegial, purposeful, and goal-directed.

As we mentioned in the introduction, a variety of persons may be involved in improving classroom and school instruction and could be referred to as supervisors or coaches. Among them are school principals, assistant principals, instructional specialists, mentor teachers, instructional lead teachers, clinical teachers, counselors, social workers, school psychologists, program directors, and central office personnel. Whenever any of these persons commits time to developing knowledge and a repertoire of applied skills in developmental instructional supervision and coaching, we would call them supervisors or coaches.

FORMATIVE VERSUS SUMMATIVE SUPERVISION

Formative developmental supervision implies that the process is nonevaluative. It is most often conducted between teachers and requires confidentiality, reciprocity, and a high degree of trust built over many months. Formative developmental supervision may be freely sought by two teachers or mandated by law. For example, many states have required that mentor teachers be assigned to beginning teachers. However, the mentor is typically not in an evaluative role, serving instead as a coach and trusted colleague. Formative supervision also implies work between two equals. In a formative supervisory relationship, a principal should offer summative information to assist the mentor and beginning teacher. And the processes outlined in this text can be employed by the principal. However, the mentor should not share information about the beginning teacher with the principal because it would violate confidentiality and the trust of the beginning teacher. In Chapter 7 we discuss the "getting-acquainted conference" as a vehicle for maintaining open communication between a novice teacher, a mentor or lead teacher, and the principal.

Evaluation is one of the defining attributes of summative developmental supervision. Summative supervision implies a gatekeeping function, regulating who is legitimized to enter or stay in the world of teaching. An example of summative supervision would be the work between a college supervisor and a student teacher. College supervisors provide instructional supervision but also are required to evaluate whether the student teacher should receive an initial teaching license. Both kinds of supervision are necessary in professional programs, and the theory and practices described in this text can be used in both summative and formative supervision. However, we recommend that the type of supervision (formative or summative) be discussed between colleagues at the onset of the relationship. This topic is featured in Chapter 10.

DEVELOPMENTAL SUPERVISION AND MENTORING OCCURS OVER TIME

A third element of our definition of developmental instructional supervision and mentoring is that the intervention extends over considerable time. It is therefore distinct from brief and episodic workshops that might update staff on the latest policies or that intend to impart awareness about a new staff development program available in the school system.

Because it is ongoing over many months, developmental instructional supervision encourages sustained reflection on experience, and permits rich opportunities for personal and professional growth. There are three phases in teachers' careers that are representative of extended supervision. The first phase is preservice teacher education—early field experiences, college coursework, and student teaching. The second phase is induction— the first two to three years of a teacher's career. And the third phase is in-service education—those years after a teacher has received a permanent license to teach.

PREPARATION OF SUPERVISORS, COACHES, AND CLINICAL MENTORS

If behind every successful school is an effective supervision and coaching program, then it stands to reason that persons who wish to become supervisors, clinical mentors, or coaches should commit themselves to adequate training for this important role in school success. Further, the preparation needs to be sustained and should model effective theory, research, and practice. We submit that such preparation for supervisory and coaching roles should be multifaceted, and include both formal coursework and guided practical or laboratory experiences in which basic helping skills, supervision and coaching principles, and knowledge of the developing adult learner are acquired.

 ## SUPERVISOR AS THEORETICAL PRACTITIONER OR PRACTICAL THEORIST?

C. P. Snow (1963) in a classic work described the problem of *theory versus practice* as a disparity between two cultures, the scientific and the humanistic. When Snow defined the two cultures, he meant different societies or world views. Neither view is the correct one; rather, they may be different sides of the same coin. The behavioral psychologist would study learning as the imprinting or conditioning of the individual by the outer environment. A study might include hundreds of trials with rewards and punishment in order to draw conclusions about behavior. Teachers, on the other hand, must make hundreds of decisions daily as they work with students. It seems that little time is available for a painstaking study of "best methods of teaching."

The same split observed by Snow can be seen in the discipline of instructional supervision. On one end of the continuum are humanistic educators who view supervision as discovery. The supervisor stays out of harm's way as supervisees hopefully discover for themselves some of the key elements of teaching. At the other end of the continuum are educators who

EXHIBIT 1-1 VIEWS OF SUPERVISION

EDUCATIONAL/ PSYCHOLOGICAL THEORY	HUMANIST	BEHAVIORIST
Supervisory guidance	Low (indirect)	High (direct)
Learning	"Naturally unfolds"	Is conditioned
Method of supervision	Discovery	Reinforcement with high structure

choose to supervise from a behaviorist stance. Their actions are very directive and performance outcomes for the supervisee are clearly defined. Exhibit 1-1 shows these different views of instructional supervision.

As you begin to work with supervision, you will realize that it is an emergent discipline that attempts to synthesize several fields: education, psychology, philosophy, and sociology, and that how it is practiced is related to the person's dominant cultural view (Snow, 1963). Exhibit 1-1 enumerates concisely the two ends of the cultural continuum.

Let's look at the theory versus practice question more closely. The purpose of theory is to provide a set of clear, logically coherent reasons and principles. It is descriptive as opposed to prescriptive. Practice, on the other hand, requires immediate responses to given activities, and is therefore prescriptive. The question you may be presently asking is, "Are both needed?" "Why should I rely on theory that is typically general and abstract? It leaves me with only a vague sense of what to do." In many respects, we agree. Theory is general, the knowledge abstract, and its goal successive approximations in our understanding of what it means to be human. "If this is so," you may say, "I am probably better served by relying on my own intuition of what is best. Besides, I learn so much from my colleagues and their suggestions." The problem with this interpretation is that you may end up with one method of teaching for all kids. Further, if something works, you may not know why it works or when it is not effective. Perhaps this is why Mosher and Purpel (1972) remarked that without theory, practice is one more fad that wanders aimlessly between the cosmic and trivial without understanding the difference. The point is that both theory and practice are needed.

Donald Schön has entered this debate by investigating how professional schools like nursing, architecture, and music prepare their students for their chosen careers (1987). His term "the reflective practitioner" has become common coinage in the field of education. His point is that practice and theory must coexist. In a sense, *theory must be visible in practice*. The novice architect's design and execution need to apply the central principles and rules of design. However, *practice must also be visible in theory*. The architect needs to account for unique aspects of the design problem that may not be part of the theory of design, what Schön calls "indeterminate zones of practice."

This dynamic interchange between theory and practice is the raison d'être for professional schools. However, before we can look at how to encourage both in supervision we must address another issue that has surfaced in the discipline of supervision.

ONE THEORY OR MANY?

If both theory and practice are important, which theory is to be selected? Certainly in the discipline of supervision it is clear, at least in some cases, that competing theories are guiding supervisory practice. It also is evident that there is no grand "unified" theory in use. How then does one choose? The scientific community evaluates theory on the basis of two basic principles: parsimony and reductionism. The term *parsimony* means that "less is more." Theory should be succinct and clear. Some of the Chinese silk screen paintings convey this principle beautifully. A few carefully placed brush strokes portray the branches of a lone pine tree in the foreground, and a few more brush strokes create mountains in the distance. The overall effect is one of simplicity and immensity. Similarly, a theory should not be more abstract than it needs to be to explain the facts.

A medieval philosopher, William of Occam, chafed at overly complex or zealous theorizing in his time. It was during the time of Occam that a religious controversy was raging over the number of angels that could dance on the head of a pin. Elaborate theories were constructed to resolve this debate. In response, Occam wrote a searing criticism, pointing out the need for parsimony. His view became immortalized as "Occam's razor," a tool that cuts away needless information and elaboration.

THE GOLDILOCKS PRINCIPLE

Katz and Raths (1985) have contemporized the dilemma of broad gauge versus narrow gauge theory with their "Goldilocks principle." Some theory is extremely broad and abstract creating a theoretical bed that is too big for the actual process. Certainly some humanistic theories stand as good examples of such excessively broad propositions.

Yet Katz and Raths also note the other side of the problem. Theory and research can be so focused on specifics that the framework becomes too narrow. Some theorists, fearing Occam's razor, have carved theories down to the barest of essentials. This principle is called *reductionism*. The goal is to eliminate as many assumptions and suppositions as possible. However, the risk is that you might dismiss too many relevant ideas. In the urgency to create the barest and most lean theory, valuable ideas may be discarded. This tendency is sometimes called "tossing the baby out with the bath water." The process-product behavioristic approach to effective teaching represents just such an instance of reducing human complexity to a few simpleminded propositions. Thus the behavioristic model creates a theoretical bed that is far too small. Goldilocks as a metaphor for supervision and teacher development then wanders from place to place seeking a better fit as the field itself tries to build theory, research, and practice. Without a careful integration of the three components, Goldilocks will continue to traverse from fad to fad perhaps blissfully unaware of the distinctions between the cosmic and the trivial.

Our original question was, one theory or many? Effective theory can probably be judged as being at the midpoint on the theory continuum. On one end of this continuum are the theorists creating overly abstract frameworks, much like the theories developed to explain the number of angels dancing on the head of a pin. On the other end are the reductionists, paring theory down to a few spare elements, always risking "tossing the baby out with the bath water." In the middle is parsimony with Occam's razor ensuring that the theory is only as abstract as it needs to be. The developmental approach described in this text offers a set of theories that are somewhere near the midpoint on the theory continuum. It reflects the work of a global network of educators, psychologists, and philosophers who have explored how persons develop and change. And it is a theory that has gone through a series of revisions as new information comes forth.

As we move to a more careful description of developmental instructional supervision, mentoring, and coaching remember that both theory and practice are important. Further, theory is dynamic and is reframed as new information emerges. It is not an answer to all of life's questions. Once you have a hammer, everything can't become a nail. However, effective theory can become the basis for informed judgments to guide professional actions. Exhibit 1-2 shows an expanded view of supervision that includes developmental theory. Think of it as existing somewhere near the midpoint on the theory continuum.

Later we will enumerate other characterisitics of developmental instructional supervision. It is a theory that comprehends a number of domains of human development that we have found visible in effective supervision between teachers, administrators, and counselor practitioners. You also will

EXHIBIT 1-2 VIEWS OF SUPERVISION INCLUDING DEVELOPMENTAL THEORY

EDUCATIONAL THEORY	HUMANIST	DEVELOPMENTAL	BEHAVIORIST
Supervisory guidance	Low (indirect)	Indirect and direct	High (direct)
Learning	"Naturally unfolds"	Guided	Is conditioned
Method of supervision	Discovery	Repertoire	Reinforcement

see that the supervisory practice of literally hundreds of educators has enlarged the theory, another case of practice visible in theory. As David Hunt
said, "There is nothing quite as theoretical as good practice" (1981, p. 64),
and there is nothing quite as practical as good theory. We hope you will appreciate the importance of both theory and practice.

 # APPLICATIONS OF DEVELOPMENTAL SUPERVISION AND MENTORING

Developmental supervision encompasses a number of tasks and skills that
promote instructional dialogue and learning and teacher personal growth
and development. Given that the organizational context of the school and
the career phase of teachers mediate the support, resources, and approach
to supervision and coaching, this book reviews research and practices on
developmental supervision across the career spectrum from preservice
teacher education, through induction, and into inservice applications. A
brief summary of each of the teacher career phases that are addressed in the
text follows.

PRESERVICE

Applying developmental supervision to the preservice arena typically involves a triad (student teacher, cooperating teacher(s), and university supervisor). The goal is to assist the student in applying concepts learned in
teacher preparation courses to the public school setting. Student teachers acknowledge the important role played by their cooperating teacher
(Copeland, 1982), and single studies and research summaries suggest that
training promotes more effective supervision of the student teacher by
the cooperating teacher (Glassberg & Sprinthall, 1980; Grimmett &
Ratzlaff, 1986; Howey, 1996; Knowles & Cole, 1996; Guyton & McIntyre,
1990; McIntyre, Byrd, & Foxx, 1996; Watson & Fullan, 1991; Zeichner & Liston, 1987). And university supervisors, who traditionally struggle to balance
supervisory responsibilities with teaching and research, are frustrated that
too little time is available to do the needed supervision (Koehler, 1984).

The importance of supervision for student teachers, and the need for
training of cooperating teachers and university supervisors, are two reasons
why some states have organized professional development consortia of universities and school systems that are undertaking innovative new strategies
for preparing cadres of clinical teachers and clinical faculty (i.e., teachers with substantive specialized training in supervision—see Learning to
Teach, 1992).

The teacher educator, cooperating teacher, or clinical teacher will be able
to use this book in a variety of ways: to assist in the training of cadres of cooperating teachers or clinical teachers, or to prepare university supervisors.

In fact, one trend we see is the development of graduate curriculum to support the preparation of cadres of clinical faculty. Such an effort is underway in a number of states including North Carolina. This is a promising innovation for teacher education.

INDUCTION

Recently, there have been a spate of commission reports and studies detailing the plight of the beginning teacher. Teachers begin their careers facing the most difficult assignments (Huling-Austin, 1990; Reiman & Parramore, 1994; Veenman, 1984), inadequate resources such as a lack of time for lesson planning and supervision (Odell, 1986), few opportunities to dialogue with other beginning colleagues (Gold, 1996), and the "sink-or-swim" mentality of some administrators and veterans who see the need for a weeding out of weak beginning teachers (Griffin, 1985; Veenman, 1984). Yet the assignment of a mentor may be the most valuable and cost-effective way to support beginning teachers (Huling-Austin, Putman, & Galvez-Hjornevik, 1986). However, once again, preparation and training for the role are needed (Little, 1990; Thies-Sprinthall, 1986). Effective supervision and coaching programs at the induction level have been found to ameliorate beginning teacher concerns, and to increase beginning teacher focus on student learning (Huling-Austin, 1990; Reiman, Bostick, Cooper, & Lassiter, 1995).

SPOTLIGHT ON EDUCATIONAL LEADERS

SUPPORTING SUCCESSFUL TEACHER INDUCTION

Although there is no perfect formula for success in developing comprehensive induction programs, research does show that quality programs address a number of interrelated needs of beginning teachers. These needs include:

- Sustained help in developing as competent persons—not screening.
- Mentors who are on-site, committed, and skilled.
- Time to develop new skills and to be involved in coaching.
- Opportunities to talk with other novice teachers in a setting free of evaluation.
- Orientation to the school system, school, curriculum, and community.
- Realistic assignments (e.g., number of preparations, type of classes, and the number of extracurricular activities).

Educational leaders in school districts support successful teacher induction in the ways they respond to these beginning teacher needs. For example, the system superintendent can recommend that all staff develop strategic plans that address the systemwide needs of beginning professionals and beginning teachers. Resources can be earmarked for beginning teacher professional release time. Further, central office staff and school-based staff can identify strategies for preventing the assignment of beginning teachers to the most challenging classroom assignments.

Staff development directors can provide opportunities for new teachers (or student teachers) to talk about their concerns and instructional and curriculum issues without fear of retribution. Renewal credit can be provided. Additionally, staff development directors can design coaching and supervision training experiences for experienced teachers interested in becoming mentors to beginning teachers.

Principals can set a positive and welcoming tone for beginning teachers, offering an orientation to the school campus and staff, and sponsoring a luncheon to honor new colleagues. They can provide opportunities for trained mentor teachers to support beginning teachers on a weekly basis. Such a provision, however, may necessitate releasing the mentor from other school duties.

Ultimately, successful induction programs require creativity, advance planning, careful preparation of a cadre of mentors, and sufficient resources to support program design, implementation, and evaluation. Given that novice teachers are future educational leaders, and that their success translates into student success, there may be no better investment.

Therefore staff developers and directors of human resources interested in building a quality induction program that focuses on mentor support and supervision as a key component that is cost-effective will be interested in the assistance strategies described in this text. Further, if the school system is planning to implement a mentor training program, the organization of the chapters could serve as a major text for such a staff development program.

INSERVICE

The literature on successful schools is replete with references to sustained and professional interactions between administrators and teachers (Glickman & Bey, 1990; Little, 1982; Rosenholtz, 1985), or between teachers (Joyce & Showers, 1995; Oja & Smulyan, 1989; Phillips, 1989; Thies-Sprinthall & Sprinthall, 1987), with a focus on instruction. The supervision of instruction appears to be vital to school success (Sergiovanni & Starrat, 1993). When administrators and teachers work in concert to provide time to plan and discuss various means of promoting students' learning and development, they counter trends of isolation and lack of discourse that are so prevalent in many unexceptional schools (Glickman & Bey, 1990; Goodlad, 1990). Developmental supervision encompasses many of the change processes (Guskey,

1986; Guskey & Huberman, 1995; Richardson, 1994) that promote planning, dialogue, learning, and development such as instructional coaching, cycles of assistance that include classroom observation, collaborative action research, teacher reflection, and ethical inquiry. Persons involved with inservice education will therefore find this book most helpful as a bridge to promoting one-to-one or group instructional assistance with teachers and administrators.

 # SUMMARY

This chapter began with several focus questions. We hope you kept these questions in mind as you read the chapter. How is C. P. Snow's metaphor of two cultures related to supervision? Can formative and summative supervision coexist? Who might be involved in developmental instructional supervision and coaching? If you can answer these questions, congratulations. If answers are not forthcoming, we encourage you to quickly review these sections of the chapter as they will be important foundations for subsequent chapters.

In introducing you to the discipline of developmental supervision, this chapter presented some of the broader issues with which the discipline of supervision has struggled. C. P. Snow used the metaphor of separate cultures to describe the tensions and ambiguities that exist between the humanistic and scientific traditions. This same split can be seen in contemporary supervision and in education, in which theory and practice often seem to operate at cross-purposes. However, both theory and practice are needed. William of Occam reminded us that effective theory must be lean and clear. Effective theory, therefore, is judged on how well it achieves parsimony without becoming overly reductionistic. Our hope is for a theoretical practitioner and a practical theorist. Schön called this process "reflection-in-action," in which the exigencies of the moment are guided by reflection on the practice.

Developmental theory will serve as the organizing framework for our discussion of instructional supervision. As you read the following chapters you hopefully will see how adult developmental theory can become a powerful bridge for understanding the supervision and coaching process. As we have worked with hundreds of educators in a variety of educational settings, we have discovered that such a theory can guide more humane supervisory practice, whether it is formative or summative in nature.

The bridge between theory and practice in subsequent chapters has been bolstered by the support, encouragement, and practical examples of developmental supervision from many persons including teachers, counselors, speech therapists, school psychologists, lead teachers, curriculum specialists, superintendents, staff development personnel, and even the co-operative extension agency. Further, a cadre of teachers called administrators, clinical teachers* and clinical counselors, and school-based teacher educators have implemented the ideas expressed in the text. Whenever possible, we will credit the ongoing work they are doing in schools and classrooms.

---

*In our program, a *clinical teacher* is defined as an exemplary practicing teacher who has participated in extensive preparation in order to assist novice and experienced teachers. The preparation involves two courses. The first course is a 45 contact hour seminar in developmental supervision. The second course is a reflective practicum. During this course participants practice skills in building and maintaining a helping relationship and using cycles of developmental supervision. A *school-based teacher educator* is a clinical teacher who has assumed the additional role of conducting his or her own local school system programs, employing the curriculum from the two courses to prepare cadres of clinical teachers.

SUPERVISION FOR TEACHER DEVELOPMENT ACTIVITIES

APPLIED

1. Chapter 1 examined the importance of theory in practice. The following questionnaire can help you decide where you stand on your own theoretical orientation as a supervisor.

	VERY IMPORTANT	SOMEWHAT IMPORTANT	UNIMPORTANT
The role of a supervisor is:			
1. To impart knowledge and skills.	_____	_____	_____
2. To employ a discovery approach.	_____	_____	_____
3. To respond to the interpersonal needs of the colleague.	_____	_____	_____
4. To view supervision as inquiry.	_____	_____	_____
5. To focus on basic skills as building blocks for future growth.	_____	_____	_____
6. To discern the developmental needs of the teacher and to select the supervisory strategy based on colleague need.	_____	_____	_____

7. To focus on the personal
   concerns of the colleague.   _____   _____   _____
8. To transmit the culture of the
   school.   _____   _____   _____
9. To encourage reflection
   based on the teacher's ability
   to draw meaning from the
   experience.   _____   _____   _____

The survey gives you a general picture of where you are now in your assumptions and philosophy of supervision. We suggest that you reexamine it near the end of the semester. What attitudes changed? What attitudes remained the same? Ratings of Very Important on items 1, 5, and 8 indicate that you have a strong preference for a direct and skill-based approach to supervision. High ratings on items 2 and 4 indicate that you prefer an inquiry-discovery approach to supervision. Items 3 and 7 indicate that you value highly a humanistic and interpersonal emphasis in supervision; and items 6 and 9 indicate that you value developmentally based supervision.

2. Answer the following questions:
   a. What theories do I include in my supervisory practice?
   b. Recall an experience in which you were supervised. What stands out as most significant in terms of helpful or unhelpful behaviors?

REFERENCES

Burden, P. (1990). Teacher development. In R. Houston (Ed.), *Handbook of research on teacher education*. New York: Macmillan.

Cogan, M. L. (1973). *Clinical supervision*. Boston: Houghton Mifflin.

Copeland, W. D. (1982). Laboratory experiences in teacher education. In H. E. Mitzel (Ed.), *Encyclopedia of educational research* (pp. 1008–1019). New York: Free Press.

Dewey, J. (1974). *John Dewey on education: Selected writings*. (R. D. Archambault, Ed.). Chicago: University of Chicago Press.

Fessler, R., & Christensen, J. (1992). *The teacher career cycle: Understanding and guiding the professional development of teachers*. Boston: Allyn and Bacon.

Furth, J., & Pajak, E. (1997). *Handbook of research on school supervision*. New York: Macmillan.

Glanz, J. (1992). Curriculum development and supervision: Antecedents for collaboration and future possibilities. *Journal of Curriculum and Supervision, 7*(3), 226–244.

Glassberg, S., & Sprinthall, N. A. (1980). Student teaching: A developmental approach. *Journal of Teacher Education, 31*(2), 31–38.

Glickman, C., & Bey, T. (1990). Supervision. In R. Houston (Ed.), *Handbook of research on teacher education* (pp. 549–566). New York: Macmillan.

Glickman, C. , Gordon, S., & Ross-Gordon, J. (1995). *Supervision of instruction: A developmental approach.* Boston: Allyn and Bacon.

Gold, Y. (1996). Beginning teacher support: Attrition, mentoring, and induction. In J. Sikula (Ed.), *Second handbook of research on teacher education* (pp. 548–594). New York: Macmillan.

Goodlad, J. (1990). *Teachers for our nation's schools.* San Francisco: Jossey-Bass.

Griffin, G. (1985). Teacher induction: Research issues. *Journal of Teacher Education, 36*(1), 42–46.

Grimmett, P. P., & Ratzlaff, H. C. (1986). Expectations for the cooperating teacher role. *Journal of Teacher Education, 37*(6), 41–58.

Guskey, T. (1986). Staff development and the process of teacher change. *Educational Researcher, 15*(5), 5–12.

Guskey, T. R., & Huberman, M. (1995). *Professional development in education: New paradigms and practices.* New York: Teachers College Press.

Guyton, E., & McIntyre, J. (1990). Student teacher and school experience. In R. Houston (Ed.), *Handbook of research on teacher education* (pp. 514–534). New York: Macmillan.

Houston, R. (Ed.) (1990). *Handbook of research on teacher education.* New York: Macmillan.

Howey, K. (1996). Designing coherent and effective teacher education programs. In J. Sikula (Ed.), *Second handbook of research on teacher education* (pp. 143–170). New York: Macmillan.

Huling-Austin, L. (1990). Teacher induction programs and internships. In R. Houston (Ed.), *Handbook of research on teacher education* (pp. 535–548). New York: Macmillan.

Huling-Austin, L., Putman, S., & Galvez-Hjornevik (1986). *Model teacher induction project study findings* (Report No. 7212). Austin, TX: University of Texas at Austin, R & D Center for Teacher Education.

Hunt, D. (1981). Teachers' adaptation: "Reading" and "flexing" to students. In B. Joyce, C. Brown, & L. Peck (Eds.), *Flexibility in teaching* (pp. 59–71). New York: Longman.

Joyce, B., & Showers, B. (1995). *Student achievement through staff development* (2nd ed.). New York: Longman.

Katz, L., & Raths, J. (1985). Dispositions as goals for teacher education. *Teaching and Teacher Education, 1,* 301–307.

Knowles, G., & Cole, A. (1996). Developing practice through field experiences. In F. Murray (Ed.), *The teacher educator's handbook: Building a knowledge base for the preparation of teachers* (pp. 648–690). San Francisco: Jossey-Bass.

Koehler, V. (1984, April). *University supervision of student teaching.* Paper presented at the annual meeting of the American Educational Research Association, New Orleans.

Kozol, J. (1992). *Savage inequalities.* New York: Harper-Collins.

Learning to Teach (1992). Chapel Hill, NC: University of North Carolina.

Little, J. (1982). Norms of collegiality and experimentation: Workplace conditions for school success. *American Educational Research Journal, 19*(3), 325–340.

Little, J. (1990). The mentor phenomenon and the social organization of teaching. In C. B. Cazden (Ed.), *Review of research in education: Vol. 16* (pp. 297–351). Washington, DC: American Educational Research Association.

McIntyre, D. J., Byrd, D. M., & Foxx, S. M. (1996). Field and laboratory experiences. In J. Sikula (Ed.), *Second handbook of research on teacher education* (pp. 171–193). New York: Macmillan.

Mosher, R., & Purpel, D. (1972). *Supervision: The reluctant profession.* Boston: Houghton Mifflin.

Odell, S. (1986). Induction support of new teachers: A functional approach. *Journal of Teacher Education, 37*(1), 26–29.

Oja, S. N., & Smulyan, L. (1989). *Collaborative action research: A developmental approach.* New York: Falmer Press.

Phillips, J. (1989). *A case study evaluation of the impact on teachers of the implementation of a peer coaching training program in an elementary school.* Unpublished doctoral dissertation, University of Georgia.

Reiman, A. J., Bostick, D., Cooper, J., & Lassiter, J. (1995). Counselor- and teacher-led support groups for beginning teachers: A cognitive-developmental perspective. *Elementary School Guidance and Counseling, 30*(2), 105–117.

Reiman, A. J., & Parramore, B. (1994). Beginning teacher assignments, expectations, and development: A collaborative investigation. In M. O'Hair and S. Odell (Eds.), *Teacher Education Yearbook I.* Association of Teacher Educators. Orlando: Harcourt Brace Jovanovich.

Richardson, V. (Ed.) (1994). *Teacher change and the staff development process.* New York: Teachers College Press.

Rosenholtz, S. J. (1985). Effective schools: Interpreting the evidence. *American Journal of Education, 93,* 352–388.

Schön, D. (1987). *Educating the reflective practitioner.* San Francisco: Jossey-Bass.

Sergiovanni, T. (1990). *Value-added leadership: How to get extraordinary performance in schools.* San Diego: Harcourt Brace Jovanovich.

Sergiovanni, T., & Starrat, R. (1993). *Supervision: A redefinition* (5th ed.). New York: McGraw-Hill.

Snow, C. P. (1963). *The two cultures: And a second look.* New York: Mentor.

Thies-Sprinthall, L. (1986). A collaborative approach for mentor training: A working model. *Journal of Teacher Education, 37*(6), 13–20.

Thies-Sprinthall, L., & Sprinthall, N. (1987). Experienced teachers: Agents for revitalization and renewal as mentors and teacher educators. *Journal of Education. 169* (1), 65–79.

Veenman, S. (1984). Perceived problems of beginning teachers. *Review of Educational Research, 54*(2), 143–178.

Watson, N. & Fullan, M. (1991). Beyond school-university partnerships. In M. G. Fullan and A. Hargreaves (Eds.), *Teacher development and educational change.* London: Falmer Press.

Zeichner, K., & Liston, D. (1987). Teaching student teachers to reflect. *Harvard Educational Review, 57*(1), 23–48.

C·H·A·P·T·E·R
2

Supervision as a Profession

• • • • • •

From Reluctance to Promise

 INTRODUCTION

In Chapter 1 we introduced you to developmental supervision and mentoring, examined the dialectic between theory and practice, and identified those persons who are responsible for supervision. We pointed out that most successful schools integrate effective supervision and assistance into a total school program.

In Chapter 2 we take a closer look at clinical supervision as it has developed since the 1960s. The major rationale and assumptions of a cycle of assistance are described, and we examine research on the effectiveness of clinical supervision. Teachers, administrators, and graduate students are encouraged to give careful attention to the discussion of preparation for emerging supervisory and leadership roles for teachers that can be bolstered by the meta-skills described in this text. This chapter also continues our discussion of the need for more coherent theory and serves as a bridge to Chapters 3, 4, and 5, which present an extensive theoretical framework for developmental supervision and assistance.

As you read this chapter keep the following questions in mind:

- Why did Purpel and Mosher describe supervision as the reluctant profession?
- Can you identify at least five of the elements of a cycle of assistance?
- If you were asked to develop a preparation program for supervisors, what would be the major units of your training program?

THE RELUCTANT PROFESSION

Educational supervision was described by Ralph Mosher and David Purpel as a near reluctant profession in their classic work *Supervision: The Reluctant Profession*. Their thesis was that persons often view supervision as a difficult and burdensome practice. Ambivalence about supervision could be discerned in many educators' deep-seated distrust of direct supervisory interventions in the classroom. In general, Mosher and Purpel observed: "Though lip service is routinely paid to the importance of supervision, the most widespread attitude is probably suspicion—suspicion that supervision is at best ineffectual and at worst a harmful form of interference with the work of the teacher" (1972, p. 2). Cogan and Goldhammer similarly had noted that most supervision appeared to be more like tampering and teachers were better off being left alone if supervision could not transform itself.

It is important to note that the pioneering work of Cogan, Goldhammer, Mosher, and Purpel must be viewed in historical context. Two important educational events were catalysts for educators to look anew at the role supervision plays. The first was a call by Harvard president emeritus James B. Conant (1963) for a new model of the teacher professional. Using the medical model, he called for "teaching hospitals" to be developed. "Clinical teachers and clinical professors," specially prepared for educating future teachers, would work side by side in the hospitals. The idea never caught on in education but it did bolster work by persons such as Cogan who recognized that a new model was needed for the preparation of clinical teachers and clinical professors.

The second event was the advent of Masters of Arts in Teaching programs. These advanced degree programs for teachers were our national response to Sputnik and the call for more rigorous teacher preparation. Yet neither Cogan's work with instructional supervision or the MAT approach achieved a solid theory base because developmental theory was still viewed as only fitting child/adolescent stages.

Some years ago we began to explore "reluctance" in supervision. Is suspicion a given in supervision? Why are teachers hesitant to appropriately guide novice teachers? Are there exceptions to reluctant supervision and, if so, why? Is it possible to prepare large cadres of clinical professors and clinical teachers who assume significant responsibility for school-based supervision? Naturally our questions seemed important if we were to unlock the potentials inherent in the supervision process. We investigated the questions with teachers, counselors, principals, staff developers, and college teacher educators, and we were encouraged by the results. Indeed it did appear that supervision, performed thoughtfully and compassionately, could lead to promising outcomes. In this chapter we look closer at the origins of clinical supervision, and pursue some tentative answers to the questions just raised.

 ORIGINS OF CLINICAL SUPERVISION

As was mentioned in Chapter 1, Morris Cogan (1973) and Robert Goldhammer (1969) are responsible for developing the original model for clinical supervision as a practice. Recognizing that much supervision is merely tampering, Cogan hoped to design a system of supervision that, in the words of one commentator, "had enough weight to have impact and enough precision to hit the target." Cogan believed that any system of supervision that could accomplish such a goal would require a sizable cadre of "clinical teachers and supervisors" capable of implementing the system. Such a venture would not be cheap. However, he believed that such an approach was far cheaper than poor teaching and failure.

Realizing that there are many forms of educational supervision, for example, the general supervision (out of class) that might occur during cooperative curriculum development, Cogan and Goldhammer concentrated on one-to-one, in-class observation and assistance. Their system came to be known as clinical supervision, an intensive supervisory process that promotes teacher learning of new instructional skills.

Rationale for Clinical Supervision

Cogan observed that most of the literature on supervision in preservice and inservice education was at the phase of "natural history" in its evolution. What he meant was that the field of supervision was based on observation and description that was not systematized or based on relevant theory. He went on to argue that one of the defining characteristics of a science is that it collects and categorizes data for the development of theory and research. Cogan, therefore, felt a professional responsibility to shift the field of supervision toward a more systematic analysis of practice. He was not sanguine, however, that a theory would emerge from his efforts. Instead, he believed that his work might lay an empirical foundation for the eventual creation of theory.

MORRIS COGAN

If you were to ask anyone in instructional supervision to list the five most influential scholars in the field, you would be sure to find Morris Cogan's name in that select group.

Cogan, himself a classroom teacher in the Trenton Public Schools for 12 years, began his scholarly career at Harvard University in 1954. During Cogan's tenure at Harvard, he worked to actualize a vision promoted by James Conant, Harvard's president, to reform and revitalize teacher education by creating "teaching hospitals." Although Conant's vision never took flight, Cogan, along with an extraordinary group of graduate students including Robert Goldhammer, David Purpel, and Ralph Mosher, studied the potential of clinical instructional supervision. This small group were all colleagues in creating a special summer program for the then new model for teacher preparation, The Master of Arts in Teaching (MAT). In addition to a heavy emphasis on liberal arts, the most critical problem was to convert these highly skilled academically oriented graduate students into gifted teachers in classroom interaction. Entering with superior GPAs and extremely high GRE scores, the students were nonetheless awkward, hesitant, and often fumbling in the classrooms. Clearly such students could "think" but not necessarily "do."

With Cogan's leadership the students were formed into small teams each with a master teacher. Then came the creativity of uncovering the approaches to supervision through pre- and post-conferences, focused observation, and structured yet humane feedback through a series of discussions each day during the six-week program. The intensity of the experience and the shrewd observations of the Cogan group created the foundation for all that was to follow for teacher supervision. Also, as befits an ideal professor, his core of doctoral students soon launched their own versions of complementary methods of supervision.

Cogan's particular genius was his ability to synthesize university research with ongoing practice in classroom teaching and supervision. Although theory and research about adult development were in their infancy at the time that Cogan was writing his seminal text, *Clinical Supervison*, he anticipated emerging trends in teacher personal and professional growth (e.g., self-knowledge, ego, conceptual complexity, in-class coaching and observation). However, his major contribution was the explication of a system of in-class supervision that was sufficiently robust to accomplish significant learning in a teacher's classroom instruction. Without such a system, Cogan submitted that "teachers are better left alone than being tampered with" through perfunctory or brief and episodic supervisory experiences.

Cogan finished his academic career at the University of Pittsburgh where he chaired the Division of Teacher Education. It was during his time at the University of Pittsburgh that Cogan began to test out the idea of creating a cadre of school-based clinical teachers with adjunct appointments at the university who would have an extensive knowledge base in supervision, curriculum, and instructional innovations, and who would support teachers and conduct action research. Through clinical teachers and school-based "teaching clinics" Cogan hoped to make schools the breeding ground for research and the testing ground for new theory. One can see that Cogan's ideas foresaw contemporary work with collaborative inquiry and professional development schools.

REFLECTION QUESTIONS

What was the impetus for Cogan's work in supervision?

How did Cogan's work with the MAT program at Harvard shape contemporary instructional supervision practices?

How might clinical supervision complement contemporary professional development school initiatives?

Cogan was astute to point out that the role of clinical supervision was anticipated by William James, American psychology's founding father. Devoted to improving the quality of classroom education, James's famous lectures, *Talks to Teachers on Psychology*, illustrated his conviction that the entire enterprise of education is determined by the classroom teacher. A central theme for James follows: "Psychology is a science, and teaching is an art; and sciences never generate arts directly out of themselves. An intermediate inventive mind must make the application, by using its originality" (1925, pp. 7–8). Morris Cogan believed that James was precisely right; the transformation of educational theory and research into practice was better accomplished through an intermediary. The rationale for clinical supervision, therefore, casts the supervisor (clinical educator) in a role envisioned by James: "An intermediate, inventive, trained professional committed to working with the teacher to help him make his own original application of the science available to him, in his own style" (Cogan, 1973, p. 18).

Cogan submitted that a move to a more intellectually rigorous system like clinical supervision, based on general rules and principles, was far more promising than relying on intuitive approaches that were more or less random. As one can discover from a careful review of his work, he was fully committed to the principle of parsimony and to the need for an emerging theory of supervision. He realized that unless supervision could internalize the standards of evidence and proof that are characteristic of science, the field would gravitate "toward uncritical enthusiasms and the formation of supervisory cults" (1973, p. 19). By now some of you may be recalling the image of William of Occam, honing his razor, as he sits midway between the angels dancing on the head of pin and a baby who has been tossed out with the dirty bath water. Certainly Cogan realized the need for Occam's razor. We now turn to a description of a cycle of clinical supervision.

THE CYCLE OF ASSISTANCE

The cycle of assistance developed by Morris Cogan and his associates (1973) consisted of eight phases. Each phase was derived from study of the supervisory process, and the phases were considered partially interdependent. The phases are as follows:

1. *Establishing a "helping and trusting" relationship.* This all-important phase in the cycle includes becoming acquainted, establishing roles and expectations, discussing learning styles, reviewing preferred ways of communicating, and clarifying how clinical supervision is implemented.
2. *Planning lessons and units with the teacher.* Plans would include clear objectives and student learning outcomes, anticipated problems, special learning circumstances, and strategies for teaching the lesson or unit.
3. *Planning for the observation.* The teacher and the supervisor discuss what will be observed during the lesson and how data will be collected. This phase is sometimes referred to as the pre-conference.
4. *Observing the instruction.* The supervisor watches the lesson and records data on classroom events.
5. *Analyzing the data for important patterns in the teaching process.* The supervisor and the teacher independently analyze the instruction.
6. *Planning for the conference.* Both the teacher and the supervisor develop general plans to discuss outcomes, classroom management, and the teaching/learning process. Possible follow-up strategies may be outlined.
7. *Conferencing to review the classroom event.* Typically, this conference includes the supervisor and the teacher.
8. *Renewed planning.* The colleagues complete the cycle of supervision by determining the next steps for professional and personal growth and development. This phase may include a written plan that identifies specific steps in the next cycle of supervision.

In general, research on clinical supervision has found that it can change a teacher's instructional repertoire (Kagan, 1988) and that supervisors using the clinical approach seem more open and accepting in post-observation conferences than those using more traditional approaches (Reavis, 1977).

More recent adaptations of clinical supervision include scientific clinical supervision, accountable supervision, artistic supervision, and ego counseling (Glatthorn, 1984). Scientific clinical supervision focuses on discrete teacher instructional behaviors that clearly are supported by research. The goal is the development of a teacher's instructional repertoire (Joyce & Weil, 1996).

A second adaptation is that of accountable clinical supervision. Here the focus is less with the teacher and more with what the student learns. Specifically, measurable learning outcomes are emphasized during the planning conference. How these outcomes are assessed becomes the raison d'être of the cycle of supervision. Perhaps the major criticism of an exclusive focus on learning outcomes is that affective and higher-order learning goals may be missed in the press to assess discrete outcomes. However, there also is evidence that first-year teachers struggle with learning outcomes and could benefit from supervision that focuses on this area.

A third adaptation is artistic supervision, promoted by Elliot Eisner (1982). This approach to supervision borrows extensively from supervision as it is practiced in professional schools of design and architecture. The supervisor is artistic critic, offering impressionistic renderings of the observed teaching.

The final form of clinical supervision was called ego counseling by Mosher and Purpel (1972, pp. 113–148). They undertook to analyze what happens to the student teacher psychologically during practice teaching. Arguing against a more traditional approach in which the analysis of teaching is restricted to the issues of curriculum, content, and pedagogy, they stated that clinical instructional supervision must be responsive to the teacher as person. The focus of ego counseling is on careful appraisal by the prospective teachers of themselves and their contexts, and subsequent revision of their thinking and actions in the classroom when the situation warrants. The supervisor (counselor) questions, interprets meanings and, when necessary, challenges the teacher's reasoning when contradictions exist between two aspects of the person's thinking or behavior.

So how are you to proceed? Clinical supervision, as described by Cogan, offered a systematic approach to supervision, yet adaptations of the system in the 1970s and 1980s also seem to have merit. By now you may be wondering if eclecticism is the answer. "After all, each of the strategies has strengths and weaknesses. I'll simply incorporate all the strategies into a grand unified supersystem of supervision." Before you embark on that rather ambitious journey, it may be helpful to review recent research trends in supervision.

What Can We Learn from Recent Research?

Two exhaustive reviews of supervisory research have been conducted by Glickman and Bey (1990) and Kagan (1988). Their work is illuminating because it spans research on the supervision of student teachers and beginning teachers, as well as inservice programs and supervision of counselors-in-training. Roles played by supervisors within each career phase and/or professional field are very similar. Bernard (1979) described three roles of the counselor supervisor: teacher, counselor, and consultant. The teacher role entails the Jamesian notion of intermediary. The supervisor interprets activities and demonstrates intervention techniques. As a counselor, the supervisor focuses on personal growth and acknowledges the feelings of the person. Finally, as a consultant the supervisor focuses on the trainee's own clients. In many respects, this terminology is similar to Housego and Grimmett's (1983) description of deliberative versus facilitative supervisory styles; Copeland's (1982) directive versus nondirective supervision; Glickman and Bey's (1990) directive, nondirective, and collaborative supervisory styles; and Tabachnick and Zeichner's (1984) technical-instrumental, personal-growth centered, and critical supervision. Certainly John Dewey's description of laboratory experiences as a means for developing self-reflection integrates these roles. Even a fairly recent special issue of the *Journal of Curriculum and Supervision* (Fall, 1989), which explored Schön's concept of the reflective practitioner, integrates the roles.

Content of Supervisory Conferences. A number of studies of preservice and inservice teacher supervision (Christensen, 1987; Pajak & Glickman, 1989; Zeichner & Liston, 1985) have examined the content of supervisory conferences. The findings are remarkably consistent. They have found that conferences are dominated by supervisors with discussion rarely moving beyond the immediate concerns of the cycle. Similar findings are found in counseling supervision. Holloway and Wampold (1983) found that supervision of counselors was almost entirely devoid of cognitive engagement, divergent thinking, and debate. It is notable to report that Pajak and Glickman (1989) found that teachers preferred informational to controlling language. It appears that novice teachers need a plan of action if they are to change instructional behaviors. When the supervisor offers specific suggestions while allowing the teacher to choose whether or not to act on or revise the recommendations, the conference is enhanced. In one of our own studies we also found that the controlling nature of conferences is influenced by supervisor development (Reiman & Gardner, 1994). Specifically, those teacher supervisors at more complex conceptual and justice reasoning levels practiced more democratic styles of conferencing. Novice teachers were allowed more time to talk and the supervisor incorporated more acceptance of feelings, specific encouragement, clarification of ideas, and higher-order questions.

Effectiveness of Supervisory Techniques. Studies in this arena largely have investigated different types of feedback (Belanger, 1962; MacGraw, 1965; Seager, 1965). Using Flanders-type rating scales, Belanger and Seager both examined the effectiveness of student feedback in changing student teacher behavior. For example, the Belanger study provided students with electrical switches which they used to report their understanding of the subject matter as presented by student teachers. Records of the student feedback were shared with the student teachers. Over the experimental period, each of the student teachers changed from primarily lecture to discussion format, and instructional presentations became clearer. More recent studies in clinical supervision (Preston & Baker, 1985) have supported the importance of systematic planning, observation, and feedback.

Thus recent research has provided information on aspects of the supervision process, styles of influence, and the importance of feedback. None of this, however, has gone beyond a description of process, nor has the research been connected in any direct way to an underlying theory. As we point out next, the directing constructs for supervision theory and practice are still ambiguous.

STILL MISSING: ADEQUATE THEORY FOR SUPERVISION

In one of her most recent works, *The Dialectic of Freedom* (1988), Maxine Greene stressed the importance of a broad definition of freedom that includes learning how to learn as well as social responsibility. As a fellow colleague Norman Sprinthall, who has traced Greene's contributions to education and human development, puts it, "Freedom is not rampant individualism, but rather helping each person become a self-reflective individual in full recognition of our common democratic goals of equality, an equality that includes sharing of the benefits as well as the burdens" (Sprinthall, Sprinthall, & Oja, 1994, p. 18). What both Sprinthall and Greene recognize and promote is a Deweyan assumption that education is not only about intellectual development but also about human development, and that theories of human development can bolster educational practice. Yet supervision largely has progressed without adequate guiding theory.

Cogan and Goldhammer raised the concern about lack of theory and research in the 1970s when they developed clinical supervision. In fact, Morris Cogan was very clear on this point. He argued that too often schools, school boards, and superintendents are unwilling to hold innovations up to the light of empiricism. Instead, they prefer to "buy blind" educational fads and styles that live for a season or two. Once the innovation has been bought, it is then promoted without being tested. Adding insult to injury, the innovation, once adopted, is handed over to teachers for implementation with few resources or support to help them in their efforts. After the passage of a few years, the innovation is allowed to wither on the vine as new ideas come along (Cogan, 1973, pp. 2–3).

Cogan further recognized the need for adequate theory to guide supervisory practice. As we mentioned in Chapter 1, however, Cogan realized that theory building would need to wait until systematic practice and supervision were mature enough to support promising theoretical frameworks. Yet he worried that if intellectual rigor and emerging theoretical frameworks were not developed, then the door would be opened for "much pseudoscience in supervision." And he wisely recognized that the cornerstone for our understanding of supervision would be the continuing work of educational psychologists who were investigating the teaching/learning process and human development.

Unfortunately, like the field of teacher education, instructional supervision has not been able to develop guiding theoretical frameworks. Saundra Tracy (1994) expressed dismay that research had not sufficiently progressed beyond general description of practices (Gordon, 1994). Similarly, John Keedy in a piece entitled *Ten Critical Research Questions in Instructional Supervision* (1994) argued for greater coherence and implicitly called for an emergent theory (pp. 4–5) when he observed that supervision must "give way to school-based collegial processes, self and collegial reflection, and problem solving based on interactions between subject knowledge and instruction." Keedy saw the need for frameworks that relate to principal and teacher intellectual growth. Perhaps the work of Glickman and Gordon has been some of the first to build a theoretical framework (1987).

Clearly the field of clinical instruction is at an important crossroad. Numerous leaders in supervision have called for greater coherence, more focus on school-based supervision, greater emphasis on shared decision making, increased attention to moral and intellectual growth, and enhanced opportunities for teachers to assume leadership roles. Yet adequate theory largely has been absent. Remember our earlier point that effective theory can be judged as somewhere near the midpoint on the continuum between wild fads and excessive reductionism. The developmental approach that we will shortly be introducing does incorporate many of the features of a theory somewhere near the midpoint on the continuum. It is a framework that continues to evolve as new research becomes available. As we describe an emerging developmental framework for supervision in succeeding chapters, we hope that you will hold it to the light of your own experience. Does the theory bridge to your practical experiences? Is the theory neither too speculative nor too narrow? And can the theory be both descriptive as well as prescriptive, in that it points the way for supervisory practice? Before we turn to the developmental framework, however, there is one final issue that must be raised.

STILL MISSING: PREPARATION FOR NEW ROLES

Long ago John Dewey described the importance of preparation: "Recognition of the natural course of development . . . always sets out with situations which involve learning by doing" (Dewey, 1974, p. 364). Dewey, as it turned out, spent a great deal of his professional life exploring ways to better prepare teachers for their important mission as educators. He realized the tragic ramifications if teachers are not prepared. Every generation of learners encounters teachers who are inadequately prepared for their complex responsibilities. To cap it all, one commentator has said that half of what we learn is wrong—and we don't know which half.

The causes for our current challenges in education are complex. Certainly a part of the problem stems from the difficulties that surround the preparation of future teachers. The challenges begin with the processes in teachers' preservice program and they escalate as teachers enter their own classrooms. Take for example the well known finding that first-year teachers often receive teaching assignments that are more difficult and challenging than their more seasoned colleagues (Huling-Austin, 1990; Reiman & Parramore, 1994).

One of the reasons for this state of affairs is the inadequacy of preservice, induction, and inservice supervision and coaching programs (Oja & Reimann, 1997). Too often, there is an absence of faculty who are able to offer instructional supervision for their novice colleagues. Cogan observed: "The profound underestimation of the difficulties teachers face in learning how to teach and in improving their teaching on the job is at the root of the major problems in the preservice and inservice education of teachers" (Cogan, 1973, p. 15). Yet as recently as 1986, Lanier and Little have observed that teacher education was characterized by "consistent chaos in the coursework" (p. 546). We also worry that too often there still is an assumption that learning to teach is easy and that the preparation of teachers, therefore, also should be simple. Coupled to these issues is a reluctance to adequately fund teacher education in general, and mentoring and supervision in particular. As a result, too little attention, too few resources, and little substantive preparation are provided for prospective supervisors (e.g., principals, assistant principals, lead teachers, mentor teachers, central office personnel, and teacher educators). Instead, we end up with brief and episodic assistance and assessment of teachers that has little chance of leading to in-depth change in teaching behaviors.

It is our belief that an important part of the delay in realizing school reform and teacher education reform is attributable to the lack of well-prepared mentors and supervisors who can offer direct in-class support to preservice teachers, beginning teachers, and inservice programs.

For 10 years we have worked in earnest to realize the goal of preparing supervisors, mentors, and clinical educators in selected school systems, and we have encountered some success in that goal. However, we are not sanguine when we realize the scope of the needs. The present corps of clinical educators, mentors, and supervisors is so minuscule in proportion to the needs of our own state that many student teachers and new teachers are not adequately supported, and many experienced teachers receive little assistance. Further, until policy makers and local school personnel change the teaching and extracurricular assignments given to new teachers, chances are that such a powerful innovation as mentoring and induction programs will be greatly reduced. This said, we still believe that one of the best hopes for education is dependent on developing cadres of new kinds of teacher professionals that we are calling mentors, clinical educators, and school-based teacher educators. These educators would have extensive preparation for their roles and would be rewarded for their new responsibilities. Exhibit 2-1 identifies a core set of needs that beginning teachers and their mentors have.

EXHIBIT **2-1**   NEEDS OF THE BEGINNING TEACHER
                   AND MENTOR TEACHER

NEEDS OF BEGINNING TEACHERS	NEEDS OF MENTOR TEACHERS
1. Help in developing as a competent person—not screening.	1. Support of administration.
2. Assistance from a clinical teacher who has been prepared for the role.	2. Education based on currently available curriculum.
3. Time to work together and to plan for growth.	3. Time to do coaching and to provide sustained support.
4. Orientation to the school, curriculum, and community.	4. Opportunities to talk with other mentor teachers.
5. Reasonable assignment.	5. Reasonable assignment which includes only one novice teacher and reasonableness in other responsibilities.

Meeting these needs better assures that the program can be sustained over many years with some certainty of success. In Chapter 7 we further explore the promise of new roles for experienced teachers. In particular, we will discuss how complex new helping roles like a school-based teacher educator can encourage the acquisition of new skills and can actually promote adult growth and development.

 SUMMARY

As a response to the ineffectiveness of most instructional supervision in the 1960s and 1970s, Cogan and Goldhammer developed clinical supervision. Their goal was to create a pedagogy of instructional supervision that would be rigorous, that could be tested empirically, and that could lead to more consistent positive changes in the instructional behavior of the teachers supervised. Cogan admitted, however, that his work must be seen as a conceptual rather than a theoretical framework. The major components of his cycle of supervision were planning, observing, analyzing, and providing feedback. More recent adaptations of clinical supervision have been scientific clinical supervision (focus on discrete teacher instructional behaviors), accountable supervision (focus on student learning outcomes), and artistic supervision (focus on the gestalt of the classroom).

Research on supervision in helping professions like teaching and counseling indicates that supervision is beginning to evolve from a discipline characterized by reluctance, to one distinguished by promise. Research has shown the following facets of supervision as key elements: sustained supervision, use of cues and feedback, positive supervisory atmosphere, use of higher-order questions, and the use of advance organizers like written plans to guide the supervision cycle. Thus supervision has begun to build a knowledge base for effective practice.

Still needed, however, is a theoretical framework to guide practice. In the following chapters, we will elaborate on a cognitive-developmental framework for supervisory practice. We remind you that all the theories about human development are not as complex as a single person. Further, the theory we present does not resolve all the questions about human behavior. Rather it represents our best current understanding, which is subject to modification as new knowledge comes forth. Perhaps this is why we often invoke the words of Harvard psychologist Gordon Allport. We are "wholehearted but half-sure."

SUPERVISION FOR TEACHER DEVELOPMENT ACTIVITIES

APPLIED

1. As you reflect on the four adaptations of clinical supervision: scientific, accountable, artistic, and ego counseling, write the strengths and weaknesses of each from your perspective. Also identify which of the four you would have an interest in using. If you need more information on each adaptation use the Suggested Readings at the end of this Activities section.

2. If you have used clinical supervision yourself, complete the following questions:
   a. I felt dissatisfied   I felt competent

               X_____X

   Place an x where you see yourself.

   Why did you have these feelings?

   b. What evidence do you remember that indicated your work as a clinical supervisor was helpful?
   c. What do you wish you would have done differently?
3. If you have been supervised by someone who used clinical supervision, answer the following:
   a. How did the process help you to develop as a teacher?
   b. What do you wish the supervisor would have done differently?
   c. What feelings do you remember having?
4. What theories do you use to guide your practice of supervision? It was noted in the chapter that there has been an absence of a theoretical

framework in the past and that one is just emerging. Write a short summary of the theorists you use to guide your practice.

PORTFOLIO DEVELOPMENT

1. Place your responses to the Applied section (just completed) in a binder. In Chapters 6 and 7 the supervisor's portfolio will be directly addressed.

SUGGESTED READINGS

1. Cogan, M. (1973). *Clinical supervision.* New York: Houghton Mifflin.

   Chapters 1 and 2 offer an overview and rationale for clinical supervision. It is rumored that Cogan rewrote this text six times before he was satisfied with the final product. Both chapters provide numerous insights for the contemporary supervisor.

2. Mosher, R., & Purpel, D. (1972). *Supervision: The reluctant profession.* New York: Houghton Mifflin.

   Of special interest is the authors' chapter on the importance of ego counseling theory and technique for supervision. Although the text is dated, there are many ideas and practices that have yet to be fully implemented.

REFERENCES

Belanger, M. L. (1962). *An exploration of the use of feedback in supervision.* Unpublished doctoral dissertation, Cambridge, MA: Harvard University.

Bernard, J. M. (1979). Supervisor training: A discrimination model. *Counselor Education and Supervision, 19,* 60–68.

Christensen, P. S. (1987). *The nature of feedback student teachers receive in post observation conferences with university supervisors.* Paper presented at the annual meeting of the American Educational Research Association, Washington, DC.

Cogan, M. L. (1973). *Clinical supervision.* Boston: Houghton Mifflin.

Conant, J. B. (1963). *The education of American teachers.* New York: McGraw-Hill.

Copeland, W. (1982). Student teachers' preferences for supervisory approach. *Journal of Teacher Education, 33*(2), 32–36.

DeAngelis-Peace, S. (1992). *A study of school counselor induction: A cognitive-developmental mentor/supervisor training program.* Unpublished doctoral dissertation, North Carolina State University, Raleigh, NC.

Dewey, J. (1974). *John Dewey on education: Selected writings.* (R. D. Archambault, Ed.). Chicago: University of Chicago Press, 1974.

Eisner, E. (1982). An artistic approach to supervision. In T. Sergiovanni (Ed.), *Supervision of teaching* (pp. 53–66). Alexandria, VA: Association for Supervision and Curriculum Development.

Firth, J., & Pajak, E. (1997). *Handbook of research on school supervision.* New York: Macmillan.

Glatthorn, A. (1984). *Differentiated supervision*. Alexandria, VA: Association for Supervision and Curriculum Development.

Glickman, C., & Bey, T. (1990). Supervision. In R. Houston (Ed.), *Handbook of research on teacher education* (pp. 549–566). New York: Macmillan.

Glickman, C., & Gordon, S. (1987). Clarifying developmental supervision. *Educational Leadership, 44* (8), 64–68.

Goldhammer, R. (1969). *Clinical supervision: Special methods for the supervision of teachers*. New York: Holt, Rinehart, and Winston.

Gordon, S. (Ed.) (1994). *Instructional supervision AERA/SIG Newsletter*.

Greene, M. (1988). *The dialectic of freedom*. New York: Teachers College Press.

Holloway, E. L., & Wampold, B. (1983). Patterns of verbal behavior and judgments of satisfaction in the supervision interview. *Journal of Counseling Psychology, 30,* 227–234.

Hopkins, D. (1990). Integrating staff development and school improvement: A study of personality and school climate. In B. Joyce (Ed.), *ASCD Yearbook: Changing school culture through staff development* (pp. 41–67). Alexandria, VA: Association for Supervision and Curriculum Development.

Housego, B. E., & Grimmett, P. P. (1983). The performance-based/developmental debate about student teaching supervision: A typology and a tentative resolution. *Alberta Journal of Educational Research, 29*(4), 319–337.

Huling-Austin, L. (1990). Teacher induction programs and internships. In R. Houston (Ed.), *Handbook of research on teacher education* (pp. 535–548). New York: Macmillan.

James, W. (1925). *Talks to teachers*. New York: Henry Holt.

Joyce, B., & Weil, M. (1996). *Models of teaching*. Englewood Cliffs, NJ: Prentice-Hall.

Journal of Curriculum and Supervision (1989, Fall). A symposium on Schön's concept of reflective practice. 5(1).

Kagan, D. (1987). Cognitive level of student teachers and their perceptions of cooperating teachers. *Alberta Journal of Educational Research, 33,* 180–190.

Kagan, D. (1988). Research on the supervision of counselors- and teachers-in-training: Linking two bodies of literature. *Review of Educational Research, 60*(3), 419–469.

Keedy, J. (1994). Ten critical research questions in instructional supervision. In S. Gordon (Ed.), *Instructional supervision AERA/SIG Newsletter* (pp. 4–5).

Lanier, J., & Little, J. (1986). Research in teacher education. In M. Wittrock (Ed.), *Handbook of research in teaching* (pp. 527–569). New York: Macmillan.

MacGraw, F. M. (1965). *The use of 35mm time lapse photography as a feedback and observational instrument in teacher education*. Unpublished doctoral dissertation, Stanford University, Stanford, CA.

Mosher, R., & Purpel, D. (1972). *Supervision: The reluctant profession*. Boston: Houghton Mifflin.

Oja, S. N., & Reiman, A. J. (1997). Describing and promoting supervision for teacher development across the career span. In J. Firth and E. Pajak (Eds.), *Handbook of research on school supervision*. New York: Macmillan.

Pajak, E., & Glickman, C. (1989). Informational and controlling language in simulated supervisory conferences. *American Educational Research Journal, 26*(1).

Preston, R., & Baker, R. (1985). An exploratory study of the clinical observation system: A systematic approach to student teacher observation during field experiences. *The South Pacific Journal of Teacher Education, 13*(1), 29–43.

Reavis, C. A. (1977). A test of the clinical supervision model. *Journal of Educational Research, 70*(4), 311–315.

Reiman, A. J., & Gardner, J. (1994). *Relationships between supervisor cognitive complexity and conference style.* Technical paper 94-1. North Carolina State University, Raleigh.

Reiman, A. J., & Parramore, B. (1994). Assignment, expectations, and development: A collaborative investigation. In M. O'Hair & S. Odell (Eds.), *Teacher education yearbook II: Partnerships in education.* Orlando: Harcourt Brace Jovanovich.

Seager, G. B. (1965). *The development of a diagnostic instrument of supervision.* Unpublished doctoral dissertation, Harvard Graduate School of Education, Cambridge, MA.

Sprinthall, N.A., Sprinthall, R., & Oja, S. N. (1994). *Educational psychology: A developmental approach.* New York: McGraw-Hill.

Tabachnick, B., & Zeichner, K. (1984). The impact of the student teaching experience on the development of teacher perspectives. *Journal of Teacher Education, 35(6),* 28–36.

Tracy, S. (1994). A message from the chair. In S. Gordon (Ed.), *Instructional supervision AERA/SIG Newsletter (p. 1).*

Zeichner, K., & Liston, D. (1985). Varieties of discourse in supervisory conferences. *Teaching and Teacher Education, 1(2),* 155–174.

Three Dimensions of Teacher Development

. . . .

*O*ur understanding of adult growth and development has been revised considerably during the last couple of decades. In Part II we take a special look at three dimensions of teacher development: cognitive development, phases of concern, and career cycles. As the reader will discover, teacher development is not influenced by just nature or nurture. Instead, teacher development involves an interaction between nature, nurture, and a critical third variable—*time*.

If you presently are preparing teachers for the new role of supervisor or on-site teacher educator you can use the developmental framework as a basis for providing differentiated support and challenge for the program participants. If you are a mentor, cooperating teacher, or school-based teacher educator you can apply the developmental framework to your work with interns and novice teachers.

C·H·A·P·T·E·R
3

A Developmental Framework

• • • • • • •

The Teacher as an Adult Learner

 INTRODUCTION

This chapter looks at the teacher as a developing adult learner. In particular, it examines the first dimension of adult development, namely teacher cognitive development. After a brief review of the major assumptions about teacher cognitive development, it describes three domains of teacher cognitive development: conceptual, ego, and moral. Each of these domains of teacher development is discussed with relevant examples from supervisory practice examined. Implications of the developmental framework for supervision are explored.

As you review this chapter check your comprehension by answering these questions:

- What is meant by the teacher as an adult learner?
- Does higher cognitive development imply more effective problem solving?
- How do the different domains of cognitive development overlap?

The choice of a developmental perspective is intended to give theoretical coherence to supervisory practices. "Standing on the shoulders" of such giants as Jean Piaget, Jane Loevinger, Lawrence Kohlberg, and David Hunt, a next generation of developmental researchers and practitioners from all corners of the globe has begun to explore adult development. At times it seems that a basic theory is proceeding at the pace of a glacier. Nonetheless, there is growing evidence that adults do not have to begin their "slow slide into senility" at the tender age of 18. Our own experiences also have shaped some of our understandings of cognitive development.

We have been working during the last 15 years to prepare and develop teachers for new roles in their schools. It has been an enterprise that is continually striving to find the middle ground, respecting both Kurt Lewin's dictum that "there is nothing quite as practical as good theory" as well as John Dewey's dictum that "there is nothing quite as theoretical as good practice." Working hard in our own backyard, we have made an important discovery. Teachers are enthusiastic about learning how to become skilled supervisors and coaches of their fellow novice and experienced colleagues (Reiman & Edelfelt, 1990). They acknowledge that teacher development is a key, and in the process, they as well as their colleagues are revitalized. No longer does supervision or "snoopervision" have to be done to teachers.

THE TEACHER AS AN ADULT LEARNER: STAGES

One of the most important changes in behavioral science has been a major revision in our understanding of directing constructs for adult development in general and teacher development in particular. For what must appear in hindsight as an unbelievable omission, psychological theories virtually ignored the process of adult growth. There were a few exceptions such as Levinson (1978) and Sheehy (1976), who implied a sequence of phases of adulthood, or Erik Erikson and his stages of personality (1982). The research base for these claims, however, was thin. Instead the far more common view was that adulthood from a growth stage perspective was a period of stability or gradual decline. Certainly psychoanalytical theory posited that adulthood was largely a recapitulation of early experience. Also trait and factor psychology, the major theory of personality in this country, was based on the assumption that there was no psychological growth beyond the age of 17 or 18. The many personality tests such as the Edwards Personal Preference Scale, the Cattell Sixteen Personality Factor Scale, or the Omnibus Personality Inventory (OPI) and others all assumed that personality was set in stone by the time a person reached adolescence. For example, the manual of the OPI states that "the ability for reflective thought, the use of abstractions, and problem solving, is fixed by the age of 17" (Heist & Yonge, 1968, p. 2). This also means that items on the scale itself were selected on the basis of indicating stability and reliability over time. Thus the concept of a trait such as conceptual complexity becomes static and item reliability becomes a self-fulfilling prophecy, and thus no growth can be measured.

Since many of the early developmental theorists shared this same view of the relative stability of growth potential, their models showed no major qualitative stage shifts after adolescence. Adult development was conceptualized as possibly involving quantitative change but not in a stage or sequence format. These views whether from psychoanalytical theory, trait and factor psychology, or indeed from cognitive stage theorists presented a similar paradigm for adults. That paradigm, however, soon evaporated. It could no longer account for new research about adult learning. There were two dimensions to these discoveries which changed our understanding of the adult growth process. The first was from research by Baltes and Schaie (1976) and the second was from a fortuitous mistake by developmental theorists themselves.

Baltes and Schaie (1976) conducted a series of important longitudinal studies (that is, they studied the same adults over extended time periods). Most of our previous information about adults had come from cross-sectional studies (studies with different adults from different age groups). Unfortunately, most cross-sectional studies presented a picture of the gradual erosion of cognitive abilities over the life span, the slow slide to senility, as a cynic might put it. Baltes and Schaie found the opposite. Three major intellectual factors (inductive reasoning, spatial ability, and verbal ability) actually showed slight increases well into adult lives. The only declines in function were the obvious ones: eyesight and hearing, as well as short-term memorizing of nonsense syllables. In the latter case it could be simply the result of motivation factors. How many adults are willing to apply great amounts of psychological energy to learning nonsense syllables at a researcher's behest? As a result the researchers clearly disproved the degeneration hypothesis and replaced it with a new view, adult "plasticity." Under certain conditions adults can improve in problem solving, generalization, and concept formation, which are crucial cognitive characteristics.

At the same time cognitive developmental researchers taking a cue from one of Piaget's lost papers (1972) began to revise that paradigm. Longitudinal studies by Kohlberg (1978); Kitchener, King, Wood, and Davison (1989); Loevinger (1976); and Arlin (1984), among others, all found that at least some adults demonstrated a clear pattern of stage and sequence growth.

Certainly the most crucial piece of evidence in this regard comes from the longitudinal study of Lee and Snarey (1988). With a sample of over 600 adults, they examined stage growth in two domains, ego or self-development based on Loevinger's theory (1976) and moral judgment based on Kohlberg's theory (1969). Adults demonstrated a pattern of slow growth in both domains, yet with important differences in the sequence. During early adulthood (ages 19 to 29) ego development with its emphasis on self-knowledge and interpersonal relations was found to be in advance of moral development. In other words, the test scores of the same subjects demonstrated a higher level of ego stage than moral stage. The cross-tabulation method, however, revealed during middle adulthood (ages 30 to 49) that the scores were equal in stage level, that is, ego and moral level were equivalent. In the older group (ages 50 to 80) there was yet another shift whereby moral stage was higher than ego stage. Theoretically, these findings outline important changes that adults may use as they construct meaning from experience. Questions of self and self-in-relationships appear to have greater salience in early adulthood, while questions of social justice, fairness, and integrity become more salient in the older phase of adulthood. These developmental trends have also been cross-validated recently by a longitudinal study by Rest and Narváez (1994) demonstrating that growth to higher and more complex stages of development is a definite potential.

The overall results of this basic research then are to depict a different picture of adult growth. We now apply these new assumptions about adult development to the teacher. Does the teacher as an adult learner progress through a sequence of stages of cognitive development? And what are its implications for teacher supervising and mentoring?

ASSUMPTIONS ABOUT TEACHER COGNITIVE DEVELOPMENT

There are a number of basic assumptions that underlie cognitive development. It is important to preface their description by acknowledging that a single human being is more complex than any theory or cluster of theories about human development. We believe, however, that it is possible to gain on the mystery of human understanding by drawing on recent research and application from a developmental perspective. Several key propositions guide cognitive developmental theory.

1. *All persons process experience through cognitive structures.* Robbie Case (1992) in his provocative synthesis of Piagetian and neo-Piagetian theory describes and extends the discussion of cognitive structures, demonstrating that considerable evidence supports their presence both within and across cultures. His work is an elaboration of constructivism. Constructivism means that each person builds or constructs meaning from experience. Piaget used the metaphor of a child as a natural philosopher or physicist in building concepts of time, space, and causality as a result of interacting with the real world. Constructivists view the mind as a gradually developing erector set in which a person's cognitions become more elaborated with increasingly complex scaffolds as a base to understand experience (Arlin, 1990). And, as we have just seen, we can now think of the adult as a constructivist in building increasingly complex cognitive structures to interpret meaning.

2. *Cognitive structures are organized in a hierarchical sequence of stages or plateaus from the less complex to the more complex.* John Dewey (1963) was one of the first educators to describe students moving through stages or cognitive structures in their intellectual growth and development. In this view, young children are not midget-sized adults, smaller yet essentially the same in their cognitive abilities. Instead children, adolescents, and adults develop through a series of qualitatively distinct stages or plateaus across a number of interdependent domains.

3. *Each shift in stage represents a major transformation in how the person makes meaning from his or her experience.* These cognitive transformations

could be compared to the metamorphosis from larva to caterpillar to butterfly. And just as with the butterfly, the growth is both invariant and irreversible. You never can go home again. For example, once a young teacher is able to use principles of justice and fairness in complex social dilemmas within the school, the capacity remains forever. She or he will, from that point on, find the use of rules and laws as necessary but not sufficient to the ultimate vitality of the school and the well-being of her or his students and colleagues.

4. *Development is not automatic.* Instead, persons need appropriate interactions with their environment. Our own research indicates that, in the case of the young adult learner, significant new "helping" experiences with appropriate reflection can promote more complex cognitive structures (Reiman & Parramore, 1993). Without these significant new experiences persons often stabilize at stages that are below their developmental potential. For example, a significant new experience for an experienced teacher might involve assuming a mentoring role for a novice colleague. If the experience is long-term (at least a year) with opportunities for reflection, the mentor teacher may well develop new ways of understanding the world that are qualitatively different from and more complex than previous understandings.

5. *Behaviors can be determined and predicted by a person's particular stage of development.* Predictions, however, are not exact and require repeated observations of the person in complex problem-solving settings. For example, participating in a post-observation conference with a novice teacher offers a unique and potent opportunity to observe how the beginning teacher is constructing meaning from his or her experiences as a teacher.

THREE FACES OF TEACHER COGNITIVE GROWTH

As was mentioned earlier, our understanding of adult growth and development has been revised considerably during the last 20 years. One change of particular significance concerns the question of stage itself. Is it a unitary concept or is it actually composed of an interlocking series of cognitive domains? In fact, early developmentalists such as Heinz Werner (1948) clearly suggested that a stage was a holistic framework or in the words of a song from the 1960s, a kind of singular and gigantic "eggplant that ate Chicago." We now know, however, that such a view was much too broad. Instead researchers now posit a series of developmental domains, or arenas, that are connected but not synonymous. Each domain itself is a highly important component of growth and deserves special attention. As a result this section provides a focused look at three domains of teacher cognitive development: conceptual complexity, ego complexity, and moral reasoning (see Figure 3-1).

FIGURE 3-1   THREE DIMENSIONS OF TEACHER
              DEVELOPMENT

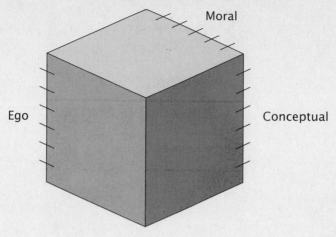

Perhaps it is obvious why these three domains are important in teaching. Conceptual complexity refers to the ability to understand abstract concepts; ego complexity refers to levels of self-knowledge; and moral reasoning is the ability to make ethical judgments. Also as you will discover, teacher cognitive development is not influenced by just nature or nurture. It is not an either-or proposition. Instead, teacher development involves an interaction between nature, nurture, and a critical third variable—*time*.

A number of major theorists have explored the area of cognitive development; among them are Hunt (1971), Loevinger (1976), Kohlberg (1969), and Piaget (1970). Each of these theorists has found that how persons reason is illustrative of a cognitive structure called a stage and that development to more complex plateaus or stages proceeds according to the assumptions that were briefly reviewed: that is, development proceeds through a sequence of qualitatively different stages in an invariant and hierarchical manner. The theorists just mentioned have concentrated their efforts on studying particular domains of human growth.

DAVID HUNT AND CONCEPTUAL LEVEL

Hunt (1971) examined adolescent and teacher development, in particular conceptual level. Conceptual level refers to a person's *current preferred style of solving problems in human interactions;* it is not a permanent classification but a description of interpersonal development (knowing how to relate to others). Hunt and his associates at the Ontario Institute for Studies in Education documented, through natural setting research, that teachers at more complex conceptual levels were more effective classroom teachers. They were more adaptive in teaching style, more flexible, and more tolerant of

Successful teachers "read and flex" according to the needs of students.

ambiguity. The teachers also were more empathic, accurately "reading and flexing" to the emotions and learning needs of the students. Hunt found teachers at lower conceptual levels to be more concrete in their thinking, less responsive to students, and preferential to one "tried and true" method of teaching.

Hunt termed the behaviors he found in more complex functioning teachers as the "new three R's"—responsiveness, reciprocality, and reflexivity. These skills represent a teacher's ability to "read and flex" with students. More abstract conceptual level teacher's were more effective at reading and flexing instruction to best match the needs of students. Hunt presents a three-stage model of conceptual level, as follows:

Stage A   Concrete conceptual level: Thinking tends to be concrete. Rules are considered fixed and unalterable. There is a preference for the single "tried and true" approach to teaching. Pleasing others is desirable. There is a strong preference for high structured learning activities.

Stage B   Concrete/abstract conceptual level: There is greater awareness of alternative strategies for solving problems as well as a growing awareness of the importance of feelings. Teachers are more open to new ideas and can tolerate some ambiguity.

Stage C   Abstract conceptual level: Teachers weigh and balance alternatives, take risks, value collaboration, and exhibit evidence of synthesis and integration in complex intellectual and interpersonal functions. There is a full acceptance of the consequences of one's behavior. Teachers can "read and flex" with students and employ a large repertoire of teaching strategies.

The whole approach to the teacher education process in general and teacher supervision (Calhoun, 1985) in particular needs to include the theory and applications of David Hunt. In the final chapter of this section we discuss how Hunt's theory forces teacher educators, supervisors, and mentors to examine the importance of differentiating their strategies to more effectively meet the learning needs of new teachers. Now it is time to look at another giant in cognitive developmental research—Jane Loevinger.

JANE LOEVINGER AND EGO (PERSONAL) DEVELOPMENT

Loevinger conducted an extensive series of field interviews. From this research emerged a framework for understanding the development of ego or intrapersonal growth (knowledge of one's self). Loevinger submits that ego frames how decisions are made. Ego is that part of the personality that acts as an executive: coordinating, choosing, and directing a person's actions. At higher stages of ego functioning persons accept or coordinate more aspects of a given situation, tolerate more ambiguity in complex decisions, and commit to actions based on review of a larger variety of possible actions. Each of Loevinger's successive milestones or stages of ego development is qualitatively different, with higher stages expressing greater integration (relating or synthesizing information) and differentiation (dividing or sorting information). Although Loevinger's theory was originally standardized on a large sample of women, it has more recently been cross-validated for males as well (Loevinger, 1987). There are no significant differences by gender. Exhibit 3-1 elaborates on Loevinger's sequence of developmental ego stages.

As one can see from Exhibit 3-1, Loevinger's developmental theory describes how persons move from *symbiotic and impulsive ego levels* (in which the person is dependent on others for decisions) to *conformist ego levels* (in which reasoning is framed by what is socially acceptable with little awareness of personal choice) to *autonomous ego levels* (in which the individual has a rich inner life, can reconcile contrasting or conflicting ideas, and has a high tolerance for ambiguity). Jane Loevinger acknowledges development as a transformation of structures with the highest ego stages showing evidence of coping with and accepting inner conflict.

EXHIBIT 3-1   SOME MILESTONES OF EGO DEVELOPMENT

STAGE	CODE	IMPULSE CONTROL, CHARACTER DEVELOPMENT	INTERPERSONAL STYLE	CONSCIOUS PREOCCUPATIONS	COGNITIVE STYLE
Presocial			Autistic		
Symbiotic	I-1		Symbiotic	Self vs. non-self	
Impulsive	I-2	Impulsive, fear of retaliation	Receiving, dependent, exploitative	Bodily feelings, especially sexual and aggressive	Stereotyping, conceptual confusion
Self-Protective	Δ	Fear of being caught, externalizing blame, opportunistic	Wary, manipulative, exploitative	Self-protection, trouble, wishes, things, advantage, control	
Conformist	I-3	Conformity to external rules, shame, guilt for breaking rules	Belonging, superficial niceness	Appearance, social acceptability, banal feelings, behavior	Conceptual simplicity, stereotypes, cliches
Conscientious-Conformist	I-3/4	Differentiation of norms, goals	Aware of self in relation to group, helping	Adjustment, problems, reasons, opportunities (vague)	Multiplicity
Conscientious	I-4	Self-evaluated standards, self-criticism, guilt for consequences, long-term goals and ideals	Intensive, responsible, mutual, concern for communication	Differentiated feelings, motives for behavior, self-respect, achievements, traits, expression	Conceptual complexity, idea of patterning
Individualistic	I-4/5	*Add:* Respect for individuality	*Add:* Dependence as an emotional problem	*Add:* Development, social problems, differentiation of inner life from outer	*Add:* Distinction of process and outcome
Autonomous	I-5	*Add:* Coping with conflicting inner needs, toleration	*Add:* Respect for autonomy, interdependence	Vividly conveyed feelings, integration of physiological and psychological, psychological causation of behavior, role conception, self-fulfillment, self in social context	Increased conceptual complexity, complex patterns, toleration for ambiguity, broad scope, objectivity
Integrated	I-6	*Add:* Reconciling inner conflicts, renunciation of unattainable	*Add:* Cherishing of individuality	*Add:* Identity	

Printed with permission from Jane Loevinger, *Ego Development*, Copyright © 1976. Jossey-Bass Inc., Publishers. All rights reserved.

In Loevinger's test samples as well as some of our own studies, adults tend to stabilize between Stage I-3 and Stage I-4. Very few adults consistently function at a level of ego development higher than Stage I-4. Whereas Hunt's theory of conceptual level looked at interpersonal development (how one deals with others), Loevinger's theory of ego development addresses intrapersonal growth (knowledge of one's self).

KOHLBERG AND MORAL / ETHICAL DEVELOPMENT

Last but not least is the work of Lawrence Kohlberg. Using Piaget's method of clinical interviews Kohlberg was interested in how persons think about problems of social justice. Interviewing persons of different ages, different social and economic classes, and different cultures, he discovered that all persons think about social justice. Moreover, the ways that persons think about issues of fairness and ethics form a developmental sequence of six stages. Each stage is distinct and qualitatively different from the other stages of moral reasoning. The levels and stages are outlined in Exhibit 3-2.

Exhibit 3-2 shows how a person's moral development moves from the pre-conventional level (in which decisions are based on "might makes right" and the notion of trading or exchanging favors—"you scratch my back and I'll scratch yours") to the conventional level (in which decisions are based on "what the majority wants" or what the laws prescribe) to the post-conventional level (in which decisions are based on principles—both written and unwritten, such as Immanuel Kant's categorical imperative: "Act only as you would be willing that everyone should act in the same situation," or John Stuart Mill's conception of the greatest good for the greatest number). Although Kohlberg's original sample in the 1960s was white males from the Midwest, substantial longitudinal research with both males and females and including studies from over 50 different countries now provides a firm research base for the stage and sequence model (Snarey, 1985; Lee & Snarey, 1988).

STAGE AND BEHAVIOR: IS HIGHER BETTER?

The critical question is, of course, what is the relation between cognitive developmental stage domains and actual behavior? Many a psychological theory has foundered on this question. Yet from our standpoint, the key issue is whether theory is visible in practice and practice is visible in theory (see Chapter 1). Theory, no matter how elegant or how much longitudinal research validates a stage sequence, would remain useless without a behavioral connection. The connection to behavior forms the rationale for our objectives. If we find that higher stages predict more adequate behavior we will have the keystone for mentoring and supervision objectives. However, before we review a selected set of studies as the basis for devel-

Exhibit 3-2 KOHLBERG'S STAGES OF MORAL DEVELOPMENT

Level I Pre-Conventional Level

At this level moral judgment resides in external happenings rather than in persons or standards.

Stage 1 Concern about self. Obedience and punishment orientation. One sees oneself as being dominated by other forces. Actions are judged in terms of physical consequences.

Stage 2 One-way concern about another person (what he or she can do for me, how we can agree to act so I will benefit). The basic motive is to satisfy my own needs.

Level II Conventional Level

At this level moral judgment resides in performing good or right roles, in maintaining the conventional order, and in meeting the expectancies of others.

Stage 3 Concern about groups of people, and conformity to group norms. An orientation to approval, and to pleasing others.

Stage 4 Concern for order in society. Honor comes from keeping the rules of society. The motive is to preserve society.

Level III Post-Conventional Level

At this level moral judgment resides in commitment to shared or sharable rights, principles, or duties.

Stage 5 Social contract, legalistic orientation. What is right is what the whole society decides. There are no legal absolutes. The U.S. Constitution is written in Stage 5 terms.

Stage 6 Universal ethical principles. What is right is a decision of one's conscience, based on ideas about rightness that apply to everyone (all nations, people). These are called ethical principles. An ethical principle is different from a rule. A rule is specific (Thou shalt not kill). An ethical principle is general (All persons are created equal). The most important principles deal with justice, equality, and the dignity of all people. These principles are higher than any given law.

opmental rationale, there is one major point often overlooked in this framework.

Higher, more complex developmental stages determine a more adequate set of behaviors *only* under certain conditions. Recall that we stressed the interactive nature of development, that is, behavior as a function of the person interacting with the environment espoused in the B f P × E model. This means we need to examine the environmental task demands. To problem-solve or to problem-frame means we need to know what kind of a problem we have to solve. Is it simple or complex? Thus we must always keep in mind what kind of activity is requisite before we can predict the behavior from developmental stage.

For example, an important study of brain activity (the amount of glucose burned during problem solving) indicated two important outcomes. Subjects assessed at higher stages of cognition on Piagetian formal operations were more efficient (burned less glucose) when the task required more complex problem solving. The subjects were asked to solve increasingly more difficult abstract patterns on Raven's Progressive Matrices. The reverse was also true. When the task was simple, rotelike and boring, requiring visual vigilance, the abstract thinkers were less efficient than the concrete thinkers (Hoestetler, 1988). Thus when it comes to predicting behavior from cognitive stage, one must always examine the complexity of the task requirements. In light of this let us look at some research in the three developmental domains (ego, conceptual, and moral) as it pertains to a complex human activity such as teaching or supervision.

CONCEPTUAL COMPLEXITY

The results of research on conceptual complexity have been reported in extensive studies of teachers and are summarized in a meta-analysis by Miller (1981). After analyzing some 60 studies which employed the Hunt Conceptual Systems Test (CST) as a measure of cognitive stage complexity, he concluded that persons functioning at higher stages on the CST exhibited behaviors such as:

1. A reduction in prejudice
2. Greater empathic communication
3. Greater focus on internal control
4. Longer decision latencies
5. More flexible teaching methods
6. More autonomy and more interdependence
7. Superior communication and information processing

Hunt (1976) noted that higher CST scores for teachers allowed for "reading and flexing" in the classroom, which meant the ability to change the learning environment in accord with pupil needs (see Exhibit 3-3).

A similar set of findings was reported by Thies-Sprinthall (1980) with an added dimension of significance for teacher supervision. She found that higher cognitive level (CL) supervising teachers were more accurate in their evaluations of student teachers, as Miller's meta-analysis would suggest. She also found what can be termed a disordinal interaction between the stage of the supervisor and the stage of the student teacher. The disordinal match was noticeable in one quadrant focused on the supervising teachers at lower CL stages than their student teachers. In that quadrant (high CL student teacher and low CL cooperating teacher) the cooperating teacher evaluations were both inaccurate and negative. The low CL cooperating teachers were excessively judgmental and perceived the flexi-

EXHIBIT 3-3   DESCRIPTIONS OF HUNT'S CONCEPTUAL STAGES:
TEACHERS' ATTITUDES TOWARD TEACHING
AND LEARNING

Stage A

Strong evidence of concrete thinking

Knowledge seen as fixed

Employs a singular "tried and true" method

Exhibits compliance as a learner and expects the same from pupils

Low on self-direction and initiative

Does not distinguish between theory and facts

Teaching is "filling the students up with facts"

Stays on Bloom's Levels 1 and 2 regardless of student level*

Enjoys highly structured activities for self and for pupils

Very uncomfortable with ambiguous assignments

Does not question authority

Follows curriculum as if it is carved in stone

Verbalizes feelings at a limited level and has difficulty discerning feelings in pupils

Reluctant to talk about own inadequacies

Stage B

Growing awareness of difference between concrete versus abstract thinking

Separates facts, opinions, and theories about teaching and learning

Employs some different teaching models in accord with student differences

Evidence of teaching for generalization as well as skills

Can vary structure of lesson according to the needs of pupils

Some openness to innovations and can make some appropriate adaptations

Shows sensitivity to pupils' emotional needs

Enjoys some autonomy

Employs Bloom's Taxonomy Levels 1 (memory) through 4 (analysis) when appropriate

Evaluations are appropriate to assignments

Stage C

Understands knowledge as a process of successive approximations

Shows evidence of originality in adapting innovations to the classroom

Comfortable in applying all appropriate teaching models

Most articulate in analyzing one's own teaching in both content and feeling

High tolerance for ambiguity and frustration. Can stay on task in spite of major distractions

EXHIBIT 3-3   *(continued)*

Does not automatically comply with directions—asks for rationale.

Fosters an intensive questioning approach with students

Can use all levels of Bloom's taxonomy—memory through evaluation

Responds appropriately to the emotional needs of all pupils

Can match and mismatch with expert flexibility

Exhibits careful evaluations based on objective criteria

Continuously reflects on experiences, making adjustments when necessary

*The description of Bloom's levels refers to his taxonomy of educational objectives. The system specifies a sequence of six stages or levels of objectives that can be matched to assessment strategies (e.g., basic knowledge, comprehension, application, analysis, synthesis, and evaluation).

ble teaching methods of the student teachers as inadequate. Such a study should serve as a reminder of the downside of cognitive developmental findings.

A study of McKibbin and Joyce (1981), also rarely reported, revealed a similar set of positive and negative findings concerning developmental stage and teaching performance. They provided teachers with a series of workshops on innovative strategies for the classroom and returned one year later to assess generalization in actual practice. With a measure of psychological development assessed at pretest, they found a direct relationship between higher-stage teachers and employment of innovative methods from the workshops. They also found the opposite. The lower-stage teachers resisted and virtually failed to employ any but the most simple and concrete methods when assessed one year later. Exhibit 3-4 displays the outcomes.

A comparable study by Hopkins (1990) explored the link between stage, implementation of innovations, and school climate. The major conclusion of the study was that the more abstract and cognitively complex teachers employed new models of teaching at a rate that was four times greater than their counterparts at concrete and less complex psychological stages. He also found that school climate and, in particular, the disposition of the principal also influenced the implementation of new innovations.

EXHIBIT 3-4   McKIBBIN AND JOYCE: TEACHER ADOPTION OF NEW TEACHING MODELS

	PRETEST	**POSTTEST**
High-stage teachers	High	High
Low-stage teachers	Moderate	Low

These findings then serve as a reminder of both aspects of the developmental question. Higher cognition is more adequate and lower cognition is less adequate when the task is complex. The McKibbin-Joyce study and the Hopkins study also explain the truism that new curricular guides are not teacherproof and the fact that so many of those guides end up gathering dust in the bottom drawers of teachers' desks.

The research of Penelope Peterson represents further confirmation of the relation between cognitive complexity and teaching behaviors. In Peterson et al. (1989) the results compared teaching performance and student achievement in mathematics between two groups of experienced first-grade teachers. Employing an elaborate set of multiple measures of teacher beliefs (interview, questionnaires, content knowledge), they could classify the teachers' cognitive/conceptual complexity into two general modes, less cognitively based (LCB) and more cognitively based (CB). The actual teaching performance of the two groups was substantially different. The CB group employed higher-order teaching skills, for example, problem posing, active listening, ongoing assessment, and continuous adaptation. The LCB group exhibited an opposite set of rigid, fact-based, rote approaches to instruction. The results for student achievement cut two ways. Both sets of students in LCB and CB classrooms did equally well on number-facts achievement tests, but the students in the CB classes also did much better on problem-solving tests. These findings, though only from one study, are in fact remarkably consistent with the huge number of research studies employing the Hunt test, as noted earlier.

EGO DEVELOPMENT

A general study on the relationship between ego stage in the Loevinger system and behavior was conducted by Bielke (1979) with a sample of over 200 young mothers. Parenting behavior was coded through direct observation over 6- and 12-month intervals. Higher stages on the Loevinger scale predicted effective parenting behavior (e.g., more empathic, authoritative, and democratic). Also a highly revealing finding indicated that as the task requirements became more complex, for example, parenting an 18-month-old versus a 6-month-old baby, the mothers at lower stages of ego development demonstrated a *decrease* in effective parenting. Such findings can be generalized to the tasks of formal instruction.

A more direct relationship between Loevinger's ego stage and teaching was reported by Cummings and Murray (1989). In a study of 58 experienced teachers in Canada there was a strong relationship between ego level and the teachers' conceptions of the instructional role. At Stage I-3 (Conformist), the role was as a presenter of information; at Stage I-4 (Conscientious) the role included modeling, concerns for students, and a mastery of teaching skills. At the highest stages, I-4/5 and I-5 (Autonomous), the role included challenge, concern for the whole child, and teaching-learning as a search. Importantly, they found that the concept of caring for students also had different meaning according to ego level. At the conformist level the teacher, "likes children." At the conscientious level the teacher "is empathic and understands the needs of the child." At the autonomous level the teacher is "a model, a catalyst, and a facilitator of growth." Each conception clearly represents a qualitatively different meaning for the teacher as a caring person. They also reported an indirect effect between ego level and performance through path analysis. A major difficulty was the narrow dependent variable (grades and instructor ratings). In an overall sense, however, the study adds to the validity and the importance of cognitive stage variables such as ego development and teaching not only for experienced teachers but also for student teachers as well. They comment that student teachers at I-3 (Conformist) simply copy the teaching style of their cooperating teachers, thus behaving in accord with their developmental level (Cummings & Murray, 1989, p. 31).

Oja and Smulyan (1989) found that a teacher's cognitive-developmental stage perspective frames his or her understandings of classroom action research. They found across a variety of developmental domains—ego, conceptual, and moral—that stage defines the context of the meaning system through which the teacher interprets and acts on issues related to the school environment and action research. At higher ego stages, for example, teachers assumed multiple perspectives, used a wider variety of coping behaviors, employed a broader repertoire of group process and change strategies, were more interpersonally sensitive, and tended to be more self-reflective.

MORAL JUDGMENT

A general meta-analysis conducted by Blasi (1980) indicated that there was a consistent and positive relationship between moral and ethical judgment in well over two-thirds of the 74 studies reviewed. It is also noteworthy that there is an increasing body of contemporary research documenting the relationship between moral cognition and ethical behavior for adults in a variety of professions. Rest and Narváez (1994) report studies indicating that professional accountants at higher stages of reasoning are far more likely to detect fraudulent practice than those at lower stages. Similar findings are reported for groups of dentists, nurses, and veterinarians. These outcomes are highly consistent with earlier research but also add new insights. For example, in the large sample study of accountants, age and experience were not related to stage score or to fraud detection. In fact, the senior officials reasoned at lower levels and were less likely to discover unethical practice. Thus there is substantial evidence to support the generalization of higher stage as a predictor of democratic principled action as well as the reverse.

What about research focused on teachers and other educators? Similar outcomes have been reported. For example Reiman and Parramore (1994) found first-year teachers at higher moral reasoning and conceptual complexity levels to have greater concern for the instructional needs of the students. Also a recent study by MacCallum (1993) examined teacher moral judgment in the Kohlberg system and approaches to student discipline. Teachers at higher stages exhibited more complex perspective-taking, were more sensitive to students' rights, and employed rules to promote student understanding. Their cohorts at lower levels of moral judgment were primarily concerned with maintaining order. There were no gender differences in moral judgment. The connection between democratic student discipline strategies and level of teacher moral/ethical reasoning was documented in an earlier study by Libby (1980). Her results from a study of middle school teachers in this country were highly congruent with the MacCallum results from Australia.

The universality of the stage-behavior relationships was documented most recently by Oser (1991, 1994) in his work in German schools. Teachers at more complex stages of moral reasoning employed more interactive teaching methods, a reduced security orientation, and "less single-handed conflict resolution" (p. 225). The latter phrase may be a euphemism for a dictatorial management style. Rulon (1992) in this country found a similar relationship between moral judgment and the ability to use a dialogue teacher-learner mode of discourse in democratically organized schools.

One of our own studies (Reiman & Gardner, 1993) looked more specifically at the relationship between supervisory dispositions and moral and conceptual reasoning. A small sample of prospective clinical teachers was assessed for moral and conceptual levels. All the participants were engaged in an extensive program to prepare them for roles as school-based supervisors of novice teachers. The program spanned one year. During the final seven months of the program each prospective clinical teacher completed four pre-observation conference audiotapes and four post-observation conference audiotapes as part of a guided practicum experience. These tapes were analyzed. Results indicated that clinical teachers at higher moral reasoning levels were more participatory in their conferencing styles encouraging supervisee talk. Further, they acknowledged more ideas and feelings expressed by the novice teachers.

The most recent summary of research on teacher performance and moral reasoning stage is highly congruent with these individual studies. Chang (1994) has shown that teachers at higher stages are more effective in discipline strategies, more empathic to student needs, more adept at individualizing instruction, and create an intellectual and participative classroom climate.

COGNITIVE-DEVELOPMENTAL SYNTHESIS

In sum, then, the research across the three domains is clear and consistent. Higher stage is more often associated with more effective performance in complex human interactions. Lower stages most often lead to less competent performance. Exhibit 3-5 summarizes the characteristics of each level.

EXHIBIT 3-5   COGNITIVE DEVELOPMENT ACROSS DOMAINS

DOMAIN	HUNT'S CONCEPTUAL	LOEVINGER'S EGO/SELF	KOHLBERG'S MORAL
	Impulsive	Presocial-impulsive	Obedience-punishment
	Concrete-Dogmatic	Self-protective	Naively egotistic
Stage	Dependent, abstract	Conformist	Social conformity
		Conscientious	Authority maintaining
	Self-directed, abstract	Autonomous	Principled reasoning

Viewing the strands of cognitive development together provides a general description of the teacher at various stages of cognitive-structural growth. At the least complex stage the teacher tends to see the world in concrete terms. Choices are perceived as black or white, authority figures are held in high regard, conformity is rewarded, instruction tends to be "tried and true," and there is little tolerance for ambiguity (Oja, 1979). Teachers at moderate levels are particularly vulnerable to the expectations of colleagues, rules are explicit, and there are some attempts to enlarge their repertoire of instructional skills. At the highest stages, teachers are inner directed, interested in collaborating with colleagues, "read and flex" with the varied instructional needs of their students, encourage more complex functioning in the students (and their supervisees), and have achieved a synthesis in their classrooms between an emphasis on achievement and an interpersonal orientation (Sprinthall & Thies-Sprinthall, 1983).

In a sense the findings on the behavior-stage relationship can be construed as supporting the concept of Attribute Treatment Interaction (ATI) (Snow, 1987). In this case the attribute is the developmental stage of the adult professional as he or she interacts with pupils, curriculum materials, or beginning professionals in supervision (Peterson, 1988). As a result, the current research base provides strong support identifying the relationship between stage and complex behavioral task requirements. That relationship clearly indicates two sets of findings. In problem-solving situations requiring complex and humane response, adults in general and teachers specifically who process experience at higher stages of development are more competent, effective, and efficient. Adults in general or teachers specifically who process experience at lower stages of development perform at increasing levels of incompetence when faced with complex tasks.

SPOTLIGHT ON EDUCATIONAL LEADERS

THE ZONE OF NEXT DEVELOPMENT

Many states are outlining performance standards for educational leaders (e.g., superintendents, principals). These standards describe broad domains of contemporary school administration. For example, North Carolina's Standards Board for Public School Administration is developing high standards for the qualification, training, and experience of public school administrators. Their ten performance dimensions follow. As you review them, note which dimensions relate to the moral/ethical, conceptual, and ego domains described in Chapter 3.

1. Facilitates the development, implementation, and communication of a shared vision of learning that reflects excellence and equity for all students
2. Promotes the development of organizational, instructional, and assessment strategies that enhance learning
3. Works with others to ensure a working and learning climate that is safe, secure, and respectful of diversity
4. Demonstrates integrity and behaves in an ethical manner
5. Facilitates school improvement by engaging the school community's stakeholders in collaboration, team-building, problem solving, and shared decision making
6. Uses excellent management and leadership skills to achieve effective and efficient organizational operations
7. Employs effective interpersonal, communication, and public relations skills
8. Demonstrates academic success, intellectual ability, and a commitment to lifelong learning
9. Promotes the appropriate use of reliable information to facilitate progress, to evaluate personnel and programs, and to make decisions
10. Fosters a culture of continuous improvement focused on teaching and learning

As you can see, an educational leader is ethical, able to problem-solve, and is empathic, among other things. Thus the educational leader becomes a model for teachers involved in supervision, coaching, mentoring, or other professional development programs.

Educational leaders have a special obligation to understand thoroughly the psychology of cognitive, social, and moral development. Devising and validating experiences that genuinely affect the full development of teachers and students are far more complex tasks than rewriting policy manuals. Like Dewey (1938) we believe that schools are democratic to the extent that they contribute to the all-around growth of every student and teacher. Educational leaders organize programs and experiences that promote full human development. Such an approach requires the educational leader to be just beyond a person's comprehension and current problem-solving ability. Thus, it encourages "stretching" and growth. Stated differently, the educational leader operates in "the zone of next development" (Vygotsky, 1978) encouraging colleagues to think and behave in more complex ways.

THE GENDER QUESTION

Ever since Carol Gilligan's (1982) remarkable book there has been a challenge to stage theory as biased against women. Somewhat ironically there have been very few studies and even fewer research studies to support her claims. Her research samples were small and local, including 25 Harvard college students in one of her classes, a follow-up study of 29 women having abortions in the Boston area, and a cross-sectional study of 36 male and female subjects between the ages of 6 to 60 years old (Loevinger, 1987). Nonetheless her view has become almost a standard criticism of stage theory as male oriented on one hand and bereft of empathy and caring on the other.

A careful review of research by both male and female scholars, however, reveals quite a different finding. Male researchers such as Rest (1986) and Walker (1984, 1986) have summarized studies of from 6,000 to 10,000 subjects and consistently report either no gender differences or slight trends in favor of females. Female scholars such as Braebeck (1982), Scott-Jones (1991), Mednick (1989), and King and Kitchener (1994) also report no significant gender differences in stage scores. The longitudinal study already noted by Lee and Snarey (1988) was composed of 400 females and 225 males, with no gender differences on either ego or moral stage. Finally, Lind (1993) reported no gender differences in a large scale (N = 4000) cross-cultural study in Europe.

These findings are highly congruent with gender findings in more general areas. For example, Case (1992) has found no gender differences in children and adolescents across six comparisons on Piaget tasks. Hyde and Linn (1988) in a meta-analysis of some 1.5 million subjects, found no gender differences by verbal ability. These same researchers (Linn & Hyde, 1989) in another meta-analysis, had shown only one difference by gender in mathematical and scientific abilities across 18 comparisons.

Thus the general summary indicates that earlier research reports and case studies suggesting gender differences are not valid. In fact Linn and Hyde (1989) suggest that the only bias may have been from male editors rejecting articles showing no differences and publishing articles that emphasized gender differences. And, of course, it is equally important to point out that the stage domains predict teaching behaviors that are more flexible and more humane.

SUMMARY

This chapter looked at the teacher and supervisor as a developing adult learner. In particular, it reviewed the first dimension of adult development, namely teacher cognitive development. The major assumptions of cognitive development were reviewed. They include (1) all persons process experience through cognitive structures; (2) the structures are organized in a hierarchical sequence of stages or plateaus from the less complex to the more complex; (3) each shift in stage or plateau represents a major transformation in how the person makes meaning from experience; (4) a person's development requires appropriate interactions with the environment; and (5) behaviors can be predicted by a person's particular stage of development.

A review of the three domains of teacher cognitive development followed. These domains include conceptual, ego, and moral reasoning and demonstrate a consistent relationship between each stage domain and complex behavior. Finally, the evidence clearly supports the assumption that stage levels are not biased against females.

SUPERVISION FOR TEACHER DEVELOPMENT ACTIVITIES

APPLIED

1. Learning About Jane Loevinger and David Hunt

   Since both theorists use the research method of open-ended sentence stems, you can observe differences in conceptual complexity through a written role play. For example, review Loevinger's descriptions of ego development at the following three levels (see Exhibit 3-1): Self-protective (Delta), Conformist (I–3), and Autonomous (I–5). Next, write an answer to a Loevinger stem at each of the three levels in the *role of a new teacher*.

   Stem: My main goal . . .
   a. Delta Self-protective
   b. I-3 Conformist
   c. I-5 Autonomous

   At Delta the main ego value is to protect yourself and externalize blame so a response might be, "To keep my thoughts to myself and figure out shortcuts."

   At I-3 with social conformity as the main value, "To find out how to please my supervisor and make sure the kids like me."

At I-5 with autonomy and self-direction as the main value, "To learn as much as I can about teaching to help children grow and develop."

You can do the same exercise with Hunt's conceptual stages (see Exhibit 3-3). Examine the characteristic learning style of the A, B, and C levels and then answer the following stem:

Stem: "When I think about rules . . ."

Note the differences in complexity for responses at A, "Rules are for the birds"; B, "Rules are necessary for an orderly society"; and C, "I try to distinguish between rules that are arbitrary or social conventions and ones based on democratic ethics. I follow the latter and try to change the former."

2. Learning About Kohlberg's Stages and Values

One method of improving your understanding of Kohlberg's stages of ethical reasoning is to pick out some current issue of controversy. Then review the reasons that participants employ in justifying, or in some cases, rationalizing their position. For example, a problem arose when four single lay religious women wanted to buy a house. The covenant for the housing development indicated that no more than two different families could live in one house to prevent the growth of sub-rental units. Some reasons in opposition were:

a. Our house value will go down. We will lose money.
b. We don't want these women in our neighborhood; their religion is different from ours.
c. We need to enforce the covenant. If we permit them to live in the house, what will happen next?

See if you can classify these reasons according to Kohlberg's system (see Exhibit 3-2). For example, which set of reasons are primarily materialistic or money based (Stage 2)? Which are based on social conformity (Stage 3)? Or based on following the law (Stage 4)? Then see if you can come up with reasons in favor of a covenant change such as:

a. The community as a whole will benefit from these new neighbors. They have good ideas and will help us become more diverse.
b. Well, let's just change the definition of a family. A religious group of four people can be considered as one family.
c. Who knows? Maybe our property values will go up.

3. Read the following three case studies. Underline statements used as clues to determine the conceptual complexity level of each person (see Exhibit 3-3).

1. Case Study—Bill

Bill moved to your state after six years of teaching. He is very excited about teaching humanities to academically gifted middle school students. After an initial observation, you determine that Bill is relating well to his students and that he uses a variety of methods to present subject matter to his students. Also you note that he helps some of the quietest kids in the class verbalize some of their scared feelings about using inquiry.

In your post-conference he was attentive but often asked for some additional resources to back up suggestions. He was at ease nonverbally. Just as you left the class, he was outlining a mini-lecture on the blackboard: "Why do some native Americans not regard Thanksgiving as a national holiday?" You felt like staying.

Bill attended a seminar that the Director of Exceptional Children sponsored concerning Renzulli's inquiry method. A ninth-grade English teacher, Beth, attended that same session. They have collaborated on a new unit going beyond the Renzulli inquiry method and you are impressed with the changes.

Bill and Beth want to develop lessons that both can use in their respective classes using the inquiry method. Bill often takes information he has received in workshops and adapts the materials to fit the classes at his school.

Now designate the stage/mode and level of supervisory structure needed for Bill based on the clues underlined.

Conceptual Level   *Level of Structure Needed*

A_____ B_____ C_____   High_____ Moderate_____ Low_____

2. Case Study—Tom

Tom is an experienced math teacher who has moved to the state to look after his ailing parents. He has eight years of teaching experience.

When you initially observe Tom, you are impressed with his knowledge of subject matter. However, you are concerned that he relies on one pattern of instruction. He introduces a concept, does a few problems on the board, assigns seatwork to be started in class and completed at home as homework, and walks around while the students start the work. The next day, he checks the homework by having students put the problems on the board, row by row, student by student.

During your first observation, Tom lost his temper with Rick, a student who is learning disabled. He yelled at him when he made the same mistake the second time, "No, you dummy! I told you, not that!"

When you discussed the incident, he apologized profusely for losing control and said it would never happen again. He says he really does like all children but has to insist on very high standards. He seems very uncomfortable with you. You have overheard him expressing his dissatisfaction with the peer coaching program.

Now designate the stage/mode and level of supervisory structure needed for Tom based on the clues underlined.

Conceptual Level   *Level of Structure Needed*

A_____ B_____ C_____   High_____ Moderate_____ Low_____

3. Case Study—Carole

   Carole is a first-year teacher. This past summer she attended a Teacher Expectations and Student Achievement (TESA) workshop that the Department of Public Instruction sponsored. Carole is interested in working with May Lynn, an experienced, successful fifth-grade teacher who also attended the TESA workshop.

   You are Carole's mentor. Carole has a comprehensive understanding of lesson design, but you have noticed she has difficulty identifying the learning outcomes for her lessons. She shows flexibility and adaptability to her students' needs most of the time. However, Carole could use some refinement of her responsiveness to students. Occasionally she doesn't pick up on the "cues" students send her. Once in a while she makes snap judgments about a student.

   She is excellent on the higher-order questioning, open-ended questions, and direct teaching method. She is a little uncomfortable with student feelings and the use of cooperative learning. In one of your planning conferences she seemed confident; however, she showed some discomfort when you showed her several readings on how to set up cooperative groups. She said, "I think I may lose control of the class if I don't teach to the whole group."

Now designate the stage/mode and level of supervisory structure needed for Carole based on the clues underlined.

Conceptual Level   *Level of Structure Needed*

A_____ B_____ C_____   High_____ Moderate_____ Low_____

SUGGESTED READINGS

1. Case, R. (1992). *The mind's staircase.* Hillsdale, NJ: Erlbaum.

   This is the most comprehensive review of recent research outlining the stage and sequence of Piaget's theory. Case and his associates examine cognitive development across a series of domains: cognitive, interpersonal, etc., with a variety of samples. It is a strong validation of cognitive-developmental theory.

2. Kuhmerker, L. (1991). *The Kohlberg legacy.* Birmingham, AL: REP.

   Kuhmerker and her associates present a synthesis of Kohlberg's monumental research over the past 20 years. Included are studies of cross-cultural validation, the gender bias question, and a variety of recent intervention studies.

3. King, P., & Kitchener, K. (1994). *Developing reflective judgment: Understanding and promoting intellectual growth and critical thinking in adolescents and adults.* San Francisco: Jossey-Bass.

   King and Kitchener detail their longitudinal studies of adult development focused on stages of reflective judgment, their conception of levels of conceptual complexity, and problem solving.

4. Loevinger, J. (1987). *Paradigms of personality.* New York: Freeman.

   Loevinger reviews a wide variety of theories of personality development including an update on her own stages of ego development, an excellent discussion comparing and contrasting different models with her stage and sequence view.

5. Hunt, D. E. (1974). *Matching models in education.* Toronto: OISE.

   Though dated, Hunt's work outlines the substantive basis for his theory of conceptual levels and teaching behavior. He is also able to show the importance of "matching" learning activities to the current preferred stage and then how to gradually "mismatch" by varying the amount of structure to promote growth.

6. Rest, J., & Narváez, D. (1994). *Moral development in the professions: Psychology and applied ethics.* Hillsdale, NJ: Erlbaum.

   This is the most recent and comprehensive review of the "higher cognitive complexity is better" issue. Various chapters detail the relationship between levels of moral judgment and professional behavior in fields such as medicine, veterinary medicine, accounting, dentistry, teaching, journalism, and nursing. Higher stages of moral reasoning predict higher levels of ethical practice.

REFERENCES

Arlin, P. (1984). Adolescent and adult thought: A structural interpretation. In C. Armon, M. Commons, & F. Richards (Eds.), *Beyond formal operations: Late adolescent and adult cognitive development* (pp. 258–271). New York: Praeger.

Arlin, P. (1990). Wisdom: The art of problem finding. In R. J. Sternberg (Ed.), *Wisdom: Its nature, origins and development* (pp. 230–243). New York: Cambridge University Press.

Baltes, P., & Schaie, K. W. (1976). On the plasticity of intelligence in adulthood and old age: Where Horn and Donalson fail. *American Psychologist, 31*(10), 720–725.

Bielke, P. W. (1979). *The relationship of maternal ego development to parenting behavior and attitudes.* Unpublished doctoral dissertation, University of Minnesota, Minneapolis.

Blasi, A. (1980). Bridging moral cognition and moral action. *Psychological Bulletin, 88,* 1–45.

Braebeck, M. (1982). Moral judgment: Theory and research on differences between males and females. *Developmental Review, 3,* 274–291.

Calhoun, E. F. (1985, April). *Relationship of teachers' conceptual level to the utilization of supervisory services and to a description of the classroom instructional improvement.* Paper presented at the annual meeting of the American Educational Research Association, Chicago.

Case, R. (1992). Neo-Piagetian theories of intellectual development. In H. Beilin & P. Pufall (Eds.), *Piaget's theory.* Hillsdale, NJ: Erlbaum.

Chang, F-Y (1994). School teachers' moral reasoning. In J. Rest & D. Narváez (Eds.), Moral development in the professions: Psychology and the applied ethics. New York: Lawrence Erlbaum Associates.

Cummings, A., & Murray, H. (1989). Ego development and its relation to teacher education. *Teaching and Teacher Education, 5*(1), 21–32.

Dewey, J. (1938). *Experience and education.* New York: Macmillan.

Dewey, J. (1963). *Experience and education.* New York: Collier.

Erikson, E. (1982). *The life cycle completed.* New York: Norton.

Gilligan, C. (1982). *In a different voice.* Cambridge, MA: Harvard University Press.

Heist, P., & Yonge, G. (1968). Omnibus Personality Inventory. Center for Studies in Education, University of California, Berkeley.

Hoestetler, A. (1988). Smart brains work better, not harder. *APA Monitor, 19*(5), 15.

Hopkins, D. (1990). Integrating staff development and school improvement: A study of personality and school climate. In B. Joyce (Ed.), *ASCD Yearbook: Changing school culture through staff development* (pp. 41–67). Alexandria, VA: Association for Supervision and Curriculum Development.

Hunt, D. (1971). *Matching models of education.* Toronto, Ontario: Institute for Studies in Education.

Hunt, D. (1976). Teachers' adaptation: Reading and flexing to students. *Journal of Teacher Education, 27,* 268–275.

Hyde, H., & Linn, M. (1988). Gender differences in verbal ability: A meta-analysis. *Psychological Bulletin, 10*(4), 53–69.

King, P., & Kitchener, K. (1994). *Developing reflective judgment.* San Francisco: Jossey-Bass.

Kitchener, K. S., King, P. M., Wood, P. K., & Davison, M. L. (1989). Consistency and sequentiality in the development of reflective judgment: A six-year longitudinal study. *Journal of Applied Developmental Psychology, 10,* 73–95.

Kohlberg, L. (1969). Stage and sequence: The cognitive-developmental approach to socialization. In D. Goslin (Ed.), *Handbook of socialization theory and research.* New York; Rand McNally.

Kohlberg, L. (1978). Revisions in the theory and practice of moral development. In W. Damon (Ed.), *New directions for child development: Moral development.* San Francisco: Jossey-Bass.

Lee, L., & Snarey, J. (1988). The relationship between ego and moral development: A theoretical review and empirical analysis. In D. Lapsley & C. Power (Eds.), *Self, ego, and identity: Integrative approaches* (pp. 151–178). New York: Springer-Verlag.

Levinson, D. (1978). *The seasons of a man's life*. New York: Ballantine.

Libby, P. (1980). *Teachers' conceptions of discipline: A cognitive-developmental framework*. Unpublished doctoral dissertation, University of Minnesota, Minneapolis.

Lind, G. (1993). *Moral und Bildung*. Heidelberg: Roland Asanger Verlag.

Linn, M., & Hyde, H. (1989). Gender, math, and science. *Educational Researcher, 18*(8), 17–27.

Loevinger, J. (1976). *Ego development*. San Francisco: Jossey-Bass.

Loevinger, J. (1989). *Paradigms of personality*. New York: Freeman.

MacCallum, J. (1993). Teacher reasoning and moral judgment in the context of student discipline situations. *Journal of Moral Education, 22*(1), 3–18.

McKibbin, M., & Joyce, B. (1981). Psychological states and staff development. *Theory Into Practice, 29*(4), 248–255.

Mednick, M. T. (1989). On the politics of psychological constructs: Stop the bandwagon, I want to get off. *American Psychologist, 44*(8), 1118–1123.

Miller, A. (1981). Conceptual matching models and interactional research in education. *Review of Educational Research, 51*(1), 33–84.

Oja, S. N. (1981, April). *Toward a theory of staff development*. Paper presented at the annual meeting of the American Educational Research Association, Los Angeles.

Oja, S. N., & Smulyan, L. (1989). *Collaborative action research: A developmental approach*. New York: Falmer Press.

Oser, F. (1991). Professional morality: A discourse approach. In W. Kurtines & J. Gewirtz (Eds.), *Handbook of moral behavior and development* (vol. 2, pp. 191–228). Hillsdale, NJ: Lawrence Erlbaum Associates.

Oser, F. (1994). Moral perspectives on teaching. In L. Darling-Hammond (Ed.), *Review of Research in Education* (pp. 57–128). Washington, DC: American Educational Research Association.

Peterson, P. (1988). Selecting students and services: Lessons from aptitude-treatment interaction research. *Educational Psychologist, 23*(4), 313–352.

Peterson, P., Fennema, E., Carpenter, T., & Loef, M. (1989). Teachers' pedagogical content beliefs in mathematics. *Cognition & Instruction, 6*(1), 1–40.

Piaget, J. (1970). *Science of education and the psychology of the child*. New York: Viking.

Piaget, J. (1972). Intellectual evolution from adolescence to adulthood. *Human Development, 15*(1), 1–12.

Reiman, A. J., & Edelfelt, R. (1990). *School-based mentoring programs: Untangling the tensions between theory and practice*. Report No. 90-7. Raleigh, NC: North Carolina State University. (ERIC Document Reproduction Service No. ED 329 520).

Reiman, A. J., & Gardner, J. (1993). *Does developmental supervision make a difference?* Technical Paper, North Carolina State University.

Reiman, A. J., & Parramore, B. (1993). Promoting preservice teacher development through extended field experience. In S. Odell & M. O'Hair (Eds.), *Diversity and teaching* (pp. 111–121). Orlando, FL: Harcourt Brace Jovanovich.

Reiman, A. J., & Parramore, B. (1994). The first year of teaching: Assignment, Expectations, and Development. In S. Odell & M. O'Hair (Eds.), *Partnerships in Education*. Orlando, FL: Harcourt Brace Jovanovich.

Rest, J. (1986). *Moral development: Advances in research and theory*. New York: Praeger.

Rest, J., & Narváez, D. (1994). *Moral development in the professions: Psychology and applied ethics*. Hillsdale, NJ: Erlbaum.

Rulon, D. (1992). The just community: A method for staff development. *Journal of Moral Education, 21*(3), 217–224.

Scott-Jones, D. (1991). From "voice" to "fugue," in females' development. *Educational Research,* 31–32.

Sheehy, G. (1976). Passages: *Predictable crises of adulthood.* New York: E. P. Dutton and Company.

Snarey, J. (1985). Cross-cultural universality of socio-moral development. *Psychological Bulletin, 97*(2), 202–232.

Snow, R. (1987). Aptitude-treatment interaction models. In M. Dunkin (Ed.), *The international encyclopedia of teaching and teacher education* (pp. 28–35). New York: Pergamon.

Sprinthall, N. A., & Thies-Sprinthall, L. (1983). The teacher as an adult learner: A cognitive-developmental view. In G. A. Griffin (Ed.), Staff development: Eighty-Second Yearbook of the National Society for the Study of Education (pp. 13–35). Chicago: University of Chicago Press.

Thies-Sprinthall, L. (1980). Supervision: An educative or miseducative process? *Journal of Teacher Education, 31*(2), 17–30.

Vygotsky, L. (1978). *Mind in society.* Cambridge, MA: Harvard University Press.

Walker, L. (1984). Sex differences in the development of moral reasoning: A critical review. *Child Development, 55,* 677–691.

Walker, L. (1986). Sex differences in the development of moral reasoning: A rejoinder to Baumrind. *Child Development, 57,* 522–526.

Werner, H. (1948). *Comparative psychology and mental development.* New York: International Press.

White, R. (1959). Motivation reconsidered: The concept of competence. *Psychological Review, 66,* 297–333.

C·H·A·P·T·E·R
4

Promoting Development

• • • • • • •

A Framework for Action

INTRODUCTION

In the previous chapter we carefully outlined the case for cognitive development in three domains as an important objective for teacher education. We showed that adults who construct experience at more complex levels of cognition perform more adequately when confronted with complex problems of human interaction. This is only part of the story. If higher is better can anything be done to promote such growth? Douglas Heath (1986) puts it another way. We should develop teachers, not just techniques. Simply providing teachers with new skills and methods will not necessarily change anything. Recall the McKibbin and Joyce (1981) study and the Hopkins study (1990), which tracked teachers' ability to adopt innovations, or the Peterson study (1989), which examined teachers' ability to use more complex guided instruction. If we don't focus on developing teachers we shall repeat history. A few teachers or supervisors may adopt new skills effectively; the majority, however, will remain at the same growth stage.

In this chapter we review research and theory focused on developmental instruction. A theory of development in the previous chapter validated John Dewey's original view of the importance of human growth as a determinant of human behavior in a democratic society. Now we turn to the other half of the Dewey question, moving from a theory *of* development to a theory *for* development, from description to action and prescription.

JOHN DEWEY'S VISION

John Dewey, a prominent educational theorist and philosopher, significantly contributed to our understanding of the crucial forces in human growth and development. During his lifetime he passionately advocated for careful, guided experiences for the learner (active learning) that were arranged according to a learner's interests and capacities. He also identified the important ecological concept of person-in-environment. His often-used phrase, "some organism in some environment" (Dewey, 1916), was his way of emphasizing the need to study learning in its broader context. Dewey believed this ecological view was a fundamental requirement for the educator. "A primary responsibility of educators is that they not only be aware of the general principle of the shaping of actual experience by environing conditions, but that they also recognize in the concrete what surroundings are conducive to having experiences that lead to growth "(Dewey, 1938, p. 40).

As you can see from the passage, Dewey intimated the idea of stages in growth and development. Early in his work he began to realize that many educators treated children as miniature adults, the same in every respect except for size. This erroneous conception of children was addressed in his writings. "The boy was a little man and his mind was a little mind—in everything but size the same as that of the adult. . . . Now we believe in the mind as a growing affair, and hence as essentially changing, presenting distinctive phases of capacity and interest at different periods" (Dewey, 1956, p. 102). Thus for Dewey the role of the educator was to promote growth and development through active learning in the form of a curriculum that balanced experiential learning with careful analyis and reflection on the experiences.

EDUCATIVE VERSUS MISEDUCATIVE EXPERIENCE

We mentioned earlier the tendency in human beings to be curious and to ask questions about oneself and others. The question Dewey explored for much of his lifetime was how to build a theory of experience that tapped this curiosity. Early on he recognized that not all educational experiences were treated equally, and thus he coined the terms "educative" and "miseducative" experiences. "For some experiences are miseducative. Any experience is miseducative that has the effect of arresting or distorting the growth of further experience" (Dewey, 1938, p. 25). Hence, for Dewey, everything depends on the quality of the experience.

Supervision in schools needs to assure that the experiences for the teacher are not miseducative in a Deweyan sense. Take, for example, the novice teacher who is in his or her second month of initial teaching. The wise supervisor recognizes that he or she must offer support and encouragement frequently, because typically the early months of teaching are extraordinarily challenging. Asking the novice teacher to assume responsibility for chairing the yearbook committee is inviting stress and overload. As you will discover shortly, we plan to look much more closely at those conditions that supervisors can use to encourage quality educative experiences.

THE ROLE OF INTERACTION

Yet another key idea in Dewey's work was the assertion that teaching and learning interacted. Dewey believed that the school building, the classroom, and the surrounding community represented different dimensions of the ecology. Further, all the persons in the school and community represent a set of possible interactions. For Dewey the quality of the interaction was a chief means of interpreting the educative potential of an experience.

Once again, Dewey foreshadowed later developmental educators when he criticized traditional education for paying *too little* attention to the person's stage of development as a crucial part of educative interactions. Instructional supervision is an example of one kind of interaction. Yet Dewey would caution us to remember that it is not just the interaction between the supervisor and supervisee. Both persons are working within the larger ecology of school and community. Although we will apply Dewey's concept of interaction directly to work between two persons, we realize that there are many other interactions that occur. Thus we are advocating a broad human-development systems framework.

CONTINUITY

A final principle Dewey advocated was the importance of continuity. He recognized that an experience could be engaging and educative, yet be disconnected from future experiences. When this is the case, time and energy are dissipated, and the total growth potential of experiences over time is diminished. Certainly traditional instructional supervision offers a plethora of examples of experiences that lack continuity. How often do we see a college supervisor who has no overall plan for the supervision of a student intern and who does too little to link the experiences together into a coherent whole. Thus, a goal for supervisors is to promote continuity in the experience. Such continuity lends quality to the experience and heightens its educativeness. We will discuss in more detail the principles of interaction and continuity shortly.

Dewey's work continues to be relevant to our long quest to gain knowledge about how persons grow and develop. His notions of interaction, continuity, experience and reflection, and growth through phases have guided much educational inquiry during the twentieth century. Certainly his famous dictum of learning by doing has as much relevance to current developmental instructional supervision practices as it does to the broader educational enterprise.

JOHN DEWEY

Born in 1859, Dewey's prolific life spanned almost a century. During this time he dramatically influenced educational thinking and practice in this country. Raised in the heartland of New England, he was one of three sons of a merchant and spent much of his youth on a farm. His early years fostered in him a great regard for hard work and a respect for how one's setting promotes or hinders growth and development. Early in his career he emphasized a theme that would follow him throughout his academic life, that being the crucial interplay between the person and environment. Perhaps it is no surprise that his marriage to Alice Chipman, a prominent social worker and educator, bolstered his interest in social activism, and the role education plays in social and moral development.

John Dewey's academic life moved swiftly. After earning his Ph.D. at Johns Hopkins at the age of 25, he quickly rose up the academic ladder to eventually serve as chairperson of the Department of Philosophy and Pedagogy at the University of Chicago. It was here that he established the nation's first laboratory school and, along with Francis Parker, where he tested his theories on experienced-based curriculum to promote more effective learning, greater self-understanding, moral competence, and maturation in living.

His contributions to our thinking about human development and developmental supervision are numerous. He made the germinal point early in his writings that Rousseau's notion of natural development (i.e., human beings, like plant seeds, have latent capacities that, if left to themselves, will flower and bear fruit) had two fallacies. The first was that people were vastly more complex in their development than plants, and second was that development required qualitative interaction between the organism and the environment. He went on to argue that the quality of interaction was a significant challenge and opportunity for educators. "The problem, a difficult and delicate one, is to discover what tendencies are especially seeking expression at a particular time and just what materials and methods will serve to evoke and direct a truly educative development" (Archambault, 1964, p. 7).

Dewey's ideas set in motion several generations of research on what constitutes quality of interaction, and what constitutes human development. His prophetic notion of "the tendencies especially seeking expression at a particular time," opened the gate for research into genetic epistemology, developmental psychology, and developmental education and supervision.

Perhaps Dewey's most significant assertion was that teaching and learning interacted and that human development requires a balance between experience (action) and guided analysis (reflection). Dewey's writings and experiences have become a foundation for much of today's view of developmental supervision.

After his formal retirement in 1930, Dewey entered a new phase in his life characterized by remarkable productivity and a synthesis and refining of his ideas. He added to his already huge bibliography until his death in 1952, and his dictum "learning by doing," considered revolutionary at the turn of the century, continues to resonate for contemporary educators.

REFLECTION QUESTIONS

How might Dewey's ideas of the interplay between the person and the environment relate to coaching and supervision?

How might mentor teachers incorporate opportunities for beginning teachers to reflect on their experiences?

Does "learning by doing" have meaning in contemporary supervision and coaching programs?

Archambault, R. D. (1964). *John Dewey on education*. Chicago: University of Chicago Press.

 THE RESEARCH BASE FOR DEVELOPMENTAL INSTRUCTION

Although Dewey's framework for growth was a very significant ground plan for both education and teacher education, developmental theory and research had lagged behind his vision. As we noted, comprehensive theory for adult development has only begun emerging in the last two decades. Also assessment methods in the important domains of conceptual complexity, ego, and moral/ethical aspects of growth are of recent vintage. We now trace these changes in our knowledge base as a means of defining the basic architecture for a growth model.

A series of studies first with adolescents and later with adult teachers and counselors was conducted to test Dewey's contentions. Exhibit 4-1 outlines the results from some of these studies. These studies provided evidence in two ways. The first series of studies with adolescents achieved very positive results, but the results were less positive for adult teachers. The measures of developmental growth included estimates of conceptual complexity, ego development, and moral/ethical reasoning. The trends were

Exhibit 4-1 EFFECTS OF COGNITIVE-DEVELOPMENTAL INSTRUCTION ON HIGH SCHOOL AND
COLLEGE STUDENTS AND ON ADULT TEACHERS

Study	Subjects	Role Taking	Effects
Mosher & Sullivan (1976)	High school students	Peer counseling	Significant developmental growth
Hedin (1979)	High school students	Service internships	Significant developmental growth
Cognetta (1980)	High school students	Peer teaching	Significant developmental growth
Sprinthall & Scott (1989)	High school students	Cross-age teaching	Significant developmental growth
Reiman & Parramore (1993)	Undergraduates	Cross-age teaching	Significant developmental growth
Sprinthall & Oja (1978)	Experienced teachers	Counseling skills and indirect teaching	Marginal developmental growth
Sprinthall & Bernier (1978)	Experienced teachers	Counseling skills and indirect teaching	Marginal developmental growth
Thies-Sprinthall (1984)	Experienced teachers	Supervision and mentoring	Significant developmental growth
Reiman (1988)	Experienced teachers	Supervision and mentoring	Significant developmental growth

much stronger for the students than for the teachers, even though both sets of studies were promising. We realized that it was necessary to refine our procedures to increase the impact on adult teachers. The more recent research (Thies-Sprinthall, 1984; Reiman, 1988; Reiman & Parramore, 1993) included such refinements and produced more noticeable developmental stage growth.

From this work then we have found that stage growth requires, as a minimum, at least five interacting conditions. Sprinthall and Thies-Sprinthall posited these five conditions in 1983. We now offer these as a framework for teacher development. If we wish to raise the cognitive developmental level of the teacher as an adult learner these five conditions are requisite.

ROLE TAKING

George Herbert Mead's early work (1934) indicated that the concept of social role taking could effect moral/ethical development. By placing a person in a more complex helping role, the person would need to construct new thoughts and behaviors to meet the new task demands. Increased responsibility would also be involved in the new role.

Many years ago Julius Caesar is reported to have said, "I would rather be a mayor of a small Ionian village, than a citizen of the great state of Rome." The responsibility of such leadership would be the discernible difference.

Another way to view role taking is that it contains a set of positive growth producing experiences. Recall Dewey's categorization of experience as educative or miseducative, or the philosophical truism that, "Push-pin is not the same as poetry," or Jane Loevinger's update that pinball doesn't equate to poetry (1976).

Research has shown clearly that the comparison groups who had role-playing experiences, through activities like values clarification, did not change in their level of development. Also as some of our comparison groups indicate, regular academic and professional coursework does not engender developmental growth. Role playing, simulations on one hand or sitting in an academic classroom on the other, is no substitute for actual participation in a constructive social role. All of the successful programs required some type of helping or educative activity.

REFLECTION

Our research has shown time and again that complex new experiences without reflection make no impact on the moral and conceptual development of the helper (Reiman & Parramore, 1993; Sprinthall, Hall, & Gerler, 1992; Sprinthall, Reiman, & Thies-Sprinthall, 1993). What does make a difference are sequenced readings, dialogue journals, and discussions of the role-taking experience. Further, we have found that teacher supervisors do not necessarily have a sophisticated capacity for reflecting on their own experiences or in guiding the reflection of a colleague. Thus we have found it helpful to structure reflection experiences and to educate teachers in how to guide the reflection of others.

John Dewey reputedly made the point through an example. A teacher applying to his laboratory school supposedly said, "I have ten years of experience." Dewey queried, "Was it ten years or one year ten times over?" Did the teacher reflect on the experience or merely repeat past activities?

In a sense these first two elements comprehend a *model of praxis*. The famous Brazilian educator Paulo Freire (1986) has noted that action without reflection leads to activism while reflection without action leads to pedanticism. The role-taking experience contains the seeds of growth. Guided reflection helps the person extract meaning from the experience.

BALANCE

Our work also indicates that the cycles of action and reflection need to be balanced to promote an effective interplay. The philosopher Bishop Berkeley could apparently remain in his cave in Newport, Rhode Island for incredibly long stretches of time for reflection. We have found, on the other hand, that a tighter framework works more effectively. The action-reflection interplay on a weekly basis, for example, allows for clarification of puzzlements and reflection on new issues without long time lags. This also allows for the last two conditions—*continuity* and *support and challenge*—to reach greater levels of effectiveness.

CONTINUITY

Dewey's principle of continuity has held true. We have found that to achieve the complex goal of impacting cognitive structures in ego, conceptual, and moral/ethical domains requires a continuous interplay of action and reflection. Usually at least one semester is needed for significant structural growth to occur. Certainly all of the research on both short-term discontinuous workshops for teachers indicates the opposite. The national survey by Howey, Yarger, and Joyce (1978) clearly demonstrated just how ineffectual the workshop approach was. If we recall the Piagetian framework such outcomes were not only understandable but predictable.

Piaget has shown that cognitive structural change results from his classic assimilation/accommodation process. Basically this means that each of us employs a consistent method of problem solving, our modal stage which we use quite consistently. We have assimilated a system that we are comfortable using. However, there are times when a new problem situation arises, called a "knowledge perturbation." Our current system becomes inadequate, inefficient, and ineffective. We need to reach new insights and new behaviors to be successful. This means our cognitions need to adapt, to accommodate, to use new strategies of problem solving. It also means that

Assimilation	Accommodation
Fitting experiences into our current preferred stage of development and understanding. One of our nephews at approximately 3 years of age, on seeing a cow in the distance, insisted that it was a doggie.	Changing or modifying our present stage of cognitive processing to make room for new perspectives and understandings. When any child driving in the back seat of a car at night finally realizes that the moon actually isn't following the car.

we have to forsake some of our old and comfortable methods. Exhibit 4-2 describes the accommodation/assimilation framework.

Developmental growth is not simply a process of adding on new systems in pack-rat fashion. Instead growth requires new cognitions *at the expense* of old cognitions. The old is gradually discarded. Sometimes this is referred to as the Thomas Wolfe hypothesis, "You can't go home again." The new and more complex system changes how a person understands experience. Piaget was adamant on this issue. Such change does not happen quickly but rather at a slow pace, a process he referred to somewhat arcanely as gradual "decentration." In any case continuity over time is an important necessary condition. Whether or not new cognitions actually emerge and take over depends on the last condition.

Support and Challenge

The last condition is easily the most difficult. It appears almost as an oxymoron or at least as a paradox. Yet when the objective is cognitive structural growth both support and challenge must form the pedagogical atmosphere. If we review the Piagetian framework of assimilation and accommodation together with the insights from two other developmentalists, Hans Furth and Lev Vygotsky, the rationale becomes clear.

During the shift created by a knowledge disturbance, the previous equilibrium between assimilation (old learning) and accommodation (new learning) is upset. During such a disequilibrium a person's affective (emotional) processes become more fully engaged. It is precisely at such a point that cognition and affect intersect. Piaget uses very obscure and seemingly circular language when he refers to the cognitive as the affective and the affective as the cognitive, a parallel process during decentration (Piaget & Inhelder, 1969, p. 95). As you can readily see it is difficult to interpret his meaning from such language. If , however, we think of a situation in our own experience when our method of problem solving and understanding no longer fits and then think of the feelings aroused, we have a clearer sense of the effects of disequilibrium during new learning.

NORMAN A. SPRINTHALL

Norman Sprinthall's most important contribution to education lies in his steadfast commitment to linking theory, research, and practice in the service of teacher and counselor development. In his view, not only does good theory and research ensure that we direct our national resources to the most important educational needs, but it also helps cut through the highly charged rhetoric that so often clouds needed solutions to some of the most vexing problems for schools and teachers. However, it would be a mistake to think that his emphasis on bridging developmental theory, research, and practice results in the reductionist tendency of science to become absorbed with the parts. Instead, Sprinthall recognizes that the whole of the education enterprise is greater than the sum of its parts. And it is the complexity of the whole education enterprise that inspires us and moves us to become involved in nourishing public education.

Born in Attleboro, Massachusetts in 1931, his early years were marked by curiosity and a thirst for knowledge. He excelled in the classroom and earned his A.B. at Brown University in 1954. In 1963 he received his Ed.D. in counseling psychology at Harvard and became an assistant professor in the guidance and counseling program. It was during his time at Harvard that he initiated a series of field-based studies examining the relationship between complex new social role taking and moral and conceptual development. Working with Ralph Mosher, Lawrence Kohlberg, and Robert Selman fostered a rich environment for the exploration and study of human development and, particularly, moral development. That working group struggled against two prevailing views in the 1960s: (1) that effective teaching was a spontaneous model; the teacher finds his or her own style and is teaching optimally and (2) that all children learned best through an inductive/discovery model. Employing the insights from cognitive-developmental theory (it may sound strange but Piaget's work was just coming into vogue), they realized that the conception of teaching and learning had to be radically revised. To start at the learner's present developmental level requires an understanding of growth stages and how each learner "constructs" meaning from experience. Meaning is not given to the learner but is created by the learner. It was not until Sprinthall left Harvard for Minnesota that such a framework was expanded.

At Minnesota he again worked with a group of developmentalists including Dan Blocker and Howard Williams, but it was his interaction with Ken Howey that uncovered the crucial concept. Howey maintained that cognitive-developmental theory ought to be expanded in scope. Official theory had suggested that stage growth ended somewhere during the college years and that further growth was only quantitative. Howey argued persuasively for a conception of the teacher as an adult learner. He was prescient and, as we noted previously, developmental theorists using new longitudinal research studies clearly validated the view of stage growth for adults. In a manner similiar to children and adolescents, adult growth can be conceptualized in a stage and sequence format. The next problem, then, became how to build a pedagogical framework for adult developmental growth. For that phase of his career, the move to North Carolina State University was the important shift as was his collaboration with his partner Lois.

A prolific writer, he has authored or edited over one hundred articles and his texts are considered "must reads" by educators interested in the cognitive-developmental perspective. One of Sprinthall's most far-reaching efforts is his work to explicate the five conditions needed for adult psychological growth and development, which is the basis also of developmental teacher instruction. Along with his partner, Lois Thies-Sprinthall, he explored how supervision and coaching could promote development. He and his spouse have encouraged teachers and counselors to take seriously the adage that "great teachers are neither born nor made, but they may be developed." Now in retirement, he maintains an active interest in adult development and moral education.

REFLECTION QUESTIONS

How does new role taking by the teacher relate to discoveries made about constructivism in the 1960s?

Do you agree or disagree with the statement that "great teachers are neither born nor made, but they may be developed"?

How do Sprinthall's ideas connect to schoolwide reform?

When we need to give up our old methods it means the knowledge disturbance is also an affective upset. William Perry (1970) has pointedly commented that if development is so positive then why is it so hard? Similarly, Hans Furth (1981) has specifically enumerated how a period of relaxed reflection is required during such a growth disequilibrium. Exhibit 4-3 outlines Furth's sequence. In other words psychological support in a relaxed atmosphere is needed so the person can gradually let go of an old method.

EXHIBIT 4-3   FURTH'S PHASES OF DEVELOPMENTAL LEARNING

EQUILIBRATING THE NEW PERSPECTIVE WITH THE PAST PERSPECTIVE

1. Awareness of a moderate discrepancy arises in understanding the meaning of an event or idea.
2. A feeling of curiosity or uneasiness arises.
3. More new information accumulates that doesn't fit with prior understanding.
4. During periods of relaxed reflection, one tries to fit the new information into the prior perspective; talking to oneself.
5. A new balance is reached. The new information moves from accommodation to assimilation.
6. After sufficient time the new information becomes "old" information and can be adapted to other situations.
7. A new moderate discrepancy or "perturbation" arises and the process of equilibration continues.

One final point on the support and challenge question. Originally Piaget viewed the growth process as an internal dialogue, in which the person attempted to figure out new solutions. Metaphorically Piaget saw us as either Charles Lindbergh or Amelia Earhart, a kind of lone eagle. Lev Vygotsky, a very important Russian developmental psychologist, however, stressed the critical importance of dialogue and discussion with others as central to the growth process. Supportive social interactive talk would promote growth. Group dialogue could contain different perspectives which could enlighten the learner's current system. In Vygotsky's framework, what a person could do with the assistance of others was considered more indicative of mental development than what he or she did alone.

In addition to such group discussion, Vygotsky presented a major insight through his concept of a *zone of proximal growth*. The zone is an arena of thought and feeling that is slightly ahead of the current equilibrium. Sometimes this is referred to as a minor discrepancy, a slight mismatch, or an arena of manageable dissonance. Cognitive growth occurs in the zone and thus requires both support and challenge. Too much support or support without challenge essentially creates a condition of no growth. A person may wish to avoid the upset feelings caused by the perturbation, resist the change, and remain in place. William James (1890) many years ago cited an example of this tendency from observing one of his children in resisting new learning. His son on seeing an orange for the first time called it a ball, and a corkscrew "bad scissors." Such old fogeyism, as James called it, is a central part of the human condition to avoid the new and preserve our present emotional equilibrium, and we would add, regardless of age.

All this does not mean that support is unnecessary and we can simply challenge and confront a person to induce growth. Too much challenge is just as miseducative as too much support. Creating expectations that may be far more complex than the current preferred stage of problem solving will have the same behavioral outcome as too little support. The person will sim-

CONTEMPORARY ISSUES

APPLICATIONS OF THE FIVE CONDITIONS IN PRESERVICE TEACHER EDUCATION AND INSERVICE SUPERVISION

The implications of the cognitive-developmental model are numerous. Take, for example, preservice teacher education. The model suggests that spaced practice over time is superior to an intensive practicum, and that careful reflection on the practice must be continuous (Cognetta & Sprinthall, 1978). Thus, we can see that the traditional "student teaching semester" with six to eight weeks of intensive methods instruction followed by the student teaching internship is less educative than one in which methods instruction and field experience overlap.

The model also implies that persons in supervisory roles will need preparation for their helping roles. This preparation must include an understanding of the five conditions necessary for supervisory development, how they apply to the young adult learner, and how to guide the reflection of the colleague. The preparation must also provide a balance between the new experience (action) and reflection. In fact, we have found that helping prospective teacher supervisors to understand their role in guiding reflection represents an important breakthrough in teacher development. Reflection is a kind of Rosetta stone for practice.

The implications of this model for teacher induction are significant. Certainly the beginning teacher is in a complex new helping role. However, if he or she has no opportunities for support and reflection on the new experiences it is unlikely that growth will occur. Therefore, teacher induction represents a formidable opportunity for teacher growth and development. Unfortunately, most beginning teachers face staggeringly complex initial teaching assignments with little or no opportunity for reflection on the experience.

ply withdraw psychologically into the safe haven of the current stage of growth.

Without question, learning how to manage the support and challenge paradox is the most difficult of all the five conditions. First it is clearly a balancing act for the developmental educator and second, the ratio for each individual differs. If that isn't enough a third factor, time, also comes into play. Individuals vary in the amount of support versus the amount of challenge according to stage. Some require massive support with small amounts of challenge. Others may thrive with an equal balance and still others may require more challenge than support. We outline a system of assessment and feedback loops that we have found very helpful in managing this ratio in the activities section at the end of the chapter. For now the main point is simply the developmental truism, given that new learning takes place during the assimilation-accommodation imbalance or disequilibrium, that a ratio of support and challenge is necessary to create a manageable mismatch.

SUMMARY

In this chapter we outlined the developmental rationale for educational programs designed to promote stage growth. It is well to remember that in Chapter 3 we provided extensive evidence that more complex stages of development predict more effective behavior in resolving complex tasks. Higher cognitive complexity is better when such behavior is required in the short term for this result. This chapter shifted the focus from prediction or a theory *of* development to programs or a theory *for* development.

The research studies on promoting developmental growth were reviewed and indicated that five conditions (complex new roles, guided reflection, balance between experience and reflection, continuity, and support and challenge) are central to developmental objectives. Each condition was detailed and tied to theory as examples of practice visible in theory and vice versa. We also noted that the fifth condition, balancing support and challenge, is clearly the most difficult to manage.

Probably the most important aspect of the chapter is the focus on developmental growth as the objective of all this effort. The goal is stage change, not simply the acquisition of some new teaching or supervising techniques. Douglas Heath's comment is most germane: we need to develop teachers, not just techniques. This is also clearly what Dewey had in mind when he pointed out that human development *should* be the aim of education. In our view, given the recent research evidence outlined in Chapter 3 we can apply Dewey's conditions to the education of adults in professional programs. And, as we have shown in some detail in this chapter, there is a valid ground plan for such developmental instruction.

In the next chapter we turn to two other aspects of teacher growth, namely teacher concerns and career phases with implications for the supervisor or peer coach.

SUPERVISION FOR TEACHER DEVELOPMENT ACTIVITIES

APPLIED

1. *In the shoes of another person.* One of the key elements we have stressed in the review of intervention research is the need for guided role-taking activities as a method of promoting growth along with the other four conditions. Role taking is the ability to see events and problems from another person's cognitive and affective growth states. To give you a sense of how widely role-taking ability varies, consider the following activity:

   At different points in your life write down the name of a person who gave you the best gift you ever received and what the item was.

Also write down the opposite. Then do the same thing for yourself as a gift giver to others at different ages in your life.

	Best Gift and Giver	*Worst Gift and Giver*
Elementary Age	_____	_____
Teenager	_____	_____
College Student	_____	_____
Young Adult	_____	_____

For example, imagine during adolescence receiving a child's book from a distant aunt who thought you were still 8 years old, or getting the same present two years in a row from an unthinking uncle. Compare that with getting guitar lessons (if that was a secret wish) when you were 13 years old or a special trip for graduation.

And, on the other hand, imagine how you might feel if you gave a young person with significant artistic talent in freehand drawing a "paint by the numbers" kit or clothes that were hopelessly out of fashion or gave tickets for a mud wrestling show to an opera fan.

In any case by reviewing gifts given and received you can quickly discern the ability to either place or misplace yourself in the shoes of another person and vice versa.

2. *The five conditions: A self test.* To see if you can remember the five conditions for developmental growth, identify/classify the following activities as a representation or a violation of the elements. You . . .
   a. Employ a series of value clarification role-play exercises.
   b. Set up a two-day training program "Orientation for Tutoring" for college tutors and dispense with any further meetings.
   c. Ask the participants, after a semester-long training program without weekly journals, to summarize their thoughts and feelings in an end-of-term reflection paper.
   d. Revise, due to a busy schedule, the seminar discussions to once per month for review and sometimes cancel meetings.
   e. Introduce dialogue journals as part of an early field experience course offered for teacher education majors at a local college, but rarely respond to the substantive thoughts *and* feelings of the students.
   f. Organize a new program for teacher leaders that provides a week-long internship in a complex new leadership role.
   g. Cut back on feedback to students' written journals due to time constraints, and use check marks to indicate you have reviewed the journal entries.
   h. Encourage the school system's leadership to develop a new character education program for students and staff that is based on once-a-week mini-discussions of selected virtues like courage and responsibility.

   In reviewing the eight scenarios, see if you can pick out an example of role playing versus *role taking*, of violations of *reflection, balance, continuity*, and *support/challenge*. Then see if you can rewrite each scenario to bring it into concordance with the five conditions, for example, in the first case eliminate values clarification role playing. Instead, provide a genuine mentoring role that takes place over one year and includes a weekly guided reflection.

SUGGESTED READINGS

1. Kohlberg, L., & Mayer, R. (1972). Development as the aim of education. *Harvard Educational Review*, 42(4) 449–496.

   This is the clearest statement of John Dewey's educational philosophy in recent years. Kohlberg and Mayer show how the developmental model of Dewey answers the problem of the so-called naturalistic fallacy. They detail the issue that if, in fact, we know what development "is," we then know what education "ought" to be.

2. Sprinthall, N. A., & Thies-Sprinthall, L. (1983). The teacher as an adult learner: A cognitive developmental view. In G. A. Griffin (Ed.), *Staff development: Eighty-second Yearbook of the National Society for the Study of Education*, (pp. 24–31). Chicago: University of Chicago Press.

3. Sprinthall, N. A., Reiman, A. J., & Thies-Sprinthall, L. (1993). Roletaking and reflection: Promoting the conceptual and moral development of teachers. *Learning and Individual Differences*, 5(4), 283–299.

REFERENCES

Cognetta, P., & Sprinthall, N. A. (1978). Students as teachers: Role taking as a means of promoting psychological and ethical development during adolescence. In N. A. Sprinthall and R. L. Mosher (Eds.), *Value development as the aim of education* (pp. 53–68). Schenectedy, NY: Character Research Press.

Dewey, J. (1916). *Democracy and education*. New York: Macmillan.

Dewey, J. (1938). *Experience and education*. New York: Macmillan.

Dewey, J. (1956). *The child and the curriculum: The school and the society*. Chicago: University of Chicago Press.

Friere, P. (1986). *Pedagogy of the oppressed*. New York: Continuum Publishing.

Furth, H. (1981). *Piaget and knowledge*. Chicago: University of Chicago Press.

Heath, D. (1986). Developing teachers, not just techniques. *Educational Leadership*, 43.

Hedin, D. (1979). Teenage health educator: An action learning program to promote psychological development (Doctoral dissertation, University of Minnesota, 1979). *Dissertation Abstracts International, 40*, 754A.

Hopkins, D. (1990). Integrating staff development and school improvement: A study of personality and school climate. In B. Joyce (Ed.), *ASCD Yearbook: Changing school culture through staff development* (pp. 41–67). Alexandria, VA: Association for Supervision and Curriculum Development.

Howey, K., Yarger, S., & Joyce, B. (1978). *Improving teacher education*. Washington, DC: Association of Teacher Educators.

James, W. (1890). *The principles of psychology*. New York: Holt.

Loevinger, J. (1976). *Ego development*. San Francisco: Jossey-Bass.

McKibbin, M., & Joyce, B. (1981). Psychological states and staff development. *Theory into Practice, 29*(4), 248–255.

Mead, G. H. (1934). *Mind, self, and society*. Chicago: University of Chicago Press.

Mosher, R., & Sullivan, P. (1976). A curriculum in moral education for adolescents. *Journal of Moral Education, 5*, 159–172.

Perry, W. (1970). *Forms of intellectual and ethical development in the college years*. New York: Holt, Rinehart, and Winston.

Peterson, P., Fennema, E., Carpenter, T., & Loef, M. (1989). Teachers' pedagogical content beliefs in mathematics. *Cognition & Instruction, 6*(1), 1–40.

Piaget, J., & Inhelder, B. (1969). *The psychology of the child*. New York: Basic Books.

Reiman, A. J. (1988). *An intervention study of long-term mentor training: Relationships between cognitive-developmental theory and reflection*. Unpublished doctoral dissertation, North Carolina State University, Raleigh.

Reiman, A. J., & Parramore, B. (1993). Promoting preservice teacher development through extended field experience. In M. O'Hair & S. Odell (Eds.), *Diversity and teaching: Teacher Education Yearbook I* (pp. 111–121). Orlando: Harcourt Brace Jovanovich.

Sprinthall, N. A., & Bernier, J. E. (1978). Moral and cognitive development of teachers. *New Catholic World, 221*, 179–184.

Sprinthall, N. A., Hall, J., & Gerler, E. (1992). Peer helping: Counselors and teachers as facilitators. *The Peer Facilitator Quarterly, 9*(4), 11–15.

Sprinthall, N. A., Reiman, A. J., & Thies-Sprinthall, L. (1993). Roletaking and reflection: Promoting the conceptual and moral development of teachers. *Learning and Individual Differences, 5*(4), 283–299.

Sprinthall, N. A., & Oja, S. N. (1978). Psychological and moral development of teachers. In N. Sprinthall & R. Mosher (Eds.), *Value development as the aim of education* (pp. 117–134). Schenectady, NY: Character Research Press.

Sprinthall, N. A., & Scott, J. (1989). Promoting psychological development, math achievement and success attribution of female students through deliberate psychological education. *Journal of Counseling Psychology, 36*, 440–446.

Thies-Sprinthall, L. (1984). Promoting the developmental growth of supervising teachers: Theory, research programs, and implications. *Journal of Teacher Education, 35*(3), 53–60.

CHAPTER 5

Concerns and Career Phases

• • • • • •

Dimensions of Teacher Change

$\mathcal{T}$hus far in our discussion of mentoring and supervision for teacher development, we have focused on the dimension of cognitive development. As you recall, we described the theory and research of David Hunt, Jane Loevinger, Lawrence Kohlberg, and Jean Piaget. In particular, we addressed three domains of development that were represented by stages or plateaus, namely, cognitive, personal or ego, and moral development. Further, in Chapter 4, we moved from a theory *of* development to a theory *for* development, examining how action and reflection are joined together to promote growth and development.

In this chapter we extend the discussion of teacher development to the important concept of teacher change, which is based on Frances Fuller's model of phases of concerns and Fessler and Christensen's career phases. Since teacher development depends on interaction between the learner and the learning environment, we will look at the special role these models play in describing the change process.

As you review the chapter, check your comprehension by answering these questions:

- What are the levels of concerns described by Frances Fuller?
- How are Fuller's concerns related to Piaget's concept of disequilibrium?
- How should mentoring and supervision account for teacher career phases?

 # TEACHER CHANGE AND CONCERNS

We have often proclaimed that all the theories about human development are not as complex as a single person. Yet we find ourselves striving to describe the extraordinarily intricate processes of adult development. The limitations of words on a printed page further exacerbate the problem, requiring us to describe complex ideas in rather simple terms. If multidimensional phenomena appear to be unidimensional, we apologize. Describing how teachers change and grow may be like trying to define concepts like dignity, compassion, or aesthetics. Given these constraints, however, we now embark on a discussion of one part of teacher change that has garnered growing attention, namely, the concerns of teachers.

FULLER'S PHASES OF CONCERN

The late Frances Fuller, of the University of Texas, spent much of her academic life attempting to understand the personal dimensions of student teaching. She practiced a dictum set forth by William James at the turn of the century, "Start where the learner is, then proceed." Fuller realized that the observations, thoughts, questions, and concerns raised by student teachers and beginning teachers were important sources of "scientific" feedback. Further, Fuller realized that these observations could not be made in the laboratory, but instead needed to be gathered in the school setting.

Fuller's observations led to the discovery that almost all student teachers and beginning teachers experience a similar sequence of concerns in their professional life as they encounter the complexities of the classroom. She grouped the phases into three broad categories: (1) survival, or self, (2) task, and (3) impact concerns (Fuller, 1969). In Fuller's words, "When concerns are mature, i.e., characteristic of experienced teachers, concerns seem to focus on pupil gain and self evaluation as opposed to personal gain and evaluation by others" (1969, p. 221). Fuller found that only when teachers reached the impact level were their concerns focused on the learning of the students. Unfortunately, her work also showed that student teachers and beginning teachers generally do not reach this level. Instead, some stay at the personal-survival level, although most reach the task level. Before we rush to judge these teachers as "slow starters" and underqualified for the teaching profession, we need to recognize that the levels discovered by Fuller in her pioneering work appeared to show a natural sequence that all new teachers progress through. The fact that so many new teachers remain at the task level may be due to the lack of professional support they receive during their initial years in the profession (Veenman, 1984). Beginning

teachers often receive the toughest teaching assignments. It is not uncommon for them to have multiple classroom preparations, challenging students, inadequate resources, and little sustained assistance from a mentor
teacher or buddy. In one of our own studies, we found that 30 percent of our
new teachers did not have their own classroom for teaching during their
first year in the profession. Instead, they roamed from classroom to classroom with their curriculum on a cart (Reiman & Parramore, 1994). It is
therefore hardly surprising that many beginning teachers stay at the survival and task levels.

CONCERNS-BASED ADOPTION MODEL

Later work on teachers' concerns by Hall, Wallace, and Dossett (1973) and
Hall and Loucks (1978) refined Fuller's original work by adding additional
levels of concerns within each of the three general categories of self, task,
and impact. Their work led to the development of the Concerns-Based
Adoption Model as well as the Stages of Concern Questionnaire (SoC), a paper-and-pencil assessment that identifies the dominant concerns a person
has. Exhibit 5-1 outlines the components of the model. At the lowest cluster

EXHIBIT 5-1   PHASES OF CONCERN

PHASE	EXEMPLAR	FEELINGS	GENERAL LEVEL
6. Refocusing	I'd like to adapt the curriculum to better meet the needs of the students.	Confident	
5. Collaboration	I am eager to share these ideas with my teammates at school.	Excited	*Impact*
4. Consequence	Are all the students connecting with the lesson?	Puzzled Successful	
3. Management	I never have enough time to do everything that is needed. How can I keep up with all this paperwork?	Frustrated	*Task*
2. Personal	How will this new program affect me? Will the parents like and respect me?	Anxious	
1. Informational	I need more information about the district curriculum guidelines.	Curious	*Self*
0. Awareness (lack of)	I'm not the least bit concerned about the new program.	Apathetic	

of concerns—*self*—the teacher is primarily concerned about whether he or she can succeed in handling the demands of teaching or managing the demands of the new innovations. Teachers worry that they somehow don't measure up. We mention innovations because there is growing evidence that as experienced teachers encounter new roles or major educational innovations, they also progress through the levels identified by Hall and Loucks (1978); however, their movement through the levels *may be at a faster rate*, due to experience and/or cognitive-developmental level. The main point is that the teachers at the self level of concern are focused on their own survival.

Within the general level of self are three phases of concern. The first is *awareness*. At this phase the teacher is unconcerned, and this largely is due either to a lack of awareness of the innovation or an indifferent attitude. The feelings expressed may be ones of indifference or apathy. In a sense, teachers don't know that they don't know and they don't care. Clearly this is the most disquieting level of concern. Hopefully, once the teacher has learned more from the initial experiences he or she will move on to the *informational* phase of concern. At the informational level the teacher is eager to learn more. You might recall the *Dragnet* television series in the 1950s with Sergeant Friday saying, "Facts m'am, just give me the facts." For the teacher, it is a similar case of wanting just the information. However, as information concerns are met, teachers' concerns will shift to the *personal* phase. For example, a teacher might proclaim, "It is all well and good to have information, but now I realize that this program has the potential to affect me personally and, frankly, I am worried." We now know that many beginning teachers have an array of personal concerns during the initial months of their employment. Without adequate orientations, assistance from support teachers and supervising principals, and realistic assignment, chances are that new teachers will spend a great deal of time in their first year with personal concerns. As personal concerns are resolved, however, and this is a crucial point, the teacher will shift to the next general level of concern called task.

At the *task* level, the major concern is with *management*. This phase is perhaps the dominant one for teachers in their first year. The self-consciousness of the earlier phases gives way to concerns about time and task. If you were at this phase, you might find yourself asking questions such as, "How will all this paperwork be completed?" "Where can I find the time I need to adequately prepare lessons?" "How can I manage all my teaching duties with only one planning period?" "Won't I lose control of the class if I use cooperative learning?" As you can see, the questions revolve around learning to manage planning, presentation, and paperwork. Maintaining order and finding time are major preoccupations for a teacher at this phase. By the way, we have heard that many gifted teachers, counselors, and administrators, when introduced to the phases of concern, have management concerns. Does this mean that all of them are at the management level? For most of these teachers and administrators, the obvious answer is no. Clearly each new school year brings its own unique demands. It is only natural that, at

FRANCES F. FULLER

Frances Fuller was born in New York City on March 17, 1918. She later attended New York State University receiving her B.A. After serving in the Army during World War II, she joined Macy's as a personnel executive working there until 1947. Wanting to contribute to public education, she joined the Eagle Pass Independent School District (Texas) in 1947 and worked as a counselor there for five years. By 1960 she had earned her Ph.D. in educational psychology at the University of Texas at Austin and immediately took an active role as a professor in the counseling psychology program at the University of Texas.

Fuller's research and study focused on the development of affective components for teacher education drawing on her extensive research and practice in counseling and behavior change. Her seminal paper, "Concerns of Teachers: A Developmental Conceptualization," created a new generation of programs and research studying relationships between new teachers' concerns and their teaching behavior. She pioneered an approach to the personal aspects of teaching effectiveness that continues to affect teacher education, supervision, and recent inquiries into the school change process.

Her background in counseling turned out to be a major aspect of her ability to view the teaching process in developmental phases. It also meant that she was able to see that Bloom's taxonomies, which separated cognition from affect, were at base a false dichotomy. Instead she recognized that our emotions, and particularly those of student teachers, were often at least as important as ideas. She innovated a concerns approach to teacher education by creating a series of group meetings designed (today we call them focus groups) to provide an open arena for discussions of both personal and professional issues. Her keen clinical insights became the groundwork for her research.

Frances Fuller found that almost all student teachers and beginning teachers experience a similar sequence of phases of personal growth. The phases can be grouped into three general categories: (1) self-concerns, (2) management or task concerns, and (3) impact (student, colleague, and curriculum) concerns. Fuller showed empirically that student teachers and beginning teachers have a heightened self-conciousness at the beginning of their careers. She showed that the concentration of concern on self was a natural part of beginning to teach. In Piagetian terms, the need of the teacher to accommodate, to learn a new role, and to adjust to a new professional setting created disequilibrium. Recognizing the need to better understand the dynamics of concerns, Fuller then showed how support and time can ameliorate the concerns about self, which permits concerns about management and task to become more dominant.

Unfortunately, Fuller's research showed that student teachers and beginning teachers often do not reach the level of impact. Instead, some remain at the personal level, and a majority reach the management or task level. Without sufficient professional support (e.g., planning and reflection time, a caring and well-trained mentor, reasonable class assignment), it is not surprising that the beginning teacher might not move to the level of impact.

During the final stages of her career, in a series of invited addresses to the American Educational Research Association during the early 1970s, Fuller repeatedly challenged researchers, teacher educators, and educational practitioners to move out of a narrow cognitive stance, and to acknowledge the role affective concerns play in teaching behavior and effectiveness. Throughout her career she embraced the importance of better understanding healthy human and teacher growth. Her work represents a "gold standard" for present inquiries into how teachers adapt and adopt innovations.

REFLECTION QUESTIONS

What is the relevance of Fuller's work to beginning teacher induction programs?

Do you agree or disagree with Fuller that supervision is more than a cognitive endeavor?

If you have participated in a support group, how effective was it in ameliorating your personal concerns?

least initially, most educators will be working through management concerns as they strive to plan lessons and units of study and establish classroom or school routines. For most of you, however, there is a need to move on to the more important question of how to meet the instructional needs of the students or teachers. This leads us to the impact level.

The *impact* level of the concerns-based model includes consequence, collaboration, and refocusing. As Fuller and her associates discovered, it is the shift to impact that prompts a concern with student learning outcomes, colleagues, and the broader concern for school vitality. This makes a lot of sense when you think about it. A teacher who is concerned about survival or security is probably unable to be greatly concerned about other person's well-being or learning, let alone the welfare of the larger school community.

Only after you have attained some control of your classroom environment, are you able to concentrate on the learning needs of the students. The *consequence* phase represents a concern for students, the *collaboration* phase represents a concern for colleagues, and the *refocusing* phase represents a concern for adapting or reframing a specific teaching innovation, for example, cooperative learning.

As more research has been conducted, we are beginning to see that the work of Fuller and her associates can be applied to a variety of educational settings. For example, Richard Kimpston conducted a four-year study of teacher and principal phases of concern regarding the implementation of benchmark testing (Kimpston, 1987). His voluminous findings showed a gradual but steady increase in the phase of concern for the majority of teachers (144) in the study. The study also reported that teachers, in general, had more intense higher-level concerns than principals, and that those teachers who participated in staff development activities requiring active and sustained involvement moved to higher phases of concern than teachers who participated in brief and episodic staff development.

CONCERNS AND EQUILIBRATION

One of the most significant concepts in Piaget's theory of intellectual growth is equilibration. As we mentioned in Chapter 4, cognitive growth is the process of balancing what we already know (assimilation) with what we may want to learn that doesn't quite fit with our cognitive state (accommodation). Piaget theorized that persons develop through interaction with their environment. This interaction can lead to curiosity about new ideas or viewpoints that run counter to our past views or assimilations. As the new information is accommodated or internalized, the result is the gradual development of increasingly complex cognitive structures. Hans Furth calls these new ideas or events that don't quite fit *knowledge disturbances* (1981). But how does the process of equilibration relate to the phases of concern described by Fuller?

The work of noted educational psychologist Norman Sprinthall is instructive. He has spent much of his professional life examining how complex new helping roles (experience/action) contribute to adolescent and young adult growth and development. Always striving for the integration of affect and cognition, he is a noted Piagetian scholar in his own right. He points out that under the conditions of accommodation and disequilibration, we sense that a new or more comprehensive explanation is better. As this awareness emerges, part of us may be anxious and apprehensive. After all, we are exploring something that we don't fully understand. Additionally, another part of us may be resisting any change. Sprinthall's main point is that the feelings associated with new learnings gradually have to be worked through during equilibration. This requires "relaxed reflection" as we try to fit the new pieces of information into the old scheme. Sprinthall calls this process "talking to oneself" (Sprinthall, Sprinthall, & Oja, 1994, pp. 120–121).

The concerns identified by Fuller and her associates may be a partial description of the equilibration process. Certainly we know that strong feelings are associated with any change process. Piaget's concept of disequilibrium embodies the disruption and disquiet felt by persons as they encounter knowledge disturbances. As we have discovered, most complex new helping roles require the person to learn new ways of problem solving. The new role *also requires the person to give up previous ways of problem solving that are less adequate.* Thus persons in complex new roles initially are in a state of disequilibrium, and move through Fuller's concerns just as the theory predicts. It is only as the teacher reaches the impact level that the equilibration process is relatively complete and self-confidence again reigns. Understanding how equilibration relates to the phases of concern also explains why additional personal support is needed.

READING AND FLEXING TO TEACHER CONCERNS

Only recently have American psychologists and educators become more familiar with the significant research of Lev Vygotsky. His scholarship has much in common with that of Jean Piaget. He believed that human growth occurs through stages involving a series of radical transformations of the cognitive structures. As we mentioned in Chapter 3, his most important contribution is his description of the role played by social interaction. Breaking ranks with Piaget, who conceptualized growth as occurring largely in our heads, Vygotsky emphasized that formal and informal discussions are basic to cognitive growth. Vygotsky also invented the term "zone of proximal development" to describe the developmental principle that new learnings should be only slightly ahead of one's current preferred mode of thinking and problem solving (Vygotsky, 1962).

David Hunt has added to Vygotsky's concept of a zone of proximal development by describing how the educator must "read and flex" according to the needs of the learner. According to Hunt, the teacher or supervisor must tune the material and methods in accordance with the learning preferences of the student or colleague. The phrase "read and flex" means that first the supervisor must attend to the needs of the learner. He called this step reading the learner. Next the supervisor needs to flex the curriculum or study to meet the needs of the learner. Hunt referred to this process as a kind of attribute treatment interaction (ATI). This rather obtuse phrase simply means that the learner's needs (attributes) interact with the teaching or supervision method (treatment). Hunt explored ATI through his model of conceptual level that was described in Chapter 3.

Essentially, Hunt's three-stage framework characterized three qualitatively different modes of problem solving. As a brief review, the Stage A person used thinking that was concrete, believed in a single "right" way to teach, and showed little awareness of student feelings. The Stage B person used a combination of concrete and abstract thinking, showed some openness to new ideas, and was more aware of personal feelings as well as the needs of students. At Stage C the person exhibited evidence of integration and synthesis in complex intellectual and interpersonal arenas. Hunt went on to study how structure needed to be varied according to the problem-solving mode. Persons in Stage A preferred a more structured cognitive and teaching environment, whereas the Stage C person preferred a less structured context. This differentiation of structure is a fundamental aspect of developmental mentoring or supervision. In a sense, the mentor or supervisor must ascertain the zone of proximal growth of his or her colleague.

The work of Hunt overlaps with Fuller's model of phases of concern. Persons at concrete levels may hit a ceiling in terms of concerns. We have found few novice or experienced teachers at Stage A who were able to move higher than the management level of concern. Stage B teachers, who used a combination of concrete and abstract thinking, were able to reach consequence concerns. And Stage C teachers were able to reach the highest concerns, as described by Hall and Loucks (1978) (see Figure 5-1). Thus it becomes important for you the supervisor to be able to provide assistance and coaching that match and mismatch to the teacher's current conceptual level. The supervisor's goal is promoting teacher growth to more complex concep-

FIGURE 5-1   RELATIONSHIPS BETWEEN LEVELS IN THE CONCERNS-BASED ADOPTION MODEL AND HUNT'S CONCEPTUAL LEVELS

	A Concrete*	B Low Abstract	C High Abstract
1. Information			
2. Personal			
3. Management			
4. Consequence			
5. Collaboration			
6. Refocusing			

* Rate of movement through phases in the concerns-based adoption model varies. Persons in Stage A of Hunt move more slowly and recycle concepts often, B-stage persons move more quickly with some recycling of concepts, and Stage C persons move very quickly with little recycling of concepts.

Sources: Based on studies by R. Herring, *Psychological Maturity and Teacher Education: A Comparison of Intervention Models for Preservice Teacher Education,* 1989, Unpublished dissertation, Raleigh, NC: North Carolina State University, and J. Riggsbee, *A Developmental Reflective Seminar for Student Teachers,* 1995, Unpublished dissertation, Raleigh, NC: North Carolina State University.

EXHIBIT 5-2   DIFFERENTIATION OF STRUCTURE FOR CONCERNS

FACTORS	HIGH STRUCTURE	LOW STRUCTURE
Concepts	Concrete	Abstract
Affect	Supervisor discloses	Both colleague and supervisor disclose
Advance organizers	Multiple use	Few advance organizers needed
Complexity of learning tasks	Learning tasks divided into small steps and repeated	Learning tasks are clustered as wholes
Questioning	Tied to concrete examples and the colleague's experience	Relate to broader educational issues, ethics, and theory
Supervisor feedback	Frequent and specific	Emphasize self-critique

tual levels and to impact concerns. In Exhibit 5-2 we outline some of the factors that can be differentiated by structure.

Two Qualifications. As our understanding of the concerns-based model has enlarged, we have come to realize that two important qualifications must be considered as you apply the concepts. First, although the general rule holds that teachers at higher-level concerns prefer less structure, more participation, and more inquiry, development occurs across a series of partially independent domains. Therefore, a teacher who integrates and synthesizes knowledge in his or her subject-matter field of history and who has concerns at the impact level (focus on students and colleagues), may be at a more concrete level if the subject is mathematics with concerns that are at the task level (focus on time and management). Perhaps this is why integrated and interdisciplinary teaching is so challenging. Although the goal of integrated teaching is laudable, it demands of the teacher the ability to integrate abstract concepts and knowledge across a variety of domains. Therefore, as a mentor or supervisor, you will need to apply the general rule of low-structured context for teachers at abstract levels of cognitive complexity and offer assistance with impact concerns yet be prepared for systematic gaps. When you recognize that your colleague has switched to a more concrete level of reasoning with personal or management concerns, it is a signal that your mentoring or supervision must be modified toward higher structure, and more support and encouragement.

The second qualification has to do with stress. When teachers are in severe states of disequilibrium they may lower their level of problem solving for some period of time. Concerns at the personal level then predominate. Certainly this makes sense. Most of us have experienced times of extraordinary stress and anxiety as we accommodated to a career change, a significant personal loss, or an avalanche of professional pressures that have occurred simultaneously. If your colleague is in one of these states of disequilibrium, it is necessary for you to shift your supervision to a more structured, more direct approach. Stress also occurs as a person is shifting from one developmental level to the next. During these transitions anxiety runs high. Once again, concerns at the personal level may arise, and you will need to shift your supervision to a more structured approach.

How to Assess Concerns

There are several answers to the assessment question. One technique is a paper-and-pencil questionnaire developed by Hall and his colleagues (1987) designed to assess concerns of educators. Early work addressed reliability and validity issues, and only later was the questionnaire applied in cross-sectional and longitudinal studies (Burden, 1990). Recently Hall and Rutherford (1990) revisited the theory of concerns and conducted a review of studies that employed the Stages of Concern (SoC) questionnaire. Although not exhaustive, their review summarizes a 20-year history of research with the SoC questionnaire. As Hall and Rutherford acknowledge, "Most data collections have been one time occurrences. In only one study is there a control group, and when multiple data assessments of Stages of Concern have been made, the time interval has not been very long" (1990, p. 11). Nonetheless, the general dynamics of concerns across studies tend to be consistent.

A second type of assessment is the written response to open-ended questions (stems). The use of the SoC questionnaire in a colleague-to-colleague consultation or supervisory relationship may be perceived as too time-consuming or too obtrusive. One less obtrusive strategy is to ask a colleague to respond in writing to the following open-ended statements: *When I think about teaching, I am most concerned about. . . . and I feel. . . .* The written responses to these stems could be incorporated into an end-of-the-week debriefing conference or into a written dialogue journal that is shared between colleagues. The outcome, however, is the same. The written responses will reflect the dominant concerns of the colleague. An example of a written response by a beginning teacher to these stems is illustrative. See if you can identify the dominant concerns.

> *When I think about teaching, I am most concerned about . . .*
> Time, time, time. There is never enough time. I am driving myself crazy trying to prepare lesson plans and deal with all the other paperwork that has nothing to do with teaching. I can't remember the last time I had an entire weekend to myself.
> *I feel . . .*
> Frustrated and exhausted.

What are the dominant concerns? If you identified management and personal concerns you are batting one thousand.

A third kind of assessment is sometimes referred to as the one-legged conference. In effect, you are attempting to ascertain the concerns of a colleague in the amount of time you can stay balanced on one leg. For most of us, that isn't very long. Essentially, this method could be used as two colleagues are passing in the school hallway. It only requires a quick question like, "How is it going?" or "How is the disequilibrium?" If some trust and colleagueship has formed, the response to the question will be a brief but more than a perfunctory response. It may be a stricken look or a joyful burst about a successful lesson. The point is that these brief encounters can be opportunities to see how your colleague is faring. Although a supervisor should not rely on only this method, it is an unobtrusive, quick, and helpful strategy.

CASE STUDIES

We now turn to three case studies. Each case is a journal entry from Tom, Carole, and Bill, three teachers who were introduced in the applied activities for Chapter 3. As you read each journal entry, underline sentences that reflect a concern. After each case select possible action steps from Exhibit 5-3.

> *Tom.* "When I think about teaching I am most concerned about salary. I am working so hard but I don't think that I am rewarded appropriately. It is unbelievable how little respect teachers receive. I also am worried about the school's new emphasis on performance-based outcomes for teachers. I don't understand why the program was instituted and I worry that it will hamper me."

Reread the brief journal entry from Tom to his mentor. What passages did you underline? What concerns appear to be dominant for Tom? Tom has primarily expressed personal concerns, for example, "I am concerned about

EXHIBIT 5-3   ACTION STEPS BASED ON PHASES OF CONCERN

CONCERN	SOME POSSIBLE ACTION STEPS
0—Lack of Awareness	Provide information.
1—Informational	Clarify expectations and rationale for innovation.
2—Personal	Describe how the innovation will affect the person. Actively listen. Organize a concerns-based support group.
3—Management	Provide concrete management tips. Have the teacher observe another teacher successfully managing the class. Make sure the observing teacher collects data for follow-up discussion. Identify workshops that might be helpful.
4—Consequence	Actively listen. Provide opportunities for collegial observation and self-evaluation.
5—Collaboration	Help initiate planning meetings or teaming.
6—Refocusing	Support innovation and adaptation. Check for logic and usefulness.

salary," and "I worry that it [performance-based outcomes] will hamper me." Now identify possible action steps for the mentor to initiate.

> *Bill.* "When I think about teaching I am most concerned about how to adapt the new "hands on" mathematics curriculum for our school. I am planning to talk with my grade-level colleagues to brainstorm on how best to implement the new curriculum with the students. I have a number of concerns about the curriculum. Foremost, is my apprehension that several teachers will balk at the difficulty of the concepts introduced to students. I am hoping we can collectively develop some strategies for implementation."

As you probably have surmised from this brief journal entry from Bill to a peer coach and colleague, Bill's concerns are very different from Tom's concerns. What are the dominant concerns for Bill? Bill seems most concerned about collaboration, and how he will work with his colleagues to implement a new mathematics curriculum. Now turn to Exhibit 5-3 and identify possible action steps the peer coach might take to assist with Bill's concerns. Now read the journal entry for Carole.

> *Carole.* "When I think about teaching I am most concerned about managing my time effectively. There is so much paperwork that I often feel frustrated and overwhelmed. I want to give quality time to the students' needs but I sometimes think I shortchange the students because I have some form that must be turned in to the principal by 4:00."

Carole's concerns are at the management level (e.g., "I am most concerned about managing my time effectively,") and the consequence level (e.g., "I want to give quality time to the students' needs). However, her concerns converge on the management phase. Review Exhibit 5-3 for possible action steps a supervising colleague might take to assist Carole.

THEORY INTO PRACTICE: CONCERNS-BASED SEMINARS

The concerns-based model, as we have seen thus far, is an important addition to our understanding of teacher development. However, applying the theory is a challenge that faces teacher professional development in general, and mentoring and supervision in particular. Although it is beyond the scope of this chapter to discuss all the potential applications in detail, we can describe several programs that have showed promise. The following three perspectives are drawn from work by practicing cooperating teachers, mentor teachers, mentor counselors, principals, and teacher educators. In each case, the programs have employed some aspect of Fuller's theory to guide practice. As you will discover, theory is visible in practice and practice is visible in theory.

Student Teacher Supervision. As you will recall, many student teachers have an abundance of personal and management concerns during their student teaching. It is not unusual for student teachers to feel like they are on an emotional roller coaster as they ride the "white-water rapids" of student teaching. How often have you seen student teachers in tears or in a complete state of fatigue? Certainly almost every teacher educator can recite numerous examples of student teachers, who, stressed and strained by the demands of their new role, end up in bed for two or three days.

Recognizing that student teachers are struggling with the challenges of their assignment, some school-based teacher educators and college faculty at our institution have initiated support seminars for student teachers during their practicum experience. As part of the seminars, the student teachers are encouraged to discuss their most pressing concerns. Read the following comments by student teachers shared in seminars.

> "The cooperating teacher will be turning over the afternoon lessons to me next week, and my number one worry is classroom discipline. She makes it look so easy but I know it will be a different story when I take over."
>
> "I wonder if the cooperating teacher likes me. He seems so formal and distant."
>
> "I spent the entire weekend on lesson plans and unit plans. I am thoroughly exhausted and it is only Tuesday."

As these comments demonstrate, student teachers have a number of pressing personal and classroom management concerns. After sharing concerns, the student teachers also discuss strategies for addressing these concerns. Strategies may include taking time each week to celebrate successes, developing a flowchart of all the major responsibilities for the student teaching experience, regularly reviewing progress through formal and informal conferences, getting enough rest, and gathering "trade secrets" for being more organized. As a final activity, seminar leaders ask several student teachers to share a success story.

Acknowledging concerns in a seminar is a healthy way of managing the normal stress associated with student teaching. The dialogue also alerts student teachers to the realization that, until their concerns are resolved, it is unlikely that they can progress to a higher level of concern. It is important to note that research has been initiated to assess the impact of support seminars. Glassberg and Sprinthall (1980) showed that the seminar approach offered a time for quiet reflection on the student teaching experience and encouraged growth.

Support Groups for Beginning Teachers. As was mentioned earlier in the chapter, beginning teachers often encounter an enormous number of challenges during their first year in the classroom. Too often, it is a "trial by fire." Recognizing that more adequate professional support is needed for beginning teachers, some school systems have begun to look for ways to offer more support and guidance to beginners. Support groups have evolved as one form of professional support. Thies-Sprinthall and Gerler (1990) provide an excellent review of how these groups can be structured.

What we have generally found is that many beginning teachers are overwhelmed in the early months of their experience, and many of them believe that no one else can really appreciate how difficult things are. Further, they are hesitant to reveal their feelings to a trusted colleague for fear of appearing inadequate to the demands of the job. The support group, however, breaks down this isolation and fear, by bringing a number of beginning teachers together to share concerns, to identify possible strategies, and to celebrate successes. In fact, research has shown that novice teachers in support seminars proceed more quickly through the phases of concern (Paisley, 1990).

In one of our own initiatives with a sample of over 100 beginning teachers, we have found that support groups encourage a gradual but steady increase in progression through the levels of concern with a majority of the teachers beginning to shift to impact concerns during the final months of their first year (Reiman, Bostik, Lassiter, & Cooper, 1995). Furthermore, the mentor teachers and counselors who cooperatively lead the support groups have found that an awareness of the concerns model is tremendously helpful to their work. All of the facilitators have encouraged the beginning teachers to write written reflections as part of the support meetings. The personal and management concerns of the new teachers consistently surface in the written reflections. Thus the support team facilitators have been able to carefully track the progress of the concerns of each beginning teacher. In fact, the facilitators write responses back to each beginning teacher. In their responses, they make sure to accept and acknowledge the concerns shared by the beginning teachers. Support groups for beginning or experienced teachers are yet another form of supervision that we believe will become more pervasive in the next millennium.

Preparation of Mentor Teachers. It probably comes as no surprise that we incorporate Fuller and her associates' pioneering work into the coursework that prospective mentor teachers and mentor counselors receive. The overall emphasis of the specialized training is developmental supervision. As part of the program, the prospective mentors participate in a reflective practicum while they work with a novice professional. The practicum lasts one semester and follows a semester of coursework that introduces them to developmental supervision.

As part of the practicum, the teachers or counselors are asked to identify the current dominant concerns of their protégé. This is accomplished through review of tape-recorded formal pre-conferences and post-conferences, and review of written reflections completed by the novice teacher. The direct application of Fuller's model encourages the prospective mentor to more quickly and more competently attend to the personal needs of his or her protégé. Mentors also are encouraged to use active listening with their protégé. As trust is developed, the beginning teacher will reveal his or her concerns. Many concerns may be shared. Being knowledgeable about the theory, the mentor is able to more adequately respond to the needs of his or her protégé.

As a result of our efforts, we have found that teachers and counselors can be taught to apply Fuller's model to their work as mentors, and the use of the model actually enhances the assistance they provide. As one mentor puts it, "I have found the concerns model to be very helpful to my work as a mentor. It gives me an overall picture of where my colleague's concerns are, and what types of support she most needs from me" (Corzine, 1994).

Up to this point we have discussed two dimensions of teacher development. The first dimension is cognitive development, which describes how persons grow through stages. Each stage represents a more complex and abstract meaning-making system. Developmental instructional supervision can promote this growth through stages. A second dimension involves the work of Fuller and her associates with the concerns approach to change. As we demonstrated, this description of adult change is important because it allows us to better understand the disequilibrium that a person experiences as he or she undertakes a complex new role such as teaching for the first time. We now turn to the related work on career phases, and its linkage to developmental mentoring and supervision.

 ## TEACHER CAREER PHASES

Teacher career phases of change have their origins in age and life cycle theories. As is the case with the previous two dimensions of change, we will strive to integrate career transitions with developmental stage theory and the concerns model.

CAREER TRANSITIONS

When developmental psychology gradually shifted its focus from childhood and adolescence to adults, it was Erik Erikson who became the major theorist in such a change. His case studies of adults (Martin Luther, Mahatma Gandhi), his observations of native American tribes (the Sioux and Yurok), and his insights from the psychoanalytical treatment of adults formed the basis for creating an epigenetic principle of development throughout the life cycle (Erikson, 1963, 1975). Erikson's theory essentially described four very comprehensive psychosocial tasks for adults: early adulthood as identity achievement versus foreclosure and intimacy versus isolation, then adulthood as generativity versus stagnation, and finally old age as integrity versus despair.

These bipolar tasks were revised in more recent work (Erikson, 1982). In these revisions, Erikson outlined in greater detail how the bipolar tasks can be resolved successfully or unsuccessfully depending on the individual's current interaction with the environment. The recent revisions by Erikson described how each adult stage may be resolved with a basic strength, *love, care, wisdom,* or a basic antipathy, *exclusivity, rejectivity, or disdain.* It also is clear that his recent work shifted attention to the dynamics of adulthood itself. In particular, he examined the unique place held by the stage of generativity versus stagnation. He views that stage as a generational link between the young and the old. There is an urgency at this stage to practice what, "Hindus call 'maintenance of the world'" (1982, p. 66). And it is the commitment to care as the most appropriate integration of the polarities. Erikson stressed that such care is not limited to one's own circle but rather to a universal focus, the qualitative improvement of life for all, and a sense of communitarianism.

RECENT WORK IN TEACHER CAREER DEVELOPMENT

Recent work on teacher career development by Fessler (1985), Fessler and Christensen (1992), and Huberman (1993) can be considered as variations on the Erikson model. The work is largely descriptive, interview based, and seeks to sketch phases of the professional life cycle of teachers. Fessler (1985) developed a model to describe the dynamics of a teacher's life cycle. His work identified three major influences: personal, organizational, and career. The personal sphere includes family experiences, developmental stage, family, and significant positive experiences or crises. The organizational sphere includes professional organizations, management style and expectations, policy, public trust, and societal expectations. Fessler's third sphere, career, includes a hierarchy of eight levels as follows: preservice, induction, competency building, enthusiastic and growing, career frustration, stable but stagnant, career wind-down, and career exit. Figure 5-2 outlines these three major spheres of influence.

While the Erikson approach has been to chart the relationship between the psychological aspects of development and chronological aging, and the concerns model assesses concerns and attitudes toward change and educational innovations, teacher career development has focused on ages and phases of occupational progression. In Fessler and Christensen's recent revision of their work (1992), they have incorporated data from interviews with 160 teachers across the career span. Figure 5-2 illustrates how each sphere interacts with the others. Some elaboration of the career cycle sphere is needed. As mentioned previously, the framework includes eight levels: preservice, induction, competency building, enthusiastic and growing, career frustration, stable but stagnant, career wind-down, and career exit. The framework acknowledges that a teacher's career cycle is influenced by personal experiences such as family and crises, as well as organizational influences such as management style and societal expectations. It is important to note that the career cycle is not unidirectional. Instead, it represents an ebb and flow with teachers moving in and out of positions in the cycle in response to professional experiences as well as personal and organizational influences.

The first four positions in the career cycle sphere (Figure 5-2) (preservice, induction, competency building, and enthusiastic and growing) in general are characterized by high motivation, high task accomplishment, teacher identity formation and, particularly during the enthusiastic and growing po-

FIGURE 5-2 THREE SPHERES OF INFLUENCE ON CAREER

Organizational Sphere
1. Professional organizations
2. Management style
3. Policy
4. Public trust
5. Societal expectations

Personal Sphere
1. Family experiences
2. Developmental stage
3. Significant positive experiences (e.g., new roles)
4. Crises (disequilibrium)

Career Cycle Sphere
1. Preservice
2. Induction
3. Competency building
4. Enthusiastic and growing
5. Career frustration
6. Stable but stagnant
7. Career wind-down
8. Career exit

Source: Adapted from "A Model for Teacher Professional Growth and Development," by R. Fessler, 1985. In P. J. Burke and R. G. Heideman (Eds.), *Career-Long Education* (pp. 181–193), Springfield, IL: Charles C Thomas.

sition, a time of generativity and giving back to the profession. The remaining four career positions (frustration, stable but stagnant, career wind-down, and career exit) represent the other side of the career coin, so to speak. Each position signifies a diffusion of expectations about teaching and a waning of career satisfactions. For example, the career frustration position is characterized by feelings of frustration and disillusionment with teaching. This waning of job satisfaction typically occurs at the midpoint of a teacher's career. It is at this point that teachers more frequently question their self-worth and the worth of teaching. As we mentioned earlier, the career cycle is not unidirectional. Therefore, if a teacher at the career frustration position became involved in professional development that was revitalizing, the teacher most probably would return to the enthusiastic and growing position in the career cycle. Exhibit 5-4 elaborates each position in the career cycle.

EXHIBIT 5-4   THE TEACHER CAREER CYCLE

CAREER POSITION	DESCRIPTION
1. Preservice	Preparation in a college teacher education program.
2. Induction	Generally, the first three years in the teaching profession.
3. Competency building	Improving teaching skills.
4. Enthusiastic and growing	Expressing high levels of job satisfaction.
5. Frustration	Feeling frustration and disillusionment with teaching.
6. Stable but stagnant	Doing what is expected and little more.
7. Career wind-down	Preparing to leave the profession, and either reflecting on the positive experiences or anxious to leave an unrewarding job.
8. Career exit	Retiring or exploring a career alternative.

Supervisors need to recognize that teachers at different career positions may need different kinds of assistance. Naturally a teacher at the enthusiastic and growing level will respond differently to coaching and assistance than a teacher who has shifted to the career frustration position.

Huberman (1993) offers yet another iteration of teachers' career development. His research has traced how teachers' lives are ameliorated or constrained by the passage of time and the normal crises that are part of the social and cultural milieu. Huberman's model of career trajectories has much in common with the original theory of Erikson as well as the more recent work of Fessler and Christensen. His in-depth case studies of 160 teachers confirm that remarkable consistencies exist in career socialization, even when unique personal contexts are taken into account. In many respects, the research of Huberman has reasserted Lewin's famous insight that what it means to be human is influenced by both social influences and maturational factors.

The work of Huberman (1993) and of Fessler and Christensen (1992) adds another layer to our understanding of teacher development. Knowing a colleague's current career position allows the supervisor to tailor assistance that is in accordance with the unique needs of a particular career position. Certainly a teacher in the induction position needs a more direct and structured type of assistance, whereas the colleague who is at the frustrated position could benefit from staff development opportunities or new roles.

HOW DOES CAREER DEVELOPMENT RELATE TO COGNITIVE DEVELOPMENT?

The career development view emphasizes the importance of societal and professional conditions on the teacher during the process of aging. In many respects, the view places heavy emphasis on the external determinants of a person's development. The structural developmentalists, on the other hand, emphasize how each individual interprets the meaning of those events according to the complexity of one's cognition. For example, all teachers go through an induction phase in their career. However, how each teacher makes meaning out of those early teaching experiences greatly depends on her or his current cognitive complexity. As Noam, Powers, Kilkenny, and Beedy (1990) point out, a 13-year-old, a 30-year-old, and even a 70-year-old, may all structure the experience of interpersonal relationships at a similar stage of development in spite of contextual differences.

Thus the problem is how to synthesize the impact of career and sociological life-span forces with the cognitive-structural stage considerations into a richer and more meaningful theory for adult development in general, and teacher supervision in particular. At present, you may want to interpret the career development theories as general descriptions of teachers at different points in their careers. Cognitive-structural stage theory, on the other hand, offers you a lens for understanding the internal determinants of a teacher's development.

 ## SUMMARY

Frances Fuller (1969) identified three major phases of concern that novice teachers move through in their personal growth as they are learning about teaching. These concerns were further explained by the work of Hall, Wallace, and Dossett (1973) and Hall and Loucks (1978). Their work extended the model by identifying a total of seven phases of concern. The concerns model assists the supervisor in understanding how the colleague is making personal meaning from experience. Concerns also may be a window into the equilibration process described by Jean Piaget.

The main point is that promoting growth requires attention to both assimilation and accommodation. When new information is presented that does not fit with your supervisee's current level of problem solving, a knowledge disturbance exists. If the colleague takes in the new information, they are accommodating to it. The next step is to fit the new information in with the old or preexisting views. This balancing of accommodation and assimilation is called equilibration. Piaget's concept of equilibration fits in nicely with the concerns model because we know that feelings of worry and frustration often accompany the struggle to give up old ways of thinking. When Vygotsky talks about the zone of proximal development he is highlighting the fact that the new ideas must not require too great a cognitive adjustment on the part of the learner.

The work of David Hunt with conceptual level overlaps with the concerns-based model and explains why supervisors need to adjust their supervision according to the current preferred level of problem solving of the supervisee as well as his or her level of concern. The general rule is to use more open-ended supervisory approaches with more abstract cognitive-structured teachers at the impact level. However, two qualifications are needed.

First, there is variation across domains and across academic subject matter and, second, when there is high anxiety, persons may shift to personal concerns and need higher-structured supervision.

The work of Fessler and Christensen outlined major career phases for the teacher. Their work is based on an interview study with 160 teachers at different phases in their career. There are two most important points in the chapter. First, supervisors' attention to teacher concerns and career phases promotes better supervision. Second, the model requires mentors supervisors to be flexible in their approach. There is no single "tried and true" approach that will work with everyone. Michael Fullan (1991) has commented that the original vision of clinical supervision was to confront the complexities of teaching and learning through discourse. When teacher development is viewed as interactive and formative, he sees a whole array of possibilities unfolding. As we have reviewed different dimensions of teacher growth and change, hopefully you have begun to see how your own role encourages wise interaction and discourse. In Chapters 6 and 7 we turn to a more practical aspect of developmental supervision, the importance of developing a positive and trusting relationship.

SUPERVISION FOR TEACHER DEVELOPMENT ACTIVITIES

APPLIED

1. To practice identifying phases of concern and feeling, see if you can classify the following statements. Use the following codes (phase numbers): 0 = awareness; 1 = information; 2 = personal; 3 = management; 4 = consequence; 5 = collaboration; 6 = refocusing. Also write a feeling word that might be associated with the phase. Check your responses with the answers at the end of Suggested Readings on p. 104.

EXPRESSION	PHASE	FEELINGS
a. I tried some small group work this morning and I found I could learn a lot about the students.	____	____
b. I just can't seem to reach Tara. Something needs to be changed in my instruction.	____	____
c. The principal is making a "surprise" visit to my classroom for an evaluation.	____	____
d. Good grief, will I ever dig my way out from under all this paperwork?	____	____
e. Where can I go to get more information about teacher benefits?	____	____
f. It was terrific to work with my grade-level team last week.	____	____
g. This will be my first set of parent conferences. Frankly, I am worried what they think of me.	____	____

2. You have already learned how to identify the concerns of the person you are supervising and you have a framework for assisting with those concerns. Now use this information about levels of concern for your own benefit. Use one of the following procedures:

   a. If you keep a journal, write an entry today and include a paragraph describing what concerns you most about becoming or being a developmental supervisor. Include the feelings you have from these concerns. Tomorrow read your journal entry and list your current level of concern. Look at Exhibit 5-3 for possible action steps and write an action step you will take to remove this concern.

   b. During the next class session, ask the teacher to have a discussion about the class and discuss your responses to this activity.

3. If you are mentoring or supervising someone now, and the person is keeping a journal, read it carefully to identify the person's level of concern. There is more information about this in Chapter 11. You may want to peruse that chapter now.

SUGGESTED READINGS

1. Fuller, F. F. (1969). Concerns of teachers: A developmental conceptualization. *American Educational Research Journal, 6,* 207–226.

   Frances Fuller was one of the first researchers to document the sequence of personal issues that student teachers experienced. Using a "grassroots" approach she listened carefully to their concerns and then was able to classify the issues on a sequential hierarchy, an excellent example of field-based research with immediate implications.

2. Thies-Sprinthall, L., & Gerler, E. (1990). Support groups for novice teachers. *Journal of Staff Development, 11,* 18–23.

   The authors provide an update on Fuller's original research, outlining how Fuller's model might be applied to the first year of a teacher's employment. The authors also provide a support group practicum for persons learning to become developmental supervisors.

3. Reiman, A. J., Bostick, D., Lassiter, J., & Cooper, J. (1995). Counselor- and teacher-led support groups for beginning teachers: A cognitive-developmental perspective. *Elementary School Guidance and Counseling, 30*(2), 105–117.

   The authors spent three years designing and implementing support groups for beginning teachers. The interprofessional approach was one of the first of its kind in a large metropolitan school system. The results of the study indicate the positive effect of helping beginning teachers move beyond concerns about "self" to classroom management and then to the impact of their teaching for students. The study is a strong rationale for including such support groups as part of a teacher induction program.

4. Erikson, E. (1982). *The life cycle completed.* Norton: New York.

> *The best way to understand the significance of Erikson's theory of adult stages is to read at least a few excerpts from one of his last publications. The clarity and power of his prose illuminates his wisdom on the important issues that we face during middle and later adulthood.*

5. Fessler, R., & Christensen, J. (1992). *The teacher career cycle: Understanding and guiding the professional development of teachers.* Boston: Allyn and Bacon.

> *Fessler and Christensen update their work on teacher career cycles with new information on how to integrate career cycles with the theory and research on cognitive development.*

6. Sprinthall, N. A., Reiman, A. J., & Thies-Sprinthall, L. (1996). Teacher professional development. In J. Sikula (Ed.), *Second handbook of research on teacher education.* New York: Macmillan.

> *This is a lengthy, almost encyclopedic, review of teacher development and includes major sections on various theories of career phases and stages. Also included is a very extensive bibliography detailing the wide variety of approaches to the question of career models. It is not easy reading but it is comprehensive:*

ANSWER KEY TO ACTIVITY ONE

	CODE	PHASE	FEELINGS
a.	4	Consequence	Successful
b.	4	Consequence	Challenged
c.	2	Personal	Worried
d.	3	Management	Frustrated
e.	1	Information	Curious
f.	5	Collaborative	Excited
g.	2	Personal	Worried

REFERENCES

Burden, P. (1990). Teacher development. In R. Houston (Ed.), *Handbook of research on teacher education* (pp. 311–328). New York: Macmillan.

Corzine, I. (1994). *Personal note.* Wake County Public School System. Raleigh, NC.

Erikson, E. (1963). *Childhood and society.* New York: Norton.

Erikson, E. (1975). *Life history and the historical moment.* New York: Norton.

Erikson, E. (1982). *The life cycle completed.* New York: Norton.

Fessler, R. (1985). A model for teacher professional growth and development. In P. J. Burke & R. G. Heideman (Eds.), *Career-long education* (pp. 181–193). Springfield, IL: Charles C Thomas.

Fessler, R., & Christensen, J. (1992). *The teacher career cycle: Understanding and guiding the professional development of teachers*. Boston: Allyn and Bacon.

Fullan, M. (1991). *The new meaning of educational change*. New York: Teachers College Press.

Fuller, F. F. (1969). Concerns of teachers: A developmental conceptualization. *American Educational Research Journal, 6*(2), 206–266.

Furth, H. (1981). *Piaget and knowledge* (2nd ed.). Chicago: University of Chicago Press.

Glassberg, S., & Sprinthall, N. A. (1980). Student teaching: A developmental approach. *Journal of Teacher Education, 31*, 31–38.

Hall, G. E., & Loucks, S. (1978, September). Teacher concerns as a basis for facilitating and personalizing staff development. *Teachers College Record, 80*, 36–53.

Hall, G. E., & Hord, S. M. (1987). Change in schools, facilitating the process. New York: State University of New York Press.

Hall, G. E., & Rutherford, G. (1990). *A preliminary review of research related to stages of concern*. Paper presented at the Annual Meeting of the American Educational Research Association, Boston.

Hall, G. E., Wallace, R. C., Jr., & Dossett, W. A. (1973). *A developmental conceptualization of the adoption process within educational institutions*. Austin: Research and Development Center for Teacher Education, University of Texas.

Huberman, M. (1993). *The lives of teachers*. New York: Teachers College Press.

Kimpston, R. D. (1987). Teacher and principal stage of concern regarding implementation of benchmark testing: A longitudinal study. *Teaching and Teacher Education, 3*(3), 205–217.

Noam, G., Powers, S., Kilkenny, R., & Beedy, J. (1990). The interpersonal self in life-span developmental perspective: Theory, measurement and case studies. In P. Baltes, D. Featherman, & R. Lerner (Eds.), *Life-span development and behavior* (vol. 10, pp. 60–104). Hillsdale, NJ: Lawrence Erbaum Associates.

Paisley, P. (1990). Counselor involvement in promoting the development of beginning teachers. *Journal of Humanistic Education and Development, 29*, 20–29.

Reiman, A. J., Bostick, D., Lassiter, J., & Cooper, J. (1995). Counselor- and teacher-led support groups for beginning teachers: A cognitive-developmental perspective. *Elementary School Guidance and Counseling, 30*(2), 105–117.

Reiman, A. J., & Parramore, B. (1994). First-year teachers' assignments, expectations, and development: A collaborative investigation. In M. O'Hair & S. Odell (Eds.), *Partnerships in education. Teacher Education Yearbook II*. Orlando: Harcourt Brace Jovanovich.

Sprinthall, N. A., Sprinthall, R. C., & Oja, S. N. (1994). *Educational psychology: A developmental approach* (6th ed.). New York: McGraw-Hill.

Thies-Sprinthall, L., & Gerler, E. R., Jr. (1990). Support groups for novice teachers. *The Journal of Staff Development, 11*, 18–23.

Veenman, S. (1984). Perceived problems of beginning teachers. *Review of Educational Research, 54*(2), 143–178.

Vygotsky, L. (1962). *Thought and language*. Cambridge, MA: MIT Press.

DEVELOPMENTAL SUPERVISION AND COACHING FOR TEACHER DEVELOPMENT

• • • • • •

*I*n Part I we introduced you to mentoring and supervision, and identified the need for a guiding theory. In Part II we introduced recent research and theory on teacher development and how it can be applied to mentoring and supervision. In Part III, we shift our focus to the effective practice of developmental instructional mentoring and supervision. As you read, we hope you will see the inherent potential in mentoring and supervision as a connecting discipline between the typical world of professional knowledge and the world of practice.

In Chapter 6 we review three dispositions that constitute the personal domain. Chapter 7 shifts to interpersonal skills and the importance they play in mentoring and supervisory relationships. Chapter 8 examines models and methods of instruction and how to use anecdotel observation data to gain knowledge about successful teaching. Following this, a discussion of developmental cycles of assistance (pre-conferences, observations and data collection, and post-conferences) is presented in Chapters 9 to 11. In Chapter 12 coaching plans are described, and in Chapter 13 we discuss how guided reflection through journal keeping promotes both growth and development and deeper thinking about students and instruction. In Chapter 14 we describe strategies for documenting mentoring and supervisory assistance and teacher developmental efforts.

C·H·A·P·T·E·R
6

The Personal Domain

. . . .

As we noted in Parts I and II, the research basis for understanding the process of supervision and teacher development has expanded gradually during the last decade. In this chapter we discuss the personal domain of mentoring and supervision. Specifically, we describe how dispositions toward the teaching/learning process, colleagues, and ourselves shape the personal domain.

As you review the chapter, check your comprehension by answering these questions:

- How does conceptual level influence our attitudes toward the teaching/learning process?
- What are the myths about mentoring and supervision?
- Why mentor or supervise?

SELF-KNOWLEDGE AND EGO (PERSONAL) DEVELOPMENT

As one of the mentor teachers at an elementary school in North Carolina, the first author (AR) considered himself to be a very supportive and effective mentor for the beginning teachers at the school. In reviewing notes, however, a different picture emerged. "I remember one beginning teacher in particular. We met every Friday morning to review significant events and to plan for the next week. We also jointly planned field trips and units of study for the students. I tried to actively listen when my colleague shared prob-

FIGURE 6-1   ADAPTATION OF JOHARI WINDOW—HOW WE KNOW
SELF AND OTHERS

	Known to Self	Not Known to Self
Known to Others	1. Public self	2. Blind self
Not Known to Others	3. Private self	4. Unknown to self and others

Source: Adapted from Joseph Luft, *Group Processes: An Introduction to Group Dynamics.* New York: National Press Books, 1970.

lems and we also interacted outside of the classroom. From my perspective, the mentoring relationship was extraordinarily successful. However, at the end of the school year my teaching assistant and I were reviewing some curriculum materials I had developed and she casually mentioned that it would have been helpful for me to share some of the materials with my mentee. To my chagrin, I realized that I had been unaware of my lack of willingness to share some of my newest ideas."

The Johari window (Luft, 1970) offers a useful way of looking at what we know and do not know about ourselves. The system was created by a group of psychologists in Minnesota as a means of identifying different domains of self-awareness. The four aspects, however, were not connected to stages of development. In our view the window can be used as a general model of self-awareness and can be transformed into a stage-linked framework. In Figure 6-1 we see the various behaviors of both self and others.

In Frame 1, the public self, are the behaviors that the self is aware of (supervisor or supervisee) and that others know are used as well. For example, a teacher is aware that he or she prefers individual as opposed to team-teaching experiences and the staff know of this preference. Frame 2 represents the blind self. Included here are behaviors that are unknown to the self but are known to others. For example, as a supervising mentor teacher I was unaware of my reluctance to share new curriculum innovations with my colleague; however, my teaching assistant was aware of the behavior.

In Frame 3 are those behaviors known to the self but not to others—the private self. For instance, in my early days as a mentor teacher (AR), I worried that I was not giving enough time to my colleague. The colleague, how-

FIGURE 6-2   ADAPTATION OF JOHARI WINDOW—EGO STAGES: SELF-PROTECTIVE TO CONFORMIST (Δ–I 3)

	Known to Self	Not Known to Self
Known to Others	1. Public self	2. Blind self
Not Known to Others	3. Private self	4. Unknown to self and others

Source: Adapted from Joseph Luft, *Group Processes: An Introduction to Group Dynamics*. New York: National Press Books, 1970.

ever, was unaware of these feelings. Finally, in Frame 4 are those behaviors that are unknown to both the self and to others. In supervision, for example, the supervisor and the colleague may be unaware that during post-observation conferences, the supervisor always frowns when asking a question about whether there are any changes the teacher would make to the lesson's learning outcomes. In this case, both the supervisor and the supervisee or mentor and protégé are unaware of the nonverbal behavior at a conscious level.

The Johari window can also portray how one's knowledge of self changes with ego development. As we mentioned in Chapter 3, Jane Loevinger (1976) has shown how persons' knowledge of self develops gradually through stages over time. What is known and unknown to the self partially determines ego complexity, which grows through stages over time. The Johari window in Figure 6-2 shows how the size of the frames changes for a supervisor or supervisee at the Self-Protective and Conformist ego stages. In this scheme the frames for the public self and the private self are actually small. There are a narrower set of behaviors that are known by the self (supervisor or supervisee) and others. For example, a person at the Self-Protective and Conformist stages would have a limited awareness of how his or her teaching affects the students . Likewise, Frame 3, private self is relatively small. However, Frame 2, the blind self and Frame 4, unknown to self and others, are large. There are a larger number of behaviors that are either unknown to self, but known to others, or unknown to both self and others.

Supervisors and teachers at the midrange of Loevinger's ego development are aware of a broader range of thoughts and feelings. Thus, in the

FIGURE 6-3   ADAPTATION OF JOHARI WINDOW—EGO STAGES:
CONSCIENTIOUS-CONFORMIST TO INDIVIDUALISTIC
(I 3/4–I 4/5)

	Known to Self	Not Known to Self
Known to Others	1. Public self	2. Blind self
Not Known to Others	3. Private self	4. Unknown to self and others

Source: Adapted from Joseph Luft, *Group Processes: An Introduction to Group Dynamics.* New York: National Press Books, 1970.

Johari window, all the frames in the window are about equal in size (see Figure 6-3).

In the case of a supervisor, the public and private selves are larger at this level. The supervisor is aware of himself or herself in relation to colleagues, and publicly shares short-term and long-term goals with peers. There also is a greater willingness to express feelings with associates (public self). At this level, the supervisor is self-critical and often feels guilty for consequences that may be beyond his or her control. My own earlier shared account (AR) is a case in point. As the supervising mentor, I felt worried and guilty for not spending more time with the beginning teacher, even though a significant amount of shared planning and discussion had occurred.

Finally, at the highest stages of ego development, we see another qualitative shift in how the Johari window is portrayed (see Figure 6-4). At this level, the knowledge of self is large, whereas the blind self (Frame 2), and the unknown to self and others (Frame 4) are significantly smaller. Thus, the supervisor or supervisee has a much larger awareness of self that matches what is known by others. Doug Heath (1994) has commented that one of the hallmarks of a psychologically mature person is the increased congruence between self-knowledge and what is known to others. As an example, a principal at this level would be able to convey both his or her visions and commitments for the school while maintaining an openness to teachers' ideas and concerns (public self)—the hallmark of the kind of leadership needed in schools that are self-renewing (Goodlad, 1994; Joyce, Wolf, & Calhoun, 1993; Sergiovanni & Starratt, 1993). Rather than being aloof and unapproachable, the person at this level is accessible and genuine.

FIGURE 6-4 ADAPTATION OF JOHARI WINDOW—EGO STAGES: AUTONOMOUS TO INTEGRATED (I 5–I 6)

	Known to Self	Not Known to Self
Known to Others	1. Public self	2. Blind self
Not Known to Others	3. Private self	4. Unknown to self and others

Source: Adapted from Joseph Luft, *Group Processes: An Introduction to Group Dynamics.* New York: National Press Books, 1970.

Additionally, the supervisor at this level is, in the language of Carl Rogers, more "transparently real (private self—Frame 3)." Because there is so much more information that is available to self, the private frame enlarges. Yet the self also is more willing to share events from his or her private life when it adds to the collegiality and shared goals of a group.

 ## WHAT ARE YOUR ASSUMPTIONS?

Although the Johari window can portray the public, private, blind, and unknown selves, it does not portray the quality of what is known or unknown. If, for example, in your role as supervisor, your basic assumptions are that teaching means employing a "tried and true" kind of instruction with most of the interactions being teacher-to-student, then most likely, your behaviors will reflect these assumptions. Moreover, as a supervisor, you will most likely encourage this kind of teaching and be inclined to model only this type of instruction.

If, on the other hand, your assumptions are that teaching is both a science and an art and requires the use of a large repertoire of teaching models and strategies, once again, your behaviors will reflect these assumptions. Furthermore, in your supervision you will value, and, if you teach, model that repertoire of skills.

The evidence that beliefs and assumptions shape one's teaching are extensive. Sometimes referred to as the "hidden curriculum," Mark Ginsburg and Renee Clift (1990) have summarized research on the implicit messages that are sent by principals, teachers, schools, school systems, and teacher education institutions. The findings show an unmistakable link between beliefs, assumptions, and actual practices. Unfortunately, the consequences of the hidden agenda, particularly how it plays itself out in interactions between the teacher and child, can be most destructive, for example, racism and sexism. On a hopeful note, Ginsburg and Clift's analysis indicates that preservice teachers and teachers in their first two to three years of teaching (induction) "can learn to confront the messages in the hidden curriculum and, thus, avoid being accidentally influenced by them." (1990, p. 460).

Thus, we need to check the validity of our perceptions about supervision and the teaching/learning process. Before you read any further, we encourage you to make three copies of the following Inventory of Educational Beliefs (Exhibit 6-1). Give one copy to a colleague, and one to a student (he or she would only complete the first two parts). Ask each of them to complete the inventory on you. Mention to them that their input will be confidential, and that you will use their input to improve your work. You also should complete the inventory before scoring it (see Exhibit 6-1).

DISPOSITIONS TOWARD THE TEACHING/LEARNING PROCESS

David Hunt believed that there is nothing quite as theoretical as good practice, which is illustrative of an important point we want to make. Supervision plays an invaluable role in translating educational research and theory into practice. It is also probably true that your dispositions toward the teaching/learning process affect how you will supervise or coach a colleague. As a supervisor or mentor, you serve as a kind of instructional ombudsman, helping your colleague to translate "book learning" into effective practice. If novice teachers, for example, are left on their own, the learning of teaching becomes a "hit or miss" process. Unfortunately, we know that it is very difficult to unlearn teaching habits that are constructed during the initial years of teaching. In fact, some commentators, invoking the work of Konrad Lorenz, have suggested that the first year of teaching leaves an indelible imprint on the teacher, for good or bad. If history is a good teacher, we also know that studies of classroom interactions between teachers and students have shown recurring patterns in educational method that appear to be very resistant to change. Take as an example a study of 156 randomly selected elementary-school classrooms. The authors of the study (Goodlad & Klein, 1974) noted:

> At all grade levels, the teacher-to-child pattern of interaction overwhelmingly prevailed. This was one of the most monotonously recurring pieces of data. The teacher asked questions and the children responded, usually in a few words or phrases. . . . It is fair to

> say that this teacher-to-child interaction was the mode in all but
> about 5 percent of the classes. (p. 11)

A more recent observation was made by Ted Sizer (1984) when he poignantly argued that the fictional high-school teacher named Horace could never become a great teacher using a single tried and true method of teaching. In a sense, Horace has compromised his vision of what teaching can be when faced with the daily realities of the school.

"Horace is a gentle man. He reads the frequent criticism of his profession in the press with compassion. Johnny can't read. Teachers have low Graduate Record Examination scores. We must vary our teaching to the learning styles of our pupils. We must relate to the community. We must be scholarly, keeping up with our fields. English teachers should be practicing, published writers. If they aren't all these things, it is obvious that they don't care. Horace is a trooper. He hides his bitterness. Nothing can be gained by showing it. The critics do not really want to hear him or to face facts. He will go with the flow. What alternative is there?" (Sizer, 1984, p. 19)

As a student of supervision and the teaching/learning process you would probably shake your head after reading the above quotes, sadly noting that there is such a rich array of instructional strategies available to teachers in this day and age. "Why must so many teachers rely on rapid-fire question and answer and the safety of "going with the flow? I can't believe that teaching hasn't evolved beyond this." If you are thinking that such methods at best encourage the recitation of textbook facts and continuation of the status quo, we agree.

Perhaps this problem is inexorably linked to the lack of adequate sustained assistance between new teachers and mentors. We know that without support, demonstrations, and practice with feedback, most educational innovations are doomed to failure. We also know that it is the classroom where the new methods of teaching must be elevated, but where, in too many cases, they break down. We believe this breakdown is primarily due to the lack of in-class supervision by a cadre of highly skilled mentors. Such a cadre would need to be able to describe the research that supports innovative practice in forms understandable to new teachers, to model the practices, and to provide opportunities for the colleague to practice the new skill in a setting free of evaluation. Only in this way can we begin to break the historical pattern in which teachers, faced with little or no sustained support and assistance, rely on safe and comfortable methods of teaching. If this is to become a reality, however, it means that your own dispositions toward the teaching/learning process are important and should be held up to the bright light of self-examination.

A related issue is our perception of knowledge. Do we as supervisors treat truth as a fixed list of facts that must be transmitted to our colleague and/or students? Do we encourage a rapid-fire interchange of question and "correct" answers? Or do we find joy in the exploration, realizing that how we are solving problems is far more important than the "right" answer.

EXHIBIT 6-1   INVENTORY OF EDUCATIONAL BELIEFS

	VERY IMPORTANT	IMPORTANT	MODERATELY UNIMPORTANT
Attitudes toward students:			
1. To listen to and respond to students' learning needs and difficulties.	_____	_____	_____
2. To view students as reluctant learners who learn best from constructive criticism.	_____	_____	_____
3. To engage students as participants in the educational process.	_____	_____	_____
4. To withhold judgments about students' ability and performance until there is adequate evidence.	_____	_____	_____
Attitudes toward teaching:			
5. To literally adhere to the lesson plan as a guide for what the class will do.	_____	_____	_____
6. To rely on one or two teaching methods for the bulk of instruction.	_____	_____	_____
7. To impart knowledge and skills.	_____	_____	_____
8. To view teaching and learning as a discovery process.	_____	_____	_____
Attitudes toward the goals of schooling:			
9. To prepare students for their fullest potential to be participants in a democratic society.	_____	_____	_____
10. To respond to the developmental needs of students and then to select the appropriate model of teaching.	_____	_____	_____
11. To transmit the culture.	_____	_____	_____
Attitudes toward supervision:			
12. To display a variety of supervisory models that are matched with supervisee need.	_____	_____	_____
13. To set long-range goals for teachers based on administrative experiences.	_____	_____	_____
14. To model empathy and caring as an important part of effective supervision.	_____	_____	_____
15. To combine action and reflection at different levels depending on the needs of the supervisee.	_____	_____	_____

EXHIBIT 6-1 *(continued)*

Scoring your own inventory:

There are no right or wrong answers. Rather, the inventory is designed to encourage you to reflect on your attitudes about teaching/learning and supervision. Ratings of Very Important for Items 2, 5, 6, 7, 11, and 13 indicate that you have a strong preference for direct instruction and supervision as methods. Ratings of Very Important for Items 1, 3, 4, 8, and 14 indicate that you value student and supervisee-centered teaching and supervision, and ratings of Very Important for Items 10, 12, and 15 indicate that you value a developmentally based approach to teaching and supervision. Now compare your responses with those of the colleague and student. If there is little discrepancy in the rankings, it most likely is an indication that your public self (Frame 1) is either moderate or large in size.

Certainly most of us have sat in classrooms where facts were truth, where the teacher dispensed these facts in a steady and unalterable stream, and where success was defined by the number of correct answers attained during the day's instructional ministrations. The conditioning runs deep. The same probably holds true for those of us who have had cooperating teachers, mentors, and/or peer coaches. When a teacher supervisor is perceived as an "expert" it is very tempting to exploit such situations. Such omniscience manifests itself through a variety of verbal and nonverbal messages. For example, it might be tempting to reinforce student teacher dependence on your own rich depository of wisdom. Such a stance, however, has numerous unfortunate consequences from a developmental standpoint. As we mentioned in Chapters 3 and 4, young adult teachers may be at David Hunt's Stage A of conceptual complexity. They tend to see teaching as "tried and true" methods and are reluctant to try new innovations. If we as supervisors promote dependence in novice teachers, we undermine a person's opportunities for further growth.

DOES CONCEPTUAL LEVEL MAKE A DIFFERENCE?

The answer to this question is an important one. Is conceptual level an interesting theory that loosely connects to teachers' assumptions about teaching and learning, or is there a more direct relationship between conceptual level and actual classroom behaviors? In fact, the research of Alan Miller (1981) showed important linkages between teacher conceptual level, assumptions about teaching, and actual teaching behaviors. At Stage or Mode A of Hunt, teachers believe that teaching is "filling the students up with facts," and there is a single correct way to teach students. Furthermore, they tend to clump all the students together as having basically the same learning needs, and curriculum is viewed as being "carved in stone."

But what about actual teaching behaviors, you may ask? As one might expect, the Stage A teachers' assumptions about the teaching/learning process are observed in practice. Miller (1981) found that Stage A teachers offer large amounts of information in a direct and typically didactic fashion. Factual questions predominate and students are expected to show little initiative and to be passive receptors of the knowledge being dispensed. If problems arise in the instruction, students are blamed almost exclusively.

In contrast, Stage C teachers view students as participants in the teaching/learning process and believe that knowledge is open-ended. Further, these teachers assume that teaching requires tremendous adaptability and flexibility. Do these assumptions translate into teaching practice for Stage C teachers also? Research suggests that they do. Stage C teachers utilize a repertoire of teaching strategies, adapt their instructions according to the needs of the students, exhibit empathy toward all students, and "read and flex" with the students.

For teachers in coaching or mentoring roles, this information becomes very important. Knowing a colleague's assumptions about the teaching/learning process will be suggestive of their teaching practices. More conceptually complex teachers will "read and flex" their teaching according to student needs, whereas less complex teachers will utilize a few "tried and true" instructional approaches with little adapting of the instruction for students.

It is important to note that teachers' conceptual level represents their *current preferred way of solving complex problems*. It is not a permanent classification. In fact, as was discussed in Chapters 3 and 4, we are now learning that teachers can grow toward more complex conceptual levels when the conditions of complex new role, guided reflection, support and challenge, and continuity are present. We now turn to three personal dispositions that influence supervision. We might add that Katz and Raths (1985) have employed the term "dispositions" to describe developmental stages of teachers.

 # DISPOSITIONS TOWARD COLLEAGUES

Supervisors' attitudes toward a colleague are important in determining the kind of relationship that will exist. As we now know, your feelings about another person are communicated both verbally and nonverbally. If you have high regard for a colleague, your tone of voice and body posture will communicate that regard. Conversely, if you distrust an associate or if you consider her or him lazy or ineffectual, these feelings, too, will be communicated to the colleague. Thus, if we are genuinely interested in helping other teachers grow both professionally and personally, we must be attuned to our feelings about our colleagues.

Certainly Robert Rosenthal's pioneering work with teacher expectations is a powerful reminder of the role played by expectations. There were two major findings in his now famous Oak-Hall School study (Rosenthal & Jacobson, 1968). First, when teachers expected some students to experience a growth spurt, the students improved in academic performance and intelligence. Second, the students who made it on their own in spite of the prediction that they would not do well, were perceived negatively by the teacher. Recent studies by Babad, Bernieri, and Rosenthal (1991) have demonstrated just how quickly the expectations are communicated. They found that students could serve as observers of unfamiliar teachers in videotaped sequences and accurately detect teacher expectations in as little as 30 seconds. In fact, a mounting number of studies show that we cannot hide our true attitudes toward our colleagues. Tone of voice, facial expression, eye contact, and body posture send clear messages about how we feel. *Because these messages often are sent unintentionally, we must not ask ourselves how well we are doing, but instead ask the colleague with whom we are working.*

 ## DISPOSITIONS TOWARD SELF

Socrates said that the unexamined life was not worth living. Certainly how mentors and supervisors feel about themselves is a major factor for supervision. We know that a person's self-concept, the unspoken feelings and thoughts about oneself and one's relation to others, can play a significant role in supervision.

The so called "hidden agenda" that was reviewed earlier is, in some respects, the effect of the teacher's self-talk. Although research is limited on the role played by the hidden curriculum in mentoring and supervision, research has shown dramatic and unintentional effects on students, as was just discussed in the studies of social psychologist Robert Rosenthal. Perhaps part of the problem is the erroneous beliefs that we have about ourselves.

SPOTLIGHT ON EDUCATIONAL LEADERS

KNOW THYSELF

Experts agree that there is no single leadership style that is considered to be most effective. However, there are skills and dispositions that are commonly demonstrated by dynamic principals. Among the skills are communication (especially listening) and organizational ability. Among the dispositions are modeling strong character and democratic principles, displaying flexible problem-solving skills, and conveying caring and empathy.

Roland Barth (1990), a long-time teacher and educational scholar acknowledges three reasons why good schools need good principals. The first reason is that the quality of the educational program depends on the school principal. Second, the principal mightily contributes to teacher growth or to teacher stagnation. And third, the principal sets the tone for school climate.

More recently, researchers acknowledge that leadership skill and potential should be seen as a developmental process. The skills and dispositions outlined above are trademarks of principals whose schools are characterized by a caring attitude and mutual respect.

Principals who value teacher collegiality and professional development, and novice teacher learning and development can practice the following:

- Explicitly state expectations for cooperation and collegiality among all staff.
- Reward collegiality and peer coaching and supervision by granting release time, recognition, and funds for teachers.
- Protect beginning teachers and their mentoring colleagues or peer colleagues who are engaging in assistance programs.

Ultimately, the principal as educational leader must have a high level of self-understanding. Such self-understanding empowers principals in their leadership roles. Warren Bennis (1990) says it succinctly: "Becoming a leader is synonymous with becoming yourself. It's precisely that simple, and it's also that difficult."

Sources: Barth, R. (1990). *Improving schools from within*. San Francisco: Jossey-Bass.
Bennis, W. (1990). *Why leaders can't lead*. San Francisco: Jossey-Bass.

Myths About the Mentor and Supervisor

A starting point in this discussion must be a review of typical myths about mentoring and supervision. For example, we have encountered a large number of administrators, mentor teachers, clinical teachers, and peer coaches who feel guilty that they are not living up to their potential as supervisors. It is not uncommon for a teacher mentor to say:

> I struggle all the time with how to balance my work as a teacher with my work as a mentor. When I am with my colleague, I worry about the students. When I get involved in my teaching, I worry that I am not spending enough time with my colleague. It can be very frustrating.

Some might suggest that this problem has to do with the overwhelming workload of most administrators and teachers. "How can a teacher teach and mentor too?" "How can a principal administrate and also be involved in classroom instructional supervision, particularly with a large staff?" Still others might suggest that this concern is as much a policy problem as a school problem. "After all, the mentor program was never fully funded in the state, which is why teachers must resort to squeezing a little time here and there to assist the novice teacher." Although all of these reasons may contribute in some way to the challenges faced by the supervisor or coach, we think an important part of the problem is related to some common myths we have about our supervisory role.

As you read, check whether you have adopted one or more of the myths of the effective mentor or supervisor:

1. Effective supervisors can and should hide feelings from the colleague they are supervising.
2. Effective supervisors should never admit to any thoughts or feelings of racial prejudice, gender bias, or sexual orientation. They must be outwardly color-blind, gender fair, and paragons of universal acceptance.
3. Effective supervisors should appear as knowledgeable as possible. If you don't know something, fake it.
4. Effective supervisors must demonstrate unflagging energy and enthusiasm at all times, irrespective of the personal and professional demands faced. Picture Kathryn Hepburn in *African Queen*, Opray Winfrey, or Mr. Rogers of *Mr. Rogers' Neighborhood*.

Thus, the effective supervisor must be a wise, knowledgeable person who demonstrates a just and caring attitude at all times. In short, he or she must rise above the human condition with all of its quirks, injustices, and inequities, becoming the model democratic citizen, communitarian, and a model educator.

If you found yourself believing one or more of these myths then you probably have an idealized vision of the mentor or supervisor. Unfortunately, such myths do more harm than good, because they require you to deny your own humanity. Therefore we think it is important to be honest with yourself. If you do have preferences or prejudices, acknowledge them as part of what it means to be human. This does not mean that you are content to keep your sexist beliefs. Rather, honesty is the first step toward eliminating prejudice and injustice. Only through honesty can you become a more authentic human being and a more responsible and effective supervisor or mentor.

Motives for Mentoring or Supervising

If you are planning to supervise, either as a college teacher educator, principal, or as a school-based mentor or peer coach, you may encounter one of the following experiences during your initial work in the role:

1. You are sitting across the desk from a teacher in her third year of teaching. As you prepare to conduct a post-conference discussion you think back on the mess she made of the lesson. You are really angry and worry that the teacher's performance is a reflection on your work as a supervisor and the conference begins with you confronting the teacher. "You really had some problems with that lesson didn't you? I thought you realized how important it is to keep the kids organized and on task."
2. You are a mentor who has been asked to work with a beginning teacher who is struggling with classroom management. Because you are new to the role of mentor you have a desire to refine your supervisory skills, particularly how to conduct conferences and focused observations on discrete instructional strategies. Thus, you are looking forward to your work with the beginning teacher. You do worry, however, that the lack of time may impede your work together.

3. The chair of the education department has asked you to supervise six student teachers during fall semester. Although this request comes as a surprise, and requires you to reprioritize some of your goals for the semester, you are eager to work with the prospective teachers. As a beginning step, you schedule getting acquainted conferences with each student teacher and each cooperating teacher prior to the internship, hoping to build rapport, identify strengths, and formulate a common set of expectations about the student teaching experience.

4. You have been teaching for 15 years. During the last three or four years you have felt a yearning to give back to the profession. It is a real pleasure to work on projects with your colleagues. Recently you have learned of an opportunity to participate in coursework through the school system's Center for Professional Development. The staff development course will better prepare you for offering supervisory assistance to novice teachers. You register for the course, recognizing that this is just the kind of new role you have been looking for in your work.

Can you see yourself having any of these motives? The four scenarios above illustrate some common motives for mentoring and supervision. The four motives are:

1. The desire to protect or credit oneself as well as the need to dominate others
2. The desire to improve one's skill with the function of mentoring or supervision
3. The desire to help novice teachers learn, grow, and develop
4. The desire to contribute to the larger education enterprise through collaboration with colleagues

Certainly this list of scenarios is not exhaustive of the implicit and explicit motives that might exist for mentors or supervisors. It also is likely that we may experience competing motives for why we are supervising. Furthermore, this list of motives makes a complex phenomenon appear too simple. Nonetheless, if you recall the work of Frances Fuller with phases of concern as well as the discussion of cognitive development and career phases, you may see how concerns, developmental stage, and career phases overlap with one's motivations. If a person primarily has personal concerns and frequent feelings of insecurity, his or her supervision or coaching of a teacher will most likely replay some aspect of the first scenario. Conversely, if the supervisor or mentor has become more autonomous and interdependent, concerns for students and colleagues will predominate and it is far more likely that he or she will give primary attention to the supervisee and the larger schooling community. Our main point is that motives, like developmental stages, concerns, and career phase, do help shape a supervisor's or a colleague's behavior, and that it is important for you to be aware of your motives for wanting to mentor or supervise.

SUMMARY

In this chapter we discussed the personal domain of mentoring and supervision. Specifically, we described how dispositions toward the teaching/learning process, colleagues, and ourselves shape the personal domain. The Johari window was employed as a graphic means of portraying self-knowledge. Our main point was that knowledge of self (ego development) grows over time. We also discussed how conceptual level shapes our assumptions about teaching and learning, as well as our behaviors.

Dispositions toward our colleagues represent a second part of the personal domain, and as was discussed, there is growing evidence that our expectations and attitudes about others do affect their ability to learn and to be productive. Thus, your own attitudes and expectations toward a colleague will affect them, for better or worse. A goal of supervision is to enlarge our self-knowledge of these subtle expectations and attitudes.

In the final part of the chapter we centered on dispositions toward self. Socrates said that the unexamined life was not worth living. Certainly how supervisors feel about themselves is a major factor for supervision. We know that a person's self-concept, the unspoken feelings and thoughts about oneself and one's relation to others, can play a significant role in supervision.

This "hidden agenda," sometimes discussed in educational literature is, in many respects, the effect of the teacher's self-talk. We also discussed four myths you may believe as a supervisor, mentor, clinical teacher, or peer coach. Unfortunately, such myths do more harm than good, because they require you to deny your own humanity. Therefore we think it is important to be honest with yourself. If you do have preferences or prejudices, acknowledge them as part of what it means to be human. This is the first step toward eliminating prejudice, and only through honesty can you become a more authentic mentor or supervisor.

The chapter concluded with a discussion of some common motives for mentoring and supervising. Some motives may be self-centered, whereas other motives may be more altruistic and other-centered. Also motives probably overlap with a person's current stage of development. However, we cautioned the reader that it is impossible to portray the full range of human motivations a supervisor might have.

SUPERVISION FOR TEACHER DEVELOPMENT ACTIVITIES

APPLIED

1. Write a reaction to this chapter. Include in the reaction paper the following:
   a. What do you agree or disagree with in the chapter? Why?
   b. Identify your main learnings.
   c. What will you do differently now that you have read the chapter?

2. Write a description of your basic assumptions toward the goals of schooling, how children learn, your role as an educator, and the role of supervision. Also locate a goal statement for your school system or school. After completing your own statement, read it critically to compare it with the goal statement of the school system and/or school. Write a paragraph describing the similarities and differences. Research shows that your supervisory (and teaching) behaviors are based on attitudes and assumptions. It will be important to share your assumptions with your supervisees and to find out their assumptions.

3. Report the results of the Inventory of Educational Beliefs (see Exhibit 6-1). In the summary discuss whether there was a small or large discrepancy between your own inventory and the completed inventories of the principal and student.

4. Write reflections and reactions according to your own interests and hand them to your instructor.

5. Interview a supervisor in a local school system. Ask him or her to discuss the public and private self (Johari window) as it relates to their own supervision. Afterward, prepare a report of the interview.

PORTFOLIO DEVELOPMENT

1. Prepare a large three-ring binder for use as a personal portfolio. As a beginning to your supervisory portfolio, include the paper on your assumptions about students, teaching, schooling, and supervision.

2. Prepare a section for all written reflections. Date the reflection entry. It is helpful if the instructor reads and responds to your reflection entries.

3. Tape-record a typical supervisory conference. Label the tape "assessment." It can be reviewed at a later date. Place the tape in a brown envelope and place the envelope in the binder in a section called "pre-assessments."

4. Tape-record a typical lesson. Label the tape "teaching pre-assessment." Place the tape in a brown envelope and place the envelope in the binder in a section called "pre-assessments."

Suggested Readings

1. Gordon, T. (1979). *Teacher effectiveness training* (3rd ed., chaps. 2 and 3). New York: Longman.

   These two chapters review effective communication and its role in good teacher-student relationships. Feedback from hundreds of teachers has been overwhelmingly positive about the content and the presentation of the ideas in the chapters.

2. Sprinthall, N. A., Sprinthall, R., & Oja, S. N. (1994). *Educational psychology: A developmental approach* (6th ed., chap. 1). New York: McGraw-Hill.

In this chapter the authors present some of the major issues with which the field of educational psychology has struggled. We think it is a helpful reading for persons who are struggling to identify their own philosophy and assumptions about education and supervision.

REFERENCES

Babad, E., Bernieri, F., & Rosenthal, R. (1991). Students as judges of teachers' verbal and non-verbal behavior. *American Educational Research Journal, 28*(1), 211–234.

Ginsburg, M., & Clift, R. (1990). The hidden curriculum of preservice teacher education. In R. Houston (Ed.), *Handbook of research on teacher education* (pp. 450–465). New York: Macmillan.

Goodlad, J. (1994). *Educational renewal: Better teachers, better schools.* San Francisco: Jossey-Bass.

Goodlad, J., & Klein, M. F. (1974). *Looking behind the classroom door.* Worthington, OH: Jones Press.

Heath, D. (1994). *Schools of hope: Developing mind and character in today's youth.* San Francisco: Jossey-Bass.

Joyce, B., Wolf, J., & Calhoun, E. (1993). *The self-renewing school.* Alexandria, VA: Association for Supervision and Curriculum Development.

Katz, L., & Raths, J. (1985). Dispositions as goals for teacher education. *Teaching and Teacher Education, 1*, 301–307.

Loevinger, J. (1976). *Ego development.* San Francisco: Jossey-Bass.

Luft, J. (1970). *Group processes: Introduction to group dynamics.* New York: National Press.

Miller, A. (1981). Conceptual matching models and interactional research in education. *Review of Educational Research, 51*(11), 33–85.

Rosenthal, R., & Jacobson, L. (1968). *Pygmalion in the classroom.* New York: Holt, Rinehart, and Winston.

Sergiovanni, T., & Starratt, R. (1993). *Supervision: A redefinition.* New York: McGraw-Hill.

Sizer, T. (1984). *Horace's compromise.* Boston: Houghton Mifflin.

C·H·A·P·T·E·R
7

The Interpersonal Dimension

· · · · · · ·

Successful mentoring and supervision in all its various forms involves a unique kind of relationship between two or more persons. Further, if this relationship is to prosper there must be a "connection" or "bond" between the colleagues. This chapter reviews several strategies and communication skills that help to build more successful connections.

The strategies and skills described require that you set aside time for talking, getting to know your colleague, and developing clear expectations for the supervisory relationship. Without taking enough time, the connections with your colleague or colleagues probably will not be strong enough to sustain the kinds of mentoring and supervision that are discussed in this book.

As you will discover, listening is a critical skill that facilitates the mentoring or supervisory process and actually accelerates learning. We hope you will see that effective communication fosters strong relationships, which paves the way for real learning to occur.

As you review the chapter, check your comprehension by answering these questions:

- How should one begin a "helping" supervisory relationship?
- What is effective communication?

COLLEAGUE AS SIGNIFICANT OTHER

In 1952, Carl Rogers presented some personal reflections on teaching and learning to a group of teachers that had gathered at Harvard University (Rogers, 1969). Rogers concluded that he could not teach someone how to teach. He observed that when he tried to teach others, he was appalled by the results, which were either damaging or inconsequential. Instead, he argued, most learning of significance can only be self-discovered. The teachers in the audience were aghast. Feelings ran high. Rogers listened and acknowledged the views and concerns of the teachers. Gradually, after much storm, the conversation evolved to a thought provoking discussion about the meaning of teaching and learning.

Taken at face value, one might conclude that Rogers had forsaken all teaching. However, the deeper structure of the interaction between Rogers and the teachers reveals another story. By acknowledging his own apprehensions about teaching and his journey as a learner, he opened the door for teachers to explore what teaching meant to them. First he modeled for others by sharing his deepest reflections, and then, when the teachers initially stormed, by refusing to become defensive.

"Mutual-needs meeting" means that both persons' needs must be met, but never at the expense of the other person.

This drama portrays three conditions required of a helper, which were at the very heart of Carl Rogers's work. These conditions are genuineness (congruence), empathy, and regard. *Genuineness* or *congruence* means that the helper is being honest, authentic, and trustworthy. It also implies that the verbal communication and the nonverbal communication are aligned. In effect, one is being honest in both word and behavior. Another dimension of genuineness is openness or transparency. This means that you are willing to share your own feelings.

Empathy is the ability to communicate to others that we understand the emotions they are experiencing. Rogers described empathy as the capacity to "step into another person's shoes." We express empathy for another person when we acknowledge the feelings mentioned by a colleague. For example, if a colleague stepped into your classroom scowling and mentioned frustration because of a recent decision by the principal to unilaterally enforce a suspension policy that made no allowance for student input, your ability to accurately recognize the main feelings that she or he expressed is a measure of your empathy.

The final condition, *regard,* was described by Rogers as the ability to accept another human being for what he or she is without passing judgment. In fact, he thought that "unconditional positive regard" was crucial to helping relationships. When there is regard, there is no room for bargaining, "If you will agree to do these things, I will agree to be your supervisor."

MUTUALITY IN RELATIONSHIPS

Thomas Gordon (1974) adds another condition to effective relationships. He submits that *mutual-needs meeting* is essential. What this means is that in any relationship, both persons' needs must be met, but never at the expense of the other person. Why is this so important to supervisory or mentoring relationships? At least part of the answer has to do with the traditional nature of supervision or mentoring. Both have tended to involve relationships in which one person has more power than the other person. In such a situation, one person's needs prevail. The mentoring or supervision described in this text, in contrast, encourages assistance in which relationships have far greater equitability and mutual-needs meeting. Teachers involved in peer coaching, school leadership programs (principals and teachers), or mentoring can provide valuable assistance to teachers. At times, however, the investment could be great. After all, effective supervision and mentoring requires careful planning, implementation, and ongoing reflection. The point we want to make is that a supervisor's or mentor's needs must also be met. Administrators or teacher educators may think that their work is mainly one of giving and supporting. Such an approach is misguided, however, if the administrator's or teacher's own needs are ignored. Eventually the well runs dry. Thus, we assert, that effective supervisory relationships must include mutual-needs meeting.

In summary, the conditions described by Rogers and Gordon are necessary for healthy human relationships. Certainly supervision needs these conditions. Effective supervisors must be helpful and caring (i.e., showing

EXHIBIT 7-1   THREE MAIN ROLES OF THE SUPERVISORY TEACHER

A supervisor is:
1. **Helpful and caring**
2. **A model of effective instruction**
3. **Supportive and challenging**

---

empathy, genuineness, regard, mutual-needs meeting), models of effective teaching, and supportive and challenging. Support is a necessary first step in any new relationship. However, as the relationship develops, you will need to challenge the colleague. Exhibit 7-1 summarizes the three main roles of the supervising teacher. We now turn to a discussion of selected communication skills that can enhance your work as a supervisor.

EFFECTIVE COMMUNICATION IS ESSENTIAL

Communication can build a strong mentor or supervisory relationship if it is the right kind of communication. Thomas Gordon has been able to blend theory and practice in his work with supervisors and teachers on how to employ effective communication skills. In fact, we have found that Gordon's concept of a "language of acceptance" can become a constructive force for positive change in communication among principals, teachers, and teacher educators. Although too few supervisors possess these skills, we have found that the skills can be learned. We hope you will discover that what you say has a tremendous influence on whether you will be helpful or not. The concepts that follow are based on a commonly accepted model of communication between two persons.

Figure 7-1 demonstrates communication between two persons, a sender and a receiver, and the importance of accurate feedback. The sender rarely communicates a direct and clear message; rather the sender codes his or her feelings in unique ways that require decoding by the receiver. In Figure 7-1, three different responses are offered by the receiver or listener to the sender's uniquely coded message. In the first, silence is provided. In the second, a simple acknowledgment is given, and in the third, feedback about feelings is offered. This third type of feedback often is referred to as *active listening*. Each type of listening is now reviewed.

SILENCE

One of the most difficult ideas for teachers to accept is that merely listening quietly is very facilitative. Called *passive listening* by some, we have learned that when teachers or teacher educators listen without comment to their colleagues, it invites the colleague to share concerns and encourages him or her to explore more deeply the different feelings and ideas that may be a part of the problem.

FIGURE 7-1   MODEL OF ACTIVE LISTENING

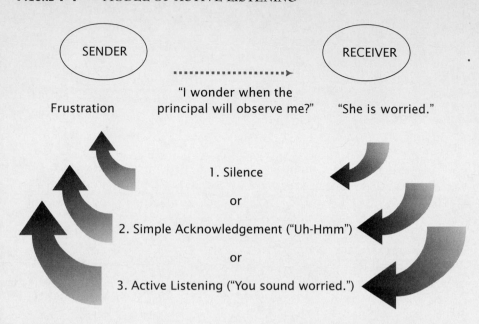

Silence is the least complex kind of listening. It only requires that you are quietly paying attention. The difficulty for many teachers, however, is that we are convinced that the best solution to any problem is to provide potential answers or solutions to the colleague's concern or problem, that is, to talk. We think telling is the best kind of help. You might find yourself thinking, "Any personal problem can be remedied, and boy do I ever have the perfect solution for your problem." Unfortunately, such proposed solutions are roadblocks to effective communication and end up hurting more than helping, and, perhaps more importantly, *they take away an opportunity for the colleague to solve his or her own problem, which can lead to growth and development.* Recall in our earlier discussion of cognitive development that guided reflection is a necessary condition for growth. Listening is one way to promote greater reflection because it encourages your colleague to actively think and feel more deeply as he or she constructs meaning from an experience. If you regularly attempt to offer solutions to a colleague's concerns or problems, you forfeit a growth opportunity.

SIMPLE ACKNOWLEDGEMENTS

At the next level are simple acknowledgements by the listener that alert the colleague that you are listening. All of us have employed simple acknowledgements when listening. Examples include, "uh-huh," "go on," "tell me more," or "gosh, that's interesting, care to elaborate?" Sometimes referred to as affirming grunts, they are verbal cues to your colleague that you are tuned in to what he or she is saying. These brief statements require you to occasionally interject statements that encourage the colleague to offer greater elaboration on his or her ideas or feelings. The following example from a teacher mentor demonstrates this kind of listening:

> *Protégé:* I am really struggling with classroom management.
>
> *Mentor:* Oh.
>
> *Protégé:* Yes, it seems like I barely have my head above water. I haven't even had a chance to grade any papers.
>
> *Mentor:* Hmm.
>
> *Protégé:* I have realized that something has to change in my classes. I'm not sure what the problem is and I haven't had any time to try to sort out the problem.
>
> *Mentor:* (Silence)
>
> *Protégé:* I'd like to better understand the problem. Could I observe your classroom sometime this week? It might give me some ideas.

As you can see, simple acknowledgements can encourage the speaker to elaborate on her or his concern. However, this kind of listening, while facilitative, does have limitations. Perhaps the major drawback is that it does not inform the speaker about your own interpretation of the concerns. Described differently, the speaker has no way of knowing whether you comprehend. Instead, she or he only knows that you are attentive and tuned in to what is being said. For this reason, Rogers and Gordon saw a need for a more active kind of listening that could encourage deeper communication in which feelings and thoughts are shared and *acknowledged* by the listener.

The above example also may offer insights into the protégé's cognitive-developmental stages and concerns. Reread the example. Do the comments by the protégé suggest superficial or highly differentiated understanding of the problem? Are feelings shared? Do the expressed concerns relate to self, task, or impact (students)? Although the passage is brief, it suggests that the protégé may be approaching the problem from a more concrete and narrow perspective. Feelings are not shared and the concerns have to do with task—classroom management. No mention of students is given. Review the Johari window for teachers at Self-Protective and Conformist levels (see Figure 7-2). The blind self (Frame 2) may be relatively large. Thus, active listening is a valuable strategy for enlarging Frame 1, the public self, by encouraging the protégé to elaborate on his or her concerns, and it offers an important means of assessing the developmental stage of the colleague.

At the level of simple acknowledgement, then, listening is an affirmative act, but requires the feedback provided in active listening to be effective.

ACTIVE LISTENING AND THE TEACHING/LEARNING FRAMEWORK

Work by Rogers and Gordon with thousands of teachers, parents, and educational leaders eventually led to the creation of a method of active listening that provides feedback to the speaker of the listener's understanding. This

FIGURE 7-2 ADAPTATION OF JOHARI WINDOW—EGO STAGES: SELF-PROTECTIVE TO CONFORMIST (Δ–I 3)

	Known to Self	Not Known to Self
Known to Others	1. Public self	2. Blind self
Not Known to Others	3. Private self	4. Unknown to self and others

Source: Adapted from Joseph Luft, *Group Processes: An Introduction to Group Dynamics.* New York: National Press Books, 1970.

form of communication, as opposed to silence or simple acknowledgements, requires greater interaction between the speaker and the listener, and allows the speaker to stay informed of the listener's understanding.

The relationship between active listening and the teaching/learning framework for action and reflection that was introduced in Chapter 4 is direct (see Exhibit 7-2). Active listening is responsive to several of the conditions in the framework. With regard to the conditions for growth and development, active listening relates to the second condition, guided reflection, and to the fourth condition, support and challenge. Because active listening encourages persons to think more deeply about their problems, it is a kind of guided reflection. As we mentioned earlier, reflection is not necessarily an automatic process. By offering to actively listen to a colleague, you are pro-

EXHIBIT 7-2 TEACHING/LEARNING FRAMEWORK

SKILLS BUILDING	GROWTH AND DEVELOPMENT
1. Rationale and/or theory	1. Significant new role
2. Demonstrations	2. Guided reflection
3. Practice with feedback	3. Balance between role and reflection
4. Adapt and generalize	4. Support and challenge
	5. Continuity

viding an opportunity for the colleague to make meaning from his or her experience. Active listening also provides support. For example, beginning teachers will experience significant personal dissonance during the initial months of their teaching. By listening actively to the beginning teacher during this time span, the supervisor permits the teacher to more fully explore his or her thoughts and feelings, and to resolve some of the dissonance.

Likewise, with the steps for learning a new teaching model or skill, active listening can be effectively employed during the demonstration and practice steps of instructional coaching by a supervisor. Listening provides ample opportunity for a colleague to think about his or her new learnings. Thus, listening is important to teacher development.

An example of active listening follows in which a clinical teacher, responsible for supervising student teachers from a nearby college, meets with one of the student teachers at the end of the day. The student teacher mentions that she is wondering about a visit from the college supervisor next week. An observation is planned along with a post-conference. Imagine yourself as the clinical teacher.

> *Student teacher (ST):* My college supervisor is going to observe me next week.
>
> *Clinical teacher (CT):* You sound worried.
>
> *ST:* Yeah, I guess I am. This will be the first formal observation and I really want everything to go well, but I won't know when she will arrive.
>
> *CT:* Not knowing the time of the observation has you rattled.
>
> *ST:* Not exactly rattled. It is just that I feel some pressure to make sure the whole day goes well. However, that may be unrealistic. After all, I haven't been student teaching for long and I think it is unreasonable of the college supervisor or me to expect perfection.
>
> *CT:* So you realize perfection isn't realistic but the planned visit still makes you nervous.
>
> *ST:* Yeah, I guess it is a little like stage fright. There is some nervousness but things tend to turn out okay.
>
> *CT:* (Silence)
>
> *ST:* I guess the best thing for me to do is to be well organized and let the chips fall where they may.
>
> *CT:* Since you have some concerns, let's discuss the plans for the day and how the lessons will match the needs of the students.

In this short interchange several things have happened. The clinical teacher has accurately decoded the student teacher's opening statement, keying into a feeling. When you hear the comment by the student teacher, "My college supervisor is going to observe me next week," the content of the message is clear. The supervisor will be at the school next week to observe. However, listening "between the lines" the clinical teacher hears another message from the student teacher, which is that she is anxious about the upcoming visit. Such reading between the lines requires a person to make inferences about what is being communicated. However, without interaction, the person has no way of knowing whether the inferences are accurate or inaccurate. Further, the student teacher has no way of knowing whether her message is understood. Thus, offering some feedback about the message checks for accuracy. "You sound worried." This kind of feedback is what Rogers and Gordon called active listening. It requires that you feed back the ideas and feelings that you have heard.

You also probably noted that in one case, the clinical teacher slightly missed in the feedback, "Not knowing the time of the observation has you rattled." The student teacher clarifies, "Not exactly rattled. It is just that I feel some pressure to make sure the whole day goes well. However, that may be unrealistic. After all, I haven't been student teaching for long and I think it is unreasonable of the college supervisor or me to expect perfection." This interchange shows how active listening can clarify possible misinterpretations by the listener.

Let's move to another interview that involves two experienced teachers in a peer coaching program, and includes several examples of active listening. We will refer to the two teachers as Ashley and Tracey.

> *Ashley:* I am really struggling with these observations of other teachers. There isn't enough time in the day for me to work with students, grade papers, and also plan for observations of other teachers.
>
> *Tracey:* You sound pretty frustrated.
>
> *Ashley:* I am. I didn't realize when I volunteered to participate in this program that it would be so time-consuming. I just don't think it is reasonable to ask teachers to take time away from teaching for observations.
>
> *Tracey:* Even though you volunteered, the time commitment seems unrealistic.
>
> *Ashley:* Actually, it isn't so much the time. It has just been kind of frustrating to plan for the visits. Once I am in the teacher's classroom I learn so much and so does she.
>
> *Tracey:* So making the arrangements is the frustrating part.
>
> *Ashley:* Exactly.

In this illustration Tracey accurately paraphrased both thoughts and feelings shared by Ashley. As Ashley talked, Tracey checked out what she heard without judging the ideas or feelings.

In the next example, the feelings are less apparent. Thus, there are greater demands on the listener to decode the messages and discover the speaker's real feelings. As you read the dialogue, note how the principal's active listening allowed the beginning teacher to uncover some underlying concerns.

Teacher:	What a day!
Principal:	Frustrating, huh.
Teacher:	I'll say. The kids were out of control. We accomplished nothing today.
Principal:	*(Nod)*
Teacher:	The problems seem to be getting worse. I just don't seem to be able to keep their attention for more than a few minutes.
Principal:	You sound worried.
Teacher:	I am. At the rate I am going, the only solution may be the suspension of some of the real troublemakers. Then I think things might improve.
Principal:	You are afraid that without some dramatic changes, no improvement will occur.
Teacher:	Yeah. There is so much yelling. I even had to break up a scuffle at the beginning of class. It really seems hopeless without the suspensions. Frankly, I can't think of any other options.
Principal:	You sound pretty overwhelmed.
Teacher:	I am *(begins to cry)*. I don't seem to connect with the students. This is far worse than student teaching. Nothing seems to be working *(grabs tissue and blows nose)*. I am disappointed in myself. I always thought I would make a great teacher. But these last three weeks have been an absolute nightmare.
Principal:	You feel defeated.
Teacher:	I am.
Principal:	*(Silence)*
Teacher:	I'm not sure I can talk any more right now. Can we arrange for another chat tomorrow afternoon?
Principal:	Sure. What about tomorrow? How does 3:30 sound?
Teacher:	Good. Thanks for listening.

In this illustration the principal was able to decode the messages accurately. A number of feelings were mentioned, and as the conversation unfolded, more of the underlying concerns of the teacher were expressed. This conversation did not reach closure and finished with an agreement to talk more about the concerns. This said however, we have found that the listening strengthens the relationship, and will encourage the colleague to begin to do his or her own problem solving.

Some Guidelines for Active Listening. At the end of a recent supervision course, we asked the participants (teachers and administrators with 8 to 23 years of experience) two questions: which elements of the course were the most meaningful, and which elements of the course were the most challenging. Somewhat to our surprise, the skill of using active listening rated high for most participants on both lists. Partly as a result of this outcome, we have reflected on our work with hundreds of teachers and administrators who have commented on the powerful force that active listening had become in their personal and professional lives. Listening to their comments, we have compiled an abbreviated set of guidelines for administrators, teachers, and teacher educators wishing to develop their active listening skills.

1. *Realize that novice teachers* (student teachers and beginning teachers) *probably harbor many strong feelings* as they begin their journey as a teacher. If the mentor teacher or cooperating teacher earns the novice teacher's trust, there will be many opportunities to actively listen.
2. *Understand when to use active listening.* If a colleague is not expressing a concern or problem, active listening is less critical. It is important, however, for you to consciously and genuinely want to help your colleague.
3. *Strive to paraphrase* your colleague's ideas, concerns, or feelings in the fewest words possible. Less is more. Near word for word repetition is not encouraged.
4. *Realize that active listening is a skill that takes time to develop.* Understand that when you begin to practice the skill it may feel mechanical and uncomfortable. Accept this feeling as part of the learning process.
5. *Learn to listen for the expressed concerns of the colleague.* Some concerns will be requests for information; others will be related to personal issues, classroom management, or students. Be prepared to give the necessary information.
6. *Respect confidentiality.* Active listening encourages colleagues to reveal themselves. Recognize that what is discussed is private.
7. *Trust your colleague's ability to solve problems.* Your listening demonstrates trust and a willingness to be completely "present" with the colleague as she or he attempts to resolve the problem.
8. *Recognize that active listening takes energy.* If your "batteries are low" active listening will be difficult. Not only will it be harder to effectively listen, but it is more likely that you will find it difficult to be completely present with your colleague. It is wise to schedule a time in the near future for the sharing of concerns.

THE GETTING ACQUAINTED CONFERENCE

As we mentioned earlier, one characteristic of a supervisor is to be helpful and caring as well as a model of effective teaching practices. Building a trusting supervisory relationship communicates caring and, as you will discover, can be an opportunity to model helping skills. To begin the relationship building process we recommend that you and your colleague have a getting acquainted conference early in your professional experience together.

If you have never conducted a getting acquainted conference before, we recommend that the conference be tape-recorded. Mention to your colleague that you are building your skills as a supervisor and the tape will help you self-evaluate. Also indicate to your colleague that he or she is welcome to listen to the tape.

Use the guidelines in Exhibit 7-3 to facilitate your conference. These guidelines will help you as you begin to develop active listening.

SUPERVISOR'S SELF-ANALYSIS AND REFLECTIONS

After you have completed the conference listen to the tape and record in writing examples of listening or non–active listening that you noted during the conference. Use the following outline (see Exhibit 7-4) for your self-analysis. Hopefully, you will find active listening a personally enriching skill that enhances interactions with colleagues and family.

EXHIBIT 7-3   GUIDELINES FOR THE GETTING ACQUAINTED CONFERENCE

I. Introduction
  A. Talk about feelings you have had when you begin new relationships.
  B. Ask your colleague about his or her feelings.
     _____ Actively Listened
II. Roles and Expectations
  A. Ask how your colleague learns best.
     _____ Actively Listened
  B. As a model of effective teaching, what areas of instruction are they most concerned about?
     _____ Actively Listened
  C. How would they prefer to receive feedback during the supervisory relationship (i.e., conference, written, other)?
III. Closing
  A. Discuss your goal of being a colleague.
  B. Set the norms for a working relationship. For example, review the importance of confidentiality and how to keep it.
  C. Discuss the place and time for the next meeting.
  D. Discuss the schedule of events that will be taking place during the year.
     1. Weekly seminars and planning sessions
     2. Written reflections
     3. Coaching cycles and classroom observations
        _____ Actively Listened
  E. Close with a restatement of your interest in having the person as a colleague.
  F. Invite your colleague to summarize the meaning of the conference.

EXHIBIT 7-4   SELF-ANALYSIS OF LISTENING AND REFLECTIONS ON A GETTING ACQUAINTED CONFERENCE

HOW ACTIVE A LISTENER AM I?

Part I: Analysis of Listening

Level I.   Identify examples of paraphrasing for feelings.

Level II.   Identify examples of paraphrasing for content.

Level III. Identify examples of door openers ("tell me more") or acknowledgements.

Identify examples of non–active listening (roadblocks, e.g., interrogation, questioning, probing, sympathizing, diagnosing, advising, directing, or preaching)

1. Did you actively listen?

2. What were the two main levels?

3. What would you have changed?

4. Other reactions?

EXHIBIT 7-4 *(continued)*

Part II: Reflections on the Conference
1. Identify the feelings you had during the conference.

2. Complete the following:

    I was dissatisfied_____ satisfied_____
    Why?

3. My initial observation is that my supervisee is

    __ Conceptual level A __ Conceptual level B __ Conceptual level C
    Write observations used to make this decision.

4. My main learnings from holding this conference are:

5. Other comments:

SUMMARY

In this chapter we reviewed aspects of the interpersonal dimension of supervision. We pointed out that developmental instructional supervision in all its various forms involves a unique kind of relationship between two or more persons. Further, if this relationship is to prosper there must be a "connection" or "bond" between the colleagues. Whenever more open and honest communication is required, listening will help. Certainly this is the

---

CONTEMPORARY ISSUES

SUPERVISION AND HORIZONTAL DECALAGE

Novice teachers know they need additional skills but they often don't know exactly which skills are most needed. They probably need to more effectively manage their students and their classroom yet this awareness will probably be global and undifferentiated in nature, "Something has to change in my classes or I am going to go crazy." To further complicate the situation, the teachers also may be at different points in the domains of development we have discussed: conceptual, ego, and moral.

Robbie Case (1992), a post-Piagetian, has referred to this as synchronous versus asynchronous development. If the progression is uneven, referred to as *decalage*, it implies that the progression across the domains is uneven. Conducting a series of rigorous studies, he and his associates have reconfirmed the basic tenets of Piaget's stage theory. However, one additional important outcome of their work is the discovery that different domains do not represent a single larger stage but rather are parallel and somewhat independent, that is, a multilevel conception of domains. This means that we cannot think of concrete operations as a single stage, but rather as concrete operations in different domains.

The supervisor must therefore be sensitive to differences in supervisees' cognitive growth across the domains. We cannot assume that all beginning teachers, for example, are functioning at the formal/abstract level. Nor can we assume that all adults are functioning at the formal/abstract level across a variety of domains. For example, a beginning physics teacher may perform brilliantly when asked to explain the theoretical underpinnings of thermodynamics, yet shift to concrete or even preoperational levels when attempting to unravel the complexities of teacher-student relationships and classroom management, that is, never varying the classroom routine in spite of changed circumstances.

Thus, the supervisor must provide a careful balance between new experiences, guided reflection, and support and challenge in those areas of teaching activity in which development is incomplete. Given these conditions, growth can continue.

Source: Case, R. (1992). *The mind's staircase.* Hillsdale, NJ: Erlbaum.

case with supervision. Thus we described three types of listening that can facilitate communication: silence, simple acknowledgements, and active listening.

Active listening requires the most from the listener because it requires that you give feedback about your interpretations of what is being said. This kind of listening helps colleagues ventilate feelings generated from the stress of classroom teaching, encourages the colleague to do his or her own problem solving, and it facilitates more effective supervisory conferences. As you become more skilled with active listening, you will probably find yourself applying the skill to all aspects of your personal and professional life.

Certainly it is important to get acquainted with your supervisees. It requires that you set aside time for talking and listening, getting to know your colleague, and developing clear expectations for the supervisory relationship. Without taking enough time to develop a relationship, the connections with your colleague or colleagues probably will not be strong enough to sustain the kinds of supervision that are discussed in this book.

SUPERVISION FOR TEACHER DEVELOPMENT ACTIVITIES

APPLIED

1. On a piece of paper list the three levels of active listening. At the end of each day put a tally beside each type of listening you used. Continue to tally for five consecutive days.

2. Daily write four or five feelings you had during the day. Use the following structure for each feeling statement: " I was (*feeling*) when (*action of other*) because (*effect on you*). Also place a star by each feeling you shared with another person. *Example*: "I was relieved when my conference with you was finished because I learned about you as an individual."

3. Record a discussion with an individual or a small group. Use only active listening. This includes "door openers" and acknowledging responses.
   a. Ask a few open-ended questions on any appropriate topic—about someone who has recently moved, a friend, some aspect of school, etc., almost any topic about which there may be some emotion.
   b. Turn on an audiotape recorder and do some active listening. Try to hold the conversation for at least 5 to 10 minutes. Really concentrate on restating the feelings that the child, group of students, or colleague expresses either directly or indirectly.
   c. Withhold judgment on the content in order to clarify how the person feels.
   d. Replay the tape and ask the colleague if you were accurate in your paraphrasings and where you missed.

    e. After you complete the active listening, using Exhibit 7-4 to self-eval-
uate.

      (1) Jot down statements you made on the "How Active a Listener Am
I?" scale.

      (2) On the back of the sheet write the feelings you had during the
conversation *and while you were critiquing your listening skills.*

      (3) Write what you learned.

      (4) What questions do you have?

4. Write reflections and reactions to this chapter according to your own
interests.

5. Interview a school counselor. Ask her or him to identify materials that
are available for use by teachers and students interested in developing
better communication skills.

PORTFOLIO DEVELOPMENT

1. Prepare a section in your portfolio binder called "Building Helping Relationships." Include the getting acquainted conference tape and the
self-analysis in this section of the portfolio. Make sure to date and label
the audiotape.

2. Write a brief paper summarizing your thoughts about the importance
of effective communication to supervisory relationships. Place the syn-
opsis in the portfolio with the heading "My Rationale for Building
Helping Relationships."

3. If you complete an audiotape of active listening with a group or colleague, also include the tape in this section of the portfolio.

Suggested Readings and Resources

1. Gordon, T. (1970). *Teacher effectiveness training* (chap. 4). New York:
Wyden.

> *This chapter reviews the many ways that active listening can fa-
> cilitate more open and honest communication: parent confer-
> ences, content-centered discussions, student-centered discus-
> sions, etc.*

2. Funk, F., & Long, B. (1982). The cooperating teacher as most significant
other. *Action in Teacher Education, 4*(2), 57–64.

> *The paper reports a replication of a study on the effects of the
> cooperating teacher. The significance of the cooperating
> teacher–student teacher relationship in teacher training is dis-
> cussed.*

3. Aspy, D., Roebuck, F., & Aspy, C. (1984). Tomorrow's resources are in
today's classroom. *The Personnel and Guidance Journal, 4*, 455–459.

The paper reports a large-scale intervention study by The National Consortium for Humanizing Education in over 1000 classrooms. Among the many significant findings are the following:

a. *There is a positive and significant relationship between teachers' levels of interpersonal functioning and students' gains on achievement test scores (K–12).*

b. *There is a positive and significant relationship between principals' levels of interpersonal functioning and the tendency on the part of their teachers to employ interpersonal skills in their classrooms.*

4. Jackson, P., Boostrum, R., & Hansen, D. (1993). *The moral life of schools.* San Francisco: Jossey-Bass.

The text is an ethnographic inquiry into the moral complexity of classroom interactions. One of the major contributions of the text is to show how the stream of communication in classrooms, when carefully analyzed, reveals a complexity of moral meanings in both feedback and gestures.

REFERENCES

Gordon, T. (1974). *Teacher effectiveness training.* New York: Peter H. Wyden.
Rogers, C. (1969). Personal thoughts on teaching and learning (p. 7). In C. R. Rogers, *Freedom to learn: A view of what education might be.* Columbus, OH: Merrill.

C·H·A·P·T·E·R
8

Identifying Models and Methods of Instruction

• • • • • • •

The material presented in this chapter is aimed at giving you a general introduction to ways of gaining knowledge about a teacher. Just as we have recommended that you have some understanding of how teachers prefer to solve complex human-helping problems in the conceptual, ego, and moral domains, so also, it is important to gain an understanding of teachers' preferred models and methods of instruction.

Additionally, as a supervisor or mentor, you will be expected to understand and model your own strengths as an educator and to have a general grasp of research and literature on models and methods of teaching and learning. When you begin your new role as supervisor you will be spending considerable time honing your own instructional expertise as well as your self-assessment skills. Therefore, as we discuss the models and methods of instruction and the "gaining knowledge" component of developmental instructional supervision, we hope that this basic introduction enhances your ability to self-assess and to observe others. As you review the chapter, check your comprehension by answering these questions:

- How does a supervisor gain knowledge about a teacher?
- What are the major differences between the four major models of instruction?

- How does your own teaching encourage or discourage students to use their minds well?

Because you will be asked to identify which models of instruction are effectively employed by the supervisee, we consider several general models of instruction and their implications for supervision, teaching, and students.

 # FOUR MODELS OF INSTRUCTION

Because we believe that classrooms and what happens in them have enduring formative effects on children, we have sought to understand the general models that are frequently or infrequently employed by teachers as they interact with students. The work of Sprinthall, Sprinthall, and Oja (1994), and Joyce and Weil (1996) have been very instructive. A model is a cluster of strategies that is logically consistent with a certain set of assumptions about how students learn best. Our experiences have shown that expert teachers are able to use each of the models to be described with equal dexterity and effectiveness.

What we have observed in these teachers is a testament to an idea forwarded by Nate Gage, "that there is a scientific basis for the art of teaching," and it is exemplified by teachers who can flexibly employ a broad repertoire of instructional models for the end of developing students to their fullest capacities for eventual participation in a democratic society. The following four models—knowledge transmitter, inquiry, interpersonal, and teaching for understanding—are an adaptation and synthesis of the four broad families of models described by Joyce and Weil (1996), which includes behavioral systems (direct), personal systems (interpersonal), information-processing systems (direct and inquiry), and social systems (interpersonal).

KNOWLEDGE TRANSMITTER MODEL

Perhaps it is a truism that many teachers are most comfortable with the knowledge transmitter model of instruction. This model views teaching as the transmission of knowledge. It assumes that there is a well-known and fixed body of knowledge that should be passed onto the students. The teacher directs the flow of information by selecting those facts and concepts that are most important to students. An implicit assumption of the model is that students must know certain basic facts before they can be expected to think in more independent and interdependent ways. The transmission of the information often is characterized by high structure with a greater emphasis on lecture.

In the knowledge transmitter model the teacher establishes the outcomes for the lesson as well as the main point or concept of the lesson. Examples of the knowledge transmitter model include Bloom's mastery learning (1971) and Good's direct instruction (1996). In the knowledge transmitter model the general concept and the outcomes are shared with the students early in the lesson, assuring that students understand the overall objective and the expectations. Advanced organizers may be used to illustrate the main concepts or aims of the lesson (Ausubel, 1960). Ideally, before the general concept has been introduced, the teacher has assessed students' prior knowledge or has linked the concept to students' experiences.

Immediately following the introduction of the general concept and learning outcomes, the teacher shifts the instruction from the abstract concept to concrete examples. The examples help the students connect the general concept to facts. For example, a unit in biology might start with, "Today we are going to begin an exploration of how different species of plants reproduce." The students have been alerted about the major focus of the lesson. The teacher continues, "By the end of the lesson each of you should be able to describe three major ways that plants reproduce." The expectations are clear, explicit, and measurable.

Immediately following the generalized idea the teacher shifts from the abstract to the concrete. Thus, in the biology lesson example, the teacher would now provide concrete examples and connect them to the general concept. "Let me begin by describing a number of ways that plants reproduce. As I introduce each concept, please notice the examples that have been placed at each of your lab tables. After my presentation your team will have an opportunity to sort and classify the plants according to the type of reproduction."

As you can see, the presentation of examples is followed by opportunities for the students to work with the concepts at a concrete level. This is sometimes referred to as *guided practice*. In effect, the students are led through demonstrations and practice to an understanding of the same general concept that was introduced at the outset of the lesson. The major goal of the knowledge transmitter model is the maximization of student learning time, which is often referred to as *academic learning time* (ALT). Teacher direction is high, ambiguity is low, and the sequence is general concept–examples–general concept. The teacher behaviors incorporated into the knowledge transmitter model (direct instruction or mastery learning) are geared to create a structured environment in which students are actively engaged and experiencing a high rate of success (80 percent mastery or better) in the tasks they are given. It is important to note that there is substantial evidence that criticism inhibits students' achievement in the knowledge transmitter model (Soar, Soar, and Ragosta, 1971). A strength of the model is that it offers a relatively systematic approach to teaching and is, perhaps, the least complex and therefore easiest model to learn. Further, there is substantial evidence that the model affects students' success in learning.

SPOTLIGHT ON EDUCATIONAL LEADERS

PRINCIPAL AS INSTRUCTIONAL LEADER

A recent study by Brubaker, Simon, and Tysinger (1993) sheds light on the principal as instructional leader. Their study found that a large majority of respondents view the most desirable principal leadership role to be instructional leader. Yet some principals are unable to describe the development of teacher professional expertise in much detail beyond the general novice to expert sequence. The work of Leithwood (1992) offers a helpful construct for a more detailed progression of teacher learning. Based on Joyce and Weil's models of teaching, Leithwood outlines phases in the development of professional expertise as exemplified in instruction. An abbreviated summary of his framework follows:

1. Developing survival skills
   - Partially developed classroom management skills
   - Very limited skill in use of several teaching models
   - Student assessment is primarily summative
   - May be a poor link between instructional goals, instructional activities, and focus of assessment

2. Becoming competent in the basic skills of instruction
   - Well developed classroom management skills
   - Several teaching models are employed
   - Student assessment begins to reflect formative purposes

3. Expanding one's instructional flexibility
   - Interest in expanding repertoire of teaching models
   - Choice of teaching model is influenced by needs of students
   - Student assessment is carried out for both formative and summative purposes

4. Acquiring instructional expertise
   - Classroom management is integrated with the program
   - Skill in application of a broad repertoire of teaching models

5. Contributing to the growth of colleague's instructional expertise
   - Connects own competence and instructional choices to fundamental principles and values on which they are based
   - Interested in assisting other teachers in developing new instructional skills

6. Participating in a broad array of educational decisions at all levels of the education system
   - Exercises leadership, both formal and informal, with groups of adults inside and outside of school
   - Demonstrates a high level of commitment to a broad range of social and educational issues

Every effort should be made to prevent teacher stabilization at the midranges on the professional expertise domain. Thus, rather than supporting independence and isolation, principals should encourage reflection, new teacher leadership roles, and collegial instructional supervision and coaching. One commentator described this approach to instructional leadership as redefining the problem as the solution.

Sources: Brubaker, D., Simon, L., & Tysinger, N. (1993). Principal's leadership styles: The power of the "halo effect." *NAASP Bulletin, 77*(553), 30–36.
Leithwood, K. (1992). The principal's role in teacher development. In M. Fullan & A. Hargreaves (Eds.), *Teacher development and educational change* (pp. 86–103). Washington, DC: Falmer Press.

Rosenshine (1985) has found that effective teachers spend more time explaining and demonstrating new material than less-effective teachers. He also found that effective teachers:

- Ask more questions that check for understanding.
- Ensure that all students have a chance to respond.
- Ask more questions that are "matched" to students' ability (75 to 90 percent).
- Avoid nonacademic questions during instruction.

Another fruitful area of study has been in mastery learning (Bloom, 1971). This application of the knowledge transmitter model has the following characteristics:

- Mastery is based on objectives and outcomes.
- Content is divided into smaller learning units that can be measured.
- Prior knowledge is assessed.
- Supplementary instruction and practice are provided.

There are three levels of practice: highly structured, guided practice, and independent practice. For younger students practice should be short, 5 to 10 minutes interspersed over the day.

When the knowledge transmitter model is employed wisely, it can accommodate to multiple learning styles by varying the types of examples and the types of student practice. Furthermore, when careful assessment is done of students' interests and prior knowledge, the lesson can effectively link to students' experiences. The major drawbacks, however, are that it can lead to student passivity, and it can discourage student-to-student interaction.

INDUCTIVE-INQUIRY MODEL

A second major approach to instruction is the inductive-inquiry model and includes the work of Dewey—project investigation (1916); Slavin—cooperative learning (1990); Taba—inductive thinking (1966); Schwab—scientific inquiry (see review in Joyce, 1978); Suchman—inquiry (1962); Adler—Paideia approach to discussions (1982); and Gordon—synectics problem solving (1961).

As you can see from the variety of efforts, the inductive-inquiry model became popular during the 1960s. In general it recommends that the teacher's major goal is to encourage students to uncover the fundamental structure of a discipline. Facts are of less importance. Thus, in our science lesson on plant biology, having students memorize a set of concepts and facts is no longer the major priority. Depth of knowledge is more important than coverage of knowledge. Instead, the students might be presented with the general properties of plant reproduction and then posed the problem of constructing a model for a specific plant species that includes the general properties.

According to this model, the excitement of discovery is highly motivating. The curiosity and the need to make sense out of the puzzle or problem encourages learning and an understanding of the structure of the discipline (Ausubel, 1960; Bruner, 1961). As mentioned, in the inquiry model there are a variety of methods that promote discovery learning. Of course, there are problems if this model is used exclusively. It probably isn't necessary to discover everything for yourself. Sometimes, it is more efficient not to reinvent the wheel.

Additionally, important questions have been raised about the exclusive application of the inquiry model with elementary school children. The idea of a structure of a discipline is, after all, an abstract concept, which is beyond the concrete stage of thinking of most elementary school children.

The inquiry model requires more sophistication on the part of the teacher also. Whereas the knowledge transmitter model is teacher directed with high structure and low ambiguity, the inquiry model is less teacher directed, requires moderate structure, and may lead to unforeseen outcomes that the teacher would need to adapt to during instruction. Anyone who has employed a more open-ended problem-solving lesson with students knows that it requires greater teacher flexibility or what David Hunt calls "reading and flexing." The main point is that this model is more abstract, more complex, and takes more time for a teacher to master.

INTERPERSONAL MODEL

While the knowledge transmitter model emphasizes learning of facts, and the inquiry model stresses the discovery of concepts, the third and most recent model, interpersonal learning, promotes genuine and compassionate human relationships. Thus, the teacher strives to convey genuine affection, empathy, and regard.

Carl Rogers and Thomas Gordon are leading exponents of this model. They argue that the quality of teacher-student and student-student relationships holds the key to more effective teaching and learning. Rogers has even suggested that feelings and experiential learning are the most important pathways to knowledge. The main point for both Rogers and Gordon is that traditional teaching too often ignores the interpersonal nature of learning. Too often, they argue, the focus is on a cold and sterile set of facts or concepts that hold no meaning for the students. In Rogers's (1969) classic work, *Freedom to Learn* he argued that such instruction was another case of ships passing in the night. Facts travel in one ear and out the other without any noticeable effect.

From his perspective, what is needed are three conditions that promote more authentic and vibrant teaching and learning: empathy, unconditional positive regard, and congruence. Empathy is the ability to communicate understanding of the feelings of another person. Unconditional positive regard is the capacity to accept students and to not pass judgment. And congruence is the willingness to be honest or "transparent" with the students or with a colleague. If a teacher or supervisor provides these conditions, then the students or a colleague are free to learn.

Examples of this model can be seen in conflict resolution programs, getting acquainted conferences held between teachers and students before the beginning of the school year, the dilemma discussion championed by Lawrence Kohlberg, deliberate psychological education programs described by Norman Sprinthall, discussion groups, and the "democratic community" approach of Ralph Mosher. The strength of this model for teaching and for supervision lies in its acknowledgement that building and maintaining strong relationships bolsters learning and is more responsive to the whole person. After all, what it means to be human is more than just thinking. Most of us have been in situations in which we were reluctant to learn or to share because we did not feel supported or we felt judged by the teacher.

The major drawback of this model is that it is primarily concerned only with human interaction. Imagine a supervisory conference where all of the interaction is based solely on feelings and experiential learning! It seems unlikely that the entirety of the teaching/learning/supervisory enterprise is driven by the three conditions described by Rogers. Another issue regards the complexity of the interpersonal model. For many teachers and supervisors, the affective part of education may be perceived as either "warm and fuzzy" or so emotionally charged that persons are reluctant to draw on its strengths. Whatever the case, the interpersonal model requires a teacher or supervisor to stay attuned to the complex inner world of feelings. As an example, picture the biology lesson on plants, except that the main focus is on the ethical considerations related to genetic alteration of plant material. During the heated discussion several students express fears about genetic manipulation. What if an altered gene somehow changed the delicate balance of nature? Respecting and responding to the feelings of fear places additional challenges on the teacher to "read and flex," adding another layer of complexity to the teaching/learning process.

The same pattern holds true for supervision. Anyone who has assisted a beginning teacher or supervised a student teacher knows that "feelings can run high" and that effectively responding to the feelings requires more time, more energy, and more thoughtfulness from the supervisor, as well as the implicit understanding that the supervisor must also share feelings as well as thoughts.

TEACHING FOR UNDERSTANDING: A SYNTHESIS MODEL

Integrating the three models for influencing classroom practice is representative of the teaching-for-understanding perspective that has recently surfaced in the literature (Good, 1996; Perkins, 1992; Richardson, 1996). This synthesis model derives from the desire among educators and researchers to overlap the process-product studies of teaching (e.g., teacher as presenter of information) with the need to promote constructivist development in students. Thus the teaching-for-understanding model deals more systematically with how students construct meaning and achieve learning outcomes (e.g., the issue of how teachers scaffold knowledge, which encourages students both to understand concepts and to progressively assume more responsibility for directing their learning during their schooling years) (Good, 1996).

But how do you do it? Teaching for understanding requires the teacher to blend the three models of instruction previously described into a coherent and flexible whole. Thus, the teacher utilizes the process-product research (knowledge transmitter model) summarized by Good and Brophy (1994), assuring that prior knowledge is assessed, learning needs are tied to authentic tasks that include variations in structure and practice, and learning outcomes are linked to generative ideas (Perkins, 1992) that have meaning for students. Likewise, the inquiry and interpersonal models are employed so students and the teacher can gain a better understanding of students' lives and to address the informal curriculum (e.g., fairness, equity, ethical dilemmas). Exhibit 8-1 summarizes the four models and outlines the strengths of each model, its drawbacks, and the level of complexity.

As you can see from Exhibit 8-1, each model has a different focus, and the introduction of each model in supervision places a different set of expectations and requirements on the supervisor and the supervisee. Naturally the ultimate goal is the integration of the models into one's teaching repertoire. Within the teaching models are strategies or methods that a supervisor should be aware of during an assessment of the beginning pedagogical knowledge of a supervisee. We now turn to a discussion of selected methods that have been shown to affect student achievement and student growth and development.

 # METHODS OF INSTRUCTION

In this section we review recent research on effective teaching. In particular, we draw on the meta-analysis conducted by Wang, Haertel, and Walberg (1993). A caveat, however, is in order. It is impossible to share all related re-

EXHIBIT 8-1   MODELS OF TEACHING

MODEL	WHAT	HOW	SHORTCOMING
Knowledge Transmitter (least complex)	Facts	Lecture (high structure with teacher direction)	Pupil passivity
Inductive-Inquiry (moderate complexity)	Core concepts Structure of the discipline	Problem solving	Abstraction Reinventing wheel
Interpersonal (complex)	Human interaction Mutual needs meeting Building community	Empathy Positive regard	"Love alone is not enough"
Teaching for Understanding (complex)	Student construction of meaning	Prior knowledge Powerful ideas Increasing student responsibility for learning over time Integration of facts, inquiry, and interpersonal models	Requires rich conception of students

search, and you should recognize that the emerging science of teaching and learning is a process of successive approximations. Thus, with each new discovery, we move a little closer to understanding just how rich and complex learning and teaching are.

As you read the remainder of the chapter you might want to reflect on which of the strategies you model in your classroom. After all, an effective supervisor should be able to demonstrate those instructional strategies he or she hopes the intern will learn.

 ## PEDAGOGICAL STRATEGIES WITHIN TEACHING MODELS

An influential work by B. Othaniel Smith, *A Design for a School of Pedagogy* (1980), stressed the importance of pedagogy, "Pedagogical practice has made significant progress in this century largely because of the rise and growth of research. Despite this fact, negative attitudes toward pedagogical education are widespread" (p. 49).

Although the research base for how learning occurs has literally exploded, there have not been, until recently, many causal connections between teacher behavior and student learning. Additionally, the field of teacher education has been bereft of theory. As recently as 1986, Lanier and Little noted that teacher education programs could be characterized as representing "consistent chaos in coursework" (p. 546). They suggested that very little has changed since the influential Conant report (1963) that documented a largely atheoretical and ad hoc approach to teacher education with wide variation as the only common element.

However, most clinical professions have similar histories. Physician Lewis Thomas reports in his book, *The Youngest Science* (1983) the state of the medical profession in the middle of the 1930s:

> We didn't know much that was really useful, that we could do nothing to change the course of the great majority of the diseases we were so busy analyzing, that medicine, for all its facade as a learned profession, was in real life a profoundly ignorant occupation. (p. 9)

As we mentioned earlier, only recently has a research basis for understanding teaching and teacher education begun to emerge. The most comprehensive reviews of teaching effectiveness have been completed by Wang, Haertel, and Walberg (1993) and Good (1996). Using the techniques of statistical meta-analysis and extensive review of the extant literature, they have found moderate to substantial agreement on the variables exerting the greatest influence on school learning. For example, in their study Wang et al. used evidence gathered from 61 research experts, 91 meta-analyses, and 179 handbook chapters and narrative reviews, the data representing over 11,000 relationships. Instructional variables exerting particularly strong effects on student learning include:

1. Classroom management
2. Questioning
3. Cooperative learning
4. Metacognitive strategies
5. Positive reinforcement
6. Classroom atmosphere (climate and equity)
7. Frequency and quality of teacher-student and student-student interactions (Flanders)

Furthermore, although Wang et al. (1993) found few strong relationships between state, district, and school level policy and demographics and school learning, they did find home environment to be very important. They concluded that "the home functions as the most salient out-of-school context for student learning, amplifying or diminishing the school's effect on learning" (p. 278).

Each of these elements of teaching effectiveness is discussed briefly in turn: classroom management, questioning, cooperative learning, metacognitive strategies, effective use of positive reinforcement, classroom atmosphere (climate, equity, and expectations), and frequency and quality of teacher-student and student-student interactions.

CLASSROOM MANAGEMENT

Classroom management includes several strategies that appear to relate directly to student achievement. Among them are the efficient handling of routine tasks, the use of advance organizers, and engaged academic learning. Advance organizers alert the student in advance of the main concepts to be introduced. Typically these organizers include written and verbal cues. It is important to assure that the advance organizer is closely matched to the students' level of cognitive development. For example, if the advance organizer includes concepts that are overly abstract when the student or students are at a concrete level, chances are great that the advance organizer will not be helpful to the students' learning.

Engaged academic learning represents those teaching behaviors that keep the learners involved in learning. Studies have shown that the amount of engaged learning behavior can vary by as much as 40 percent from one classroom to the next (Walberg, 1988). How efficiently you handle transitions and how you handle digressions affect student learning.

QUESTIONING

Recently there has been an upsurge of interest in the "teaching of thinking" through effective questioning. Actually, effective questioning requires at least two essential skills. The first is the capacity to ask higher-level questions that encourage the student to analyze, synthesize, and evaluate ideas through reasoned discourse.

The second skill is that of wait time. The research of Mary Budd Rowe (1986) has shown that simply increasing the wait time by a few seconds both after the question is posed and after the student responds has a very positive effect on student learning.

COOPERATIVE LEARNING

As most teachers recognize, there are numerous ways to organize students in a classroom (individual seatwork, small groups, group projects, whole class). Because students have different learning styles and come from different cultural and family backgrounds, it is necessary for the teacher to organize the classroom in a variety of ways to meet the diversity of styles (Johnson & Johnson, 1990). Cooperative learning is a strategy that can help address these different needs.

For example, research on the factors associated with women's success in mathematics classrooms (Fennema & Leder, 1990) consistently show that females learn more effectively in cooperative rather than competitive situations. Hilda Hernandez (1989) has summarized research in Native American communities which strongly suggests the importance of cooperative learning activities. The cooperative learning methods of Slavin (1983, 1990) have been used to reduce student prejudices in racially mixed classes and classes in which special education students have been mainstreamed. Furthermore, the work of Knight (1982) and Deci, Vallerand, Pelletier, and Ryan (1991) has shown that cooperative learning approaches lead to higher levels of intrinsic motivation. Overall, recent meta-analyses of cooperative groups have shown that academic achievement improves on the average of about three-quarters of a standard deviation (.75 main effect) for all students (Reynolds, 1990).

Knowing that this method of teaching positively affects student learning, motivation, and involvement with peers, does not mean that teachers will necessarily use the strategy. Cooperative learning groups require that teachers relinquish some of their classroom control of learning, which can be frightening. Another complication is that teachers sometimes assume that any small group activity is cooperative learning. This is not true. Cooperative learning activities are carefully structured around a variety of learning formats (see Johnson & Johnson, 1990) that involve explicit teacher directions on outcomes, small group tasks, and individual responsibilities. The carefully orchestrated strategy promotes high engaged learning time and successful group activities. Teachers who successfully employ cooperative learning methods vary the composition of groups in order to include different ability levels in each group. Underlying effective cooperative learning is an emphasis on group goals, individual accountability, and equal opportunity for success.

Several types of cooperative learning formats have been developed by Johnson and Johnson (1990), Slavin (1990), and Sharan and Sharan (1990). Although a summary follows, you are encouraged to review the original sources if you are interested in greater detail on the methods.

- *Learning Together*. Students work on project sheets in small groups (four to six students). The project sheet is submitted to the instructor and evaluation is based on the group product.
- *Think-Pair-Share*. Students individually analyze a topic provided by the teacher; then a student pairs with another student to discuss the topic. The activity is complete after student pairs share their thoughts.
- *Student Teams Achievement Divisions (STAD)*. The teacher presents the lesson, and the students work within the teams to make sure that all team members have mastered the objectives. Students take individual quizzes. Points are awarded based on improvement over previous quiz scores.
- *Jigsaw*. Each student on the team becomes an expert on one topic by working with members from other teams assigned the same topic. When they return to the home team, each expert teaches the group members. Students are assessed on all aspects of the topic.

CONTEMPORARY ISSUES

WHAT IS AUTHENTIC INSTRUCTION?

What models and methods of instruction engage students in using their minds well? This question has been at the forefront of work by Newmann and Wehlage (1993), who argue that efforts to improve the quality of instruction for student achievement must rely on three criteria (p. 8):

1. Students construct meaning and produce knowledge.
2. Students use disciplined inquiry to construct meaning.
3. Students aim their work toward production of discourse, products, and performances that have value or meaning beyond success in school.

Their main point is that models of teaching or methods of instruction, whether they are traditional or innovative, must engage students in using their minds well. Newmann, director of the National Center on Organization and Restructuring of Schools, and Wehlage, associate director, have introduced the conception of thoughtfulness. "Dispositions of thoughtfulness" include flexibility, creativity, reflectivity, and those teacher behaviors that encourage students' higher-order thinking. Further, they have begun to articulate standards for instruction that represent the quality of students' intellectual work. The five standards are higher-order thinking, depth of knowledge, connectedness to the world beyond the classroom, substantive conversation, and social support for student achievement.

Each standard can be assessed for shallow versus deep understanding. For example, a high level of "substantive conversation" would include considerable interaction about the ideas among the students and classroom dialogue that builds toward an improved collective understanding. Shortly, you will read about the Flanders Interaction Analysis instrument. How does it connect to the work of Newmann and Wehlage? The authors believe that the Newmann-Wehlage framework represents a necessary but not sufficient structure for studying how teaching for understanding and higher-order applications can be developed.

METACOGNITIVE STRATEGIES

Information processing theory seeks to understand how information is encoded, stored, and retrieved within the brain. Metacognition (Flavell, 1985) implies having internal knowledge, awareness, and control over memory. For example, when a student summarizes a chapter just read she or he is using cognitive skills. However, when a student summarizes as a means of obtaining feedback about her or his understanding of the material, the student has engaged in metacognition. Teachers can promote this "thinking about thinking" through the use of the following cluster of strategies:

1. Providing opportunities for feedback.
2. Having students keep a journal or daily learning log.
3. Providing instruction in self-questioning and/or student-student questioning.
4. Encouraging students to self-monitor and rate their ability to comprehend and understand.
5. Prompting students to generalize concepts.

For example, if you were teaching a course in developmental psychology to high school students you might employ a conventional test to ascertain the students' comprehension of the content: who is Piaget, what are his theories about, what are his definitions of accommodation and assimilation? However, if you handed the students an article from the *New York Times* and asked them to explain the phenomena using developmental theory, you would be encouraging them to generalize the learned concepts in a new situation.

POSITIVE REINFORCEMENT

The careful and consistent use of both verbal and nonverbal reinforcements has the most significant effect on student achievement. The effect is greater than one standard deviation. Naturally there are some important guidelines for its use. Reinforcements should not be used indiscriminately with all the students all of the time. The relationship between positive reinforcement and achievement is curvilinear rather than linear. Instead, you must be selective, genuine, and tie the reinforcement to learning. Reinforcements can include the following:

- Simple acknowledgements—Okay, Good work, Nice effort
- Differentiated reinforcements—acknowledging a part of the student's answer that is correct
- Delayed reinforcement—acknowledging a student's contribution made earlier in the lesson
- Extended reinforcement
- Nonverbal reinforcement—nods of head, smiles, proximity, eye contact

JAMES BANKS

Too few educators become direct agents of social change. James Banks is an exception. After receiving a Bachelors of Education at Chicago State College in 1964 in elementary education, he worked as an elementary classroom teacher for two years. As a fifth-grade teacher in inner-city Joliet, Illinois, he encouraged his students to dramatize episodes of black history. In 1966 he began graduate study at Michigan State University. "I wanted to find a way to take my civil rights commitment to scholarship." Enrolling in "independent studies," Banks completed his M.A. and Ph.D. in the short time span of three years. His dissertation focused on the treatment of blacks in textbooks, and his research and scholarship continue to have this focus.

Moving to the University of Washington, Banks chose to study ethnic and multicultural education. Serving as a consultant to the U.S. Office of Education, as well as urban school systems, Banks showed a remarkable ability to blend his emerging interest in multicultural education with the ongoing need to develop curriculum that was more responsive to a diverse student body.

Presently he heads the University of Washington's Center for Multicultural Education, which was established in 1992. The center conducts research on equity issues, intergroup relationships, and the achievement and intellectual and social-emotional development of minority students. One of the center's projects was the first-ever *Handbook of Research on Multicultural Education*.

Although Banks' work was not directly linked to supervision, he has encouraged teacher education programs, prospective teachers, and experienced teachers to better understand how their life experiences link to the experiences of other cultures. Thus supervision and mentoring can play an important role in promoting instruction that is equitable. He has popularized a strategy that requires students or teachers in diversity training to do a cultural history of their own families. Banks' research has shown that multicultural perspective-taking and interventions at the school site can occur at increasingly complex levels. At the highest or most complex level, which he calls the social-action approach, students and teachers are engaged in new roles as data gatherers and activists. The students are encouraged by teachers to assume a problem-finding and problem-solving approach, using critical thinking and reflection as they study crime, poverty, or pollution. This is somewhat similar to the new social role-taking and reflection research that is described in the text.

Banks' work has paved the way for a better understanding of multicultural education, and his research on equity issues has enlarged a knowledge base that supervisors and teachers should be familiar with in their instruction. He has written or edited 16 books and has written over one hundred articles. Ultimately, Banks sees multicultural education as an effort to re-envision America. "It isn't about 'the other.' It's about all of us and our shared destiny."

REFLECTION QUESTIONS

How have your family experiences shaped your perspectives on culture?

How do Banks' ideas about social action relate to the role-taking model introduced in Chapter 4?

How might you incorporate diversity into a peer coaching program at a local school?

It also is important to recognize that reinforcement often varies according to student characteristics. For example, girls receive significantly less reinforcement than boys (American Association of University Women [AAUW] 1992), and boys often receive more extended and differentiated reinforcement (Sadker, Sadker, & Klein, 1991). Thus, as a supervisor, you need to give careful attention to whether the frequency and quality of the teacher reinforcements vary according to race, gender, and class.

CLASSROOM ATMOSPHERE

Although classroom atmosphere is not, strictly speaking, a teaching strategy, it does have a significant impact on learning. Feelings of cohesiveness, positiveness, high expectations, opportunity, and goal-directedness appear to make the most difference. Essential to positive classroom atmosphere is equitable instruction that respects differences in ethnicity, race, class, religion, gender, primary language, sexual orientation, learning style, and family configuration. Educators must set consistently high expectations for success for all students, and *students must believe they can achieve in the teacher's classroom.* High or low expectations can create a self-fulfilling prophecy (Rosenthal & Jacobson, 1968). Unfortunately, low expectations are conveyed in subtle ways. Babad, Bernieri, and Rosenthal (1991) found that body language sends strong messages to students about the teacher's positive or negative expectations of them. In their book, *Failing at Fairness*, Myra and David Sadker (1994) offer substantial evidence that girls are frequently denied an equal education simply because of their gender. As we learn more about classroom atmosphere and studies of teacher expectations, it becomes clear that supervisors must have an understanding of strategies for coaching equitable instruction. In Chapter 10 we return to this topic, when we discuss data collection.

FREQUENCY AND QUALITY OF TEACHER-STUDENT AND STUDENT-STUDENT INTERACTIONS

One of the weaknesses of such a massive meta-analysis as the one conducted by Wang et al. (1993) is that the results do not depict actual patterns of teaching. There is a temptation to conclude that technical precision with the elements of teaching leads to instruction that is stellar. If this were so, we might be able to rely on a cadre of robots programmed to provide the teaching elements in well-timed sequences. As you might expect, such an experiment would be doomed to failure. We now know that the frequency, quality, and pattern of teacher-student and student-student interaction is essential to effective teaching. To help us understand how the elements fit together, we now turn to the work of Ned Flanders (1970).

HOW TO ASSESS MODELS AND METHODS: THE FLANDERS SYSTEM

Flanders (1970) did extensive classroom observation of thousands of teachers at all educational levels and in all content areas. He and his associates found that teacher talk and silence could be categorized into eight areas, and student talk could be categorized into two areas as shown in Exhibit 8-2. The categories are still relevant today. In Exhibit 8-3 you can see how his framework applies to current research on teaching as well as to the models we have discussed. We use the Flanders system to account for both verbal and nonverbal teacher behaviors. When this system is combined with the concerns approach described by Fuller to address the affective concerns of teachers, the supervisor or mentor has an assessment system that is neither too broad nor too narrow in focus. As Good (1996) points out in his review of evaluation systems, good teacher-effectiveness evaluation systems should be valid (McLaughlin & Pfeifer, 1988), reliable (McLaughlin & Pfeifer, 1988), fair and easily mastered (Bridges, 1990), account for quantitative and qualitative effort, and be relevant to teacher context (Peterson & Comeaux, 1990). The Flanders/Fuller framework is relatively easy to master, can assess groups of behaviors, accounts for teachers' sense of fairness, and assesses both teacher-student interaction (quantity), and teacher and student affective concerns.

The ten categories represent the most commonly observed teaching behaviors. Nate Gage (1978), in his book *The Scientific Basis for the Art of Teach-*

Exhibit 8-2   CATEGORIES FOR FLANDERS INTERACTION ANALYSIS

INDIRECT

1. *Accepts feelings*: Accepts and clarifies the tone of feelings of the students in an unthreatening manner. Feelings may be positive or negative. Predicting or recalling feelings are included.

2. *Praises or encourages*: Praises or encourages student action or behavior. Humor that releases tension, but not at the expense of another individual; nodding head and saying "um hm?" or "tell me more" are included.

3. *Accepts or uses ideas of students*: Clarifies, builds, or develops ideas suggested by a student. As teacher brings more of her or his ideas into play, shift to Category 5.

4. *Asks questions*: Asks a question about content or procedure with the intent that the student answer.

DIRECT

5. *Lectures*: Gives facts or opinions about content or procedure; expresses his or her own ideas, asking rhetorical questions.

6. *Gives directions*: Directs, commands, or gives orders that students are expected to comply with.

7. *Criticizes or justifies authority*: Makes statements intended to change student behavior from unacceptable to acceptable pattern; bawling someone out; stating the rationale for teacher behavior or action.

8. *Student talk—response:* Talk by students in response to teacher. Teacher initiates the contact.

9. *Student talk—initiation*: Talk initiated by students.

10. *Silence or confusion*: Pause, wait time, or periods of confusion in which the communication cannot be understood by the observer.

Source: From *Analyzing Teaching Behavior* (p. 34), by N. A. Flanders, 1970, MA: Addison-Wesley.

ing examined the influence of Flanders' categories by grouping them in two major clusters: indirect teaching, Categories 1 to 4, and direct teaching, Categories 5 to 7. The major difference between the clusters is whether teaching is viewed as more participatory and question driven or less participatory and more lecture driven. In comparing the modes, Gage (1985) found that at the elementary level a more direct mode (60%) can lead to significant student achievement, whereas at the secondary and college levels, there is clear evidence that a more indirect mode leads to greater academic gains. It also should be noted that Flanders found that only 1 in every 1000 teacher inter-

Exhibit 8-3   A COMPARISON OF TEACHER EFFECTIVENESS: FLANDERS AND WANG, HAERTEL, AND WALBERG

Flanders' Type	Wang, Haertel, and Walberg's Elements of Effective Teaching
(3) Accepts and builds on student ideas (10) Silence—wait time	Higher-order questions
(4) Asks questions; a combination of indirect plus (6) clear directions	Cooperative learning
(1) Gives clear directions	Classroom management
(8) Student response (9) Student initiation (3) Accepting ideas (4) Questioning (2) Praises or encourages	Metacognitive strategies Positive reinforcement
(1) Accepts feelings (2) Praises or encourages	Classroom atmosphere
(3) Accepts ideas; a combination of indirect, direct, and student talk categories	Frequency and quality of teacher-student and student-student interactions

actions included acceptance of feelings—Category 1. When used, however, the acceptance of feelings significantly contributed to classroom learning.

These findings make sense from a developmental perspective. Younger students need more advance organizers, benefit from clear directions, and prefer low levels of ambiguity. However, the older and more mature student has acquired a number of the rudimentary skills, is developing greater capacity for abstract reasoning, and is eager to think more independently. Thus the indirect mode is favored. Naturally it is not desirable to rely exclusively on either the direct or indirect mode. Instead, a ratio is preferred, with the ratio being the use of more direct teaching in elementary school and more indirect teaching in secondary programs.

Flanders also gave careful attention to the role played by student talk. In general, he found the frequency and quality of student talk to have tremendous bearing on student achievement and on the atmosphere of the class. Classrooms in which students felt comfortable initiating ideas (Category 9) and asking questions (Category 9) also had high levels of teacher acknowl-

Exhibit 8-4   NONVERBAL BEHAVIORS: THE GALLOWAY SYSTEM

INDIRECT			
	1, 2.	**Congruent** Nonverbal behavior is consistent with words. No "mixed messages" are given. Body language shows a range of feelings.	**Incongruent** Behavior contradicts words; for example, smiles when annoyed. Body language is controlled. Feelings are rarely shown.
	3.	**Implement** As teacher uses ideas of students, nonverbals are consistently encouraging; for example, leaning forward.	**Perfunctory** Nonverbal behavior indicates no genuine interest in students' ideas; for example, distant or bored facial expression.
	4.	**Personal** Teacher maintains face-to-face contact, is "connected" with the class.	**Impersonal** Teacher avoids eye contact during questioning.
DIRECT			
	5.	**Responsive** Tone, pace of talk are designed to keep student interest.	**Unresponsive** Teacher drones on and on, with little variation in tone and little attention to student cues.
	6.	**Involve** Nonverbal behavior encourages student participation in clarifying directions and rules.	**Dismiss** Nonverbal behavior cues students to avoid participation.
	7.	**Firm** Nonverbal behavior is consistent with firm language in controlling misbehavior.	**Harsh** Nonverbal behavior is severe, aggressive, genuinely intimidating.

edgement of ideas and feelings (Categories 1 and 3). These results dovetail with the more recent work of Wang et al. (1993). Once again, this is not a discrete skill that can magically appear with a wave of the supervisory wand. Rather, the frequency, quality, and pattern of teacher-student interactions and student-student interactions require the teacher to use a cluster of strategies. It should also be noted that the Flanders system has been criticized as focusing too much on verbal interaction (see Exhibit 8-4 for Galloway's adaptation (1977) of the Flanders system), yet on balance, there is much more research supporting the framework as a valid measure of teaching effectiveness than any other system (Flanders & Morine, 1973; Gage,

1985; Walberg, 1990). And when the Flanders model integrates the work of Galloway, nonverbal interactions are accounted.

If the teaching goal for middle and secondary level students is developmental, that is, to promote the shift to formal operations, and the use of metacognitions and metaphorical concepts, then the indirect mode, and in particular, open-ended questions, cueing, building on student answers, and responding to feelings will enhance such cognitive growth (Aspy & Roebuck, 1973; Gage, 1985; Hunt & Joyce, 1967).

 # GAINING KNOWLEDGE

At the heart of the "gaining knowledge" phase of developmental instructional supervision is the goal of identifying teacher behaviors (models and methods) that promote student learning and development in the broadest sense. From this starting point, an effective supervisor or mentor can begin to provide both support for those models and methods that are exemplary, and challenge the teacher to try new models and methods of instruction that will prompt richer student learning and development. There are two major components to the "gaining knowledge" phase: prior knowledge and present assumptions about education and observation of the teacher. Each of these components is now described.

PRIOR KNOWLEDGE AND PRESENT ASSUMPTIONS ABOUT EDUCATION

Most beginning teachers arrive in their new classroom with some knowledge, explicit and implicit beliefs and assumptions about teaching and learning, and a lot of anxiety. One of the goals for you as the mentor is to ascertain the prior knowledge and the teacher's beliefs and assumptions about education.

Prior knowledge may take the form of a portfolio the teacher maintained during his or her student teaching experience. Often these portfolios include the teacher's written philosophy of education. If a portfolio was completed, ask the teacher to initially review the portfolio to see if it still is representative of his or her work. If so, the two of you can arrange a time to review the portfolio. During the review your goal is to be an effective listener, gathering as much information as possible. If the portfolio is thoughtfully prepared, it is possible that the beginning teacher will already be aware of his or her instructional strengths as well as those areas needing refinement or that presently are unexplored and untried.

If no portfolio was developed during the teacher's final internship, a conference should be planned for the purpose of discussing the teacher's prior experiences as well as his or her beliefs and assumptions about education. Prior to the conference the beginning teacher should self-evaluate his or her teaching using the guideline in Exhibit 8-5. Additionally, the teacher should respond to the questions and complete a brief summary of his or her assumptions about teaching, learning, and schooling. Make sure to answer any questions the teacher may have before he or she begins the self-evaluation. The following guideline (Exhibit 8-5) identifies topics for discussion. After you have reviewed the teacher's prior experiences and assumptions about education, you want to request a time for observation of the teacher in the classroom.

Observation of the Teacher

A second component of the "gaining knowledge" phase of developmental instructional supervision or mentoring is teacher observation. This observation should be conducted within one week of the conference to discuss prior experiences and the present assumptions about education. The goal of the observation is to gather as much information as possible about the accuracy of the teacher's self knowledge of teaching as indicated in Item 3 in Exhibit 8-5 (i.e., methods of teaching). Prior to the observation the teacher should prepare a written lesson plan that can be shared with you during a preconference. We suggest that you let the teacher use whatever format he or she is most comfortable using. This lesson plan and the observation are a sort of pretest. In fact, we encourage the beginning teacher to tape-record the lesson for his or her portfolio, which he or she should begin to prepare.

The wide-lens approach is used for this observation. This observational approach is useful for a first observation because the technique attempts to record as much teaching phenomena as possible. More information on data collection and observation is included in Chapter 10. In addition, you should script the lesson, making brief written notes of teacher-student interactions as they occur.

However, the main goal is to record what you see and hear, not what you judge as effective or ineffective. Also remember that your notes must be legible so that your colleague may read and interpret them.

The post-observation conference, which ideally should occur the same day as the observation, is an important step. But Chapter 11 gives much more detail on how to hold a post-conference. Four major topics should be discussed:

How are you feeling now that the lesson is over?

Were the learning outcomes reached?

Did the lesson corroborate your self-assessment of strengths with the models and methods of teaching?

What should we establish as the first teaching behavior focus to develop or refine?

Exhibit 8-5   GUIDELINE FOR DISCUSSION OF PRIOR EXPERIENCES

Focus

Rate yourself on each of the areas: S = strength, M = moderate, N = no experience.

1. Purpose: To review educational experiences

2. Models of Teaching
   ____Experiences with Inductive-Inquiry Model
   ____Experiences with Knowledge Transmitter Model
   ____Experiences with Interpersonal Model

3. Methods of Teaching
   ____Classroom atmosphere (active listening, response opportunities, "read and flex" to student needs, nonverbal communication)
   ____Positive reinforcement
   ____Questioning
   ____Lesson planning
   ____Frequency and quality of teacher-student and student-student interactions (Flanders Indirect/Direct)
   ____Cooperative learning
   ____Classroom management (time on task, clear directions, classroom management strategies that are positive and developmentally appropriate)
   ____Metacognitive strategies

4. The goals of schooling are . . .

5. How do children learn?

6. My role as a teacher is . . .

As these questions are asked be prepared at first to actively listen. This can be followed by your own brief comments and further probes. Remember that the goal is discerning what the teacher thinks and feels. At the end of the conference you should arrange a date and a time to prepare a coaching plan. This plan is discussed in Chapter 12.

We now turn to several case studies of the "gaining knowledge" phase of supervision. Each case study portrays how beginning teachers (induction career phase) at different stages of conceptual, ego, and moral development would complete the self-assessment. The case studies are followed by a sample of the anecdotal observation data collected during the first observation and a discussion of insights made that may be helpful to you as a mentor or supervisor.

Case Study—Tom

The first case study is Tom, a beginning teacher whom you have encountered in Chapters 3 and 4. His completed "Guideline for Discussion of Prior Experiences" is shown (see Exhibit 8-6). Recall that Tom appears to be at the Concrete conceptual stage, Self-Protective/Conformist ego stage, and Conformist moral stage. Immediately following Exhibit 8-6 is a brief anecdotal record of the observation of Tom that was conducted by the supervisor, and subsequent discussion of the case study.

Anecdotal Observation Data. Tom's class had 25 students. They were seated in rows. The first ten minutes of class were spent taking roll and answering questions. Questions were asked individually by students as they entered the classroom. The lesson began at 10:10 with Tom describing the purpose of the lesson, "Today we will discuss the concept of alliteration in poetry."

After a brief explanation of the meaning of alliteration, Tom then proceeded to read several poems to the students, asking them to mentally note when they heard alliteration in the poems.

Discussion. Tom's instructional strengths are limited and support his dominant view of effective teaching—the knowledge transmitter model. From our discussion and his self-analysis, Tom's idea of how students learn is ambiguous and global. In fact, he really doesn't anwer the question of *how* students learn. Lesson organization and whole group instruction are the central themes discussed. The observational data corroborate Tom's self-

Exhibit 8-6   GUIDELINE FOR DISCUSSION OF PRIOR EXPERIENCES—
TOM

Focus

Rate yourself on each of the areas: S = strength, M = moderate, N = no experience.

1. Purpose: To review educational experiences

2. Models of Teaching
   ____Experiences with Inductive-Inquiry Model
   _S_ Experiences with KnowledgeTransmitter Model
   ____Experiences with Interpersonal Model

3. Methods of Teaching
   ____Classroom atmosphere (active listening, response opportunities, "reading and flexing" to student needs, nonverbal communication)
   ____Positive reinforcement
   _S_ Questioning
   _S_ Lesson planning
   ____Frequency and quality of teacher-student and student-student interactions (Flanders Indirect/Direct)
   ____Cooperative learning
   _S_ Classroom management (time on task, clear directions, classroom management strategies that are positive and developmentally appropriate
   ____Metacognitive strategies

4. *The goals of schooling are . . .*   Schools have a responsibility to prepare students for the global economy. This means that schools must return to their basic mission, the 3Rs. By returning to this mission, we will assure that students can enter the workplace with the skills needed to be effective.

5. *How do children learn?*   Students benefit from well-organized lessons and clear presentation of the material. They also need to know that you can be a friend in time of need. In my educational classes at State the professors mentioned the importance of individualizing instruction. But I am not sure this is realistic given the numbers in my classes.

6. *My role as a teacher is . . .*   Classes should be well organized and the teacher needs to be knowledgable in his or her subject matter. I think this is very important to successful teaching.

---

analysis. His lesson is for the whole class, and he does little, early in the lesson, to accommodate to the needs of individual learners, such as visual aids or teacher-student questioning. Additionally, there is little interaction between Tom and the students. Compare Tom's self-evaluation with that of Carole discussed next. Also note the differences in how Carole and Tom approach teaching and learning. For example, how does Carole's approach to students vary with Tom's approach?

Case Study—Carole

Carole, the focus of the second case study, is at more moderate levels of conceptual and ego development (see Exhibit 8-7).

Anecdotal Observation Data. As students entered the classroom they placed a check by their name before taking their seat. Carole greeted several of the students as they entered. She began her class promptly at 11:00. The lesson began with Carole asking three students to review the previous day's lesson. These students raised their hands in response. Sarah began by describing how sound is caused by vibrations. After each of the students responded, Carole stated, "Okay," "An excellent summary," and "Nice work."

Discussion. Carole's self-analysis portrays another qualitative shift in stage toward moderate conceptual and ego development levels. Carole is able to represent the goals of schooling, how students learn, and the role of the teacher as multidimensional. Thus, she is beginning to recognize the complexity that is inherent in the teaching/learning process. Carole has experience with a broader range of models and methods of instruction and, most likely, is somewhat more willing to experiment with new strategies. However, descriptions of how to meet the challenges of teaching (role of the teacher) are still somewhat general in description, that is, teaching the whole child, descriptions relate to students generally rather than to the individual student.

Case Study—Bill

Finally, we turn to Bill's case study (see Exhibit 8-8). Bill is at more complex conceptual and ego stages. Contrast his self-analysis with those of Tom and Carole.

Anecdotal Observation Data. Bill greeted the students as they arrived in his classroom. He frequently smiled and, in some cases, kneeled down so that he would be face to face with some of the students. He began the lesson by reviewing the goal of the students' homework assignment—to complete their creative writing assignment. After this introduction, he explained that students would have four objectives in their task groups: (1) to describe the

EXHIBIT 8-7   GUIDELINE FOR DISCUSSION OF PRIOR EXPERIENCES—
CAROLE

FOCUS

Rate yourself on each of the areas: S = strength, M = moderate, N = no experience.

1. Purpose: To review educational experiences

2. Models of Teaching
   _M_ Experiences with Inductive-Inquiry Model
   _M_ Experiences with Knowledge Transmitter Model
   _N_ Experiences with Interpersonal Model

3. Methods of Teaching
   _M_ Classroom atmosphere (active listening, response opportunities, "reading
       and flexing" to student needs, nonverbal communication)
   _M_ Positive reinforcement
   _S_ Questioning
   _M_ Lesson planning
   _N_ Frequency and quality of teacher-student and student-student interactions
       (Flanders Indirect/Direct)
   _M_ Cooperative learning
   _M_ Classroom management (time on task, clear directions, classroom manage-
       ment strategies that are positive and developmentally appropriate
   _N_ Metacognitive strategies

4. *The goals of schooling are . . . to:*
   a. prepare students for lifelong learning
   b. prepare students for the workplace
   c. provide a safe and secure setting for learning

5. *How do children learn?*   Students learn in a variety of ways. Some students learn
   better through visual modes, whereas other students learn better through an auditory approach. Students benefit from hands-on approaches and small group
   work. I also think regular review of concepts is important to how children learn.

6. *My role as a teacher is . . .*   to meet the needs of the students. This requires me to
   arrange the learning experiences in ways that are most beneficial to the students.
   I also think it is important to arrange experiences that meet the needs of the
   whole child.

---

main idea of their story; (2) to identify questions or problems that arose in
the writing process; (3) to identify the main characters; and (4) to have a peer
read the story and write a brief description of a character they liked and
why. These objectives also were posted on chart paper at the front and back
of the classroom.

Discussion. Bill focuses on broader ranges of individual differences and
readily acknowledges that teaching is complex. He has ego strength, identi-

EXHIBIT 8-8 GUIDELINE FOR DISCUSSION OF PRIOR EXPERIENCES— BILL

FOCUS

Rate yourself on each of the areas: S = strength, M = moderate, N = no experience.

1. Purpose: To review educational experiences

2. Models of Teaching
   _M_ Experiences with Inductive-Inquiry Model
   _S_ Experiences with Knowledge Transmitter Model
   _N_ Experiences with Interpersonal Model

3. Methods of Teaching
   _M_ Classroom atmosphere (active listening, response opportunities, "reading and flexing" to student needs, nonverbal communication)
   _M_ Positive reinforcement
   _M_ Questioning
   _M_ Lesson planning
   _S_ Frequency and quality of teacher-student and student-student interactions (Flanders Indirect/Direct)
   _M_ Cooperative learning
   _M_ Classroom management (time on task, clear directions, classroom management strategies that are positive and developmentally appropriate
   _N_ Metacognitive strategies

4. *The goals of schooling are . . .* to educate students to their fullest capacities so that they can be responsible citizens in a democratic society.

5. *How do children learn?* Students learn in a variety of ways: visual, auditory, kinestetic. They also develop in a number of cognitive and social/emotional areas. Developmental growth occurs in stages. I believe that learning and development occur at different rates for students, and that the teacher must be attuned to these different rates. I also think students benefit from interaction with their peers.

6. *My role as a teacher is . . .* complex, and requires that I balance learner needs with my own goals for curriculum and instruction, as well as the needs of the whole class. I see myself as a facilitator, and I like to try to see learning problems from the students' perspectives. This strategy gives me a lot of insight into their learning. I also realize that teaching is at times joyful, frustrating, and taxing.

fying a number of feelings that are part of his experience. His list of identified strengths is diverse and he is probably a self-starter when it comes to learning new skills and strategies. Bill also is able to reconcile that he also has needs. Recall our discussion about mutual needs meeting in Chapter 7. Thus, he is able to balance the needs of the students with his own instructional goals. Finally, his observation data portray a classroom that has clear goals, carefully planned activities that are highly interactive and outcome-based, and there are some examples of effective nonverbal communication as well as some accommodation for the learners, that is, posted charts that review the objectives of the small group work. Clearly Bill is able to employ all teaching models according to the needs of the students.

SUMMARY

The question of how to represent the many different frameworks for instruction was resolved in the chapter through a discussion of three general models of teaching. In the first model the emphasis is on the direct transmission of knowledge. In the second model—the inductive-inquiry approach, the teaching is more indirect, with open-ended questioning and accepting and building on student ideas the major instructional processes. The focus of the third model is the quality of interpersonal interactions. Within these models are clusters of teaching methods and strategies.

Recent research on teaching based on a large-scale meta-analysis conducted by Wang, Haertel, and Walberg, indicates that a number of factors significantly contribute to student achievement: classroom management, positive reinforcement, cooperative learning, metacognitive instruction, higher-order questioning, classroom atmosphere, and the frequency and quality of teacher-student and student-student interactions. The system developed by Flanders shows how these factors fit together in classroom interaction.

The models and methods of teaching served as a backdrop to the "gaining knowledge" phase of developmental instructional supervision. The supervisor must ascertain the teacher's prior knowledge and present assumptions about the teaching/learning process as a starting point for supervision. Three case studies were presented that portrayed teachers' self-analysis of teaching and their assumptions about the teaching/learning process. The teachers represented different stages of conceptual, ego, and moral development.

SUPERVISION FOR TEACHER
DEVELOPMENT ACTIVITIES

APPLIED

1. Ask a colleague to complete the "Guideline for Discussion of Prior Experiences" questionnaire. Conduct an interview as a follow-up to the questionnaire to discuss the teacher's perceived areas of strength.

2. Afterward, analyze the questionnaire based on your knowledge of teacher development. Answer the following questions:
   a. Does the teacher focus on individual differences?
   b. Is there a range of individual differences or are references global?

   c. How is the complexity of teaching addressed?

   d. What might be a good starting point for supervision if it were to precede the teacher self-assessment?

3. Write a critique of the chapter. What were your main learnings? With what did you disagree? What ideas do you plan to use as a supervisor? What questions do you have after reading the chapter? Are there additional readings you would suggest?

PORTFOLIO DEVELOPMENT

1. Complete the "Guideline for Discussion of Prior Experiences." Place a copy of the guideline in your portfolio in a new section called "Coaching for Models and Methods of Teaching."

2. Observe a lesson. Use the scripting method to collect data. Record for approximately 30 minutes. As a follow-up, answer the following questions:

   a. My main learnings from the observation were: _____.

   b. I rate the data collection as:
   Inadequate _____ Marginal _____ Excellent _____ .
   Explain why.

   c. I will use the following strategies the next time
   I do scripting: _____.
   Include the observation data and the answers to the follow-up questions in a section of your portfolio called "Observation with a Purpose." Consider the data as a pretest of your scripting skills.

3. Write reflections according to your own interests. After your instructor has responded to the reflections, date and file them in your portfolio (section labeled "Reflections").

SUGGESTED READINGS

1. Amidon, E., & Flanders, N. A. (1967). *The role of the teacher in the classroom: A manual for understanding and improving teacher classroom behavior*. Minneapolis, MN: Association for Productive Teaching.

   This dated work still contains some of the most helpful information about the interpretation of the Flanders Interaction Analysis System.

2. Levine, S. (1989). *Promoting adult growth in schools* (chap. 4). Needham Heights, MA: Allyn and Bacon.

   Throughout the text Levine draws on the experiences of teachers and principals. Chapter 4 gives special attention to four teachers using the lens of cognitive-developmental theory.

REFERENCES

Adler, M. (1982). *The Paideia Proposal: An educational manifesto.* New York: Macmillan.

American Association of University Women (1992). *How schools shortchange girls.* Washington, DC: AAUW Educational Foundation.

Aspy, D. N., & Roebuck, F. (1973). An investigation of the relationship between students' levels of cognitive functioning and the teacher's classroom behavior. *Journal of Educational Research, 65*(6), 365–368.

Ausubel, D. P. (1960). The use of advance organizers in the learning and retention of meaningful verbal material. *Journal of Educational Psychology, 51,* 267–272.

Babad, E., Bernieri, F., & Rosenthal, R. (1991). Students as judges of teachers' verbal and non-verbal behavior. *American Educational Research Journal, 28*(1), 211.

Bloom, B. S. (1971). Mastery learning. In J. H. Block (Ed.), *Mastery learning: Theory and practice.* New York: Holt, Rinehart and Winston.

Bridges, E. (1990). Evaluation for tenure and dismissal. In J. Millman & L. Darling-Hammond (Eds.), *The new handbook of teacher evaluation: Assessing elementary and secondary teachers* (pp. 147–157). Newbury Park, CA: Sage.

Bruner, J. (1961). *The process of education.* Cambridge, MA: Harvard University Press.

Conant, J. (1963). *The education of American teachers.* New York: McGraw-Hill.

Deci, E. L., Vallerand, R. J., Pelletier, L. G., & Ryan, R. M. (1991). Motivation and education: The self-determination perspective. *Educational Psychologist, 26*(4), 325–346.

Dewey, J. (1916). *Democracy and education.* New York: Macmillan.

Fennema, E., & Leder, G. (Eds.). (1990). *Mathematics and gender.* New York: Teachers College Press.

Flanders, N. A. (1970). *Analyzing teacher behavior.* Reading, MA: Addison-Wesley.

Flanders, N. A., & Morine, G. (1973). The assessment of proper control and suitable learning environment. In N. L. Gage (Ed.), *Mandated evaluation of educators.* Stanford: California Center for Research and Development in Teaching.

Flavell, J. H. (1985). *Cognitive development.* Englewood Cliffs, NJ: Prentice-Hall.

Gage, N. (1978). *The scientific basis for the art of teaching.* New York: Teachers College Press.

Gage, N. (1985). *Hard gains in the soft sciences.* Bloomington, IN: Phi Delta Kappan.

Galloway, C. (1977). Nonverbal. *Theory into practice, 16*(3).

Good, T. (1996). Teaching effects and teacher evaluation. In J. Sikula (Ed.), *Second handbook of research on teacher education* (pp. 617–665). New York: Macmillan.

Good, T., & Brophy, J. (1994). *Looking in classrooms* (6th ed.). New York: HarperCollins.

Gordon, W. J. (1961). *Synectics.* New York: Harper & Row.

Hernandez, H. (1989). *Multicultural education.* Columbus, OH: Merrill.

Hunt, D., & Joyce, B. (1967). Teacher trainee personality and initial teaching style. *American Educational Research Journal, 4,* 253–259.

Johnson, D., & Johnson, R. (1990). Social skills for successful group work. *Educational Leadership, 47*(4), 29–33.

Joyce B. (1978). *Selecting learning experiences: Linking theory to practice.* Washington, DC: ASCD.

Joyce, B., & Weil, M. (1996). *Models of teaching* (5th ed.). Boston: Allyn and Bacon.

Knight, C. J. (1982, May). Cooperative learning: A new approach to an old idea. *Teaching Exceptional Children,* 233–238.

Lanier, J., & Little, J. (1986). Research in teacher education. In M. Wittrock (Ed.), *Handbook of research in teaching* (pp. 527–569). New York: Macmillan.

McLaughlin, M., & Pfeifer, R. (1988). *Teacher evaluation: Improvement, accountability and effective learning*. New York: Teachers College Press.

Newmann, F. M., & Wehlage, G. G. (1993). Five standards of authentic instruction. *Educational Leadership, 50*(4), 8–12.

Perkins, D. (1992). *Smart schools*. New York: Free Press.

Peterson, P., & Comeaux, M. (1990). Evaluating the systems: Teachers' perspectives on teacher evaluation. *Educational Evaluation and Policy Analysis, 12*, 3–24.

Reynolds, M. C. (1990). Educating teachers for special education students. In R. Houston (Ed.), *Handbook of research in teacher education* (pp. 423–436). New York: Macmillan.

Richardson, V. (1996). The role of attitudes and beliefs in learning to teach. In J. Sikula (Ed.), *Second handbook of research in teacher education* (pp. 102–119). New York: Macmillan.

Rogers, C. R. (1969). *Freedom to learn*. Columbus, OH: Merrill.

Rosenshine, B. (1985). Direct instruction. In T. Husen & T. Postlethwaite (Eds.), *International encyclopedia of education* (pp. 1395–1400). Oxford, England: Pergamon Press.

Rosenthal, R., & Jacobson, L. (1968). *Pygmalion in the classroom*. New York: Holt, Rinehart, and Winston.

Rowe, M. B. (1986). Wait time: Slowing down may be a way of speeding up! *Journal of Teacher Education, 37*(1), 43–50.

Sadker, M., & Sadker, D. (1994). *Failing at fairness*. New York: Random House.

Sadker, M., Sadker, D., & Klein, S. (1991). The issue of gender in elementary and secondary education. In G. Grant (Ed.), *Review of research in education* (pp. 269–334). Washington, DC: American Educational Research Association.

Sharan, Y., & Sharan, S. (1990). Group investigation expands cooperative learning. *Educational Leadership, 47*(4), 17–21.

Slavin, R. (1983). *Cooperative learning*. New York: Longman.

Slavin, R. (1990). *Cooperative learning: Theory, research, and practice*. New Jersey: Prentice-Hall.

Smith, B. O. (1980). *A design for a school of pedagogy*. Washington, DC: U.S. Department of Education.

Soar, R. S., Soar, R. M., & Ragosta, M. (1971). *Florida climate and control system: Observer's manual*. Gainesville: Institute for Development of Human Resources, University of Florida.

Sprinthall, N. A., Sprinthall, R., & Oja, S. N. (1994). *Educational psychology: A developmental approach* (6th ed.). New York: McGraw-Hill.

Taba, H. (1966). *Teaching strategies and cognitive functioning in elementary school children*. (Cooperative Research Project 2404.) San Francisco: San Francisco State College.

Thomas, L. (1983). *The youngest science: Notes of a medicine watcher*. New York: Viking.

Walberg, H. (1988). Synthesis of research on time and learning. *Educational Leadership, 45*(6), 76–81.

Walberg, H. (1990). Productive teaching and instruction: Assessing the knowledge base. *Phi Delta Kappan, 71*(6), 70–78.

Wang, M. C., Haertel, G. D., & Walberg, H. J. (1993). Toward a knowledge base for school learning. *Review of Educational Research, 63*(3), 249–294.

C·H·A·P·T·E·R
9

Promoting Growth Through Cycles of Assistance

• • • • • • •

As we noted in Chapter 8, a research basis for understanding both the teaching/learning models and methods as well as the frameworks that are most successful for promoting the use of these models and methods has grown dramatically in the last ten years. In Chapters 9, 10, and 11 we elaborate on the cycle of assistance originally developed by Cogan. Chapter 9 introduces the pre-observation conference. Chapter 10 describes observation methods, and Chapter 11 reviews the post-observation conference. In Chapter 12 we discuss the crucial role of instructional coaching.

The practice of clinical supervision and assistance has lacked systematic theory as a basis for its methods. This major omission lies at the root of the problems facing supervision programs today. As we mentioned in the first part of the text, without theory, the practice of supervision moves randomly, first in one direction, then, a few years later, in yet another direction. Such episodic activity, as one cynic remarked, leads to wandering between the cosmic and the trivial without understanding the difference. Thus, one of the goals of this text is to explicate a guiding theoretical framework for supervisory practice. In this chapter we provide an overview of the assumptions of a cycle of assistance and describe the pre-observation conference from the developmental perspective.

As you review the chapter, check your comprehension by answering these questions:

- How is the pre-observation conference adapted to the needs of the adult learner?
- How is a cycle of clinical supervision related to the coaching plan?

CLINICAL SUPERVISION: RATIONALE AND ASSUMPTIONS

As we mentioned in Chapter 1, the works of Morris Cogan and Robert Gold-hammer with clinical supervision are representative of this special approach to supervision. Clinical supervision is depicted as a democratic inquiry that encourages teachers to consider alternatives, to problem-solve, and to select teaching behaviors based on their unveiling of the meaning and structure of teaching. Both Goldhammer and Cogan encourage the supervisor to be a "humble questioner" who recognizes the unpredictability of classroom events, implying that there are no absolutes in teaching, instead, our understanding of teaching and learning is a process of successive approximations. The clinical supervision model has a number of assumptions (Cogan, 1973):

1. The supervisor's role is to facilitate the discovery of the fundamental structure and meaning of classroom and school events. The supervisor should lead the way for teaching according to broader concepts, rather than on the basis of just facts about "good" teaching.
2. The supervisor must be flexible; she or he must be able to employ a repertoire of assistance strategies according to the needs of the teacher.
3. "Clinical supervision" implies direct observation, analysis, and follow-up discussion, as opposed to "general supervision," which implies supervision outside of the classroom.
4. The clinical supervisor is responsive to context.
5. The supervisor is ethically responsible for ensuring the teacher's welfare and for enhancing teaching skills.

If clinical supervision cycles are a way of helping teachers to improve their teaching, then developmental clinical supervision adds four additional assumptions:

6. The supervisor is ethically responsible for promoting the teacher's cognitive-developmental growth.
7. Promoting learning and growth embodies reasonable sequences and continuities that can be bolstered by a carefully designed support program (application of the teaching/learning framework).
8. The cycle of developmental instructional supervision is one part of a larger sequence of carefully planned activities. From a skills perspective, the cycle permits an opportunity to adapt and generalize the new

model. From the growth and development perspective, the cycle permits intensive guided reflection on the the teacher's new role.

9. When a teacher and a colleague begin to analyze instruction, the effective supervisor should be able to demonstrate a repertoire of models of instruction and supervisory strategies to promote the development of the teacher, "reading and flexing" supervision according to the needs of the colleague.

As you can see from the nine assumptions, the focus is on sustained assistance that is developmental and specifically tailored to the needs of the teacher, in contrast to brief or episodic experiences. Our discussion of getting acquainted conferences, "gaining knowledge" appraisals and observations, and planning conferences for the purpose of developing coaching plans are all part of a carefully planned sequence of learnings. Such an approach helps to assure the continuity of learning and reflection.

CYCLES OF DEVELOPMENTAL INSTRUCTIONAL SUPERVISION

As Cogan remarked, "By both its form and its processes the cycle strongly conveys to the teacher the sense that classroom teaching and classroom learning must be worked out, they do not just happen" (1973, p. 29). The cycle of developmental instructional supervision includes a number of phases that are now described. The phases of a developmental supervision cycle are as follows:

Phase 1.   Establishing the teacher-supervisor relationship (Chapter 7)
Phase 2.   "Gaining knowledge" (Chapter 8)
Phase 3.   Developing and implementing the coaching plan (Chapter 12)
Phase 4.   Pre-observation conference (Chapter 9)
Phase 5.   Observing instruction (Chapter 10)
Phase 6.   Analyzing the teaching/learning processes (Chapter 8)
Phase 7.   Conducting the post-observation conference (Chapter 11)
Phase 8.   Renewed planning and new coaching plans (Chapter 12)

The ultimate goal of clinical supervision as envisioned by Cogan and Goldhammer is the emergence of a professional teacher; one who is self-analytical, responsible, and self-directing. The cycle we have described is abbreviated once the teacher exhibits these attitudes and dispositions. We now elaborate on Phase 4—the pre-observation or planning conference.

PHASE 4. PLANNING THE STRATEGY OF OBSERVATION—THE PRE-CONFERENCE

In this phase, the trained observer meets with the teacher to discuss feelings, the teaching behavior focus, lesson learning outcomes, and the physical and technical aspects of the observation and data collection (see Exhibit 9-1).

Exhibit 9-1   PRE-CONFERENCE OBSERVATION SHEET

Focus	Behavior

1. Purpose
_____ Instruction
_____ Concerns
_____ Evaluation

2. Feelings
_____ Colleague feelings
_____ Evidence of listening
_____ Supervisor feelings

3. Learning Outcomes
_____ Learning outcome
_____ Rationale for selection
_____ Lesson plan
_____ Evidence of listening

4. Teaching Behavior Focus
_____ Teaching focus
_____ Review of rationale
_____ Evidence of listening

5. Information Gathering
_____ Observation instrument for
teaching behavior focus
_____ Collect data on other three
questions
_____ Special circumstances

6. Ground Rules
_____ Notes
_____ Share notes
_____ Notes on three other areas
_____ Logistics

7. Follow-up
_____ Feedback time
_____ Self-analysis sheet

Early in the supervisory relationship, the supervisor will take a more dominant role. As the teacher becomes more familiar with the clinical processes, and as the supervisor learns more about the current development of the teacher, the process will become more collegial if the current developmental stage of the teacher indicates less structure is needed.

At the heart of the pre-conference is the opportunity for teachers to reflect on and share with supervisors the uniqueness of their classrooms. It also is an opportunity for the supervisor or mentor to learn about the classroom and to share plans with the teacher. Thus, the pre-conference engenders a sense of cooperating toward reaching specific instructional outcomes.

Some experts (Hunter, 1986) contend that this phase of a cycle is unnecessary, arguing that it is time-consuming and that a well-trained observer should be able to collect all of the necessary information without the pre-observation conference. Developmental theory suggests otherwise because the goal is more than just skills building. The pre-observation conference permits an opportunity for guided reflection and analysis. New teachers and, in particular, teachers at less complex stages of development need assistance with reflecting. The supervisor or mentor can help the teacher initiate deeper reflection on instruction, curriculum, and beliefs about education. Furthermore, the teacher may harbor anxieties about the observation. These concerns can be addressed during the pre-observation conference. Although experienced supervisors can conduct pre-conferences that address concerns and instructional outcomes, we often find that new mentors and supervisors benefit from a clearer description of pre-conference outcomes. The pre-observation conference includes seven elements:

1. Statement of the purpose
2. Discussion of feelings
3. Review of the learning outcomes
4. Discussion of the teaching behavior focus
5. Clarification of information gathering
6. Review of ground rules
7. Planning for follow-up

Each of the seven elements of a pre-conference is now described.

STATEMENT OF PURPOSE

In most cases, the purpose is to focus on instruction—building a teaching repertoire. For example, a mentor would briefly state the purpose: "You have been working on monitoring students in your coaching plan. The purpose of today's cycle of assistance is to provide the two of us with an opportunity to assess your level of mastery with this skill." However, the purpose might be evaluation or peer review. If so, this should be mentioned in the statement of the purpose. For example, "The purpose of today's cycle of assistance is to evaluate your progress in managing student behaviors." The important point is that the purpose should be clear, concise, stated, and mutually supported.

DISCUSSION OF FEELINGS

Asking the teacher to describe his or her feelings about being observed permits an opportunity to defuse feelings of anxiety and trepidation. The consequence is that the teacher will be more open to learning from the cycle of assistance. As you might guess, an understanding of phases of concern, which was discussed in Chapter 5, and your active listening skills, will come into play. We also think it is important for the supervisor to share her or his feelings about the coming observation. The following is an example:

> *Teacher:* I am a little anxious about the observation, even though I know I have been working on monitoring students' behavior during the past two weeks, and in general, I think I have greatly improved.
>
> *Colleague:* The idea of being observed is unnerving, even though you have practiced. Well, I am a little anxious and excited. After all, it is the first observation.

If the supervisory relationship is strong, and trust has been fostered, this phase of the pre-conference can help clear the air. Remember an earlier admonition that being fully human is more than just thinking. Feelings are important and they should be acknowledged in the pre-conference.

LEARNING OUTCOMES

Specific learning outcomes of the observed lesson should be reviewed, as well as the rationale for their selection. It is important that the learning outcomes represent the behaviors, attitudes, or skills that the students can perform at the end of the lesson. When and if necessary, the supervisor should use questioning to clarify the learning outcomes. A copy of the lesson plan should be available for the supervisor.

A special comment about learning outcomes is needed. As we have related, our work with thousands of mentor teachers, supervisors, and teacher educators has guided revisions in our understanding of the supervision process. It has come to our attention that a careful review of the stated learning outcomes is needed. Why? Because many of the learning outcomes are not written as outcomes. They are not measurable. In fact, we have hundreds of reports of student teachers and beginning teachers who had only an amorphous idea of what they hoped to achieve during the lesson. Supervisors can do a great service for the teaching profession by assuring that novice teachers have a clear understanding of how to write and assess learning outcomes.

TEACHING BEHAVIOR FOCUS

As you may recall, the teaching behavior focus represents that instructional model or method which the teacher is interested in learning or perfecting. It was earlier identified on the coaching plan. The assumption of the assistance cycle is that the teacher has achieved some confidence with the selected focus (e.g., higher-level questioning). Thus, the pre-conference selection of the teaching behavior focus will probably be very brief since it has already been discussed, demonstrated, and practiced during the coaching phase of supervision. A caveat is in order regarding the selection of a teaching behavior focus. Research on assistance to novice teachers (Huling-Austin, 1986; Hunter, 1979) indicates that the novice teacher struggles to compose measurable learning outcomes for lessons and to be an effective classroom manager. Thus the first order of business is to diagnose abilities in these two instructional areas, namely, writing and implementing clear learning outcomes, and second, effective classroom management. Do not move on to other teaching behavior focuses until the teacher is competent. Also realize that the teaching behavior focus should be demonstrated by the supervisor or a mentor, with follow-up practice. A coaching plan can guide this process and is discussed in Chapter 12.

INFORMATION GATHERING

Information is gathered in four areas:

1. Were the *learning outcomes* met?
2. Did the *classroom management* interfere with or support reaching the learning outcomes?
3. Was the *teaching behavior focus* met?
4. What *other teaching behaviors* should be continued or changed?

The supervisor should review each of these areas, alerting the teacher that data will be collected on the four questions. Appropriate and objective data should be collected. In the case of the teaching behavior focus, the teacher should have a working knowledge of how data can be collected and the relevant instruments that can be used, since these forms were a part of the coaching phase of supervision. More information about observations will be shared in Chapter 10.

GROUND RULES

The supervisor reminds the teacher that notes will be taken during the observation to answer the four questions previously mentioned: outcomes, classroom management, teaching behavior focus, and other teaching behaviors that should be continued. Logistics also are discussed. For example, where will the supervisor sit during the observation? If the purpose of the cycle is evaluation, you should state that observation notes will be discussed and then filed with both the supervisor and the teacher. If the focus is assistance and/or instructional coaching, you would discuss how the observation notes can be placed in the colleague's portfolio, for example, if the lesson adds value to the overall portfolio.

FOLLOW-UP

Finally, the time of the post-observation conference is identified. A second part of this step is the "self-analysis sheet." The supervisor provides a self-

Exhibit 9-2   SELF-EVALUATION OF A LESSON (to be completed by the teacher before a post-observation conference with a mentor, cooperating teacher, or supervisor)

---

1. Evaluation of Pupil's Achievement of Stated Objectives. If you did not achieve objectives, write the reason(s) here:

2. Classroom Management:
   Place a check on the scale.
   Interfered_____Supported

   Evidence:

3. Teaching Behavior Focused on_____

   _____

List behaviors you included in your lesson to show competence in the above teaching behavior.	List those behaviors you could have included.

SUMMARY: Check one:
   _____Competency achieved. New teaching behavior focus:_____.
   _____Competency not achieved. Continue same teaching behavior focus.

---

analysis sheet for post-observation self-reflection and analysis. The self-analysis sheet (see Exhibit 9-2) is most important because it provides an opportunity for the teacher to reflect on the lesson before the post-conference discussion. The supervisor will find that Stage A teachers will have some difficulty completing the self-analysis, and their reflections will be of a general nature. In contrast, the stage C teacher will provide more detail, share feelings, and relate the impact of the instruction to students' lives. In summary, the objective of this phase of the cycle is to complete a dress rehearsal for the observation.

THE SUPERVISOR'S RESPONSIBILITIES IN THE PRE-CONFERENCE

The supervisor or coach has responsibility for setting a positive and productive tone in the pre-conference. In many respects, the pre-conference becomes a kind of contract for the entire cycle of assistance. And, as we just described, the concerns, lesson outcomes, and teaching behavior focus should be discussed. However, the supervisor or coach also has a responsibility to understand the teacher as an adult learner. If, for example, the teacher is reticent about sharing feelings, the supervisor can be accepting but also share his or her feelings.

== Case Study—Tom

Another example of being responsive to the adult learning needs of the teacher relates to the need for structure. Teachers at less complex conceptual levels will desire and need more structure from the supervisor during the pre-conference (see Exhibit 9-3).

   As you can see from the pre-observation case study between Tom and his assistant principal, more structure is offered. There is more input about the supervisory process, links to concrete examples and actual classroom practice, use of encouragement, review of key concepts and terms before completing the conference, and more initiation and talk by the assistant principal. Further, Tom's focus is on self and task rather than the students as expressed in his rationales.

   Recalling the Flanders system (p. 161), we have found that prospective supervisors who are learning to differentiate structure in a cycle of assistance should conduct a conference that is 70 percent direct to 30 percent indirect. Further, the proportion of supervisor talk can be as much 60 percent to 70 percent of the conference dialogue.

   In contrast, however, the supervisor might be working with a teacher or teachers who are at moderately complex conceptual levels. Such teachers would prefer a more collaborative pre-conference, characterized by give and take. Most likely, the pre-conference should balance indirect and direct conferencing (i.e., Flanders system), and ample time should be provided for teacher input. A goal might be to have a pre-conference that is 50 percent direct and 50 percent indirect, with a balance between supervisor talk and supervisee talk. Glickman and Gordon (1987) describe this approach as collegial supervision.

Exhibit 9-3   PRE-CONFERENCE OBSERVATION SHEET—TOM
AND ASSISTANT PRINCIPAL

Focus	**Behavior**

Teacher level is High Structure. Tom's comments are in italics.

1. Purpose
   _____ Instruction
   _____ Concerns
   __x__ Evaluation
   • The purpose of today's cycle is to assess your progress with monitoring of student behavior.
2. Feelings
   __x__ Colleague feelings
   __x__ Evidence of listening
   __x__ Supervisor feelings
   • Any feelings?
   • *I am fine, I guess.*
   • You feel okay, but you are uncertain.
   • I am eager to observe the lesson you have planned. What are the outcomes?
3. Learning Outcomes

   __x__ Learning outcome
   • *I want the students to identify the three main branches of the federal government.*

   __x__ Rationale for selection
   • What is the rationale for the selection of that learning outcome?
   • *It was in the state curriculum guide.*
   • So the state curriculum is being incorporated into your curriculum. Any other reasons?
   • *I guess I am also trying to keep up with my mentor who is teaching a similar lesson.*

   __x__ Lesson plan
   • It is important to you to keep up with your mentor. Do you have a copy of your lesson plan to share with me? Thanks. (Lengthy pause). This plan includes your outcome, materials you plan to use, and key lecture comments (input). How were you planning to assess whether 80 percent of the students achieved the outcome?
   • *I was planning to give a quiz on Friday.*
   • There is merit to assessing the outcome during the lesson. Any ideas?
   • *I guess I could have students complete a worksheet. Then I could evaluate whether students mastered the concept.*
   • That is a good idea.

   __x__ Evidence of listening

Exhibit 9-3   PRE-CONFERENCE OBSERVATION SHEET—TOM
AND ASSISTANT PRINCIPAL *(continued)*

Focus	Behavior
4. Teaching Behavior Focus __x__ Teaching focus	• Your teaching behavior focus is monitoring of student behavior. I know you have practiced this focus with your mentor. • *She has been terrific.* • Uh-hm. Well, what is the rationale for this focus?
__x__ Review of rationale	• *Well, the main rationale is that in our last cycle you noted that I did not monitor student behavior.* • Okay, the last observation. Are there any other reasons? (None given.)
__x__ Evidence of listening 5. Information Gathering	• I will be using the seating chart form to collect data. You are familiar with this form. Right? Didn't you use it while observing your mentor's monitoring of behavior?
__x__ Observation instrument of teaching behavior focus	• *That's right. I have used the instrument and I like how it shows where I moved during the lesson.*
_____ Collect data on other three questions	• I will be collecting data on three other questions: Was your learning outcome met? Did classroom management support or interfere with the lesson? And what other strengths or changes are needed?
_____ Special circumstances	• Are there any special circumstances I should be aware of during the observation? • *Only that the overhead sometimes doesn't cooperate.* • Any others? • *I guess I sometimes run out of time and rush the ending to the lesson.*

6. Ground Rules
   _____ Notes
   _____ Share notes
   _____ Notes on three other areas
   _____ Logistics
	• Time problems. Okay. I will be taking notes during the observation and I plan to share them with you. Data will be collected on the other three categories we just discussed. Where would you like me to sit during the observation?
	• *In the back of the room by the gerbil cage.*

EXHIBIT 9-3   *(continued)*

FOCUS	BEHAVIOR
7. Follow-up _____ Feedback time _____ Self-analysis sheet	• Let's plan to meet this afternoon at 3:30 to discuss the observation. I also want you to complete this self-evaluation sheet before the post-conference. Give it careful thought. Any questions? None, okay. Thank you for taking time out of your busy schedule to meet with me. I will be at your class promptly at 10:00.

Case Study—Bill

At the other end of the continuum, the supervisor might encounter teachers who are at the most complex conceptual levels (see Exhibit 9-4).

Recall that teachers at Stage C have high tolerance for ambiguity, employ a wide repertoire of instructional styles, initiate reflection, and value collaboration and autonomy. As you can see from Exhibit 9-4, the assistant principal's responsibility shifts to providing low structure, encouraging Bill to assume a high degree of responsibility for the outcomes of instructional improvement. The supervisor conducts a conference that is no more than 30 percent direct and 70 percent indirect and supervisor talk would be less than 50 percent of the total dialogue. Note how Bill initiates conversation, anticipates questions, recalls related research, and focuses on learning experiences that are meaningful for students.

BUT DOES TRAINING IN THE CYCLES OF ASSISTANCE MAKE A DIFFERENCE?

Good question! The studies, although few, suggest that training in the general approaches to instructional supervision, and developmental supervision in particular, does make a difference at all points in the teacher career span. For example, Thorlacius (1980) found that training in instructional supervision altered cooperating teachers' conferences with student teachers. Confer-

Exhibit 9-4 PRE-CONFERENCE OBSERVATION SHEET—BILL
AND ASSISTANT PRINCIPAL

Focus	Behavior

Teacher level is Indirect—Low Structure. Bill's comments are in italics.

1. Purpose
   ____ Instruction
   ____ Concerns
   __x__ Evaluation

   • The purpose of today's cycle is is to assess your progress as a third-year teacher.

2. Feelings
   __x__ Colleague feelings

   • *I am pleased that you are here. I find this clinical focus on instruction to be rewarding, insightful, and energizing. And, to be honest, a bit scary.*

   __x__ Evidence of listening
   __x__ Supervisor feelings

   • Energizing yet scary. I too am energized, and I appreciate your eagerness to participate in these cycles.

3. Learning Outcomes

   • Can you tell me about your lesson and the learning outcomes?

   __x__ Learning outcome

   • *Sure. I plan to have three major outcomes. Students should be able to:*
     a. *Relate a personal decision that involved compromise with another person.*
     b. *Identify the three main branches of the federal government.*
     c. *Construct a model that symbolizes the three branches: legislative, executive, and judicial.*
   • *I plan for the lesson to develop over two days and I want the students to see how their own decisions sometimes include "checks and balances." Mom, Dad, friends, brothers, etc.*

   __x__ Rationale for selection

   I also hope that constructing a model will match their current intellectual levels. By the way, here is a copy of the lesson plan.

   __x__ Lesson plan

   • Thank you. (Lengthy pause). It is apparent that you have given the lesson careful thought and you have planned outcomes that are measurable, meaningful, and developmentally appropriate.

   __x__ Evidence of listening

EXHIBIT 9-4   *(continued)*

FOCUS	BEHAVIOR
4. Teaching Behavior Focus	• What about the teaching behavior focus?
__x__ Teaching focus	• *I am working on cooperative learning. The research supports this strategy but I have struggled to master it. In particular, I want to be able to more effectively structure the cooperative groups so that all students participate. To accomplish this I have increased the structure of the cooperative groups with clearer directions and guidelines for task accomplishment. These guidelines will be used today and I hoped you would collect data on student participation in two random cooperative groups, noting types of comments, level of participation, and effectiveness of the group guidelines.*
__x__ Review of rationale	
__x__ Evidence of listening	• The teaching behavior focus is structuring of the cooperative groups for maximized learning. Okay.
5. Information Gathering	• Would it be acceptable for me to create a seating chart form for each of the small groups to tally comments? I also could record selective verbatim statements by the students.
__x__ Observation instrument for teaching behavior focus	• *That sounds excellent.*
__x__ Collect data on other three questions	• I will also be collecting data on whether the learning outcomes were met, classroom management, and other strengths or areas in need of refinement.
__x__ Special circumstances	• Are there any special circumstances?
	• *Yes, three of my students will need to leave class at 10:30 for some testing. The students will be in cooperative groups so I do not anticipate much disruption. I have prepared a follow-up activity for the students and the cooperative groups also are charged with following up with their classmates.*

EXHIBIT 9-4   *(continued)*

FOCUS	BEHAVIOR
6. Ground Rules	

__x__ Notes
  __x__ Share notes
  _____ Notes on three other areas
  __x__ Logistics
	• I will share all of my notes with you.
	• *Thank you. Please feel comfortable moving around the classroom so that you can collect the needed data. By the way, I plan to alert the students about your observation.*

7. Follow-up
  __x__ Feedback time
  __x__ Self-analysis sheet
	• When can we meet for a post-conference?
	• *How about 3:30. I will complete the self-analysis sheet before our conference.*
	• Thank you.

ences were more differentiated and more reciprocal. Chandler (1971) found that, without training, cooperating teachers dominated the talk in conferences. Further, without training in supervisory processes the dialogue of cooperating teachers and student teachers focused on noninstructional tasks rather than the analysis of instruction. Feedback was particularistic and not tied to theory, research, or the general aims of instruction (Koehler, 1986).

Likewise research on teacher induction attests to the role of trained mentors. Odell (1986) found that clinical support teachers (highly trained in supervision, relationship skills, and coaching techniques) offered more assistance with formal teaching processes. And Huling-Austin, Putman, and Galvez-Hjornevik (1986) found the assignment of a well-trained support teacher to a beginning teacher to be the most powerful and cost-effective intervention in an induction program.

Similar results are seen at the inservice level (e.g., principals, assistant principals, lead teachers, peer coaching). Direct instructional supervision and coaching promote greater reflection (Phillips, 1989), improved collegiality (Simone, 1986), teacher revitalization (Stein, 1985; Thies-Sprinthall & Sprinthall, 1987), teacher higher-order problem solving and autonomy (Reiman & Thies-Sprinthall, 1993; Smith, 1985), and improved student achievement and student attitudes (Joyce & Showers, 1995).

 SUMMARY

The goal of this chapter was to introduce the assumptions of clinical and developmental assistance, and to describe the pre-conference, discussing its value to developmental instructional supervision. As was mentioned in

CONTEMPORARY ISSUES

Is More Practice Better?

One of the age-old questions for researchers and practitioners is the question of whether more practice is better? The assumption is that if a little bit of practice helps some, a lot of practice should really boost performance. This belief is acted out in a variety of settings. For example, many preservice teacher education programs have increased the amount of time prospective teachers spend in schools both in observation and practice teaching. Teacher educators believe that the best way to learn to teach is through real-world applications. Support for this approach comes from policy makers, administrators, teachers and teacher educators, and the preservice students. After all, how many of us have heard the refrain that beginning teachers lacked sufficient practice for their start as teachers. A similar perception exists in teacher education programs. Once again, the assumption is that more time will translate into more effective practice. Likewise programmers of inservice education argue that training should be longer to permit better acquisition of skills.

Although this view of more practice has become pervasive, emerging research suggests that more practice does not necessarily mean a more skillful or mature person (Leavitt, 1992). For example, Joyce and Showers (1995) have shown that the sequence of experiences is central to learning new models of teaching. Further, some needed learning experiences for prospective teachers are best provided in laboratory rather than field settings (Metcalf, 1995). Induction programs confuse quantity with quality. Gold (1996) found that careful training for the role of mentor teacher positively affected program quality. And Exum (1980) found that it was the reflection time, not the amount of experience, that promoted adult growth. Naturally other problems constrain the potential of practice. For example, there often is a lack of connectedness between college teacher education programs and field experiences. What is taught in the college is not reinforced in the schools, or the teachers responsible for assistance have had no preparation for their role. Nonetheless, even this limited review of research should give educators pause and raise questions about the wholehearted embracing of the belief that more practice by itself will lead to more effective teaching.

Chapter 1, the works of Morris Cogan and Robert Goldhammer with clinical supervision are representative of the special approach to supervision called clinical supervision. Clinical supervision is depicted as a democratic inquiry that encourages teachers to consider alternatives, to problem-solve, and to select teaching behaviors based on their unveiling of the meaning and structure of teaching. Both Goldhammer and Cogan encourage the supervisor to be a "humble questioner" who recognizes the unpredictability of classroom events, implying that there are no absolutes in teaching; instead, our understanding of teaching and learning is a process of successive approximations. However, developmental supervision adds four assumptions about the assistance process:

- The supervisor is ethically responsible for enhancing the teacher's cognitive-developmental growth.
- Promoting learning and growth embodies reasonable sequences and continuities that can be bolstered by a carefully designed support program (application of the Teaching/Learning Framework, p. 132).
- The cycle of developmental instructional supervision is one part of a larger sequence of carefully planned activities. From a skills perspective, the cycle permits an opportunity to adapt and generalize the new model. From the growth and development perspective, the cycle permits intensive guided reflection on the the teacher's new role.
- When a teacher and a colleague begin to analyze instruction, the effective supervisor should be able to demonstrate a repertoire of models of instruction and supervisory strategies to promote the development of the teacher, "reading and flexing" supervision according to the needs of the colleague.

In Chapter 10 the focus shifts to the role of observation in cycles of assistance. As you will note, the emphasis is on helping the teacher develop a repertoire of models and methods of teaching through classroom observation.

SUPERVISION FOR TEACHER DEVELOPMENT ACTIVITIES

APPLIED

1. Interview five teachers. Questions that might be asked include the following: When your principal observes you is a pre-conference first initiated? Have you ever participated in a pre-conference? If so, what were its advantages? If you had a choice, would you want a pre-conference conducted and why?

2. Summarize the results of the interview in writing. Select one interviewee to feature in the analysis. Liberally use quotes from the teacher. Include a brief conclusion that argues for or against pre-conferences.

PORTFOLIO DEVELOPMENT

1. Write about your own experience or lack of experience with pre-conferences.

REFERENCES

Chandler, B. (1971). *Levels of thinking in supervisory conferences.* Paper presented at the annual meeting of the American Educational Research Association, New York. (ERIC Document Reproduction Service No. ED 049 186).

Cogan, M. (1973). *Clinical supervision.* Boston: Houghton Mifflin.

Exum, H. (1980). Ego development: Using curriculum to facilitate growth. *Character Potential, 9*(3), 121–128.

Glickman, C., & Gordon, S. (1987). Clarifying developmental supervision. *Educational Leadership, 44*(8), 64–68.

Gold, Y. (1996). Beginning teacher support: Attrition, mentoring, and induction. In J. Sikula (Ed.), *Second handbook of research on teacher education* (pp. 548–594). New York: Macmillan.

Huling-Austin, L. (1986). What can and cannot reasonably be expected from teacher induction programs. *Journal of Teacher Education, 37*(1), 2–5.

Huling-Austin, L., Putman, S., & Galvez-Hjornevik, C. (1986). *Model teacher induction project study findings* (Report No. 7212). Austin, TX: University of Texas at Austin, R & D Center for Teacher Education.

Hunter, M. (1979). Diagnostic teaching. *The Elementary School Journal, 80*(1), 41–46.

Hunter, M. (1986). Let's eliminate the preobservation conference. *Educational Leadership, 43*(6), 69–70.

Joyce, B., & Showers, B. (1995). *Student achievement through staff development* (2nd ed.). New York: Longman.

Koehler, V. (1986). *The instructional supervision of student teachers.* Paper presented at the annual meeting of the American Educational Research Association, San Francisco. (ERIC Document Reproduction Service No. ED 271 430).

Leavitt, H. B. (Ed.) (1992). *Issues and problems in teacher education: An international handbook.* New York: Greenwood Press.

Metcalf, K. (1995). *A meta-analysis of laboratory experiences.* Paper presented at Annual Association of Teacher Educators, Detroit, MI.

Odell, S. (1986). Induction support of new teachers: A functional approach. *Journal of Teacher Education, 37*(1), 26–29.

Phillips, M. (1989). *A case study evaluation of the impact on teachers of the implementation of a peer coaching training program in an elementary school.* Unpublished doctoral dissertation, University of Georgia.

Reiman, A. J., & Thies-Sprinthall, L. (1993). Promoting the development of mentor teachers: Theory and research programs using guided reflection. *Journal of Research and Development, 26*(3), 179–185.

Simone, M. A. (1986). Uses of common technical language and public agenda in the supervisory process and their relationship to trust of the supervisor and teacher efficacy (Doctoral dissertation, Rutgers University). *Dissertation Abstracts International, 47,* 2838A.

Smith, S. (1985). The effects of clinical supervision on teachers' autonomy and perceptions of productive relationships (Doctoral dissertation, University of Idaho). *Dissertation Abstracts International, 46,* 3003A.

Stein, R. D. (1985). The relationship between principal supervisory behavior and teacher burnout (Doctoral dissertation, University of Illinois). *Dissertation Abstracts International, 46,* 577A.

Thies-Sprinthall, L., & Sprinthall, N. A. (1987). Experienced teachers: Agents for revitalization and renewal as mentors and teacher educators. *Journal of Teacher Education, 169*(1), 65–75.

Thorlacius, J. (1980, April). *Changes in supervisory behavior resulting from training in clinical supervision.* Paper presented at the annual meeting of the American Educational Research Association, Boston. (ERIC Document Reproduction Service No. ED 211 506).

C·H·A·P·T·E·R
10

Data Collection

· · · · · · ·

$\mathcal{T}$he material presented in this chapter provides a general introduction to some of the techniques employed by supervisors and teaching colleagues (mentors). Though as a practicing teacher, administrator, or teacher educator you may have practiced some of the techniques that are described, your understanding of these concepts will be greatly enhanced after reading this chapter. The goal is for the supervisor or mentor to have a repertoire of observation techniques from which to draw.

Comprehending a particular observation strategy does not guarantee that you will be able to master it in your supervision or coaching, but you will be able to evaluate the strengths and limitations of a variety of strategies for collecting data on instruction. As we know from the coaching research and literature, demonstrations and practice in the strategies assure a deeper understanding of the processes. Therefore the objectives of this chapter are to introduce a range of data collection strategies, identify their strengths and limitations, introduce specific techniques, review some of the problems in observation, and discuss how the techniques can be differentiated according to the needs of the adult learner.

As you review the chapter, check your comprehension by answering these questions:

- What are the major types of classroom observation strategies?
- What are the strengths and limitations of various data collection strategies?
- How can the data collection techniques be differentiated according to the needs of the adult learner?

- How might one select, adapt, or modify data collection techniques to better meet supervisory or coaching needs?

RATIONALE FOR OBSERVATIONS

In-class observations continue to be a vital way to refine and expand instructional repertoire (Showers, Joyce, & Bennett, 1987). Further, when the data on the observation instrument are consistent with what the teachers or teacher and supervisor agreed to focus on and later discuss, it promotes professional growth (Bauer, 1986; Chunn, 1985; Garman, 1986; Russell & Spafford, 1986). Data collection techniques are therefore used to describe, and they are based on prior agreement (pre-observation conference or coaching plan). An evaluation instrument, in contrast, is intended to summarize and judge professional competence, and it is implemented with all teachers using similar criteria.

As we mentioned in Chapter 8, supervisors and mentors must first become familiar with the teacher's classroom style before narrowing the coaching to address a teaching model a colleague wants to expand, or in the case of a supervisor, an area of instructional need. Therefore initial observations need to capture the wider span of classroom activities because they form the basis for subsequent planning, coaching, and supervision. As the supervisory or coaching relationship progresses, the observations will become more focused on desired areas of instruction. Typically the progression in observation instrumentation moves from wide-lens (qualitative) to narrow lens (quantitative) (Acheson & Gall, 1992). Thus the supervisor or the mentor needs to be able to employ a variety of data collection strategies (Exhibit 10-1). We now turn to data collection strategies.

DATA COLLECTION: AN ANALOGY

Imagine the production of a film documentary on baseball. The filming crew has worked over the past year to collect footage of some of the great moments in baseball history. Now the crew wants to record the World Series. On this particular day of filming the crew hopes to record game five. An

EXHIBIT 10-1 RANGE OF DATA COLLECTION STRATEGIES

Widest Lens		Narrowest Lens
(Qualitative)	(Qualitative/Quantitative)	(Quantitative)
Video/Audio	Verbatim/Selective Verbatim	Diagrams/Timelines/ Frequency

elaborate script has been developed to guide the process. Filming begins with the camera set on wide-lens, panning the stadium, the fans, the coaches, and the players as they enter the field. This footage is followed by a filmed interview with the two coaches. Selective verbatim quotes by the coaches are recorded and spliced together. This is followed by a close-up of one of the pitchers who is expected to play a key role in the game. Subsequently, the film displays the vital statistics for each team as they have progressed through the season.

As we hope you will see from the filming analogy, data collection procedures to record classroom instruction can be compared to camera filming. When the camera is placed at the back of the classroom and the widest lens is used to document the students, the teacher, and the classroom furnishings, it is much like our analogy in which the filming crew pans the stadium, fans, coaches, and players. If the lens is closed a bit, some of the panorama is lost but more detail (the interview with the coaches or focus on the pitcher) is achieved. Similarly, in a classroom the data collection might record only the types of questions asked by the teacher, an example of the selective verbatim strategy. Continue to close the lens and greater detail is achieved. Like our baseball analogy in which the camera documents the vital statistics for each team, in the classroom visual diagrams and timelines can be used to record quantity of specific behaviors over time. The focus is very narrow and specific but the supervisor or mentor loses the larger story of the classroom. Exhibit 10-1 illustrates the range of data collection techniques.

 # DATA COLLECTION STRATEGIES

As we just mentioned, a range of data collection strategies can be employed. Some forms of data collection record the broader classroom context, and are categorized as qualitative or wide-lens, whereas quantitative or narrow-lens observations reveal the amount of teacher behaviors in defined categories (Medley & Mizel, 1963). We now turn to a more in-depth description of qualitative (wide-lens) observation strategies.

QUALITATIVE (WIDE-LENS) OBSERVATION STRATEGIES

As the filming analogy shows, wide-lens observation strategies attempt to record as much information as possible. Although detail is lost, the strength of qualitative (wide-lens) strategies is their comprehensiveness. Video and audio recordings are examples of qualitative observation.

Video Recording. The camera never blinks. Video recording provides an objective record of a teacher's instruction. Video recording has become more widely used as teacher education programs and school staff development programs have integrated video into training programs. An advantage of video recording is that it includes both the verbal and nonverbal classroom interactions. Another strength of video recording is that it can be viewed by the teacher, other teachers, students, or teacher/principal, at a later date. Further, the videotape can be used for future demonstrations as part of a coaching program. In some of our own district-based developmental supervision courses, videotapes of clinical supervision and coaching are completed by prospective mentor teachers. These videotapes are used to self-assess coaching and supervision techniques.

There are, however, several limitations to video recording. The foremost is cost and accessibility. Although camcorders are present in many suburban and urban schools, we still encounter many rural schools that do not have camcorders in the media centers. Another limitation is degree of comfort. Some teachers are reluctant to learn how to use the video recording equipment. Another issue is the discomfort many of us feel when we first see ourselves on the videotape. How many of us like the way we look on videotape? A final limitation to video recording is its obtrusiveness. Students are very aware when a camera is present, and the camera can alter student behavior. Although these limitations can be daunting to many teachers and supervisors, the benefits of video outweigh the limitations. In fact, many of the limitations can be alleviated through practice or trial sessions that create comfort for both the teacher and the students. Another helpful strategy that reduces anxiety (Acheson & Gall, 1992) is to leave the videotape in the possession of the person who was observed.

Audio Recording. Audio recording is another technique for collecting data. The use of audio recording eliminates nonverbal interactions, which is problematic. However, audio tape recorders are easy to use. Most models now come with built-in microphones and operate on batteries, and it is easy for the teacher to record 30 minutes of instruction with a minimum of difficulty. Further, this technology is unobtrusive, is universally accessible, and permits fairly in-depth analysis and reflection on the classroom context. The video or audio recording, with its wide-lens focus, can be viewed or listened to during the post-observation conference. The supervisor's role is to encourage the teacher to reflect and self-analyze, recalling significant classroom events and trends, and drawing inferences whenever possible.

Narrative Observation. Narrative observation requires the supervisor to record those events, persons, and/or interactions that appear noteworthy. The supervisor begins with very little structure and the challenge is to write as much as possible about the complex and dynamic classroom events. The observation form's heading would include the name of the observed teacher, the beginning and ending time of the observation, and the name of the observer. A narrative observation might read as follows:

> The time is 11:00. The teacher is greeting the students as they enter the classroom. Some students are smiling as they enter. Others are talking with each other as they enter the room. Most of the students acknowledge the teacher in some way. The bell rings at

11:05. No students arrived late. There is a large bulletin board beside the teacher's desk. It has the heading Current Events. Newspaper clippings that the students have found are fastened to the board with student comments beside each article. The teacher begins the class promptly at 11:05 by describing the planned outcomes for the day's inquiry lesson. Students will be working in small groups. The teacher has prepared handouts for each small group and explains the process for small group work.

As you can see, a strength of this type of observation is that it can keep track of the flow of classroom events in a way that could not be recorded with a checklist. Further, this type of observation may be well suited to supervision with self-directed teachers. The shortcomings of this approach are that it is somewhat difficult to master without practice and it places greater cognitive demands on the supervisor and teacher to analyze in the post-observation conference.

Focused Questionnaire Observation. Focused questionnaire observations rely on general questions to guide the qualitative recording of events. You might think of this type of observation as a focused form of the narrative observation we just described.

For example, we have used the focused questionnaire observation with undergraduate students. Sophomore students who are visiting schools for the first time are asked to seek information on specific questions about the classroom customs. Some sample questions follow:

Observation of Classroom Customs
1. How are attendance and tardiness handled?
2. What are the procedures for greeting visitors?
3. How are materials distributed and collected?
4. When do students work together?
5. Are there any automatic privileges and/or penalties?
6. What provisions are there for the students to talk with the teacher?
7. What are the students' attitudes toward school, subjects, and teachers?

This type of observation is relatively easy to use, links well to coaching, is easily tailored to unique teacher needs, and encourages focused reflection. Thus it is a form of qualitative observation that we recommend highly.

Educational Criticism. Elliot Eisner (1985) is the major advocate of educational criticism. In this method of observation the observer *sees* and *interprets* both the explicit classroom events as well as the nuances or implicit classroom meanings (e.g., motivations, discrepancy between what the teacher espouses and what is actually practiced). As Eisner relates, the ability to be an educational critic requires a disposition to fully appreciate, respect, listen, and find meaning from the classroom observation. Eisner refers to this ability as educational connoisseurship. Like an architecture studio critique, edu-

ELLIOT EISNER

Elliot Eisner was named the Art Educator of the Year in 1996 by the National Art Education Association, and the award is a testimonial to his efforts to use critical methods employed in the arts and humanities to study classroom practice. It also is a tribute to his work to expand school curricula to address the forms of thinking and meaning that the arts and humanities make possible.

Born in Chicago in 1933, Eisner received his B.A. in Art and Education at Roosevelt University. He went on to earn an M.S. in Art Education at the Illinois Institute of Technology one year after completing his B.A. degree. Eisner taught art at Carl Schurz High School in Chicago from 1956–1958, and he taught art at the famous laboratory school at the University of Chicago from 1958–1960. In 1962 Eisner received his Ph.D. in Education at the University of Chicago and worked as an assistant professor of education at the University of Chicago from 1962–1965. Moving to Stanford University in 1965, he quickly climbed up the academic ladder to Professor of Education and Art.

Eisner's unique contribution to supervision has been the observation technique called educational criticism, in which the observer attends to the implicit classroom processes that are often missed by other forms of observation. The ability to be an educational critic depends on a person's capacity to see the subtleties of classroom interactions. Eisner refers to this ability as educational connoisseurship, and he submits that this type of observation requires that the observer be immersed in the classroom setting, using an artistic eye to see beyond obvious meanings. Although educational criticism has not entered the mainstream of classroom observation, the concept of the educational connoisseur is now a mainstay of most supervision texts.

Eisner also has endorsed recent research by cognitive scientists to expand the study of human intelligence and human development to include the arts and aesthetics. Eisner is quick to acknowledge, however, that society in general, and education in particular, have restricted opportunities to work in the arts. In addition to being selected as the president of the American Educational Research Association, Eisner has presented and/or published over one hundred papers, and it is quite clear that he will continue to enrich our understanding of the important linkages between art, education, and supervision.

A humanist at heart, he fears that in the postindustrial age of computers and high technology the individual will be lost and to quote Jacques Ellul, that "technology the servant will become the master." As a result his work and indeed his life epitomize the truism that teaching is fundamentally a human enterprise.

REFLECTION QUESTIONS

What examples of the educational critic have you seen in public schools?

What aspects of Eisner's ideas are well suited to the type of supervision or coaching you might employ?

How have Eisner's personal and professional experiences shaped his ideas about supervision?

cational criticism requires the observer to find the deep structure (underlying meanings) of the classroom events, and to disclose the interpretations to the teacher for corroboration or verification.

Perhaps the best way to clarify this type of observational skill is through a demonstration. The following excerpts are from an observation initiated by Elliot Eisner. The observation is conducted with former United States Secretary of Education William Bennett who is teaching a high school civics class (Eisner, 1986):

> "All right, let's get to work. I'm putting my name on the board so you can write me if I make mistakes."
>
> Sarcastic? Hard to tell. Neither Bennett nor the students laugh. Perhaps he is serious. With preliminaries over, our champion takes off his suit, hangs it on the chair adjacent to the desk, rolls up his sleeves, and begins to pace back and forth in front of the room. "Why read Federalist 10? Why bother? Why not watch the Georgia-Alabama game?" His voice, his slight crouch, his hand gestures—but most of all the intensity of his gaze leave no doubt that this is a serious encounter. "Let's get to work," his opening phrase, is apt. Today's lesson will be no "once over lightly," no open-ended, superficial discussion of anything on anyone's mind, but a serious examination of the ideas which he seems to care about deeply . . ." (pp. 2–4)

Even this brief excerpt of educational criticism gives you a keen insight into classroom events. The use of selective quotes, along with running interpretation, creates a vivid rendering of Bennett's instruction. You also can recognize that this type of observation requires both keen observation skills and interpretation skills, moving beyond the obvious classroom events. This technique is more difficult to learn, serves as an example of potential observer bias, and requires a high level of trust between the supervisor and the teacher; otherwise there is a high likelihood the supervisor will cause irrevocable damage to the supervisor-teacher relationship (Tracy & MacNaughton, 1993). Sergiovanni and Starratt (1993) suggest that educational criticism can be useful after more objective and less threatening data have been collected. Another limitation of this approach is that it is not that helpful in identifying specific instructional processes. Thus it does not lend itself to coaching programs. Finally, if you recall our earlier discussions of conceptual complexity, you might also surmise that this observation technique should only be used in the later phases of a supervisory or coaching relationship in which the teacher being observed is more mature and eager to try educational criticism.

QUALITATIVE / QUANTITATIVE OBSERVATION SYSTEMS

A second family of observation systems blend qualitative and quantitative strategies. As such, they blend description (the nature of teaching) with quantity (the amount of teaching behaviors).

Verbatim Observation (Scripting). Verbatim observation or scripting requires the observer to capture all verbal teacher comments, students' comments, and teacher-student interactions. Since it is extremely difficult to record all verbal behaviors, observers often resort to abbreviations to simplify the recording process. There is little bias when verbatim scripting is done because the data (verbal statements) have not been screened or selectively recorded.

There are three limitations regarding verbatim observation. As we just mentioned, verbatim observations require the observer to record *all* verbal behaviors and this can be difficult. A second limitation is that the data may be so extensive that it is challenging to draw meaning from the data. Once again, the skill and development of both the supervisor and teacher come into play. Teachers at more complex psychological states will be able to draw richer meaning from data (Oja & Reiman, 1997). If the teacher is less tolerant of ambiguity and less reflective, the post-observation conference would require the supervisor or coach to guide the discussion by drawing the teacher's attention to selected data. A final limitation is that verbatim observations leave out anecdotal information and/or nonverbal communication which could provide important information about the classroom context.

Selective Verbatim Observations. Selective verbatim observations record only a specific type of verbal behavior. For example, a teacher involved in a peer coaching program might be interested in the types of positive reinforcement statements she gives to students. Having been introduced to positive reinforcement, and recognizing that positive reinforcement has a strong relationship with student achievement (effect size of 1.17), the teacher might have a colleague selectively record only those specific verbal positive

EXHIBIT 10-2 POSITIVE REINFORCEMENT OBSERVATION FORM

Teacher:_____ Date:_____

Observer:_____

1. When a student answered a question correctly or asked a good question, did the teacher reward the student with words such as "Fine!" "Good!," "Excellent!" and give a reason for the reinforcement? Example: "Excellent thinking." "Thoughtful answer." Yes_____ No_____ Write examples of the words or phrases used:

2. Identify nonverbal cues (e.g., a smile, proximity, or a nod of the head) that the teacher used to encourage the students. Write examples:

3. When a student gave an answer that was only partially correct, did the teacher give credit for the correct part (differentiated reinforcement)? Write examples:

4. List examples where the teacher referred to positive aspects of a student's previous responses (delayed reinforcement):

reinforcements (e.g., simple acknowledgments, differentiated reinforcement statements, delayed reinforcements, and nonverbal reinforcements). A sample observation form follows to ascertain the teacher's positive reinforcement of students (see Exhibit 10-2).

There are several strengths of the selective verbatim observation. It is relatively easy to use, and the focused data collection complements the coaching process originally described by Joyce and Showers (1995) which has been integrated into this text. As we discussed, instructional peer coaching encourages teacher colleagues to expand their instructional repertoire by focusing on specific models and methods of instruction using a learning sequence of study (readings/workshops), observation/demonstration (seeing the skill or teaching model in use), practicing the skill with follow-up discussion, and then adapting the model or method (executive control which is reached through more practice and/or a clinical cycle of supervision). We have found that supervisors, mentor teachers, teachers in peer coaching programs, and teacher educators have found the selective verbatim technique to be a valuable, low inference procedure that is highly correlated with effective teaching. Acheson and Gall (1992) provide the most complete descriptions of this observation technique.

Perhaps the major criticism of the selective verbatim observation is that it might inappropriately advantage the teacher. The critics argue that because the teacher knows exactly what the observational focus is, he or she can intentionally stack the deck, so to speak, teaching to the observation form. Thus the data do not give a true picture of the teacher's actual instruction. Perhaps this critique is legitimate if the nature of the observation is evaluative, attempting to pinpoint a teacher's quality of instruction at a given point in time. If, however, the focus is on learning and formative growth, we would argue that every opportunity should be provided for the teacher to be successful. Further, the written coaching plan that we have introduced requires that the instructional focus be explicitly identified so as to promote coaching (see Chapter 12).

QUANTITATIVE (NARROW-LENS) OBSERVATION SYSTEMS

At the narrowest end of the camera lens analogy are observation systems that collect data that can be quantified. Typically these data collection procedures record frequency of specified instructional behaviors. Additionally, time may be a variable in data collection. For example, the observer might record data every 3 seconds as is required in the Flanders Interaction Analysis System (Flanders, 1970). Quantitative observation systems usually focus on discrete instructional behaviors, collect quantifiable data, and often are easy to use. An additional asset of quantitative observation systems is their adaptation to unique instructional circumstances. As Tracy and MacNaughton (1993) point out, teacher/supervisor-constructed observation instruments often are quantitative in focus. There are three broad formats for quantitative observation systems: category frequency, visual diagramming, and event or time-dependent. An example of each follows.

Categorical Frequency Format. The categorical frequency format identifies a set of behaviors to be observed. The observer then tallies when a category of behavior is employed. Thus the frequency (amount) of identified behaviors can be determined. One example of a categorical frequency format would be an observation form for questioning skills (see Exhibit 10-3).

EXHIBIT 10-3   OBSERVATION OF QUESTIONING SKILLS

FREQUENCY   CATEGORY—QUESTIONING SKILLS

_____ 1. Paused before calling on a student OR
          _____ used the student's name before question.

_____ 2. Rewarded answer.

_____ 3. Asked question in another way if the student had difficulty answering.

_____ 4. Asked for clarification if needed.

_____ 5. Answered the question if the student was unable to answer.

_____ Memory
_____ Comprehension
_____ Application
_____ Analysis
_____ Synthesis
_____ Evaluation

Visual Diagramming. A popular quantitative observation system that Glickman, Gordon, and Ross-Gordon (1995) refer to as visual diagramming requires the observer to draw a picture of classroom events for later analysis. This type of system can be very useful for ascertaining equitable or inequitable teacher-student interactions and for describing teacher or student movement. Take as an example the picture of teacher-student verbal interactions quantified by number of response opportunities (see Figure 10-1).

As you can see, diagramming is easy to interpret. The diagram not only shows response opportunities the teacher provided, but it identifies those students that responded. As you can tell, the identifying of students by gender or ethnicity enables the observer to ascertain possible trends or patterns in in-

FIGURE 10-1   VISUAL DIAGRAM OF TEACHER-STUDENT RESPONSE
OPPORTUNITIES BY GENDER

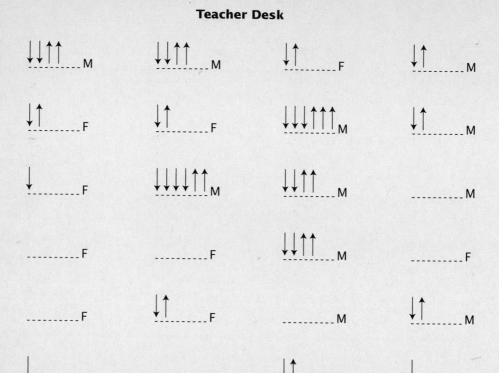

Teacher Desk

↓ = Teacher response opportunity (The teacher verbally provided an opportunity for student talk—for example, a direction or question).

↑ = Student response.

struction. This type of observation can be modified to show teacher or student movement. One caution when observing equity is the need for a high degree of trust in the supervisory relationship. The discovery that one's instruction favors males or white students can be painful and alarming. However, it is the first step toward creating more equitable instruction. Thus it is important for the teachers to be motivated to look at their own instructional equity.

Event or Time-Dependent Systems. The observation system developed by Ned Flanders (1970) is an example of the category frequency format. Flanders and his associates clustered teacher talk into seven categories and student talk into three categories (see Exhibit 10-4).

Exhibit 10-4   FLANDERS INTERACTION ANALYSIS

Who Is Talking?	Type of Influence	Type of Interaction
Teacher Talk	Indirect Influence	1. *Accepts feelings*: Accepts and clarifies the feeling tone of the students in a nonthreatening manner. Feelings may be positive or negative. Predicting and recalling feelings are included.
		2. *Praises or encourages*: Praises or encourages student action or behavior. Jokes that release tension, not at the expense of another, nodding head, or saying "uh-huh" or "go on" are included.
		3. *Accepts or uses ideas of student*: Clarifying, building, or developing ideas or suggestions by students. As teacher brings more of his or her own ideas into play, shift to Category 5.
		4. *Asks questions*: Asking a question about content or procedure with the intent that a student will answer.
	Direct Influence	5. *Lectures*: Giving facts, opinions about content or procedure, expressing his or her own ideas, asking rhetorical questions.
		6. *Gives directions*: Directions, commands, or orders with which a student is expected to comply.
		7. *Criticizes or justifies authority*: Statements intended to change student behavior from nonacceptable to acceptable pattern; reprimanding someone, stating why the teacher is doing what he or she is doing, extreme self-reference.
Student Talk		8. *Student talk-response*: Talk by students in response to teacher. Teacher initiates the contact or solicits student statement.
		9. *Student talk-initiation*: Talk by students that they initiate. If calling on students is only way to indicate who may talk next, observer must decide whether student wanted to talk. If he or she did, use this category.
		10. *Silence or confusion*: Pauses, short period of silence, and periods of confusion in which communication cannot be understood by the observer.

Source: From *Analyzing Teaching Behavior* (p. 34), by N. A. Flanders, 1970, Reading, MA: Addison-Wesley. Reprinted with permission of the author.

NED FLANDERS

It is no exaggeration to acknowledge Ned Flanders as the father of contemporary classroom observation systems. Born in 1918 and raised on the West Coast, Flanders earned an A.B. degree in chemistry at the University of California and a B.S. in electrical engineering from Oregon State College in 1944. However he changed fields, earning his master's degree and Ph.D. at the University of Chicago in educational psychology. After working as an assistant professor at the University of Chicago he moved to the University of Minnesota. It was during his time at Minnesota that his research and scholarship matured.

Flanders was fascinated by the complexities of classroom interaction and was eager to study and explain teaching effectiveness. Prior to his work, literally hundreds of studies had been conducted on teaching effectiveness, yielding few patterns and even fewer significant results. Researchers had sought teacher characteristics that could be correlated with classroom effectiveness such as warmth, overall temperament, or cultural background.

Flanders succeeded where other researchers had failed. He was able to create a practical model, based on thousands of hours of classroom observation, that broadly defined teacher-student interaction. His model is called the Flanders Interaction Analysis System. Teacher interaction is categorized as direct or indirect, and the model also accounts for the ratio of teacher talk to student talk. Implementing an extensive series of field studies, he found that with various subject matters, at different grade levels, and in different school settings, teachers with more indirect styles produced higher levels of academic learning in their students.

In later years he referred to his research as an inquiry into human interaction models. His choice of terminology was purposeful. "The use of the word human in the phrase 'human interaction model' is a reminder that my model of teaching is concerned with rich human experience and it should have the capacity to synthesize the affective and cognitive in a way that would please John Dewey or Søren Kierkegaard were they alive today" (1987, p. 20).*

Ultimately his model concerns teacher flexibility—the ability of a teacher to change patterns of interaction according to the exigencies of the moment as well as to carry out different teaching functions during various phases of the same lesson. Flexibility also concerns the supervisor or the peer coach who is attempting to support a colleague. Having retired to San Francisco, Flanders maintains an interest in teacher behavior and in the adaptation of his system to other realms of teacher and counselor reflection and professional development. He still worries, however, that his system of classroom interaction will become reified. So much so that even in his current correspondence with the authors of this volume, he carefully reiterates the need to view effective teaching as the ability to use all forms of influence. The master teacher must master all forms, direct and indirect, and student talk, and then use the ratios that enhance student learning.

REFLECTION QUESTIONS

How did Flanders' work examine "rich human interaction"?

Why does the Flanders model address teacher flexibility?

*Flanders, N. A. (1987). Human interaction models. In M. J. Dunkin (Ed.), *The international encyclopedia of teaching and teacher education* (pp. 20–27). New York: Pergamon.

The Flanders Interaction Analysis System classifies all teacher talk as either indirect or direct. Student talk is classified as response (to a question or request), or initiation. The final category is silence or confusion. In the Flanders system verbal interaction is coded on one of the ten categories every 3 to 5 seconds. Thus a minute of instruction would have 12 to 20 tallies.

When a teacher "What is the length of the hypotenuse of the right triangle?" the observer would code that statement as Category 4, question. The observer marks a category every 3 to 5 seconds or whenever the behavior changes, whichever comes first. There are several ways to analyze the data. The least difficult is to simply review the numbers noting patterns (see Exhibit 10-5).

EXHIBIT 10-5 COMPLETED FLANDERS INTERACTION ANALYSIS SHEET

1. 5	10. 8	19. 9	28. 9
2. 5	11. 2	20. 9	29. 9
3. 10	12. 2	21. 9	30. 9
4. 9	13. 4	22. 9	31. 4
5. 9	14. 8	23. 3	32. 8
6. 3	15. 3	24. 3	33. 2
7. 3	16. 3	25. 3	34. 5
8. 4	17. 6	26. 9	35. 5
9. 8	18. 10	27. 1	36. 5

In this 2-minute teaching episode the teacher and students are engaged in a discussion and there is a fairly high amount of student-initiated talk. Another way to analyze the data is to count the tallies for each category and then to determine the percentages for each category for Indirect, Direct, Teacher Talk and Student Talk. To obtain the percentage of a specific behavior in relation to the total interaction, divide the total into each subtotal. To determine the percentage of indirect or direct teacher statements, divide the total number of indirect statements (Categories 1 to 4) by the total number of teacher talk categories (1 to 7). To determine the percentage of teacher talk, divide the total number of teacher talk categories (1 to 7) by the total talk categories (1 to 9). Exhibit 10-6 displays an analysis of the data presented in Exhibit 10-5.

The strengths of this quantitative observation system are its comprehensiveness as well as the variety of kinds of data that can be summarized (e.g., ratio of teacher talk to student talk, ratio of indirect to direct teacher influence). From an adult growth perspective, we also have found that teachers can draw many conclusions from Interaction Analysis data. In fact, with moderately complex teachers it often encourages deeper reflection on the discrepancy between their espoused focus on high student interaction and the reality that much of the instruction is teacher talk (Categories 5, 6, and 7). Additionally, if the instrument is used with peer coaching programs, the teachers can focus on discrete focuses like increasing the amount of indirect instruction or increasing the amount of student talk. Naturally the limitation of the Flanders system is its difficulty to master. We have found, however, that prospective supervisors and teachers participating in school staff development programs like peer coaching can become proficient in using the system if they are provided with opportunities for practice.

EXHIBIT 10-6 FLANDERS INTERACTION ANALYSIS SUMMARY SHEET

| | (Teacher Talk) | | | | | | | (Student Talk: 8–9) | | |
	(Indirect: 1–4)				(Direct: 5–7)					
Category	1	2	3	4	5	6	7	8	9	10
Subtotals	1	3	7	3	5	1	0	4	10	2
Category %	2.7	8.3	19.4	8.3	13.8	2.7	0	11.1	27.7	5.5

Indirect %	70.0 (Divide 1–4 by 1–7)
Direct %	30.0 (Divide 5–7 by 1–7)
Teacher Talk %	58.8 (Divide 1–7 by 1–9)
Student Talk %	41.2 (Divide 8–9 by 1–9)

Source: Adapted from S. J. Tracy and R. MacNaughton, *Assisting and Assessing Educational Personnel: The Impact of Clinical Supervision,* 1993, Needham Heights, MA: Allyn and Bacon.

RECOMMENDATIONS FOR DATA GATHERING AND ANALYSIS

As you can see, there are a variety of observation techniques and your goal is to develop skill in using a number of them. The type of observation that is employed should be anchored to the requests and instructional needs of the teacher. Remember that the coaching model would require the teacher to use the observation instrument during a demonstration lesson, and as he or she practices the new skill. Therefore the teacher should be well familiar with the observation instrument and comfortable with having it used in a clinical cycle of supervision.

Further, the quantitative and qualitative observation approaches described in this chapter require analysis once they have been completed. Regardless of the type of supervision (e.g., supervisor-teacher, mentor-protégé, peer coaching partners, or teacher educator and student intern), we recommend that the data be analyzed and reflected on by both persons. For both the supervisor and teacher, the analysis should consider the following questions:

- How effectively do the data support the teaching behavior focus that was selected for the written coaching plan?
- Were the learning outcomes met?
- Did classroom management support or interfere with the lesson?

We recommend that the teacher reflect in writing before the post-observation conference (see Exhibit 10-7). Remember that the goal of developmental supervision is to promote the learning and development of the colleague. Therefore it is most important that you always let the teacher first respond to each of the questions during the post-observation conference.

COMPARING OBSERVATION SYSTEMS WITH TEACHER LEARNING AND DEVELOPMENT

As we have mentioned throughout the text the Teaching/Learning Framework guides the work of the supervisor and teacher. Recall that coaching requires a specific focus on a teaching model or method. Also recall that a crucial condition for adult growth is ongoing reflection. Further, remember that a goal for the supervisor or teacher educator is to expertly match (starting where the adult learner is), and then mismatch (providing a slight constructive challenge) cognitive approaches for teacher development. Thus developmental supervisors not only must select observation systems based on teachers' needs and motivations, they must also be aware of how a particular observation system matches or mismatches with the teacher, links to coaching, and promotes deeper reflection of teaching, learning, self, and others. Exhibit 10-8 illustrates the types of observations described in this chapter, their complexity (e.g., ease of use in data gathering and interpretation),

CONTEMPORARY ISSUES

The Assistance/Assessment Dilemma

There continues to be a raging debate over the relationship between assistance and assessment. It is generally agreed that assistance promotes learning, growth, and development. Rather than measuring the minimum competencies needed to maintain your job, assistance starts where the learner is, and then designs plans for promoting new skill acquisition and development. The coaching process and the conditions for growth described in this text lend themselves to the assistance process. The assumption is that every teacher and supervisor can expand his or her instructional repertoire and psychological maturity.

In contrast, assessment implies "quality control" (Sergiovanni & Starratt, 1993), providing organizations with a means of maintaining certain minimum standards of performance. Thus assessment can lead to decisions about dismissing a teacher (Manatt, 1983). Assessment results in judgments.

To further complicate things, assessment responsibilities are often relegated to administrative staff while assistance strategies are conducted by teachers, for example in peer coaching and mentoring programs. Yet some educators are calling for more review of performance (assessment) by teachers (peer review), similar to other professions like law and medicine. Yet McGreal (1983) reports that 98 percent of teachers are at least minimally competent, thus raising questions about the need for assessment. And Popham (1988) argues that the mixing of assessment and assistance cannot be carried out simultaneously by administrators.

How would you resolve this dilemma? Would you only employ supervision as assistance because so many teachers would benefit? On the other hand, isn't there a need to maintain "quality control" for the good of the profession? Or perhaps you would side with scholars such as Hunter (1988), who argues that assisting and assessing are sequential and inseparable processes leading to the same outcome—improved teacher performance. What about growth and development? If promoting greater flexibility, self-understanding, and principled thinking are the most important goals, doesn't it make sense to focus on assistance?

We advocate a separation of assistance and assessment responsibilities. Administrators play important roles in assessment, and they can provide the conditions in their school for effective assistance between teachers. Thus they need to be familiar with the concepts discussed in this text. However, the teacher never forgets the assessor role. Besides, as Tracy and MacNaughton point out (1993), most principals and assistant principals simply have too many teachers to blend the functions of assessment and assistance. Therefore, teachers must become key players in supervision as it relates to assistance.

Exhibit 10-7 SELF-ASSESSMENT OF A LESSON

You are encouraged to reflect on the lesson and to respond to the questions below before the post-observation conference.

1. Were the learning outcomes met?

   Evidence:

2. Was the teaching behavior focus met?

   Evidence:

3. Did classroom management interfere with or support the lesson?

   Place a check. Interfered_____ Supported

                 1   2   3   4   5

Evidence:

4. Other:
   Continue doing:

   Change:

EXHIBIT 10-8 COMPARING OBSERVATION SYSTEMS FOR COACHING AND TEACHER DEVELOPMENT

	METHOD			COMPLEXITY OF APPROACH	COACHING EXPERTISE NEEDED	REFLECTIVE POTENTIAL
TYPE	QUANTITATIVE	BOTH	QUALITATIVE			
Video			X	Mod.*	Mod.	High
Audio			X	Low	Mod.	Mod.
Focused questionnaire			X	Mod.	Mod.	Mod.
Educational criticism			X	High	Low	High
Narrative			X	High	Low	High
Verbatim		X		High	Low	Mod.
Selective verbatim		X		Low	High	Mod.
Categorical frequency	X			Low	High	Mod.
Visual diagram	X			Low	High	High
Event or time coding	X			Mod./High	High	Low to High

*Mod. = Moderate.

their adaptability to coaching, and their potential to encourage reflection on the deeper structure of teaching/learning.

As you can see, the various observation methods differ in ease of use, adaptability to coaching programs (teacher education or staff development), and reflective potential. Those methods that are easier to use and that place fewer affective and cognitive demands on a person might be more accessible to teachers at less complex conceptual levels. Fortunately many of these methods also link well to coaching. On the other hand, teachers at more complex psychological states (e.g., conceptual, moral, self) would probably be more open to and interested in more complex observation systems. However, some of these methods (i.e., verbatim and educational criticism) are not easily adapted to a coaching program. Additionally, some observation methods like Flanders interaction analysis (event or time coding) and video may be more difficult to employ but should be used because they link to coaching and encourage deeper reflection (Russell & Spafford, 1986).

 SUMMARY

The material presented in this chapter provided a general introduction to some of the techniques employed by supervisors and teaching colleagues (mentors). The goal is for the supervisor or mentor to have a repertoire of observation techniques from which to draw. The chapter introduced a range of data collection strategies including qualitative instruments like narrative observation that provide rich description of the classroom context, qualitative/quantitative methods that combine description with detail, and quantitative methods like visual diagrams or categorical frequency instruments that concentrate on the amount of a specified instructional behavior.

As you should now recognize, different methods of instruction have both strengths and limitations. For example a verbatim script of a lesson provides an abundance of information, but it does not interface with instructional peer coaching as well because coaching identifies specific methods or models of instruction that are being learned. We also pointed out that some observation methods are better suited to teachers at less complex psychological stages. For this reason, it is important for you the supervisor to be able to understand and apply a variety of observation methods according to the needs of the adult learner.

In-class observations refine and expand on teachers' instructional repertoire. Further, when the data on the observation instrument are consistent with what the teacher and supervisor agreed to focus on and later discuss, it promotes professional growth. Thus data collection techniques are used to describe, not to evaluate, and they are based on prior agreement (pre-observation conference or coaching plan). An evaluation instrument, in contrast, is intended to summarize and judge professional competence, and it is implemented with all teachers using similar criteria.

Initial observations need to capture the wider span of classroom activities because they form the basis for subsequent planning, coaching, and supervision. As the supervisory or coaching relationship progresses, the observations will become more focused on desired areas of instruction. Typically the progression in observations moves from wide-lens (qualitative) to narrow lens (quantitative) (Acheson and Gall, 1992). Note that in the applied activities we ask you to tailor an observation instrument. We consider this skill important because supervisors and mentors are confronted regularly with the need to adapt or create observation instruments that meet the needs of the teacher. In Chapter 11 we examine how the observation data can be most advantageously used in a post-observation conference. You might want to give special attention to how the methods described attempt to differentiate structure according to the needs of the adult learner. Also note how the conversation is framed by input from the teacher.

SUPERVISION FOR TEACHER DEVELOPMENT ACTIVITIES

APPLIED

1. Select one of the observation methods reviewed in the chapter. Redesign the instrument to meet an instructional focus you deem important (e.g., giving directions, cooperative learning, active listening). Name your observation instrument.

2. Try out your tailored observation instrument on a lesson you conduct (approximately 30 minutes). This will require that you audiotape or videotape the lesson and then self-assess.

3. Write an analysis of the tailored observation instrument. Label the form to identify the type of data collected (e.g., selective verbatim, narrative, visual diagram). Answer the following questions: Was your instrument easy or difficult to use and why? Could your instrument be used in a peer coaching program? How does your instrument encourage reflection? What changes would you make to improve the observation instrument?

4. Begin to build a data collection bank of observation forms.

PORTFOLIO

1. Place a copy of the tailored observation instrument in your supervisory portfolio entitled "Observation Methods." Include your written self-analysis of observation form.

2. Write reflections according to your own interests. After your instructor has responded to the reflections, date and file them in your portfolio.

SUGGESTED READINGS

1. Acheson, K., & Gall, M. (1992). *Techniques in the clinical supervision of teachers* (3rd ed.). New York: Longman.

This is the best review of classroom observation techniques.

REFERENCES

Acheson, K., & Gall, M. (1992). *Techniques in the clinical supervision of teachers: Preservice and inservice applications* (3rd ed.). New York: Longman.

Bauer, L. K. (1986). Teacher attitude toward supervisory practices of elementary school principals (Doctoral dissertation, Arizona State University). *Dissertation Abstracts International, 47*, 1540A.

Chunn, G. F. (1985). Perceptions of teachers and principals concerning behaviors and attitudes that contribute to an effective supervisory cycle (Doctoral dissertation, University of Mississippi). *Dissertation Abstracts International, 46*, 2494A.

Eisner, E. (1985). *The educational imagination: On the design and evaluation of school programs* (2nd ed.). New York: Macmillan.

Eisner, E. (1986, April). *The secretary in the classroom.* Paper presented to the American Educational Research Association, San Francisco, CA.

Flanders, N. (1970). *Analyzing teaching behavior.* Reading, MA: Addison-Wesley.

Garman, N. B. (1986). Clinical supervision: Quackery or remedy for professional development? *Journal of Curriculum and Supervision, 1*(2), 148–157.

Glickman, C., Gordon, S., & Ross-Gordon, J. (1995). *Supervision of instruction* (3rd ed.). Needham Heights, MA: Allyn and Bacon.

Hunter, M. (1988). Effecting a reconciliation between supervision and evaluation: A reply to Popham. *Journal of Personnel Evaluation in Education, 1*(3), 275–279.

Joyce, B., & Showers, B. (1995). *Staff development for student achievement* (2nd ed.). New York: Longman.

Manatt, R. (1983). *Supervising the marginal teacher: A videotape.* Alexandria, VA: Association for Supervision and Curriculum Development.

McGreal, T. L. (1983). *Successful teacher evaluation.* Alexandria, VA: Association for Supervision and Curriculum Development.

Medley, D. M., & Mizel, H. E. (1963). Measuring classroom behavior by systematic observation. In N. L. Gage (Ed.), *Handbook of research on teaching.* Skokie, IL: Rand McNally.

Oja, S. N., & Reiman, A. J. (1997). Describing and promoting supervision for teacher development across the career-span. In J. Firth & E. Pajak (Eds.), *Handbook of research on school supervision.* New York: Macmillan.

Popham, W. J. (1988). The dysfunctional marriage of formative and summative teacher evaluation. *Journal of Personnel Evaluation in Education, 1*(3), 269–273.

Russell, T. L., & Spafford, C. (1986, April). *Teachers as reflective practitioners in peer clinical supervision.* Paper presented at the American Educational Research Association, San Francisco, CA.

Sergiovanni, T. J., & Starratt, R. (1993). *Supervision: A redefinition* (5th ed.). New York: McGraw-Hill.

Showers, B., Joyce, B., & Bennett, B. (1987). Synthesis of research on staff development: A framework for further study and a state-of-the-art analysis. *Educational Leadership, 45*(3), 77–87.

Tracy, S. J., & MacNaughton, R. (1993). *Assisting and assessing educational personnel: The impact of clinical supervision.* Needham Heights, MA: Allyn and Bacon.

C·H·A·P·T·E·R
11

Supervision and Post-Conferences

• • • • • •

$\mathcal{I}$n Chapter 9 the pre-conference was described as an important formalized component of developmental supervision. Chapter 10 introduced various observation instruments and how they can be adapted to the differing needs of the developing adult learner. We now turn to the role of the post-observation conference as a penultimate event in a developmental instructional supervision and coaching program. The goal of the chapter is to introduce the purpose, structure, and techniques needed to implement the post-conference and an entire cycle of assistance with a teacher.

As you review the chapter, check your comprehension by answering the following questions:

- What are the main elements of a post-observation conference?
- How is the conference differentiated according to the developmental needs of the teacher?
- How does a supervisor link the post-conference to the next steps in the supervisory relationship?

 ## RATIONALE FOR POST-CONFERENCES

In a study reported by Kiley (1988), 96 percent of a large sample of teachers commented on their strong desire to participate in a conference following their classroom observation. Likewise, national studies indicate that teachers want to be observed more frequently, they are interested in receiving more feedback about their teaching, and they want to talk more about classroom instruction and student learning (Glickman & Rogers, 1988; Little, 1982).

Unfortunately, in the study conducted by Kiley (1988), 19 percent of the teachers surveyed indicated that they had never participated in a feedback conference. And a study by Blankenship and Irvine (1985) found that 50 percent of experienced teachers in one state had never in their careers been observed, been given feedback, or had a conference focused on instructional improvement. Further, recent studies of support groups for beginning teachers indicate that such experiences promote greater teacher self-efficacy, reduce teachers' personal concerns, and promote increased concern about student learning and student welfare (Reiman, Bostic, Lassiter, & Cooper, 1995; Thies-Sprinthall & Gerler, 1990).

Thus it would appear that the stage would be set for individual and group supervision as important and valued components of teachers' personal and professional growth (Oja & Reiman, 1997). This is certainly the case if the instructional supervision and coaching process engages teachers in authentic, intellectual, and nonevaluative learning and development (Anderson & Snyder, 1993; Cogan, 1973). In this context, the post-conference becomes a teacher-valued process that furthers peer coaching, mentoring, and supervision.

 ## POST-OBSERVATION CONFERENCES

During the post-conference the supervisor guides the teacher through an analysis of the lesson observed. Whenever possible, the supervisor or mentor solicits the perceptions of the teacher, asking what his or her response was to selected questions on the self-analysis sheet (see Chapters 9 and 10), promoting the ability to reflect on practice through questioning. It is most important that the teacher have time to complete this self-analysis before the post-conference. Only after the teacher's perceptions are shared does the supervisor offer his or her own perceptions. Once again, development makes a difference. For example, if the teacher has many personal concerns, these feelings probably will surface in the post-conference and must be addressed. Furthermore, conceptual, ego, and moral stage will affect how the conference is structured. Teachers at Stage A will have more difficulty analyzing their own actions, will be less confident, and may be prone to defer to the wishes of the supervisor (Glickman, Gordon, & Ross-Gordon, 1995). Therefore, the supervisor should be prepared to ask leading questions to elicit the information, to actively listen, and to supply his or her own perceptions as a springboard for discussion.

During the post-conference, the supervisor meets with the teacher to discuss feelings, the lesson's learning outcomes, classroom management, the teaching behavior focus, the focus for the next coaching plan, and summary. As we mentioned previously, early in the supervisory relationship, the supervisor takes a more dominant role. As the teacher becomes more familiar with the clinical processes, and as the supervisor learns more about the current development of the teacher, the process becomes more collegial. The post-observation conference includes six elements:

1. Discussion of feelings
2. Review of the learning outcomes
3. Discussion of classroom management
4. Review of the teaching behavior focus
5. Focus for the next coaching cycle
6. Summary

DISCUSSION OF FEELINGS

Once again, feelings of both the teacher and supervisor are solicited. Furthermore, the supervisor should employ active listening. This is a very important juncture in the conference. You may think the lesson went remarkably well, yet the teacher begins by reporting distress and dismay. Thus, you need to take a deep breath and be prepared to focus in on the feelings. How you ask for feelings also may determine whether feelings or thoughts are shared. If you ask, "How are you feeling about the lesson?" you may get thoughts about the success of the lesson in return. By rephrasing the question, "Now that the observation is over, how are you feeling?" you increase the chances that feelings of the person will be shared. If the feelings are particularly strong, continue listening until the strong feelings are defused and the teacher appears prepared to talk about the content of the lesson. The outcome of this strategy is more meaningful learning for the teacher.

LEARNING OUTCOMES

The supervisor asks the teacher if the learning outcomes were reached, and what evidence he or she has to support that conclusion. After listening, the supervisor can share any additional data on learning outcomes. If teachers are at Stage B or Stage C conceptual level, they most likely will go into some detail as to why the learning outcomes were reached. In these cases, the supervisor only needs to agree, "My data support your conclusions." This step in the conference concludes with the supervisor asking the teacher if there are any changes he or she would have made to the learning outcomes. This question encourages deeper reflection on student learning needs and planning for instruction.

CLASSROOM MANAGEMENT

A similar sequence ensues. The supervisor requests input from the teacher about classroom management. For example, "Did your classroom management support or interfere with the objectives of the lesson?" After the teacher has responded, the supervisor offers a listening response, and then provides additional data. Finally, the supervisor asks if any changes should be made to classroom management. This question encourages deeper reflection about management.

Teaching Behavior Focus

The teaching behavior focus is a major objective of the coaching cycle. Therefore the hope is that this focus is successfully reached. The teacher is probably well prepared to elaborate on the focus with minimal probing from the supervisor. Once again, after active listening, the supervisor can offer additional feedback, and possible changes can be discussed.

Focus for the Next Coaching Cycle

At this juncture in the post-conference the teacher is asked to identify the next focus. If learning outcomes were not reached, it becomes the focus. If classroom management interfered rather than supported the lesson, it becomes the focus. If the teaching behavior focus was not mastered, additional demonstration and practice are discussed as part of a revised coaching plan. If all areas were reached, a new teaching behavior focus is selected from data collected concerning changes needed, and a new coaching plan is collaboratively composed. Such a plan explicates a review of the rationale, demonstration, and practice with the selected focus. Obviously, this discussion may take more time than is available to the supervisor and teacher. We recommend minimally that you identify the teaching behavior focus and the initial demonstration activities. This allows the teacher to begin work on the new focus. A follow-up conference may need to be scheduled to complete the new coaching plan. How the new coaching plan is structured depends on the concerns, interests, context, and developmental stage of the teacher (see Chapter 12).

Summary

We recommend that the supervisor ask the teacher to bring closure to the post-conference by summarizing the main points or main learnings. This strategy permits the teacher to once again reflect on the experience. It also allows the supervisor to observe how the teacher is making meaning of the supervisory experiences; in effect, what he or she considers important. The supervisor should close with an encouraging statement including instructional behaviors that the teacher should continue to use.

In Exhibit 11-1 the post-observation conference sequence is outlined. We now turn to three case studies of the post-conference for teachers with different concerns and at qualitatively different cognitive-developmental stages.

CONTEMPORARY ISSUES

STRESS

A number of prominent persons in the field of supervision have acknowledged that instructional supervision entails quite a bit of stress and anxiety. They cite case studies and clinical studies that describe dissonance and anxiety as major factors to address in supervision. Can you recall the first time you were observed? For most of us the anxiety is significant. Naturally some stress is okay, but when stress becomes great, learning comes to a screeching halt. Scholars in the field of supervision have emphasized the importance of warm, trusting, and creative human relationships between the supervisor and the teacher to reduce stress. If the supervisor or mentor can convey empathy and regard, the teacher will be able to learn more effectively and take risks and creative leaps in his or her teaching.

The leading exponents of this model are Ralph Mosher and David Purpel (1972), Norman Kagan (1980), Arthur Blumberg (1980), and Elliot Eisner (1982). For example, Mosher and Purpel were very concerned about the quality of the relationship between the teacher and the supervisor. Their approach incorporates counseling as well as group supervision. The primacy of working with teachers as people comes through loud and clear in their writing:

> It is a crucial component in the process of teaching teachers, we believe, to work with teachers as people. Our reasoning is founded on the belief that what the teacher is *personally* affects what he does, how he teaches and what the pupils do and learn. In order to improve classroom instruction, implement a curriculum or affect children's formal learning, the supervisor must take into account the powerful contributing effect of the teacher's personality and his relationship with the child. (p. 4)

For Mosher and Purpel, the student teacher or beginning teacher brings significant intellectual and emotional stress to the supervisory conferences. Thus, there is a need for counseling approaches and practices attuned to the person. It is important to add that Mosher and Purpel believe that attention to the affective domain contributes to increased self-knowledge.

Likewise, Blumberg described the importance of quality human relationships between supervisors and teachers. His work is based on the repeated observation that low trust and regard, lack of empathy, defensiveness, secrecy, and competition are common attributes of supervisory relationships. Drawing on the extensive work of Ned Flanders, he fashioned a framework for analyzing one's own supervisory conference interactions. He believed that careful attention to this data could lead to more humane conferencing skills.

Perhaps the most widely known supervision approach using videotape is Interpersonal Process Recall (Kagan, 1976, 1980; Kagan & Krathwohl, 1967). Kagan asserted that there are many psychological barriers to complete communication in supervision. Among these barriers is the habit of behaving diplomatically. The process of IPR is relatively simple. The supervisor and the colleague view a prerecorded videotape of a supervisory conference, observation, or planning session together. At any point either person can stop the videotape and share an idea or feeling that occurred at that point in the session. For example, a teacher might stop the tape, saying, "I was really frustrated here. I didn't understand the student's question, and I was worried that whatever I would say would make me look like I wasn't in command of the material in the book." At this point, it is important for the supervisor not to assume the teaching role, instructing the teacher on the "correct" course of action. Instead, the supervisor actively listens and then asks additional questions, encouraging greater exploration of the concern.

Elliot Eisner, who has a disdain for the term "supervision," recommends an approach in which the supervisor acts more as a consultant, responding to the "client's" needs. The supervisor in this role would have an extensive background in the subtleties and complexities of the schooling enterprise. Furthermore, the contacts and observations would occur over an extended period of time, thus providing an opportunity to develop rapport and trust.

Each of these scholars is convinced that traditional supervision is too impersonal and aloof. The end result is that the teacher and supervisor are engaged in a kind of interpersonal warfare, characterized by defensiveness, high stress, and minimal learning. In their minds, quality human interaction catapults the supervision to new heights.

Obviously, the exclusive focus on warm trusting relationships is unsatisfactory. But the work of these individuals has reinforced what the massive meta-analysis by Wang, Haertel, and Walberg (1993) found, that the morale in a setting influences learning. Perhaps we should view the interpersonal aspects of developmental supervision as very necessary but not sufficient for effective supervision.

Case Study—Tom

On the following post-conference observation sheet, selective verbatim comments by the supervisor and Tom are noted. Recall that Tom's coaching plan focused on using more higher-level questions. He has seen demonstrations and has practiced the skill. The supervisor has concluded that Tom initially needs high structure, and that his concerns are primarily at the personal and management levels. As you read the case study, note how the supervisor uses matching or mismatching responses according to Tom's conceptual level, Stage A (see Exhibit 11-2). As a review, it might be helpful to refer to the differentiated structure table introduced in Chapter 8 (see Exhibit 11-3).

Discussion   Tom continues to be reluctant to share feelings. In response, the supervisor has identified her own feelings about observing the lesson, and she has labeled some of Tom's unstated feelings about classroom management. Both supervisor responses are mismatches for Tom, intended to

EXHIBIT 11-1 POST-CONFERENCE OBSERVATION SHEET

FOCUS

1. Feelings
   _____ Colleague feelings
   _____ Supervisor feelings
   _____ Evidence of listening

2. Learning Outcomes
   _____ Colleague shares
   _____ Evidence of listening
   _____ Supervisor shares
   _____ Changes discussed

3. Classroom Management
   _____ Colleague shares
   _____ Evidence of listening
   _____ Supervisor shares
   _____ Changes discussed

4. Teaching Behavior Focus
   _____ Colleague shares
   _____ Evidence of listening
   _____ Supervisor shares
   _____ Changes discussed

5. Focus of Next Coaching Plan
   _____ Learning outcomes
   _____ Classroom management
   _____ Refine current teaching behavior focus
   _____ Identify new teaching behavior focus
   _____ Discuss coaching plan
   _____ Evidence of listening

6. Summary
   _____ Colleague summarizes
   _____ Supervisor gives encouraging closing statement

---

prompt Tom to acknowledge feelings as an important part of making meaning out of teaching. The supervisor also asks, "What changes could be made to monitor student work during guided practice?" The question is a mismatch. How? By interjecting students into the dialogue, the supervisor is encouraging Tom to stretch his thinking to include consideration of students. This is a mismatch given Tom's present concerns about self and classroom management. Finally, you probably have noted how the supervisor has offered regular encouragement to Tom. More frequent encouragement is a match to Tom's conceptual level.

Exhibit 11-2 POST-CONFERENCE OBSERVATION SHEET—TOM

Focus	Behavior

Tom's comments are in italics.

1. Feelings
 - • Now that the lesson is over, how are you feeling?
 - __x__ Colleague feelings — • *Okay, I guess.*
 - __x__ Supervisor feelings — • You felt okay.
 - __x__ Evidence of listening — • I was excited to have the opportunity (mismatch).

2. Learning Outcomes
 - • Tell me about your learning outcomes.
 - __x__ Colleague shares — • *I think the learning outcomes were met.*
 - __x__ Evidence of listening — • Okay. Tell me more about the reasons.
 - _____ Supervisor share — • *I saw everyone label the parts except for two.*
 - __x__ Changes discussed — • Are there any changes you would make regarding the learning outcomes?
 - • *No. I thought the lesson outcomes were reached.*

3. Classroom Management
 - • Did classroom management interfere with or support the lesson?
 - __x__ Colleague shares — • *I'm not sure. A little of both. Sometimes it seemed like the class wasn't with me.*
 - __x__ Evidence of listening — • You sound uncertain and a little disappointed (mismatch).
 - • *I guess I am. I thought the lesson would be more of a success.*
 - __x__ Supervisor shares — • In general, students did raise hands. I did note 7 students who were not engaged in the lesson.
 - __x__ Changes discussed — • What changes could be made to monitor student work during guided practice (mismatch)?

4. Teaching Behavior Focus
 - • Was the teacher behavior focus reached?
 - __x__ Colleague shares — • *Yes. I had the analysis and evaluation questions written in advance. Each one was used.*
 - __x__ Evidence of listening — • Uh-hmm.
 - __x__ Supervisor shares — • My data support yours. I think the strategy of writing down the questions in advance is a terrific idea. Nice work (match).
 - __x__ Changes discussed — • Are there any changes you would make in your questioning Tom?
 - • *Not right now. I am satisfied.*

Exhibit 11-2 *(continued)*

Focus	Behavior
5. Focus of Next Coaching Plan	• What should be the next focus of the coaching plan?
_____ Learning outcomes	
__x__ Classroom management	• *You mentioned monitoring. Maybe that is an area I should work on next.*
_____ Refine current teaching behavior focus	
__x__ Identify new teaching behavior focus	• Okay. Monitoring of student behavior. I'd love to have you visit my classroom to observe my monitoring. The seating chart observation form is an excellent way to record data. Let's plan some dates and times that are convenient for visits.
_____ Discuss coaching plan	
_____ Evidence of listening	
6. Summary	• Would you summarize the main points of the conference?
_____ Colleague summarizes	
__x__ Supervisor gives encouraging closing statement	• I know you worked hard to refine your use of higher-level questioning. Nice work (match).

Exhibit 11-3 DIFFERENTIATION OF STRUCTURE

Factors	A—High Structure	→ B	→ Low Structure—C
Concepts	Concrete	Concrete Abstract	Abstract
Affect	Supervisor discloses	Mixture of A & C	Both colleague and supervisor disclose
Advance organizers	Multiple use	Moderate use	Few advance organizers needed
Complexity of learning tasks	Learning tasks divided into small steps and repeated	Less repetition	Learning tasks are clustered as wholes
Questioning	Tied to concrete examples and the colleague's experience		Relate to broader educational issues, ethics, and theory
Supervisor feedback	Frequent and specific	Moderate feedback	Emphasize self-critique

Case Study—Carole

Let's now turn to the post-conference for Carole (see Exhibit 11-4) who is at a moderate conceptual level (Stage B). As you read the case study remember that Stage B conceptual level persons exhibit more tolerance for ambiguity and uncertainty, and they have a moderate awareness of alternative instructional strategies. They are somewhat open to new ideas, are becoming more inner directed, and are moderately aware of emotions in self and others.

Discussion   As you might expect, Carole readily shares some of her feelings and she is able to recall with greater accuracy events within the lesson. The supervisor matches by offering comments and feedback more sparingly. After all, Carole appears to be thoughtful and penetrating in her analysis. For example, she revised her coaching plan with no input from her supervisor. Thus the supervisory approach begins to shift toward less stucture and toward a more collegial approach. Yet the supervisor does mismatch when he or she asks Carole to elaborate on how she anticipated "trouble spots" in the lesson. In effect, he or she encourages Carole to do some deeper reflection on how she plans and predicts student responses to the lesson.

EXHIBIT 11-4   POST-CONFERENCE OBSERVATION SHEET—CAROLE

FOCUS	BEHAVIOR
Carole's comments are in italics.	
1. Feelings	• How are you feeling?
__x__ Colleague feelings	• *Frankly, I was pretty nervous about the observation.*
__x__ Supervisor feelings	• You were anxious about being observed.
__x__ Evidence of listening	• I was excited to have the opportunity to observe.
2. Learning Outcomes	• Were the learning outcomes met?
__x__ Colleague shares	• *Two of the three outcomes were met. My evidence is the student work. The reason we did not achieve the third outcome is because of time.*
__x__ Evidence of listening	• So, two outcomes were reached.
__x__ Supervisor shares	• My data corroborates yours (match).
__x__ Changes discussed	• Are there any changes you would make regarding the learning outcomes?
	• *No. Each outcome needed student practice. You can't rush it.*

EXHIBIT 11-4 *(continued)*

FOCUS	BEHAVIOR
3. Classroom Management	• Did classroom management interfere or support the lesson?
__x__ Colleague shares	• *It supported the lesson with some qualifications. I was aware of the group's response to the lesson, and I anticipated where they might have difficulty. I do wish I would have given clearer directions for the guided practice. I had four students ask me questions because the directions were unclear.*
__x__ Evidence of listening	• You were disappointed by your direction giving. Tell me more about how you anticipated places where the students might have difficulty (mismatch). • *Carole talks at length.*
__x__ Supervisor shares	• In general, my data support yours. My data also show that you used a number of visual prompts to clarify input.
__x__ Changes discussed	• Are there any changes you would make? • *Not that I can think of now.*
4. Teaching Behavior Focus	• Was the teacher behavior focus reached?
__x__ Colleague shares	• *I don't think so. The lesson certainly had an inquiry focus; however, when time became an issue, I took control and, as a result, I think the amount of student talk was not as high as I had hoped.*
__x__ Evidence of listening	• Okay. So you don't think you reached the focus.
__x__ Supervisor shares	• Let me show you the Flanders data. It turns out 38% of the talk was students and 62% was teacher talk. Say a little more about needing to take control. • *Carole shares.*
__x__ Changes discussed	• Are there any changes you would make? • *Yes, I need to build in more small group work.*

EXHIBIT 11-4 *(continued)*

FOCUS	BEHAVIOR
5. Focus of Next Coaching Plan	• Where does this lead us with the coaching plan?
_____ Learning outcomes _____ Classroom management __x__ Refine current teaching	• *I think I'd like to practice inquiry teaching with an emphasis on small group work for several weeks and then invite you back in for an observation, if that is okay with you.*
_____ Identify new teaching behavior focus _____ Discuss coaching plan _____ Evidence of listening	
6. Summary	• Would you summarize the main points of the conference?
_____ Colleague summarizes __x__ Supervisor gives encouraging closing statement	• *Carole summarizes discussion.* • In my view, the students found a lot of meaning in the lesson. Your early attempt to link the topic with some of their experiences was laudable.

Case Study—Bill

Last we turn to Bill's case study (see Exhibit 11-5). Recall that he is at Stage C conceptual level; thus he needs low structure, and he shows evidence of integration and synthesis in both the intellectual and interpersonal arenas. He weighs and balances alternatives, and can take the perspective of students and colleagues. Futhermore, he employs principles in decision-making and has a high tolerance for ambiguity. Bill's coaching plan has as its focus, "to implement an interpersonal lesson on ethics that includes seven examples of active listening for feelings."

Discussion   This post-conference with Bill is typical of Stage C teachers. The conference is dominated by the dialogue of Bill who is "off to the races" as he recalls the lesson in great detail and with clarity. He easily shares an array of feelings and he zeroes in on a particular student who was affected by the lesson. The supervisor, recognizing Bill's depth of recall, drops the structure of the post-conference entirely, realizing that Bill's self-analysis will probably cover all of the major steps. Only the first part of the conference is given as are examples of Bill's ability to self-analyze.

EXHIBIT 11-5 POST-CONFERENCE OBSERVATION SHEET—BILL

FOCUS	BEHAVIOR
1. Feelings __x__ Colleague feelings	• So how are you feeling? • *What a delightful lesson. I am overwhelmed by the students' response, and I am thrilled by my success with the interpersonal approach to lessons. I am particularly pleased with my active listening for feelings. I used the strategy frequently and it fit so well with the focus on ethics and the environment. So many of the students had strongly felt views that it seemed quite natural for me to actively listen to both their feelings and their ideas. Did you notice how Jonathan opened up during the lesson? I have been very concerned about how to reach him. I have moved his desk, rearranged small groups, and asked for his comments about the lessons. Nothing seemed to work. What a change today. . . .*

The case studies of Tom, Carole, and Bill illustrate how a post-conference is differentiated according to the conceptual level of the teacher. Some matching and mismatching responses were highlighted for Tom and Carole. We now turn to how supervisors can self-evaluate their cycles of clinical supervision.

EXHIBIT 11-6 TEACHING/LEARNING FRAMEWORK

COACHING STEPS	CONDITIONS FOR GROWTH
1. Rationale and theory	1. Significant new role
2. Demonstration	2. *Guided reflection*
3. Practice with feedback	3. Balance between the experience and reflection
4. *Adapt and generalize*	4. Support and challenge
	5. *Continuity*

SUPERVISOR'S SELF-ANALYSIS

The clinical cycle with its pre-observation, observation, and post-observation phases represents an important milestone in the supervisory process (Thies-Sprinthall & Reiman, 1994). It brings closure to a cycle of assistance by establishing that the newly learned skill or model has been adapted and generalized (coaching framework), and it permits intensive guided reflection on the teaching/learning process (conditions for growth and development) (see Exhibit 11-6). We regularly get feedback from teachers and school-based supervisors (mentors, peer coaches, assistant principals, principals) that the coaching cycle and the final clinical cycle really do help persons to become more effective and psychologically mature teachers (e.g., empathy, commitment to principles, autonomous, and interdependent).

In the preparation of supervisors, we have found that it is important for them to analyze and reflect on their initial attempts to conduct a clinical cycle of supervision. To assist them in this process of self-evaluation, we encourage the following kinds of self-reflection once the supervisor has audiotaped a clinical cycle (see Exhibit 11-7).

1. Listen to the pre-conference.

   * Are you satisfied with your use of the supervisory behaviors?
   * Identify what kinds of active listening are used.
   * Analyze the conference for the percentages of direct and indirect supervisor talk and the ratio of supervisor talk to colleague talk.
   * Use the adapted Flanders Interaction Analysis System for Supervision (discussed in Chapter 12 in depth). Are the percentages appropriate? What matching or mismatching strategies are used?

2. Review the observation data.
3. Listen to the audiotape of the post-conference. Analyze it using the same form as shown in Exhibit 11-7.
4. Reflect on the clinical cycle.

The clinical analysis of supervision should be given the highest priority. By definition, the supervision process is a complex new role if it is being undertaken for the first time. The novice supervisor and even the experienced supervisor benefit from careful analysis of their supervisory patterns and interactions. In our reflective practica (Thies-Sprinthall, 1984) for mentor teachers and administrators new to supervision, we have found these supervisory patterns to be important and consistent, whether they are good or bad. The self-analysis of the patterns of supervisory interaction achieves two important objectives: it promotes the building of a repertoire of supervisory skills, and it encourages deeper reflection, which is necessary for growth and development.

EXHIBIT 11-7   SELF-ANALYSIS OF PRE- AND POST-CONFERENCE SKILLS

1. My overall reaction to the conference is: Place an x on the continuum.

   Not satisfied_____Satisfied
   Why?

2. On the self-observation of a conference I was able to include _____ of the supervisory behaviors.

3. On the Flanders analysis of the supervisory interaction I had:

   _____ tallies in indirect—Categories 1–4

   _____ tallies in direct—Categories 5–7

   _____ tallies 1–7

   _____ tallies in supervisee talk—Categories 8–9

   _____ tallies in Category 10

   A. I was able to hold a (an)

      Indirect conference _____%

      Direct conference _____%
      Divided 1–4 by 1–7 to find percentage for indirect.

   B. The amount of supervisor talk vs. supervisee talk was

      _____%
      Divide 1–7 (supervisor talk) by 1–9 to find this percentage.

   C. The amount of supervisor talk is appropriate.

      _____Yes _____ No Why? Link your remarks to the
      conceptual level of the supervisee.

4. Analyze observation data:

   A. Did you record data in the four parts needed (learning outcomes, classroom management, other skills to do again, and teaching behavior focus)?

      Yes_____ No_____

   B. Recorded what I saw, not what I thought. I did not use value words such as "good," or "poor," and I included behavior descriptions:
      Example: "Poor job of keeping attention." *No*
                 "Six pupils were playing while you gave directions." *Yes*

   C. Reviewed my data and recorded strengths on the coaching plan.

   D. Reviewed my data and I am prepared to suggest a new teaching behavior focus if the teacher cannot.

   E. Changes I need to make in my observation data collecting include:

5. Overall reflection questions:

   A. Identify your five main learnings from being a supervisor.

   B. Trace the feelings you experienced during the cycle.

   C. Write a coaching plan for yourself on the supervisory behavior you want to improve.

THEORY INTO PRACTICE IN DEVELOPMENTAL SUPERVISION

THE ROLE OF HIGHER-LEVEL QUESTIONING

In the mid-1950s, Benjamin Bloom and his colleagues worked to develop the now famous taxonomy of educational objectives (Bloom, 1956). Bloom recognized that a major issue confronting education was the articulation of a set of goals that might guide teachers, counselors, supervisors, and educational administrators. Bloom's classification system related the educational objectives to specific classroom or school procedures. The system also identified levels of objectives. Can these levels of Bloom's system relate to work in supervision? Perhaps the question is rhetorical. The following rubric describes Bloom's levels of objectives, and clarifies how supervising teachers might employ the various levels of questions in their supervisory practice as they employ "dialog journals" (see Chapter 13).

Level One: Basic Knowledge

Definition and Assessment. Students or teachers are responsible for information and ideas. They have to know specific facts, terms, methods, and models. Direct questions and multiple choice tests are used to assess the individuals' ability to recall the facts. No effort is made to encourage deeper analysis or evaluation of the ideas.

Supervision. An example of this level would be a mentor teacher's attempt to ascertain how much material his or her colleague recalls from a workshop presentation of cooperative discipline that both of them attended. The supervisor does not ask the colleague to evaluate the effectiveness of the workshop.

Development. As you have probably guessed, Level one is basic knowledge. This level is easily accessible to the concrete thinker.

Level Two: Comprehension

Definition and Assessment. Persons must show they understand the ideas, concepts, or theories. Asking students or teachers to restate the material in their own words would be an example. At this level, the students or teachers are needing to process the information.

Supervision. Returning to the example of the cooperative discipline workshop, the mentor might ask the colleague to explain in his or her own words the main concepts of cooperative discipline. As you can see, this question is of a different order, since it requires the colleague to act on the information he or she has heard. Comprehension of the main concepts is the goal.

Development. Clearly this level of questioning is within the grasp of concrete thinkers. Certainly, the general rule with teachers who are functioning at more concrete levels would be to use more structure, more encouragement, and more explicit connections between concepts and classroom practice.

Level Three: Application

Definition and Assessment. Students or teachers must be able to apply their knowledge in real situations. A key aspect of Level three is the demonstration of the knowledge. On the surface, assessment of the application level seems pretty straightforward. Activities must be developed that require students or teachers to try out the knowledge or skill they have learned. For example, asking students in a geometry class to construct a "right" triangle out of straws and then measure the length of the hypotenuse. However, as Bruce Joyce, a noted educational psychologist, has emphasized, education at all levels is notorious for providing too few opportunities for application of the ideas or skills. Joyce refers to this problem as one of transfer.

Supervision. Bloom's application level requires the supervisor to develop opportunities for the teacher to apply new knowledge or skills to real situations. Thus, it is not enough to know that a colleague comprehends the research and theory related to cooperative learning. The teacher must put the knowledge of cooperative learning into action, by practicing the strategy in his or her classroom, connecting the proven strategy to the varied needs of the students. Ideally, Level three of Bloom would relate to all three of the models of supervision.

Development. Although it is important to apply ideas or skills to real situations, some adapting of the situations may be needed depending on the cognitive and conceptual development of the person. Teachers at more concrete levels will need more structure and more repetitions at the application level. Another caution would be to include a variety of application activities. Howard Gardner has pointed out that too often application activities are narrowly conceived and do not require persons to apply ideas or concepts to unfamiliar real situations.

Level Four: Analysis

Definition and Assessment. Analysis requires the student, teacher, or supervisor to categorize, classify, or break down a concept into its component parts, describe the relationships between the parts, and understand the guiding principles or assumptions that support the main concept. We can assess analysis by asking teachers to identify the underlying assumptions behind a particular teaching concept or model.

Supervision. A supervisor might mention a recent local newspaper editorial that takes a position that "lean economic times call for drastic cuts to the school lunch program to help reverse the trend of an enormous federal deficit." Teachers might be asked to examine the assumptions that underly this argument. Another example might be yet another blue ribbon national commission report indicating that "American schools are quickly becoming obsolete, and that they are unable to prepare persons who can help industry compete in a global economy." Prospective supervisors might be asked to analyze the report and identify the main principles at work in the document.

Development. You probably are aware, as we move up the ladder of Bloom's levels of thinking, that we find increasing complexity and abstractness. Asking a teacher to describe in his or her own words what he or she learned from a school workshop is qualitatively different from the challenge to analyze a commission report, noting the underlying assumptions of the report. At the analysis level, you are encouraging the teacher to think critically about the teaching/

learning process. Thus, when you encourage teachers to reflect on the "structure" of their discipline, you are asking a higher-order question that is abstract and that requires logical reasoning.

Level Five: Synthesis

Definition and Assessment. Synthesis requires the teacher or student to create a "new whole" by bringing together familiar ideas or concepts in an original way. The synthesis level is perhaps the most difficult to assess because it requires subjective conclusions about whether the integration is indeed a "new whole."

Supervision. Picture a scenario where an experienced teacher in a peer coaching program has chosen to observe five different teachers as they use varied questioning activities to encourage students' critical thinking. The teacher might gather data and field notes on each teacher's strategies as well as conduct student interviews. On completion of the observations and interviews, the teacher recommends a new framework for encouraging critical thinking that clearly goes beyond the knowledge and efforts of the five teachers.

Development. Level five thinking, synthesis, requires a person to symbolize and integrate knowledge in a new way. Thus it requires both creativity—the intuitive leap—as well as abstract thinking in Piaget's formal-operations system. As a supervisor, you cannot assume that a colleague is comfortable with these modes of reasoning. If they are not, supervision will require careful, sustained, and deliberate assistance and challenge for a teacher in order to promote the growth of more abstract, and/or creative thinking.

Level Six: Objective Evaluation

Definition and Assessment. Level six, objective evaluation, requires the student or teacher to create a set of criteria or standards of judgment that are employed in the careful analysis of an issue, theory, or educational idea. Assessment requires a careful analysis of the comprehensiveness of the evaluation. For this kind of an examination to occur, the judging must follow a logical systematic framework similar to the rubrics teachers use to evaluate essays or the criteria judges might use to assess a college debate team's arguments.

Supervision. Certainly the summative aspects of supervision would be an example of evaluation. A teacher is evaluated based on some already established set of standards for what good teaching represents. There are, however, examples in formative supervision. For example, a mentor teacher and a beginning teacher might develop a rubric for self-analysis of instructional decisions. Thus, whenever the colleagues met for a formal conference, the beginning teacher already would have conducted a careful analysis and evaluation of his or her instructional decisions based on the rubric.

Development. Bloom's Level six, objective evaluation, implies an ability to create standards of judgment, yet to temporarily postpone judgment while one examines, analyzes, and weighs the evidence. Only after careful analysis and consideration is a judgment passed. A teacher or supervisor who regularly employs objective evaluation is similar to Bill Perry's notion of the "committed relativist"; he or she carefully weighs a variety of perspectives, and ultimately, takes a moral position based on the information available. Naturally, the goal of developmental instructional supervision is to promote more complex and higher-order thinking, self-development, and value judgment.

Source: Adapted from B. Bloom (Ed.), *Taxonomy of educational objectives, Handbook 1: Cognitive Domain,* 1956, New York: McKay.

A number of persons in developmental supervision have called attention to the important role questioning plays in assistance activities. Among them are Costa and Garmston's cognitive coaching (1985), Glickman, Gordon, and Ross-Gordon's developmental supervision (1995), and our own work with developmental supervision through new roletaking and reflection. Common to each of these theorists is a recognition that questions should be matched and mismatched to the conceptual complexity of the supervisee. Thus one of the goals of developmental supervision is to link Bloom's Taxonomy to cycles of assistance and responding to journals. As you have been reading we hope you have begun to see that a synthesis of goals is possible for supervision.

 # SUMMARY

Most teachers who voluntarily participate in instructional improvement that includes peer observation by a trained colleague or building administrator find it valuable. Some principals are able to offer developmental supervision, while others are not. Our main point in this chapter is that the cycle of assistance has a distinct place in both the theory and practice of mentoring and supervision. Our review of the pre-observation conference, observation, analysis, and post-conference episodes included a description of how such supervision is differentiated according to conceptual level. It goes without saying that such supervision as we described in Chapter 11 requires the following:

1. Teachers and administrators who are carefully prepared for the role of supervision.
2. A commitment and interest by teachers in participating in the supervisory process.
3. Supervisor or mentor dispositions to empathize, to be autonomous, to act based on democratic principles, and to be able to symbolize teaching in ways that are accessible to beginning teachers.

4. A willingness of the supervisor to model effective teaching and responsible ethical supervision. Implicit in such a commitment is a willingness to self-evaluate.

5. A sensitivity to the setting, situation, and organization within which the teaching and supervision take place.

If these conditions are met, there is the opportunity for significant skill building and growth and development.

SUPERVISION FOR TEACHER DEVELOPMENT ACTIVITIES

APPLIED

1. Videotape an entire developmental cycle of assistance with a teacher. Identify a colleague who also is learning about supervision to review the videotape with you. View and analyze the videotape, pausing the tape when necessary as salient points are discussed.

2. Conduct an interview with an experienced supervisor. Tape-record the interview. Ask questions about his or her strengths, style of supervision, and main learnings.

3. Write an analysis of the case studies introduced in Chapter 11. Go beyond the preliminary analysis we provided for you. Explain how the supervisors vary structure in the post-conferences to match and mismatch the conceptual level of the teachers.

4. As suggested in the chapter, complete a coaching plan for yourself in the role of supervisor. Use the format for coaching plans introduced in Chapter 12.

5. Design an observation data collecting instrument on any teacher behavior you think a beginning teacher or student teacher would be interested in developing. Label the form to identify the type of data collected, for example, selective verbatim, wide-lens, seating chart.

PORTFOLIO DEVELOPMENT

1. Place your coaching plan for building supervisory skills in the section of the portfolio entitled "Instructional and Supervisory Coaching Plans."

2. Write reflections according to your own interests. After your instructor has responded to the reflections, date and file them in your portfolio.

3. Place the written self-analysis of a clinical cycle of supervision in your portfolio. Include the tape of the cycle.

SUGGESTED READING

1. Thies-Sprinthall, L. (1980). Supervision: An educative or miseducative process? *Journal of Teacher Education, 35*(3), 53–60.

> This study was one of the first to identify the problems associated with the assignment of a "concrete" cooperating teacher to an "abstract" student teacher.

REFERENCES

Anderson, R. H., & Snyder, K. J. (1993). *Clinical supervision: Coaching for higher performance.* Lancaster, PA: Technomic.

Blankenship, G., Jr., & Irvine, J. J. (1985). Georgia teachers' perceptions of prescriptive and descriptive observations of teaching by instructional supervisors. *Georgia Educational Leadership, 1*(1), 7–10.

Bloom, B. (Ed.) (1956). *Taxonomy of educational objectives, Handbook 1: Cognitive domain.* New York: McKay.

Blumberg, A. (1980). *Supervisors and teachers: A private cold war.* Berkeley, CA: McCutchan Publishing Corporation.

Cogan, M. (1973). *Clinical supervision.* Boston: Houghton Mifflin.

Costa, A. L., & Garmston, R. (1985). Supervision for intelligent teaching. *Educational Leadership, 42*(5), 70–80.

Eisner, E. (1982). An artistic approach to supervision. In T. J. Sergiovanni (Ed.), *Supervision of teaching, 1982 ASCD Yearbook.* Alexandria, VA: Association for Supervision and Curriculum Development.

Glickman, C. D., Gordon, S. P., & Ross-Gordon, J. M. (1995). *Supervision of instruction: A developmental approach* (3rd ed.). Boston: Allyn and Bacon.

Glickman, C., & Rogers, M. G. (1988). Supervision: State of direct supervisory services. *Educational Leadership, 46*(1), 84.

Kagan, N. (1976). *Influencing human interaction.* Washington, DC: American Association for Counseling and Development.

Kagan, N. (1980). Influencing human interaction—eighteen years with IPR. In A. K. Hess (Ed.), *Psychotherapy supervision: Theory, research and practice,* (pp. 262–286). New York: John Wiley and Sons.

Kagan, N., & Krathwohl, D. R. (1967). *Studies in human interaction: Interpersonal process recall stimulated by videotape.* East Lansing, MI: Michigan State University.

Kiley, M. A. (1988). *Teachers' and administrators' views of evaluation: Differing perspectives.* Technical Report 143. Towson State University, Towson, Maryland (ERIC Document ED 300 434).

Little, J. (1982). Norms of collegiality and experimentation: Work place conditions of school success. *American Educational Research Journal, 19*(3), 325–340.

Mosher, R. L., & Purpel, D. E. (1972). *Supervision: The reluctant profession.* Boston: Houghton Mifflin.

Oja, S. N., & Reiman, A. J. (1997). Describing and promoting supervision for teacher development across the teacher career span. In J. Firth & E. Pajak (Eds.), *Handbook of research on school supervision.* New York: Macmillan.

Reiman, A. J., Bostick, D., Lassiter, J., & Cooper, J. (1995). Counselor- and teacher-led support groups for beginning teachers: A cognitive-developmental perspective. *Elementary School Guidance and Counseling, 30*(2), 105–117.

Thies-Sprinthall, L. (1984). Promoting the developmental growth of supervising teachers: Theory, research programs, and implications. *Journal of Teacher Education, 35*(3), 53–60.

Thies-Sprinthall, L., & Gerler, E. (1990). Support groups for novice teachers. *Journal of Staff Development, 11*(4), 18–23.

Thies-Sprinthall, L., & Reiman, A. J. (1994). *Curriculum for developmental instructional supervision.* Raleigh: North Carolina State University.

Wang, M. C., Haertel, G. D., & Walberg, H. (1993). Toward a knowledge base for school learning. *Review of Educational Research, 63*(3), 249–294.

C·H·A·P·T·E·R
12

Supervision and the Coaching Process

• • • • • • •

$\mathcal{A}$s we mentioned in Chapter 8, it is important to ascertain the prior knowledge and teaching assumptions of a teacher you are supervising. This phase in the supervision process entails assessing and understanding the teacher's models and methods of instruction as well as his or her current style of solving complex human-helping problems in the conceptual, ego, and moral domains.

In Chapters 9 through 11, a cycle of developmental supervision and assistance was described. In Chapter 12 our attention shifts to the rationale for instructional coaching, and to the role that coaching plans play in guiding this next phase of developmental supervisory assistance (see Exhibit 12-1). Coaching encourages persons to perform in more complex ways as they undertake their new role. Thus, coaching is the action part of the action/reflection paradigm we have described, and the coaching plan, in a very real sense, *actualizes* the complex new role.

The chapter begins with a review of the important research and follow-up work of Joyce and Showers (1995) with coaching principles and practices. We follow this discussion with an introduction to coaching plans and how they can guide differentiated supervision. Returning to the case studies introduced in Chapters 8, 9, and 11, we then examine how the coaching plans are differentiated in structure to accommodate to the needs of teachers at various developmental stages. As you review the chapter, check your comprehension by answering these questions:

Exhibit 12-1   TEACHING/LEARNING FRAMEWORK

Instructional Repertoire*	Conditions for Growth and Development†
1. Theory/rationale	1. Complex new role
2. Demonstrations	2. Guided reflection
3. Practice with feedback	3. Balance between new role and re-flection
4. Adapt and generalize through coaching	4. Support and challenge
	5. Continuity

*Adapted from B. Joyce, and B. Showers, *Student Achievement Through Staff Development*, 1995. New York: Longman.
†N. A. Sprinthall, and L. Thies-Sprinthall, The teacher as an adult learner: A cognitive-developmental view. In G. Griffin (Ed.), *Staff Development: Eighty-Second Yearbook of the National Society for the Study of Education*, 1983, pp. 13–35. Chicago: University of Chicago Press.

- What is instructional coaching?
- Why does instructional coaching make a difference?
- How does coaching accommodate to teacher development?

RATIONALE FOR INSTRUCTIONAL COACHING

Bruce Joyce and Beverly Showers (1995) have reported how limited most teachers' instructional repertoires are. They argue that exclusive reliance on any one model limits student learning. Instead, Joyce and Showers propose greater teacher flexibility among the different models of teaching.

The implications for supervision are direct. Persons involved in formative supervisory or coaching roles should avoid rigidity in their own teaching ("practice what we preach"). Further, we need to assist new teachers in learning to flexibly use the different models of instruction. The goal is to assist and coach teachers as they learn to apply the models. Joyce and Showers warn that it is very important to avoid reliance on any one model; however, the novice teacher often tends to do just this, relying on a singular approach.

Therefore, learning new models of instruction needs to be a priority for the field of supervision. We now turn to a set of conditions described by Joyce and Showers in their recent work, *Student Achievement Through Staff Development* (1995) that promotes such learning.

PROMOTING FLEXIBILITY AMONG THE TEACHING MODELS

In their most recent work, Joyce and Showers (1995) set forth a number of propositions about teaching, learning, supervision, and professional growth. Among them are the following:

1. Well-designed teacher education and staff development initiatives can be implemented and have significant effects on student learning.
2. The key to student development is educator development.
3. Any significant changes in curriculum, instruction, or technology must be supported by intensive staff development and coaching.
4. The coaching of teachers or administrators requires capacity building and technical support.

As two of the country's leading researchers on the teaching/learning process, Bruce Joyce and Beverly Showers have asserted the importance of good design in staff development for the learning of new models of teaching. The goal is designing the workplace so that teachers can work together through peer coaching, which is the key to transferring the concepts learned in a training program into the repertoire of classroom practice.

Joyce and Showers differentiate between learning that requires refinement of an existing skill and learning that requires the addition of a new model to one's repertoire. Obviously, the latter is more complex and requires more time. For example, most teachers at the outset incorporate questioning into their instruction; however, they may want to employ more higher-level questions. In these cases a training program might focus most intensively on clear description of the theory and rationale with some demonstrations (Gliessman, Pugh, Dowden, & Hutchins, 1988).

However, if an entirely new model is being learned, careful attention to the following four components should be pursued.

INSTRUCTIONAL COACHING COMPONENTS

Joyce and Showers (1995) describe four needed major components of training for maximum probability that the desired effects will be achieved:

1. *Exploration of theory and rationale.* The first component builds an understanding of the rationale behind the particular teaching model or method and the principles that govern its use. Exploration occurs through discussions, readings, lectures, and so forth.
2. *Demonstration or modeling.* The second component boosts learning of the skill. Examples of demonstrations include audiotapes, videotapes, computer simulations, and live performances.
3. *Practice with feedback.* The third component is the practice of the model or skill under simulated conditions or in a laboratory or training facility setting. Considerable amounts of skill can be achieved in this setting.

For example, peer teaching (practice with other teachers) reduces the complexity of the skill, provides a safe setting for exploration, and allows for immediate feedback from peers and the instructor.

4. *Adapt and generalize.* The fourth component—peer coaching—requires collaborative arrangements in the school setting. For example, a team of teachers interested in the interpersonal model of teaching would support and assist each other as they attempted to master the new model of teaching. It is this final component that promotes what Joyce and Showers call "executive control," that is, the consistent and appropriate use of a model or cluster of strategies during teaching. One formidable strategy for promoting executive control is the cycle of assistance that we described in Chapters 9 to 11.

The goal of the Teaching/Learning Framework is to design experiences that enable your colleague to learn new models of instruction and to assure that the new model is demonstrated when appropriate in classroom practice.

RESEARCH ON INSTRUCTIONAL COACHING

Research on the training components just described reveals some provocative insights about the different components and combinations of them (Joyce & Showers, 1995) (see Exhibit 12-2). As you can see, information or theory-only

EXHIBIT 12-2 EFFECT SIZES FOR TRAINING OUTCOMES BY TRAINING COMPONENTS

TRAINING COMPONENTS AND COMBINATIONS	TRAINING OUTCOMES		
	KNOWLEDGE	SKILL	TRANSFER OF TRAINING
Information	.63	.35	.00
Theory	.15	.50	.00
Demonstration	1.65	.26	.00
Theory/Demonstration	.66	.86	.00
Theory/Practice	1.15		.00
Theory/Demonstration/ Practice		.72	.00
Theory/Demonstration/ Practice/Feedback	1.31	1.18	.39
Theory/Demonstration/ Practice/Feedback/Coaching	2.71	1.25	1.68

Source: Data from B. Joyce and B. Showers, *Student Achievement Through Staff Development*, 2nd ed., 1995, p. 112. New York: Longman.

treatments increase teacher knowledge (comprehension) by about .50 between them (one-half of a standard deviation on a normal curve). In contrast, when theory is combined with demonstrations, practice, and feedback, the effect size increases to 1.31 for knowledge. We see similar trends in skill acquisition (application). Theory alone and demonstration alone result in effect sizes of .50 and .26 respectively, whereas when theory, demonstration, practice, and feedback are combined the effect size jumps to 1.18.

Transfer of the skill or model to classroom practice represents another qualitative shift upward in complexity. Unfortunately, only recently have supervisors, staff developers, and teacher educators begun to acknowledge the transfer question. For too long, the erroneous assumption was that once an instructional skill or teaching model was developed in the workshop setting, it would naturally transfer to classroom practice. As you can see from Exhibit 12-2, the transfer of knowledge or a skill to active classroom practice is not a given. In fact, it is only after in-class coaching is added that we observe dramatic increases—effect size 1.68—in the transfer of the skill.

IMPLICATIONS FOR THE SUPERVISOR AND MENTOR

The skills building framework described by Joyce and Showers has numerous implications for supervisors and mentors. Consider, for example, the first component: theory and rationale. The component's purpose is to build an understanding of the rationale behind the particular teaching model or method and the principles that govern its use. As the supervisor or mentor, you can encourage exploration through discussions, readings, lectures, and so forth. Such explorations, however, should be differentiated according to the teacher's conceptual level. You may recall, we discussed in Chapter 5 ways to differentiate structure according to a teacher's conceptual level. This structure is reiterated (see Exhibit 12-3). As you can see, for teachers needing high structure, the introduction of new models and methods of teaching would require the supervisor to relate the model to concrete examples and to the colleague's prior experiences. Additionally, more complex models and methods would need to be broken down into more manageable learning tasks. In contrast, teachers needing low structure would readily relate to a discussion of theory and research (abstract); thus, a new model could be introduced in its entirety.

The second component of the Joyce-Showers skills building framework is demonstration or modeling. Thus, in order to be an effective supervisor, you should be able to model a relatively large repertoire of instructional models and methods. You also need to be aware of gaps in your own repertoire. If the supervisee selects a teaching behavior focus for his or her coaching plan that is not a part of your own instructional repertoire, it is then important to identify other teachers and videotapes or audiotapes that effectively demonstrate the skill. Additionally, the number of demonstra-

Exhibit 12-3 DIFFERENTIATION OF STRUCTURE

Factors	A—High Structure ⟶ B ⟶ Low Structure—C	
Concepts	Concrete	Abstract
Affect	Supervisor discloses	Both colleague and supervisor disclose
Advance organizers	Multiple use	Few advance organizers needed
Complexity of learning tasks	Learning tasks divided into small steps and repeated	Learning tasks are clustered as wholes
Questioning	Tied to concrete examples and the colleague's experience	Relate to broader educational issues, ethics, and theory
Supervisor feedback	Frequent and specific	Emphasize self-critique

tions of the new skill would be differentiated according to the developmental needs of the teacher. High abstract-conceptual level teachers would need fewer demonstrations, whereas concrete-conceptual level teachers would need repeated demonstrations.

The third component of the Joyce-Showers model, practice with feedback, requires similar differentiation of structure. As you can see from Exhibit 12-3, the teacher at Stage A conceptual level needs more practice with sustained encouragement and feedback that is specific and carefully tailored to his or her needs. A Stage B conceptual-level teacher needs less encouragement and feedback because she or he will be able to self-monitor progress more effectively. Finally, a Stage C conceptual-level teacher is very self-directed and new models and methods are incorporated relatively swiftly into the teacher's repertoire. Joyce refers to these teachers as omnivores: "They are mature high-activity people who have learned to canvass the environment and exploit it successfully. In the formal domain they keep aware of the possibilities for growth, identify high-probability events, and work hard at squeezing them for their growth potential" (1995, p. 178).

The final component, in-class coaching, similarly requires supervisors to adjust their cycles of assistance in order to meet the instructional and growth needs of the teacher.

Thus, the work of Joyce and Showers has clarified the importance of assuring the presence of the four components—theory and rationale, demonstration, practice with feedback, and skill generalization. Supervisors, teacher educators, and staff developers need to arrange the learning environment so that these components are met. In fact, we have found that with-

BEVERLY SHOWERS

Perhaps this biography is unusual in that it portrays the work of Beverly Showers and Bruce Joyce. However, Joyce and Showers' collaboration over 20 years, in itself, is very unique and extraordinary. Both of them dashed over academic hurdles and quickly attracted increasing notice in teacher education, supervision, and staff development for their work on instructional coaching.

In the early 1980s they conducted a meta-analysis of teacher training studies in their seminal work, "Improving Inservice Training: The Messages of Research" (Joyce & Showers, 1980). Their findings created quite a controversy and dilemma for the field of education. The main conclusion was that most inservice training was ineffective and did not promote the "transfer" of new skills into teachers' classrooms.

Acknowledging the problems associated with staff development, Joyce and Showers have systematically developed and studied large-scale school-wide programs that promote both student growth and teacher growth. In fact, they believe that the key to student growth is educator growth. They have engaged administrators and teachers in the design of school work-places where teachers can work together to expand their repertoire of instructional models. This has been dubbed the "peer coaching" movement.

In their most recent work (Joyce & Showers, 1995), they have reemphasized how district and school innovations depend on concerted study and action by the faculty. If the school context is open and democratic, such faculty-wide initiatives are bolstered, but they are impeded if the school climate is not healthy. Undoubtedly, their work and study will continue to positively affect education, and to reinforce the importance of connecting all staff development to student learning. In their minds, great staff development is neither born nor made, but it may be developed when it directly relates to effects on students' personal, social, and academic learning.

REFLECTION QUESTIONS

How has the work of Joyce and Showers revised thinking about staff development?

How can the coaching concepts introduced by Joyce and Showers promote more effective teacher education?

Do beginning teacher induction and mentoring programs provide time for collegial coaching?

out a clear, concrete, written plan for how to implement the suggested new areas of instruction, the potential for coaching is limited. Thus, we now turn to what is called a *coaching plan*.

 # THE COACHING PLAN

The weekly activity of supervision and coaching can be a vehicle to accomplish the admittedly lofty goal of improving teaching and promoting personal growth and development. As we have shown, especially in the early chapters of this book, such development takes place in the cognitive, personal, and value domains. By viewing colleagues developmentally, we gain a picture of how they are currently preferring to solve complex problems (Case, 1989), as well as their potential for developing increasingly complex systems of cognitive structure, self-development, and value judgment. Whether or not such growth takes place, however, depends on the appropriate match between the learner's present level of development and the new level that he or she is moving toward. As mentioned earlier, the process of equilibration or dynamic self-organization of cognitive structures (Garcia, 1992; Piaget & Garcia, 1991) involves the person's need to learn more about the world and how to better solve complex real-life problems. Such a goal embraces the broadest definition of effective education, that is, to help persons think deeply about democratic principles (Goodlad, Soder, & Sirotnik, 1990).

As we just mentioned, a second goal of developmental instructional supervision is to help teachers become more skillful in instruction. After all, when a teacher is able to teach the whole child in a developmentally responsive manner, so that the student may grow from less complex to more complex thinking, self-development, and value judgment, the teacher is ensuring that our next generation of citizens is responsible, able to carefully weigh complex issues, and can embrace the diversity that exists in our culture. Thomas Jefferson was most eloquent on this topic: "If a nation expects to be ignorant and free, in a state of civilization, it expects what never was and never will be."

The challenge for developmental instructional supervision is how to translate these goals into a plan of action for supervision between colleagues. After all, some of our own research has shown that even experienced teachers who try out their current methods, master those, and then systematically enlarge their repertoire of models and methods of teaching are more effective teachers and show definite evidence of developmental growth (Reiman & Thies-Sprinthall, 1993; Thies-Sprinthall, 1984). However, such growth does not take place automatically without a plan of action and continuous reflection. The two processes of skills building and growth and development must go hand in hand. First you try a new approach, then you review the results, analyze, make changes, and try again.

A coaching plan is like a map. Normally, the first coaching plan is developed after the "gaining knowledge" phase of supervision. The goal is to

EXHIBIT 12-4   COACHING PLAN

Name_____ Conceptual Level _____
Amount of Structure _____ High _____ Mixture _____ Low

	FOLLOW-UP AND DATES

List strengths: _____
                                         _____
                                         _____
                                         _____
                                         _____
                                         _____

Skill to improve (write as a
teaching outcome):   _____
                                         _____
                                         _____
                                         _____
                                         _____
                                         _____

PLAN OF ACTION

1. *Review and/or read* the following: _____
                                         _____
                                         _____
                                         _____
                                         _____
                                         _____

2. *Observe* using the following
   designated observation instrument: _____
                                         _____
                                         _____
                                         _____
                                         _____

EXHIBIT 12-4 *(continued)*

FOLLOW-UP AND DATES

3. *Practice the skill* in the following ways:

_____

_____

_____

_____

_____

_____

4. *Demonstrate successful understanding* of the skill by:

_____

_____

_____

_____

_____

_____

Time needed:

_____

_____

Resources needed:

_____

_____

---

identify a model or method of instruction to add to the teacher's instructional repertoire. Once the new skill has been learned, subsequent coaching plans would be developed as part of each post-observation conference (see Chapter 11). A coaching plan should guide the work between colleagues, and it assures the right kinds of support and guided reflection for the teacher who is undertaking to learn a new model or method of teaching. Exhibit 12-4 outlines a framework for a coaching plan. Note that the framework is based on conditions Joyce and Showers (1995) recommended if instructional repertoire is a goal, as well as the conditions for growth outlined by Sprinthall and Thies-Sprinthall (1983).

As you can see, the coaching plan meets several purposes. First, it offers an opportunity for the supervisor or mentor to be responsive to the current conceptual level of the colleague, and his or her need for high, moderate, or low structure. This is very important, because the coaching plan is organized very differently, depending on the need of the colleague for structure (Costa & Marzano, 1987). Shortly we review several coaching plans, encouraging you to identify how the plan has "matched" structure to the supervisee's current conceptual level.

The category of the coaching plan called strengths provides an important starting point for discussions about instructional change. After all, most of us appreciate acknowledgments and affirmations. Identifying strengths can set a positive tone for the discussion of the coaching plan. If colleagues have less confidence, or if they are at the Stage A conceptual level (need high structure), you would want to list more strengths. Occasionally, we have had a teacher supervisor comment that it is sometimes difficult to identify many strengths with teachers who prefer high structure and the tried-and-true approach to teaching, that is, lecture with little flexibility and low expectations of student compliance. Our advice is to strive to identify authentic instructional strategies the teachers are using that make a difference for students. It might be that their lesson is clearly organized with measurable outcomes or it might be that all the materials needed for the lesson are ready.

The next step in the coaching plan is to identify the skill to improve. Once again, the "gaining knowledge" phase and the discussion of models and methods of teaching in Chapter 8 can serve as a foundation for this decision. If the teacher has done some self-assessment it will likely be clear what skills the teacher is interested in developing. As a supervisor, it is important to ensure that the skill is written as a learning outcome. For example, "The teacher will be able to use at least five higher-level questions in a lesson," is an outcome that can be measured. The more nebulous outcome, "The teacher will understand higher-level questioning," is ambiguous and difficult to measure. Naturally, the skill that is chosen should be an effective "mismatch" for the teacher (Hunt, 1974, 1981). What we mean is that some skills will challenge the teacher slightly. A goal that represents a slight challenge is more appropriate than a skill that represents high challenge. Remember, the goal is growth and success in the use of the new skill. If, for example, in your work with student teachers who prefer high structure and low risk, you develop an initial coaching plan that focuses on the ratio of indirect to direct teaching (Flanders), it will probably be too great a mismatch for the teachers, requiring them to accommodate too much new information. The result is high levels of frustration, and little success with the new skill.

As you can see from our discussion of the coaching plan, each step of the plan should be shaped by the current developmental level of the teacher, as well as his or her current instructional goals. Readings and/or discussion of theory will need to start where the learner is developmentally. Teachers at more concrete levels will prefer a few excellent readings that have plenty of practical examples, whereas teachers at more abstract levels will enjoy more extended discussion of the research and theory.

Providing demonstrations of the skill is an important part of the coaching plan. However, we regularly hear from teachers who point out that the demonstration part of the plan requires the most planning and coordination of schedules. Nonetheless, it is a crucial step. We do recommend that, when teachers are observing a demonstration lesson, they collect data on the demonstration for later discussion. The observation form focuses on the components of the experience, leads to more in-depth post-conferences, and builds an understanding of the skill. It also can serve as a scaffold (Rosenshine & Meister, 1992) to subsequent observations. The number of demonstrations planned should depend on the needs of the teacher. Once again, a teacher at a more complex conceptual level may need fewer demonstrations.

THEORY INTO SUPERVISORY PRACTICE: USE OF SCAFFOLDS

How to Employ Scaffolds to Build Higher-Order Cognitive Strategies

1. Present the new model of instruction or cognitive strategy.
    a. Introduce the concrete prompt.
    b. Model the skill.
    c. Think aloud as choices are made.

2. Regulate difficulty during practice.
    a. Start where the learner is and then gradually increase the complexity of the task.
    b. Engage in co-teaching with a particular task.
    c. Provide advance organizers to assure success.
    d. Present information in manageable steps.
    e. Anticipate colleague difficulties.

3. Provide varying contexts for colleague practice.
    a. Engage in reciprocal teaching.
    b. Have groups of teachers work cooperatively in a study group.
    c. Provide a variety of forums for teacher-led practice.

4. Provide feedback.
    a. Provide supervisor-led feedback after the teacher has thoroughly discussed the strategy.
    b. Provide self-analysis forms for the teacher.
    c. Provide models of exemplary practice (e.g., colleagues, videotape).

5. Increase teacher responsibility.
    a. Gradually diminish advance organizers and models.
    b. Gradually increase complexity of material.
    c. Gradually diminish support.
    d. Gradually increase teacher self-analysis.
    e. Gradually encourage teacher consolidation of instructional skills.
    f. Provide for independent practice.

Source: Adapted from B. Rosenshine and C. Meister, "The Use of Scaffolds for Teaching Higher-Level Cognitive Strategies," *Educational Leadership,* 1992, *49*(7), 26.

We do recommend that the demonstration lesson be audiotaped or videotaped. Thus, if it is a particularly effective demonstration, it can be reviewed repeatedly and it becomes a valuable resource. Our experiences tell us that most teachers are more reluctant to use videotape for these purposes, although they agree that the videotape provides a more complete picture of their teaching or supervision. The tape recorder, on the other hand, is very unobtrusive and convenient to use.

Practice of the selected teaching skill may occur with or without direct supervision or mentoring. Typically, teachers want to try out the skill and later discuss outcomes with their colleague or supervisor. Suppose, for example, you want to use more higher-level questioning. The coaching plan might identify that you will tape-record at least three lessons using higher-level questions. At the end of each lesson, you would review the lesson, identifying spe-

---

CONTEMPORARY ISSUES

CAN EQUITABLE INSTRUCTION BE PROMOTED?

A number of educators have asked themselves and others some hard questions about ways to break down overt stereotyping in the classroom. Two leaders in this arena are Dee Grayson and Mary Martin, who have developed a staff development program called GESA (Gender Expectations and Student Achievement). A number of assumptions frame their program. Among them are the following:

1. Deep-seated attitudes and stereotypes are difficult to change.
2. The action (doing)/reflection format is most effective. Just talking about stereotypes does little to change attitudes.
3. Rationale, demonstration, observation, and practice with feedback are necessary to the change process.

The GESA program, which spans five months, encourages teachers to look at specific observable teaching strategies that can increase student achievement and that often are employed in differential ways with students. Each month several new instructional focuses are introduced, for example, probing and listening during a three-hour workshop. This is followed by four to five observations among teachers during a three-week period. Each month a new set of instructional focuses is reviewed. Thus, the staff development cycle is one of theory/research–action/observing/practice–reflection.

Studies have found that the program reduces disparity in teacher interactions with students and increases teacher use of nonstereotypical curriculum materials and activities. A close look at the program also reveals that many of the instructional focuses described by Wang, Haertel, and Walberg (1993) are a part of the GESA program. Further, you probably have noted that the framework for the GESA program draws on the important work of Joyce and Showers (1995) described in this chapter.

cific verbatim examples of higher-level questioning. This self-analysis might be followed by a discussion with your mentor or supervisor. Once you have gained some confidence with the skill, you would move onto the final phase of the coaching plan—successful demonstration of the skill for a colleague.

In our work with supervisors and clinical mentor teachers, this final step typically has included a cycle of supervision (pre-observation conference, observation, and post-observation conference) between the supervisee and the supervisor. This final step is very interactive, and involves in-depth discussion of the lesson outcomes, the teaching behavior focus, and classroom management.

As you have probably noted, the right-hand column—Follow-up and Dates—has not yet been mentioned. It is, however, important, and it should match the conceptual level of the supervisee. For example, teachers at concrete levels will need specific dates and times for follow-up. Without this additional structure, it is unlikely the coaching plan will be completed. However, more self-directed teachers who prefer low structure probably need little follow-up. Teachers at the midpoint in conceptual level will need some specifics in follow-up.

We now turn to examples of three coaching plans for Tom, Carole, and Bill, beginning teachers introduced in previous chapters. Each plan represents a teacher at a particular conceptual level: A—needs high structure; B—needs moderate structure; and C—needs low structure. Discussion follows the case studies.

Case Study—Tom

You may recall that Tom's self-evaluation of his present knowledge of models and methods of teaching was relatively limited, and that he preferred high structure. Tom's coaching plan (see Exhibit 12-5) includes clear outcomes, a rationale that is tied to Tom's experiences, multiple demonstrations, and carefully organized practice sessions. Additionally, follow-up sessions with the supervisor/mentor are frequent with specific dates.

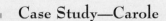

Case Study—Carole

Let's turn to our second case study—Carole. Again recall that Carole was introduced in Chapter 8. Her self-evaluation included a fairly large repertoire of models and methods that were mentioned as strengths. The follow-up observation corroborated Carole's self-evaluation and showed evidence of moderate interaction between her and the students. As you read through the plan (see Exhibit 12-6), note any marked differences from

EXHIBIT 12-5 COACHING PLAN—TOM

Tom is at conceptual level A and needs high structure.

List strengths:
    Recall and comprehension questions
    Content knowledge

Skill to improve (write as a teaching outcome):
    Use at least five higher-level questions for each lesson taught.

COACHING PLAN	**FOLLOW-UP**
1. *Review and/or read* the following:	
a. Read article on questioning skills. Write a summary.	Discuss with mentor in two days.
b. Write sample questions to use in a lesson.	
2. *Observe* using the following designated observation instrument:	
a. Observe the mentor while using the questioning levels observation form. Also audiotape the lesson.	Date:_____
b. Observe another classroom teacher, collect data, and hold a post-conference.	Date:_____
3. *Practice the skill* in the following ways:	
a. Use higher-level questions, prepared in advance, in three lessons.	Report results to the mentor at the end of the two weeks.
b. Tape-record each lesson and self-evaluate.	
4. *Demonstrate successful understanding* of the skill by:	
a. Teach a lesson using higher-level questions as the mentor observes using selected instrument.	Date:_____

Time needed: Four to six weeks.

Resources needed: Readings on questioning, tape recorder, personnel, questioning observation forms.

EXHIBIT 12-6 COACHING PLAN—CAROLE

Carole is at conceptual level B and needs moderate structure.

List strengths:
> Effective questioning at levels from recall through analysis.
> Employs a variety of teaching skills in a lesson.
> Employs some individualization of instruction.

Skills to improve (write as a teaching outcome):
> Implement an inquiry lesson that includes at least 50 percent student talk.

COACHING PLAN	FOLLOW-UP
1. *Review and/or read* the following:	
a. Read Chapters 1–3 of *Analyzing Teacher Behaviors* by N. Flanders.	None unless Carole requests.
b. Ask Carole to search out articles on Flanders Interaction Analysis System.	
2. *Observe* using the following designated observation instrument:	
a. Observe a teacher of own choice and collect data on student talk using the Flanders system.	Meet on Friday to discuss.
3. *Practice the skill* in the following ways:	
a. Plan an inquiry lesson, teach, tape-record, and self-assess using the Flanders system.	Discuss with the mentor on completion.
4. *Demonstrate successful understanding* of the skill by:	
a. Teach a second lesson in a different content area.	
b. The mentor conducts a pre-observation conference, observation, and post-observation conference.	
c. Tape-record and self-assess using Flanders analysis. If successful, report results to mentor.	Mentor assistance at Carole's request.

Time needed: Carole will report to mentor.

Resources needed: Readings, tape recorder, observation form.

Tom's coaching plan. Also try to identify how the coaching plan employs moderate structure.

How is Carole's coaching plan similar to Tom's plan? How is it different? What clues would you underline to indicate that Carole needs moderate structure? What weaknesses does the plan have? Explain why? If you concluded that the coaching plan for Tom includes more structure, more explicit follow-up, and more opportunities for demonstration and practice, you are correct. In contrast, Carole's coaching plan has moderate structure and occasional follow-up.

Case Study—Bill

Turning to the third coaching plan for Bill (see Exhibit 12-7), analyze how his plan differs from those of Tom and Carole. Once again, recall that Bill was discussed in Chapter 8. As you have learned, he needs low structure, is very self-directed, and he seeks out growth producing experiences on his own. To use Bruce Joyce and Beverly Showers' terminology, Bill is an enthusiastic omnivore. As you can see, Bill's plan provides low structure. For example, there is no follow-up on specific components of the Joyce/Showers framework unless it is requested by Bill. Also note his strengths, which include an interest in working with colleagues.

Discussion. The coaching plans we introduced were written to initially match the structure to the supervisees' conceptual level—their current preferred way of solving complex teaching/learning problems. As the supervision progresses through the school year, the plans would begin to include more mismatching activities. This particularly is the case for Tom and Carole, who are less aware of self (e.g., Johari window).

Not only does the written coaching plan outline a research-based process for learning new teaching methods and models, but the coaching plan can become a part of the teacher's portfolio. It captures both the teacher's goals for improving in instruction, and, along with the observation data and audiotapes, represents the teacher's progress or achievement in a focused instructional area.

Naturally, such a deliberate focus on supervisory interventions requires that the supervisor have background knowledge and demonstrated competence in how to effectively coach a colleague. Thus, a major challenge for the field of supervision, teacher education, and staff development in general is the design and implementation of programs that can effectively prepare

Exhibit 12-7 COACHING PLAN—BILL

Bill is at conceptual level C and needs low structure.

List strengths:
Effective questioning at all levels.
Employs the inquiry and transmission models with almost equal mastery.
Collaborates with colleagues.

Skill to improve (write as a teaching outcome):
Implement an interpersonal lesson that includes at least 7 active-listening responses for feelings.

Coaching Plan	**Follow-up**

1. *Review and/or read* the following:
  a. Read Chapters 1–3 of Gordon's *Teacher Effectiveness Training.*
  b. Ask Bill to search out articles on effective teacher-student communication.	

2. *Observe* using the following designated observation instrument:
  a. Observe mentor teacher and collect data on active listening using the observation form.
  b. Analyze data.
	None unless Bill requests.

3. *Practice the skill* in the following ways: a. Plan a lesson on ethics, teach, tape-record, and self-assess using the active listening observation form.	None unless Bill requests.

4. *Demonstrate successful understanding* of the skill by:
  a. Teach a second lesson in a different content area.
  b. Gather data using the same observation form. If successful, report results to mentor.
	None unless Bill requests.

Time needed: Bill will report to mentor.

Resources needed: Readings, tape recorder, observation form.

CONTEMPORARY ISSUES

DOES OUR NONVERBAL COMMUNICATION MAKE A DIFFERENCE?

A component of effective supervision and teaching that is discussed too rarely is nonverbal communication. Until the pioneering work of Charles Galloway (1977), nonverbal communication was practically nonexistent as a topic in teacher education and the field of supervision. This fact is made all the more remarkable because evidence indicates that 75 to 90 percent of a message's impact is communicated nonverbally. Tone of voice, facial expression, proximity, and posture all turn out to be very important. Unfortunately, too often we are unaware of the unintended nonverbal messages we send that can inhibit or discourage colleague or student involvement.

Babad, Bernieri, and Rosenthal have conducted a series of studies that have important ramifications for our understanding of nonverbal communication. One study (1987) of experienced teachers (preschool, remediation, and elementary) yielded two general patterns of nonverbal behavior. The first pattern was flexible, democratic, and warm, whereas the second pattern was hostile and dogmatic. Preschool teachers were highest in the first pattern. Elementary teachers were highest in the second pattern. A second finding was that the main channel for conveying nonverbal hostile and dogmatic messages was facial expressions. In another study, Babad, Bernieri, and Rosenthal (1991) examined how students perceive teachers' differential behavior and interpret its intent. This is an important line of research because teacher behavior seems to have substantial, accumulating effects on students. The investigators found that after as little as 10 seconds of seeing and/or hearing a teacher on audiotape or videotape, even very young students could detect whether a teacher is talking to an "excellent" or "weak" student, and could determine the extent to which the student in the video was respected.

Since nonverbal messages communicate basic attitudes and expectations a supervisor has toward a colleague or a teacher has toward students, it is important to identify supervision practices and staff development programs that have had positive effects in increasing self-awareness of verbal and nonverbal communication.

cadres of school-based supervisors, teacher educators, mentors, and clinical teachers to conduct in-class and in-school supervision and coaching. Furthermore, these persons need to be able to differentiate their coaching according to the complexity of the skill and the developmental level of colleagues. Both authors of this text have implemented such a preparation program, the details of which are provided in Chapter 17.

SUMMARY

We opened the chapter by reviewing the important work of Bruce Joyce and Beverly Showers. They have emphasized the need for teachers to learn a variety of teaching models which they refer to as instructional repertoire. Their research with hundreds of teachers and principals has helped explain why some forms of staff development are more effective and long-lasting than others. It appears that four components are needed when a teacher is learning a new model of instruction: rationale and theory of the new model, demonstration, practice with feedback, and in-class coaching for adaptation and generalization.

However, learning a new model of teaching requires that we give up using only our tried-and-true teaching methods. Piaget was one of the first theorists to help us understand why humans prefer to maintain their current ways of solving problems and often ignore new information or new frameworks. He called this assimilation.

The goal then as a developmental supervisor is to encourage the teacher, through support (matching) and challenge (mismatching), to move to the next level of awareness, in which the new teaching model is considered as a possibility (accommodating to the new). Coaching plans were introduced as a tool for helping teachers accommodate to new models and methods of instruction. However, the plans must be differentiated according to the cognitive-developmental level of the teacher. Three case studies of coaching plans were reviewed. Each plan employed a different amount of structure depending on the conceptual stage of the teacher. As research in earlier chapters illustrated, this coaching process takes time. But the outcome is teachers who are more flexible, who view their teaching analytically, who strive for meaningful and significant student learning, and who can empathize with their students.

SUPERVISION FOR TEACHER
DEVELOPMENT ACTIVITIES

APPLIED

1. Complete a coaching plan for yourself. Refer to your completed "Guideline for Discussion of Prior Experiences" (see Exhibit 8-5) for additional insight into possible instructional areas that need further development.

2. Write an analysis of the three coaching plans introduced in Chapter 12. Go beyond the preliminary analysis provided by the authors. Explain how the plans deliberately vary their structure to accommodate to the teachers' current preferred styles of solving complex problems.

Include in your analysis a critique of the plans. How sufficient or insufficient are they as guiding frameworks for the coaching process?

3. Write a brief paper entitled, "How I Learn Best." As part of the inquiry, discuss whether demonstration and practice play a significant role in your own learning.

4. Interview an instructor from an athletics program. How are the components described by Joyce and Showers (that is, rationale, demonstration, practice with feedback, and adaptation and generalization) incorporated into the athletics program? What resources are allocated for training? How are the programs evaluated? Do the programs have a parallel to the coaching plan introduced in Chapter 12?

5. Interview a director of staff development in a local school system. What system resources are allocated for training? Do the programs employ the principles of coaching?

PORTFOLIO DEVELOPMENT

1. Place your coaching plan, developed in the applied section, in a new section of the portfolio entitled "Instructional and Supervisory Coaching Plans."

2. Prepare a videotape of yourself teaching. The video should be approximately 30 minutes in length. The lesson should demonstrate one of the models or methods of teaching described in Chapter 8. Include a lesson plan, an observation form, and reflective questions with the videotape. This videotape and related materials may or may not be included as part of your portfolio; however, it should become a part of your professional collection. Building a library of videotapes facilitates the coaching process.

3. Write reflections according to your own interests. After your instructor has responded to the reflections, date and file them in your portfolio ("Reflections").

SUGGESTED READINGS

1. Joyce, B., & Showers, B. (1995). The continued search for content that has student effects (chap. 5). *Student achievement through staff development* (2nd ed.). New York: Longman.

   This chapter reviews research on promising models and methods of teaching. Although Joyce and Showers classify the models differently than we have in Chapter 8, the review of the research and theory is impressive and thorough.

2. Huling-Austin, L. (1992). Research on learning to teach: Implications for teacher induction and mentoring programs. *Journal of Teacher Education, 43*(3), 173–180.

The paper describes the importance of coaching and support for novice teachers and relates some of the significant challenges faced by beginning teachers.

REFERENCES

Babad, E., Bernieri, F., & Rosenthal, R. (1987). Nonverbal and verbal behavior of preschool, remedial, and elementary school teachers. *American Educational Research Journal, 24*(3), 405–415.

Babad, E., Bernieri, F., & Rosenthal, R. (1991). Students as judges of teachers' verbal and nonverbal behavior. *American Educational Research Journal, 28*(1), 211–234.

Case, R. (1989, June). *Situating the development of outstanding achievement in the adult life cycle.* Paper presented at the annual meeting of the Jean Piaget Society.

Costa, A. L., & Marzano, R. (1987). Teaching the language of thinking. *Educational Leadership, 45*(2), 29–33.

Garcia, R. (1992). The structure of knowledge and the knowledge of structure. In H. Beilin & P. Pufall (Eds.), *Piaget's theory: Prospects and possibilities* (pp. 21–38). Hillsdale, NJ: Erlbaum.

Galloway, C. (1977). Nonverbal. *Theory into Practice, 16*(3).

Gliessman, D., Pugh, R., Dowden, D., & Hutchins, T. (1988). Variables influencing the acquisition of a generic teaching skill. *Review of Educational Research, 58*(1), 25–46.

Goodlad, J., Soder, R., & Sirotnik, K. (Eds.) (1990). *Places where teachers are taught.* San Francisco: Jossey-Bass.

Grayson, D., & Martin, M. D. (1990). Gender/ethnic expectations and student achievement (GESA) (2nd ed.). Earlham, IA: Graymill.

Hunt, D. (1974). *Matching models in education.* Toronto: Ontario Institute for Studies in Education.

Hunt, D. (1981). Teachers' adaptation: Reading and flexing to students. In B. Joyce, C. Brown, & L. Peck (Eds.), *Flexibility in teaching* (pp. 59–71). New York: Longman.

Joyce, B., & Showers, B. (1980). Improving inservice training: The message of research. *Educational Leadership, 37*, 163–172.

Joyce, B., & Showers, B. (1995). *Student achievement through staff development* (2nd ed.). New York: Longman.

Piaget, J., & Garcia, R. (1991). *Toward a logic of meanings.* Hillsdale, NJ: Erlbaum.

Reiman, A. J., & Thies-Sprinthall, L. (1993). Promoting the development of mentor teachers: Theory and research programs using guided reflection. *Journal of Research and Development, 26*(3), 179–185.

Rosenshine, B., & Meister, C. (1992). The use of scaffolds for teaching higher-level cognitive strategies. *Educational Leadership, 49*(7), 26.

Sprinthall, N. A., & Thies-Sprinthall, L. (1983). The teacher as an adult learner: A cognitive-developmental view. In G. A. Griffin (Ed.), *Staff development: Eighty-second yearbook of the National Society for the Study of Education* (pp. 24–31). Chicago: University of Chicago Press.

Thies-Sprinthall, L. (1984). Promoting the developmental growth of supervising teachers: Theory, research programs, and implications. *Journal of Teacher Education, 35*(3), 53–60.

Wang, M C., Haertel, G. D., & Walberg, H. J. (1993). Toward a knowledge base for school learning. *Review of Educational Research, 63*(3), 249–294.

C·H·A·P·T·E·R
13

Guided Reflection: An Emerging Construct

• • • • • • •

*T*his chapter describes how supervisors and clinical teachers (e.g., mentor teachers, cooperating teachers, teachers involved in peer coaching, and school-based instructional resource teachers) can guide the reflection of their interns or colleagues. In particular, it looks at the role that interactive journals can play in the supervisory context. The concept of matching is applied to two case studies. Each of the case studies is discussed within the developmental framework. Strategies for deepening the reflection of a teaching intern or colleague are explored in the final section of the chapter.

As you review the chapter, check your comprehension by answering these questions:

- How is teacher reflection guided?
- Why is *educative mismatching* important?
- How can the principles of matching and mismatching be applied to the reflection process?

As was mentioned in the previous chapter, reflection or reflective teaching must be a central part of the teacher/learning process. Reflecting on one's experiences permits new learning to occur. In its absence one runs the risk of relying on routinized teaching and, as we have discovered, not developing as a teacher or as a person. Reflective teaching means the ability to analyze the process of what you are doing while simultaneously *adapting* your instruction so that it best matches the needs of the students. Donald Schön

(1983, 1987) called this "reflection-in-action" and considered it to be a milestone skill for professional practice. But reflection is not necessarily automatic. Fortunately, it can be developed. Just as instruction can be adapted to
the different needs of students, so reflection can be differentiated and
guided by the mentor according to the needs of the adult learner.

RESPONDING TO JOURNALS

Journals are one of the mainstays of purposeful reflective activity. Yet some
of your experiences with journals may have been less than satisfying. Often
they are used as a diary to record one's stream of consciousness. In this
chapter, guidelines are provided for focusing and guiding the reflection of
teacher interns. The goal is encouraging both novice and experienced teachers to make meaning from their experience in increasingly complex ways.
And, as you will discover, one's ideas, feelings, and symbols are rich
sources of information for both the intern as well as the teacher educator or
clinical mentor.

Journal reflection on the teaching/learning process can occur in a number of ways. It can be structured by the teacher educator or left unstructured. The journal could be shared with the teacher educator or kept private
so the account is uncensored. If it is shared, it can be highly interactive or
more one-way in communication. Further, teacher journals can record and
examine an array of experiences at a variety of levels of complexity. Teachers might reflect on instructional planning, classroom management concerns, teaching decisions during teacher-student interaction, individual student needs, teacher colleagues, or broader implications of schoolwide and
districtwide curricular and/or policy choices on the welfare of teachers, students, and parents. The challenge for clinical mentors and university-based
teacher educators who are interested in teacher development is how to *guide
the reflective process*.

For the past seven years, we have been investigating a dialogue-based
journal reflection model that is developmental in orientation. Working with
interns, new teachers, peer teachers, and mentors, a series of field-based
studies (Anson, 1989; Mann, 1992; Oja & Sprinthall, 1978; Thies-Sprinthall,
1984; Reiman & Thies-Sprinthall, 1993; Reiman & Parramore, 1993; Watson,
1995) have refined a framework for guiding reflection. Using cognitive-
developmental theory as an operational framework, educators and clinical
mentors can gain an understanding of the patterns in journal responses, the
differences in persons' abilities to reflect on and make meaning from their
educational experiences, and how the written responses and/or feedback of
the mentor must be differentiated according to teachers' problem-solving
ability.

Through our work with hundreds of interns, clinical mentors, and
teacher educators, we have developed a number of propositions about
guided teacher reflection through journals:

1. Journal writing becomes crucial when persons are engaged in complex new helping roles like teaching for the first time because the new role generates disequilibrium.
2. Sharing journals requires a trusting and accepting collegial relationship or the journals will be far less effective.
3. Provisions should be made for structured and less structured journal writing depending on the preference of the intern.
4. Journal entries reflect a person's current preferred system of solving complex "human-helping" problems.
5. Careful attention to a person's current preferred system of reflecting on teaching/learning, dilemmas, and personal issues provides the foundation for rendering a more thoughtful and "growth producing" response.
6. Journal responding "starts where the learner is" and only gradually mismatches written responses to encourage deeper intern reflection.

The first proposition may be the most important. Drawing on the social theory of George Mead (1934), we are proposing that complex new helping roles like internship teaching, first-year teaching, mentoring, peer coaching, and clinical teaching embody a unique type of reflective action or praxis. These significant new roles (Sprinthall & Thies-Sprinthall, 1983) are a fundamental catalyst for attaining a more complex sense of self as well as a sense of community. Mead believed that "all reflective thought arises out of real problems present in immediate experience" (1934, p. 7). He called this social perspective taking and submitted that the self is in a continual process of construction. Ultimately, as persons develop to more complex stages, their actions more sufficiently account for the behaviors, values, and orientations of the community.

The second proposition seems like common sense. If a person doesn't trust you, chances are that he or she will censor much of his or her journal writing. For this reason we took an extended look at how to build a trusting relationship in Chapters 7 to 9. Journal writing is mind-to-mind and sometimes heart-to-heart communication. Therefore the mentor's trust, regard, and acceptance must be present as well as thoughtfulness and insight.

Deciding on the amount of structure (proposition three) to provide in a journal may warrant choices and decisions by both the supervisor as well as the intern or supervisee. We recommend that fairly high structure be applied early in the journal writing process (see Exhibit 13-1). For example, you might ask that each intern identify the three major concerns they had during the week of internship. Such a question will most likely generate some strong feelings. "What stands out as most significant?" is a semi-structured question that has great generative potential. After several weeks of dialogic journal writing, the option of a less structured approach to journal writing with fewer stimulus questions could be made available (see Exhibit 13-2). The main point is that an initial structure for reflection can "up the ante" by encouraging the teacher to purposely reflect on significant thoughts and feelings that have occurred.

EXHIBIT 13-1   GUIDELINES FOR JOURNAL REACTIONS

1. The main learnings I got from teaching this week were:

2. When I think about being a teacher I am concerned about . . .

    I feel . . .

3. I agree/disagree with:

4. Questions I have after working this week are:

5. I rate my experiences this week as:

   Inadequate _____   Marginal _____   Excellent _____

6. Elaborate on one particularly significant event that occurred this week.

Exhibit 13-2 GUIDELINES FOR FREE WRITE JOURNAL

As you work to connect concepts and ideas you may choose not to use an outline for organizing your feelings and thoughts. Instead, you may prefer to write a collection of "Dear _____" letters. These letters can utilize whatever type of format and/or expression you see fit as long as they portray your ongoing thoughts and feelings related to supervision.

I will write responses to your ideas in the letters. At times, I may also ask you to expand on ideas or to clarify issues which you have raised. Please know that you can also ask the same of me.

The fourth proposition, that journal entries represent a person's current preferred system of solving complex "human-helping" problems, relates to our discussion throughout the text about adult development. Thus, when persons who are engaged in complex new roles are asked to reflect in writing on their experiences, their thoughts and feelings parallel their current cognitive-developmental stage. For example, a person at Hunt's conceptual level A (concrete), will most likely find written reflection difficult, prefer writing about concrete and observed events, view knowledge as fixed, and avoid sharing feelings. On the other hand, an abstract conceptual level person would enjoy relating theory to practice, see knowledge as successive approximations, and actively share feelings as he or she relates his or her experiences.

By carefully attending to the expressed "meaning making" in the journal, the supervisor or mentor can more adequately guide the written reflections in ways that can encourage deeper reflection and development. This leads us to the final proposition, which is at the heart of this chapter. Journal responding starts where the learner is (matching) and only gradually mismatches written responses to encourage deeper intern reflection. For example, if the intern's journal entries talk about the teaching/learning process in perfunctory or concrete ways, and few feelings are shared, the supervisor must fashion a response that initially matches the intern's current preferred style of reflecting. How this is managed is now described.

MATCHING GUIDED REFLECTION AND FEEDBACK WITH TEACHER DEVELOPMENT

As was mentioned earlier, guided teacher reflection is more than encouraging an intern to simply bring something to mind. Thoughts, feelings, and actions must be considered (Dewey, 1933). Unexamined experience forfeits the potential for growth. Guided reflection within the developmental framework implies that reflection can be initiated and provoked as part of social interchange and social role taking (Mead, 1934). For example, when a mentor teacher and his or her protégé discuss different possible solutions to one of the protégé's classroom management problems, and the mentor encourages the protégé to consider how the students might solve the problem, the mentor is deliberately guiding (provoking) the protégé to take the multiple perspectives of the students in the class. From a developmental perspective, spoken and written discourse between educators offers "tools" needed for thinking, feeling, and acting (Vygotsky, 1934, 1978).

Given the crucial interplay between experience and reflection, we tested the question of how to guide reflection. The dependent variables were measures of cognitive development. The independent measure was a specially designed format for guiding reflection (Reiman & Thies-Sprinthall, 1993). Two important findings emerged. The first is that guided reflection may be a keystone in teacher development. The second finding is that growth and development do not come cheaply. If development is a goal, then six months to one year is needed if any significant development is to occur. A unique aspect of the reflection format, used to assist teacher educators and clinical teachers in guiding intern reflection, was its representation of strategies for differentiating instructor responses according to the current level of cognitive-developmental functioning of the intern.

Interns at concrete conceptual levels (CL) received written feedback to their journals that was more structured, more direct, more encouraging and accepting, and less complex in the level of questions posed for consideration. Abstract CL interns received written feedback that was less structured, more indirect, more theoretical, and more complex in the level of questions posed for intern consideration. The format that guided written feedback is depicted in Exhibit 13-3 and draws on the aptitude-treatment interaction (ATI) curriculum of Hedin (1979), original teacher interaction research by Flanders (1970), theory of Sprinthall and Thies-Sprinthall (1983), and the conceptual work of Dewey (1933), Mead (1934), Schon (1983), Zeichner and Liston (1987), and Hunt (1981).

Exhibit 13-3 depicts both the journal patterns of interns and a "matching" response that would be provided by the clinical teacher, mentor, or supervisor. The first four categories, accepting feelings, praising or encouraging, clarifying ideas, and prompting inquiry, are indirect strategies for guiding reflection. Categories 5 to 7, providing information, giving directions, and addressing problems, are direct strategies for guiding reflection. Two journal patterns are described for each journal category. These patterns relate to the interns' current preferred system for solving complex problems (conceptual level). Before we explore two case studies using the journal model, let's take a closer look at the categories.

INDIRECT JOURNAL RESPONDING

Category 1. Accepting Feelings. Feelings often have an enormous influence on our ability to reflect, that is, to respond to and interpret situations. We submit that reflective thinking can be temporarily "frozen" by intense feelings such as a teacher's anger over being disrupted by the same student

EXHIBIT 13-3 SUMMARY OF CATEGORIES FOR GUIDING AND
SCAFFOLDING DIALOGIC WRITTEN REFLECTIONS

INTERACTION	JOURNAL PATTERN	INSTRUCTOR RESPONSE
1. Accepts feelings	1a. Teacher has difficulty discerning feelings in both self and others.	Share own feelings.
	1b. Teacher discerns feelings in both self and students.	Accept feelings.
2. Praises or encourages	2a. Teacher doubts self when trying new instructional strategies.	Offer frequent encouragement.
	2b. Teacher has confidence when attempting new instructional strategies.	Offer occasional support.
3. Acknowledges and clarifies ideas	3a. Teacher perceives knowledge as fixed and employs a single "tried-and-true" model of teaching.	Relate ideas to observed events and clarify how ideas affect students' lives.
	3b. Teacher perceives knowledge as a process of successive approximations and employs a diversity of models of teaching.	Accept ideas and encourage examination of hidden assumptions of pedagogy.
4. Prompts inquiry	4a. Teacher rarely reflects on the teaching/learning process.	Ask questions about observed events in teaching/learning.
	4b. Teacher consistently reflects on diverse aspects of the teaching/learning process.	Ask questions that encourage analysis, evaluation, divergent thinking, and synthesis of theory/practice and broader societal issues.
5. Provides information	5a. Teacher disdains theory, prefers concrete thinking, and has difficulty recalling personal teaching events.	Offer information in smaller units, relate to practice, and review regularly.
	5b. Teacher employs abstract thinking, shows evidence of originality in adapting innovations to the class, and is articulate in analysis of teaching.	Relate information to relevant theory and contrast with competing theories.

Exhibit 13-1   *(continued)*

INTERACTION	JOURNAL PATTERN	INSTRUCTOR RESPONSE
6. Gives directions	6a. Teacher needs detailed instructions and high structure, is low on self-direction, and follows curriculum as if it were "carved in stone."	Offer detailed instructions but encourage greater self-direction.
	6b. Teacher is self-directed and enjoys low structure	Offer few directions.
7. When problems exist	7a. Teacher has difficulty accepting responsibility for problems and blames students.	Accept feelings and thoughts, use "I" messages, and arrange a conference.
	7b. Teacher accepts responsibility for actions.	Accept feelings and thoughts.

Source: Adapted from N. Flanders, *Flanders Interaction Analysis System,* 1970, Ann Arbor, MI: University of Michigan Press; and A. J. Reiman, *An Intervention Study of Long-Term Mentor Training: Relationships Between Cognitive-Developmental Theory and Reflection,* Unpublished doctoral dissertation, 1988, Raleigh, NC: North Carolina State University.

for the umpteenth time. Feelings expressed in journals, both positive and negative, should be given special consideration by the supervisor. We also acknowledge that interns vary in their ability to discern feelings in both self and others.

If the intern has difficulty discerning feelings in both self and others, the mentor teacher or clinical teacher should share his or her own feelings. By doing so, one is acknowledging that feelings are an important part of what it means to be human. If the intern discerns feelings in both self and the students the clinical teacher should accept the feelings, "You sound frustrated."

In our society persons often ignore negative feelings, offer negative feelings in return, or marginalize their feelings, "Don't worry, this too will pass." Such responses are roadblocks to effective journal dialogue, and diminish the importance of the intern's feelings.

Category 2. Praising or Encouraging.   Praise may be a short statement: "Nice idea," "Good effort," or "I like how you described your experiences this week." Encouragement prompts the intern to elaborate and might include such statements as: "Tell me more," or "I would like to read more about your ideas on questioning."

Imagine a journal entry that expresses high self-doubt whenever the teacher intern attempts new instructional strategies. From a cognitive-developmental approach, such responses may suggest that the intern lacks confidence and avoids taking instructional risks (concrete conceptual level). In this case, the clinical teacher response should offer frequent encouragement. Conversely, if the intern expresses confidence and high interest in undertaking new instructional strategies, Hunt's theory would tell us that the person needs only occasional support. Less is more in this case.

Category 3. Accepting and/or Clarifying Ideas. This category is similar to Category 1; however, it includes only supervisor acceptance and/or clarification of the intern's ideas, values, and beliefs, not acknowledgement of feelings. Once again, interns express their ideas, values, and beliefs in qualitatively different ways depending on their cognitive-structural development. As David Hunt found, some teachers perceive knowledge as fixed and desire to employ a single "tried-and-true" model of teaching for all students. Thus when a belief surfaces in the journal, the supervisor should offer a written response that relates the intern's idea to observed events. If, on the other hand, the intern perceives knowledge as a process of successive approximations and employs a diversity of models of teaching, the supervisor should accept and/or clarify the ideas expressed. For example, when the intern writes about a lack of success with cooperative learning strategies, the supervisor could paraphrase the intern's statement, restate the idea more simply, or summarize two or three ideas that were described in the journal.

Category 4. Prompting Inquiry. This is the final category in the indirect domain of journal responding. This category implies that the supervisor is raising questions that warrant an answer. They are not rhetorical. It may be helpful to mention to interns that questions are an important part of the journal dialogue and should be given a thoughtful written response.

If the intern's journal rarely includes much reflection on the teaching/learning process, then the developmental response is to ask questions about observed events in teaching/learning vis-à-vis comprehension and application questions. If, on the other hand, the intern consistently reflects on diverse aspects of the teaching/learning process, the supervisor's matching written response would ask questions that encourage analysis, evaluation, divergent thinking, and synthesis of theory/practice and broader societal issues (see the Role of Higher-Level Questioning in Chapter 11).

DIRECT JOURNAL RESPONDING

Category 5. Providing Information. In the role of supervisor, clinical teacher, or mentor, it will be necessary to provide information, research and/or theory, opinions, and ideas. The sharing of information may serve as introduction to new material, build on the thinking of the intern, review important ideas, or focus the intern's attention on a crucial issue. However, it is important once again to offer information in ways that are responsive to the current developmental level of the intern.

Thus, if the intern's journal entries regularly disdain theory, show a preference for concrete thinking, and describe personal teaching events in perfunctory ways, the supervisor, "starting where the adult learner is," would offer information in smaller amounts, relate this information to observed practice, and review the ideas regularly. On the other hand, if the intern employs abstract thinking, shows evidence of originality in adapting innovations to the classroom, and is articulate in the analysis of his or her teaching, the supervisor's developmental matching response might relate information to relevant theory and contrast it with competing theories. Larger composite concepts could be offered, and less review is needed.

Category 6. Giving Directions. Sometimes it will be necessary, after reading the journal of an intern, to write a statement that is intended as a direction. For example, when the clinical teacher writes, "Please stop by my office tomorrow afternoon at 4:00 so that I can share some new curriculum strategies with you," the supervisor is giving a direction. This category relates to our discussions about structure that are evident throughout the text. We now know that some interns, at less complex cognitive-developmental levels, will prefer detailed instructions and high structure, be low on self-direction, and follow curriculum as if it were "carved in stone." The matching response is to offer detailed instructions and directions when appropriate. It is important to remember that the intern is doing the best he or she can at that particular point in professional development. If the intern is high on self-direction and prefers low structure, the supervisor should rarely offer directions in journal dialogue.

Category 7. Addressing Problems. Anyone who has worked as a mentor or college supervisor knows that problems can arise in the internship. How the intern adapts to the problems offers an insight into his or her conceptual level. For example, if the intern's journal portrays personal difficulty in accepting responsibility for problems and tends to blame others, the supervisor must initially accept the feelings and thoughts shared by the intern. We have transposed Category 7 of Flanders (see Chapter 8, Exhibit 8-2) to permit giving constructive feedback in the form of "I" messages or "responsibility messages." "I" messages share feelings while avoiding the negative impact that accompanies criticism. When we address "journal mismatching," you will see that the next step in responding is very important if growth and development is the aim of the teacher education program. When the intern accepts responsibility for his or her actions, the supervisor's response is to accept, in writing, the feelings and thoughts of the intern.

Now that the journal response categories have been described it is time to look more closely at two case studies that portray the different journal patterns as well as the supervisor's "matched" responses to the journal entries.

JOURNAL ENTRIES: TWO CASE STUDIES

The following two case studies include both a journal entry by an intern as well as the supervisor's response. The case studies are distinguished by the various ways that the new teachers are constructing meaning from their experiences. In the first case study, Tim writes about his experiences as an intern. He has chosen to use a structured journal format (in italic script) that was offered as a choice by the college supervisor. Tim is at the concrete-conceptual level.

Journal Entry—Tim

1. *The main learnings I made from teaching this week were*:
   that teaching is work. I thought the students would be better prepared for my course. I was mistaken. They are not disciplined or motivated enough to take on the subject matter. I plan to take points off their pop quiz next week if they misbehave again.
2. *When I think about teaching I'm concerned about . . .*
   what the students think of me. I wonder if I'm being too hard-nosed about discipline. I also wonder if they respect me. One of my teammates suggested moving the desks to better manage the troublemakers. Sounds like a good idea to me. I have shifted rows and seating assignments. Maybe this will help.
   I feel . . .
   fine I guess.
3. *I agree/disagree with:*
   you! Thanks for the suggestion on the bulletin board. I really didn't know where to start. Now if I can just find my own pair of scissors.
4. *Questions I have after teaching this week are:*
   How many more weeks till Christmas vacation?
5. *I rate my experiences this week as:*
   Inadequate   Marginal   Excellent
       X
6. *Other reactions?*
   I think my background in the subject matter will suffice for the group of kids I was given. I don't have much hope for them. I thought my lecture went well. I kept all the facts straight, but I am certain that some of it was over the kids' heads.

Having reviewed the journal entry written by Tim what conclusions did you draw about his current preferred ways of understanding the teaching/learning process? Is his thinking more concrete or is it more abstract and relativistic? Are feelings shared or avoided? Does he exhibit confidence or self-doubt? Is he assuming responsibility for his actions as a teacher or does he prefer to blame the students? You will probably agree that Tim seems to be at the concrete level of cognitive complexity as well as interpersonal maturity. He is uncertain, has high regard for persons in authority positions, blames students, is eager to follow suggestions as if they are "carved in stone," and employs a "tried-and-true" approach to teaching, namely lecturing. David Hunt described these attributes in his description of concrete conceptual level teachers, and found that they prefer high structure.

Let's now examine a supervisor's "matching" guided reflection response to Tim's journal entry. Assume that Tim and the supervisor have only recently begun to work together in the internship. As you read the response, think about the categories identified in Exhibit 13-3 for guiding written reflection: accepting feelings, praising or encouraging, clarifying ideas, prompting inquiry, providing information, giving directions, and addressing problems.

"Matching" Response to Tim

Thank you for taking some time out of your hectic schedule to reflect on some of the major events that are unfolding as you learn about teaching and learning. Your journal helps me to better understand how you are making meaning from your experience.

I am pleased that the bulletin board idea was helpful. And I am glad you are talking with other faculty about teaching. There are a lot of talented teachers in the school. You mentioned that you felt fine. Nonetheless you are frustrated by the students' lack of discipline and/or motivation. A challenge! At what point during the lecture did you sense that they were not with you? What learning outcomes did you have for the lesson?

I would like to sit down with you and discuss some strategies for connecting the lesson with the interests of the students. Interested? Let's plan on a conference Wednesday afternoon at 3:15 or Thursday afternoon at 4:00. Let me know which day is more convenient. Bring your internship guidebook as well as the lesson plan or plans that went astray. We can use them as a starting point for our conference. Also be prepared to respond to the questions I have raised here.

Thanks again for taking some time with your reflections. Remember that you are in the process of becoming a teacher. My own start as a teacher seemed filled with highs and lows (ecstasy and agony).

The response by the supervisor takes into account Tim's current conceptual level. Encouragement is frequent (e.g., "thank you for taking some time"); ideas are acknowledged (e.g., "the bulletin board idea was helpful"); and concrete questions are raised. These responses are *indirect* matches to Tim's journal entry. Direct matches include detailed directions about a planning conference, and shared information that is connected to Tim's personal experiences as an intern. If each sentence was coded using the category system, the outcome would be more direct (55 percent) than indirect (45 percent). This outcome is in keeping with David Hunt's theory of conceptual level. Persons at concrete conceptual levels need greater structure.

Let's turn to the second case study. Angela also is an intern teacher. She has chosen to use an unstructured approach to journal writing (free write method). Once again, as you read the journal entry think about how Angela is constructing meaning from her initial experiences as an intern. What might you conclude about her conceptual complexity and interpersonal self-understanding?

Journal Entry—Angela

It is both exciting and frightening to be starting my work as an intern. My eagerness to learn about teaching and learning with the cooperating teacher and the students is counterbalanced by a realization of the challenges and complexities that are inherent to effective instruction. Scary! Nonetheless, I am eager to get started, and I want to contribute to what is occurring in the classroom. I think I am optimistic but also realistic.

I expressed an interest in doing some small group teaching as part of my internship. My supervising teacher liked the idea. Together we planned several units of study that could be introduced in small groups. I tried out an inquiry lesson in one of the small groups yesterday. The students were excited by the format and they made some significant discoveries about the Krebs cycle. Thank you for informing me on this approach to lesson planning. By the way, the readings you shared that describe this approach were helpful. I found the research enlightening.

There are a number of questions I have about the structure of the school day. It is so full and intense. I can see why teachers think that TIME is their most precious commodity. Can we talk about this when we get together? Thanks for listening.

What conclusions can you draw about Angela's current preferred system of making meaning of the teaching/learning process? Does she share feelings? Is she confident or does she express self-doubt? Would you describe Angela as more concrete in her thinking or more abstract? And does she appear to need detailed instructions or is she high on self-direction?

You have probably concluded that Angela is a person who is conceptually complex with a "good share" of interpersonal maturity. She openly acknowledges contrasting feelings (e.g., "exciting and frustrating"), risks trying new teaching strategies (e.g., "inquiry approach"), enjoys relating research findings to teaching practice (e.g., "I found the research enlightening"), recognizes the important role you play in her learning, and accepts responsiblity for her work as an intern (e.g., "I expressed an interest in doing some small group work"). Now read the "matching" reflection response by her supervisor.

"Matching" Response to Angela

Your excitement and fear come through loud and clear. I gather from your comments that you perceive both feelings as healthy responses to your new role as an intern. I encourage you to continue to monitor and record your feelings during the internship. They are important windows into how you are accommodating to the "rush" of new learnings. My first days as an intern also were filled with excitement, dismay, and anticipation. It was one of the most challenging experiences of my young adult life.

Kudos! You took the initiative with your cooperating teacher, and developed some plans for small group instruction. I can tell that you were energized by the process as well as the student outcomes. I would love to hear more as the planned units evolve. Do you see yourself employing inquiry instruction once you have responsibility for the whole class? Include a written response in your next set of reflections.

Finally, you mentioned the intensity of the school day. Many educators believe that the intensity and pace of the school day leaves too little time for teachers to plan, reflect, and collaborate. Why do these conditions exist? Let's chat about your observations on this topic.

As you can see, the supervisor has fashioned a response that accounts for Angela's conceptual complexity and interpersonal self-understanding. Feelings and thoughts are acknowledged (e.g., "your excitement and fear come through loud and clear"), support and encouragement are occasional, deeper introspection is prompted through analysis questions (e.g., "why do these conditions exist?"), and less structure vis-à-vis directions is offered (e.g., "let's chat about your observations on this topic"). As a general guideline, the supervisor should respond in a more indirect fashion. If we analyize each sentence in the supervisor's response we would find that it is more indirect (62 percent) than direct (38 percent). This ratio of indirect-to-direct responses is in keeping with Angela's conceptual complexity, self-confidence, and self-directedness.

Van Manen's (1977) work with "levels of reflectivity" and Tim's (1985) "arenas of the problematic" suggest, like cognitive developmentalists, that teacher reflection can occur at increasing levels of complexity and critical-ness. At the first level, reflection is technical in orientation (see also Schön, 1987 and Kitchener & King, 1981, 1994). The dominant concern is with effi-cient and effective application of educational knowledge for the purposes of attaining certain outcomes. The second level of reflectivity is based on practical action; here the challenge is to explicate and clarify competing al-ternatives as well as their consequences. Only at the third level, critical re-flection, are principles and ethical criteria a part of the discourse about ed-ucational commitment and actions. This level of reflectivity is highly similar to Kohlberg's discussion of post-conventional reasoning, Hunt's theory and research on levels of conceptual complexity, and Loevinger's (1987) theory and research on ego development. Although the literature on reflection has been extensive, far less is known about how to *encourage* deeper, more complex reflection. The next section describes a process for encouraging deeper reflection that is based on recent theory and research in cognitive structures you might also want to refer back to the section on questioning (pp. 234–236).

HOW CAN DEEPER CRITICAL REFLECTION BE ENCOURAGED: A CASE FOR THE EDUCATIVE MISMATCH

The idea of mismatching as a goal of dialogue journals is borrowed from Snow's (1987) work with the aptitude-treatment interaction (ATI) model. The concept of ATI means that journal responding must be differentiated depending on the current system of reasoning of the teacher intern. Match-ing means starting where the intern is cognitively. But does this aid in growth and deeper reflection or does a match keep the intern at his or her current level? Mismatching implies that the supervisor or mentor should gradually shift the journal responding (as well as all supervisory strategies) to a slightly more complex level in order for the intern or protégé to think in more complex ways and to develop. The slightly higher responding creates a kind of knowledge disturbance for the intern. As the intern resolves or ac-commodates to the higher level of complexity, he or she experiences devel-opmental growth. But how do these concepts translate into supervision?

If an intern perceives the teaching/learning process as either effective or ineffective and enjoys only highly structured learning experiences, then the goal for the supervisor is to gradually mismatch the intern by raising ques-tions and ideas that are slightly above the intern's current "worldview." Again using the categories outlined in Exhibit 13-3 as a guide, the supervi-sor would want to increase Tim's awareness of feelings, gradually build greater confidence so that less encouragement is needed, promote deeper examination of the multiple dimensions of teaching and learning, encourage greater application and analysis, prompt increased acceptance of responsibility, and offer only moderate structure. The following response by the supervisor demonstrates gradual mismatching of responses to Tim's journal entry that was reviewed earlier. The sentences in italics are mismatches and the other statements are matching responses.

"Mismatching" Response to Tim

Thank you for taking some time out of your hectic schedule to reflect on some of the major events that are unfolding as you learn about teaching and learning. Your journal helps me to better understand how you are making meaning from your experience.

I am pleased that the bulletin board idea was helpful. And I am glad you are talking with other faculty about teaching. There are a lot of talented teachers in the school. You mentioned that you felt fine. *Nonetheless, it sounds like you felt very frustrated* by the students' lack of discipline and/or motivation. *Are there changes that could be made in the learning outcomes to better match the skills and interests of the students? This seems like a crucial need in your lesson planning.*

Let's sit down and discuss some strategies for connecting the lesson with the interests of the students. Interested? Let's plan on a conference. *Call me once you have identified a good time.* Bring your internship guidebook as well as the lesson plan or plans that went astray. We can use them as a starting point for our conference.

Finally, I would be interested in hearing more about one student that stands out in your mind. Thanks again for taking some time with your reflections. Remember that you are in the process of becoming a teacher.

Several mismatches are identified. Let's examine each one. The first statement, "Nonetheless, it sounds like you felt very frustrated," is a mismatch because the supervisor has explicitly labeled a feeling that Tim probably experienced but left unstated. The question, "Are there changes that could be made in the learning outcomes to better match the skills and interests of the students?" challenges Tim to take students into account as he plans his lessons. Similarly, the statement, "Finally, I would be interested in hearing more about one student that stands out in your mind," encourages Tim to begin taking the perspectives of students into account as he learns about the teaching/learning process. Lastly, the statement, "Call me once you have identified a good time," mismatches Tim because it requires him to assume responsibility for setting up a conference with the supervisor. The supervisor's response to Tim is less structured and has shifted to a ratio of 50 percent direct to 50 percent indirect responses.

Two cautions must be raised about matching and mismatching. Development varies according to the domain of development. An intern who is conceptually complex may be less mature in ego development. Thus, as the supervisor, you will need to be aware of gaps in the interns' development and adjust the structure accordingly. Second, we now know that as persons make transitions in cognitive-developmental growth it will probably be a time of high anxiety. During these transitions the supervisor should resort to a more structured approach in guiding the intern. As the colleague accommodates to the changes, you can return to a less structured, more open-ended approach to supervision.

 SUMMARY

We began the chapter by raising four questions: (1) Why is teacher reflection important? (2) How is teacher reflection guided? (3) Why is educative mismatching important? and (4) How can matching and mismatching principles be employed in the reflection process? Hopefully, the chapter has helped you form some preliminary answers to these questions.

Of course, the most important point of the chapter was that teacher reflection is a cornerstone to teacher development. It permits new learning and, when employed while the adult learner is engaged in a complex new role like teaching for the first time, presents a unique opportunity for growth and development.

How to initiate reflection framed the beginning of the chapter. Structured and unstructured journals were described as mainstays of purposeful reflective activity. The challenge for clinical mentors and supervisors is how to guide the reflective process. Drawing from ten years of research and practice, a number of propositions about guided teacher reflection through journal keeping were outlined:

1. Journal writing becomes crucial when persons are engaged in complex new helping roles like teaching for the first time because the new role is disequilibrating.
2. Sharing journals requires a trusting and accepting collegial relationship or the journals will be far less effective.
3. Provisions should be made for structured and less structured journal writing depending on the preference of the intern.
4. Journal entries reflect a person's current preferred system of solving complex "human-helping" problems.
5. Careful attention to a person's current preferred system of reflecting on teaching and learning, dilemmas, and personal issues provides a more thoughtful and "growth producing" response.
6. Journal responding "starts where the learner is" and only gradually mismatches written responses to encourage the intern's deeper reflection.

The six propositions for guiding teacher reflection were followed by a more in-depth look at the concepts of matching (starting where the young adult learner is) and mismatching (offering a slight challenge) as they relate to guided reflection. We submitted that matching and mismatching are two sides of the same coin of promoting teacher reflection. Indirect and direct supervisor journal responding were described as a framework for guiding reflection. Indirect responding included accepting feelings, praising or encouraging, accepting and/or clarifying ideas, and prompting inquiry. Direct responses included providing information, giving directions, and addressing problems.

Two journal case studies were then reviewed. Each case study explored the intern's journal as well as the supervisor's matching response. Additionally, a mismatching supervisor response was presented for Tim.

The crucial point of the chapter was that reflection or reflective teaching must be a central part of teacher education. Reflecting permits new learning. Guided reflection promotes teacher development. In its absence, one runs the risk of relying on routinized teaching and, as we have discovered, not developing to one's full capacity as a flexible, empathic, and principled adult.

SUPERVISION FOR TEACHER DEVELOPMENT ACTIVITIES

APPLIED

1. Reread Tim's journal entry. Compose your own response to Tim. Use the indirect/direct format described in the chapter to guide your written response.

2. Invite a colleague or beginning teacher to keep a journal over a period of several months. Provide the alternatives of a structured journal or a "free write journal." Each time a journal entry is submitted to you, write a "matching-mismatching" response that employs the format described in the chapter to guide your initial responses.

3. Read "Promoting the Development of Mentor Teachers: Theory and Research Programs Using Guided Reflection" by Reiman and Thies-Sprinthall (1993) for an elaboration of some of the ideas presented in the chapter. Write a paper that relates the theory and research to your personal experiences with reflection.

4. Think back to your experiences as a first-year teacher. Describe in a paper three or four significant experiences that left an indelible imprint on your work as a teacher. What feelings were present during these experiences?

5. Based on your work with interns, create a reflective case study for a novice teacher at a concrete conceptual level and at the abstract conceptual level. In each case, compose a sample supervisor response.

PORTFOLIO DEVELOPMENT

1. Maintain your weekly reflections. At the end of the month reread each journal entry. Summarize the major feelings and ideas that surfaced in the journal over the month. Having read all the reflective entries, report any "themes" that showed up across most of the journal entries. Keep this "meta-reflection" in your portfolio at the end of each month's reflections.

2. Write a summary of how your supervisee is reflecting on and making meaning from his or her teaching/learning experiences. Include in your summary
   a. What typically stands out as most significant for my colleague?
   b. What level of interpersonal understanding does my colleague have?
   c. Faced with difficult decisions, my colleague tends to resolve the issue in the following way . . .

SUGGESTED READINGS

1. Sprinthall, N. A., Reiman, A. J., & Thies-Sprinthall (1996). Teacher professional development. In J. Sikula (Ed.), *Second handbook of research on teacher education*. New York: Macmillan.

   This chapter reviews teacher professional development over the last 20 years. It includes recent cutting edge research in the cognitive-developmental arena and it summarizes the role reflection has played in supervision and teacher education programs.

2. Oja, S. N., & Reiman, A. J. (1997). Describing and promoting supervision for teacher development across the career span. In J. Firth and E. Pajak (Eds.), *Handbook of research on school supervision*. New York: Macmillan.

   This upcoming chapter summarizes recent theory and research on supervision for teacher development. Social role taking and guided reflection are central constructs for the review which ends with a discussion of the role developmental programs can play in building community.

3. King, P. M. , & Kitchener, K. S. (1994). *Developing reflective judgment: Understanding and promoting intellectual growth and critical thinking in adolescents and adults*. San Francisco: Jossey-Bass.

   This extraordinary work by the two authors reviews their 15 years of research with the reflective judgment model, which is

*based on the pioneering work of a number of cognitive-develop-
mentalists: Jean Piaget, Lawrence Kohlberg, William Perry, as
well as the influence of John Dewey. Their work is characterized
by both longitudinal and cross-sectional research that is both
provocative and robust.*

4. Gordon, T. (1974). Teacher effectiveness training. New York: Wyden.

*Chapter 5 of this text reviews the difference between "I" messages
and "you" messages.*

REFERENCES

Anson, C. M. (1989). Response styles and ways of knowing. In C. Anson (Ed.), *Writing and response: Theory, practice, and research* (pp. 332–366). Urbana, IL: National Council of Teachers of English.

Dewey, J. (1933). *How we think: A restatement of the relation of reflective thinking to the educative process.* Chicago: Henry Regnery.

Flanders, N. A. (1970). *Analyzing teacher behavior.* Reading, MA: Addison-Wesley.

Hedin, D. (1979). Teenage health educator: An action learning program to promote psychological development. *Dissertation Abstracts International, 40,* 754A. (University Microfilms No. 7918343). University of Minnesota: Minneapolis.

Hunt, D. E. (1981). Teachers' adaptation: Reading and flexing to students. In B. Joyce, C. Brown, & L. Peck (Eds.), *Flexibility in teaching: An excursion into the nature of teaching and training* (pp. 59–71). New York: Longman.

King, P. M., & Kitchener, K. S. (1994). *Developing reflective judgment.* San Francisco: Jossey-Bass.

Kitchener, K., & King, P. (1981). Reflective judgment: Concepts of justification and their relationship to age and education. *Journal of Applied Developmental Psychology, 2,* 89–116.

Loevinger, J. (1987). *Ego development.* San Francisco: Jossey-Bass.

Mann, A. F. (1992). *A quantitative and qualitative evaluation of a peer tutor-training course: A cognitive-developmental model.* Unpublished doctoral dissertation, North Carolina State University.

Mead, G. A. (1934). *Mind, self, and society.* Chicago: University of Chicago Press.

Oja, S. N., & Sprinthall, N. A. (1978). Psychological and moral development of teachers. In N. Sprinthall & R. Mosher (Eds.), *Value development as the aim of education.* Schenectady, NY: Character Research Press.

Reiman, A. J., & Parramore, B. (1993). Promoting preservice teacher development through extended field experience. In S. Odell & M. O'Hair (Eds.), *Diversity and teaching* (pp. 111–121). Orlando: Harcourt Brace Jovanovich.

Reiman, A. J., & Thies-Sprinthall, L. (1993). Promoting the development of mentor teachers: Theory and research programs using guided reflection. *Journal of Research and Development in Education, 26*(3), 179–185.

Schön, D. A. (1983). *The reflective practitioner.* New York: Basic Books.

Schön, D. A. (1987). *Educating the reflective practitioner.* San Francisco: Jossey-Bass.

Snow, R. E. (1987). Aptitude-treatment interaction models. In M. J. Dunkin (Ed.), *The international encyclopedia of teaching and teacher education* (pp. 28–31). New York: Pergamon.

Sprinthall, N. A., & Thies-Sprinthall, L. (1983). The teacher as an adult learner: A cognitive-developmental view. In G. A. Griffin (Ed.), *Staff development: Eighty-second yearbook of the National Society for the Study of Education* (pp. 13–35). Chicago: University of Chicago Press.

Thies-Sprinthall, L. (1984). Promoting the developmental growth of supervising teachers: Theory, research programs, and implications. *Journal of Teacher Education, 35*(3), 329–336.

Tom, A. (1985, April). *Inquiring into inquiry teacher education.* Paper presented at the annual meeting of the American Educational Research Association, Chicago.

van Manen, M. (1977). Linking ways of knowing with ways of being practical. *Curriculum Inquiry, 6,* 205–228.

Vygotsky, L. (1934). *Thought and language.* Moscow-Leningrad: Sozekgiz.

Vygotsky, L. (1978). *Mind in society.* Cambridge, MA: Harvard University Press.

Watson, B. (1995). *Early field experiences in teacher education: A developmental model.* Unpublished dissertation. North Carolina State University, Raleigh.

Zeichner, K., & Liston, D. (1987). Reflective teacher education and moral deliberation. *Journal of Teacher Education, 18*(6), 2–8.

C·H·A·P·T·E·R
14

Systematic Documentation for Developmental Growth

· · · · · ·

*T*hus far in Part III we have introduced the personal and interpersonal domains, described the "gaining knowledge" phase of mentoring and supervision, summarized the clinical cycle of assistance, reviewed the coaching model, and introduced guided reflection and the role it plays in teacher learning and development. We now turn to the question of how to self-assess and document work as a teacher and/or supervisor. As you review the chapter, check your comprehension by answering these questions:

- Why is documentation important?
- How have you documented your supervisory experiences?
- What changes might you make in documentation after reading this chapter?

RATIONALE FOR SELF-ASSESSMENT AND DOCUMENTATION

As you look within yourself and at teachers in your setting, you probably recognize that you are a unique and special person. No one else is quite like you. No one else has experienced the same set of life experiences and professional opportunities. No one else approaches the students in quite the same way during the first hour of a teaching session. No one else has the same unique blend of cognitive abilities, expectations, and attitudes about students, teachers, teaching, supervision, and learning. You are unique. Individual differences matter.

Similarly, you probably are aware of the many ways you are similar to other persons in general, and educators in particular. After all, we all need food, shelter, and love, and most of us cannot function without sleep. You may have a colleague who also places a high priority on greeting the students as they enter the school. Several of your peers may be involved in a peer coaching program or they may employ cooperative learning in their classrooms. And you probably would agree that many educators in any given school have recognizable similarities in how they care about education and its mission. Thus, in many ways, we are all alike or similar. Self-assessment and ongoing documentation record your unique skills and dispositions, as well as those skills that are more common to all educators.

In our view, ongoing self-assessment and documentation are essential elements of any true profession. What we mean is that professional educators should be able to show, in tangible and continuous ways, how they record learning and development. Thus, we recommend that in supervision and coaching, both the supervisor or coach and the teacher self-assess as well as maintain a record of their work together. Thus, ongoing self-assessment and documentation are two sides of the same coin—professionalism.

HOW CAN TEACHERS SELF-ASSESS?

Perhaps the most important dimension of self-assessment is the ability to reflect on one's experiences as a teacher. There is an old saying, "Ten years of experience or one year ten times," meaning, did the person learn anything new from the experience? Unfortunately for many of us, self-analysis may not be automatic. There are several ways to begin the self-assessment process. One way to begin is to record "perceived" teaching strengths and areas needing to be further refined. The general guidelines are as follows:

1. The self-assessment is a focused account of your personal, professional, and instructional strengths, as well as those areas needing development.

2. One goal is to provide you with an increasingly complex profile of your instruction. Therefore, the self-assessment needs to be ongoing. Remember our earlier discussion of the conditions for growth and development. Continuity is important.
3. A second goal of the self-assessment is to establish baseline data on those models and methods of instruction that are strengths, and that you would be comfortable demonstrating for a colleague.
4. Some teachers find it helpful to invite a colleague to observe their classroom instruction. Holding a conference afterward, you and your colleague could discuss your strengths and possible areas to develop. Other teachers have employed a camcorder or audio tape recorder to "freeze instruction" for a more in-depth self-analysis.
5. In the beginning, expect some personal dissonance unless you have done self-assessment before. You may find yourself being overly critical when you observe the videotape for the first time.
6. It also may be helpful to record your feelings as you begin the self-assessment process.

 HOW CAN SUPERVISORS SELF-ASSESS?

As we mentioned in Chapters 6 and 7, a personal style of supervision that is approachable, empathetic, supportive, enthusiastic, principled, and flexible significantly contributes to the supervisory or coaching process. For example, principals or teachers in supervisory or assistance roles need to learn not to dominate coaching discussions or post-observation conferences thus gaining more complete acceptance from their colleagues, particularly if they are willing to be observed teaching as part of the coaching cycle (demonstration, in fact, is a hallmark of the coach). If you were interested in developing your skill in this area you might self-assess your use of active listening. Systematically recording selective verbatim statements of active listening from an audiotaped conference, for example, permits you to assess your communication style. A second form of self-analysis that is more elaborate employs an adaptation of the Flanders system.

FLANDERS AND SUPERVISON: DIRECT VERSUS INDIRECT ASSISTANCE

The basic research of Ned Flanders (1970) and the later adaptation of the Flanders Interaction Analysis System to supervision by Blumberg (1980) has provided developmental educators and supervisors with a tool for assessing verbal interactions of a supervisor with his or her supervisee. To briefly review, Flanders identified ten categories of interaction that are included in Exhibit 14-1. Essentially, Blumberg adapted the Flanders system to supervision, using 15 categories of behavior. Ten of Blumberg's categories describe

Exhibit 14-1   FLANDERS INTERACTION ANALYSIS SYSTEM

INDIRECT	1. Accepts feelings
	2. Gives praise or encouragement
	3. Accepts or clarifies ideas
	4. Asks questions
DIRECT	5. Provides information
	6. Gives directions
	7. Criticizes or justifies authority
	8. Student talk—response
	9. Student talk—initiation
	10. Silence or confusion

the behavior of the supervisor, four focus on the behavior of the teacher, and one indicates silence or confusion. In our own work, we have found that the Flanders system stands on its own as a framework for analysis of the supervisory verbal interactions with only slight modifications.

Galloway's Nonverbal Behaviors' Framework

Furthermore, we have used the important work of Charles Galloway (1977), of Ohio State University who, along with a few other researchers, has found that as much as 75 percent of a message's impact is transmitted nonverbally. Essentially, Galloway and his colleagues developed a nonverbal version of the Flanders system. Instead of coding verbal messages, they rated the body language of the teachers. Exhibit 14-2 outlines the main elements of the Galloway system. The main implication of the work of Galloway for supervision is that your own nonverbal behavior will set the tone for supervision. Thus, it becomes important to become more self-aware of both the verbal and nonverbal messages that are sent. The use of videotapes of supervisory performance is a major way of building an awareness of one's communication. Such analysis can be done through self-analysis, or with the help of colleagues. In our supervision practicum, we employ both methods. After videotaping or audiotaping a cycle of developmental instructional supervision, the teacher or administrator first completes a self-analysis. This analysis is followed by further analysis and feedback from classmates in the course. Finally, the instructor gives feedback after a review of the cycle.

Exhibit 14-2   GALLOWAY'S NONVERBAL BEHAVIORS' FRAMEWORK

INDIRECT			

INDIRECT

1, 2. *Congruent*
Nonverbal behavior is consistent with words. There are no mixed messages.

Incongruent
Behavior contradicts words. Feelings are rarely shown.

3. *Implement*
Nonverbal behaviors are consistently encouraging: proximity, tone of voice, leaning, touch to shoulder.

Perfunctory
Nonverbal behaviors communicate lack of interest.

4. *Personal*
Teacher or supervisor maintains eye-to-eye contact.

Impersonal
Teacher or supervisor avoids eye contact.

DIRECT

5. *Responsive*
Tone and pace maintain interest.

Unresponsive
Tone and pace are not varied according to the needs of the student or colleague.

6. *Involve*
Direction giving includes checking for understanding.

Dismiss
Direction giving communicates compliance.

7. *Firm*
Nonverbal messages communicate consistency and firmness.

Harsh
Nonverbal behavior is controlling and severe.

Synthesizing the Frameworks

Having introduced the Flanders categories and the Galloway system, we have chosen to integrate the frameworks into a single model that could be employed in the service of promoting better supervisory practices. Our system (Thies-Sprinthall & Reiman, 1995) uses the main Flanders categories with a couple of notable additions. Category 4 (questioning) is expanded to include questions for ideas and for feelings. Category 5 (providing information) includes discussing opinions, research, or collected data from an observation. Category 7 is changed to controlling behavior and includes criticizing or justifying authority, and sending "I" messages (e.g., "When you are always late I feel frustrated because I am prevented from giving you complete feedback."). Likewise, Category 8 (colleague response) includes a place for ideas and for feelings. Similarly, Category 9 (colleague initiation) includes a place for ideas and for feelings. Exhibit 14-3 outlines the revised Flanders system.

We account for nonverbal interaction by periodically coding facilitative nonverbal communication as a plus next to the coding. An example of this

EXHIBIT 14-3 REVISED FLANDERS SYSTEM APPLIED TO SUPERVISORS

INDIRECT	1. Accepts feelings
	2. Gives praise or encouragement
	3. Accepts or clarifies ideas
	4. Asks questions
	a. Questions for ideas
	b. Questions for feelings
DIRECT	5. Provides information
	a. Opinions, information, or sharing of data
	b. Self-disclosure of feelings
	6. Gives directions
	7. Controlling behavior
	a. Criticizes or justifies authority
	b. Sends an "I" message
	8. Colleague talk—response
	a. Ideas
	b. Feelings
	9. Colleague talk—initiation
	a. Ideas
	b. Feelings
	10. Silence or confusion

coding system is included in the Supervision for Teacher Development Activities section at the end of the chapter. Our main point, however, is that supervisory behavior, by its very nature, exists in a context of social interaction. The events of mentoring, supervision or coaching, both verbal and nonverbal, cognitive and affective, can be observed as a series of patterns, and can be coded and analyzed for greater self-understanding and improved skills.

From a developmental view, it is important to address both the verbal and nonverbal interactions in supervision in a systematic way. Certainly from the perspective of the learner, whether that is a prospective supervisor or a teacher, a framework for self-evaluation is invaluable. Knowing the Flanders categories and the work of Galloway permits you to focus your analysis and interpretation of actual supervision. One of the difficult problems for developmental supervision is how to explicitly portray the complex interactions that occur between a supervisor and a supervisee. We have found the adapted Flanders system to be helpful for this purpose, because it records the amount of direct and indirect supervision that is occurring in, for example, a getting acquainted conference, a "gaining knowledge" conference, a coaching conference, or a post-observation conference.

As we mentioned at the beginning of the chapter, a primary goal of developmental supervision is being able to match the initial supervisory approach with the teachers' current preferred ways of learning and solving the complex "human helping" problems of instruction and schooling. Teachers who are functioning at Stage A conceptual level (concrete), moral reasoning (preconventional), and ego reasoning (fear of reprise), will need more structured supervision, more encouragement, and more opportunities for demonstration and practice. Thus, using the adapted Flanders system as our guide, a post-observation conference, once analyzed, might show a greater ratio of direct supervisor influence (60 percent) to indirect supervisor influence (40 percent). Furthermore, because the teacher lacks self-confidence and rarely shares feelings, there would be a greater number of supervisor Category 2 responses (praise and encouragement) as well as supervisor self-disclosures of feelings (Category 5b). As you might guess, the ratios are reversed for teachers at the more abstract and allocentric developmental levels (indirect, 60 percent to direct, 40 percent).

Up to this point, we have focused on self-assessment and the different forms it can take for teachers and supervisors. We now turn the coin, so to speak, to more closely examine the different forms of documentation that can support supervision or collegial coaching.

 THE ROLE OF DOCUMENTATION

As we mentioned earlier, documentation is a cornerstone of professional practice and nicely dovetails with the goal of self-assessment. Documentation in supervision at the preservice, induction, and inservice teacher education phases can include the following:

1. A letter of agreement for specific assistance (e.g., cooperating teacher/ student teacher, or mentor teacher/beginning teacher, teacher-principal).
2. A brief statement of the supervisor's or teacher's assumptions about schools, teaching, and learning.
3. A summary of previous experiences and learnings.
4. A summary of coaching plans.
5. Notation of all formal clinical cycles of assistance.
6. A brief statement of cases discussed and significant decisions.
7. A summary of written reflections.
8. A teaching profile.
9. A supervisory profile.
10. A record of significant problems encountered in the teaching, supervision, or mentoring.
11. A portfolio (all of the above).

As you can see from the list, self-assessment and documentation take many forms. Furthermore, such self-assessment and documentation for supervisors, mentors, and teachers account for the ways in which we are unique, as well as the ways in which we are similar. Let's take a closer look at two forms of documentation that complement the supervision process: the first is the teaching profile, and the second is the portfolio as a comprehensive form of documentation.

THE TEACHING PROFILE

Recall in Chapter 8 that we discussed the need for the supervisor to ascertain his or her own areas of teaching expertise as well as to be aware of the teacher's prior knowledge and experiences. This assessment takes three forms: review of the portfolio if it is available, discussion of the teacher's completed form, "Review of Prior Experiences," and a wide-lens classroom observation by the supervisor. Because we believe that instructional repertoire, using a variety of models and methods of teaching, has enduring formative effects on children, we have sought ways to help teachers establish baseline data on their use of the three assessment strategies, as well as the varied methods of teaching and observing teaching discussed in Chapter 8 and Chapter 10.

In some recent discussions with mentor teachers and principals over more than a year, we began to recognize that experienced teachers, beginning teachers, and student teachers appreciate being able to see exactly what kind of progress they are making in their instructional skills, particularly when they can monitor their own progress. Thus, a challenge for us was to collaboratively develop a document that would be easy to use and that could summarize formative growth in instruction. Additionally, we hoped the document could serve as a guide for instructional skills building and professional development.

The teaching profile (see Exhibit 14-4) that we have developed identifies the teaching models discussed in Chapter 8 as well as the methods of observing teaching reviewed in Chapter 10. The teaching profile is not intended to be a tool for evaluation by an outside agency. Instead, it is intended to be used between trusted colleagues who are working to improve their instructional repertoire. The profile can be completed as part of a self-assessment (gaining knowledge), and thus sets the stage for deciding on which teaching behavior focus to further refine during the coaching phase. The following experience in one of our school-based initiatives clarifies the potential of the teaching profile. Patricia is a second-year teacher who has overcome many of the first-year frustrations with classroom management. She is part of a schoolwide peer coaching program, and has teamed with another teacher, La-Keisha. Patricia is a bright, energetic teacher who is willing to take risks in her teaching, trying innovative new strategies that she has discussed with a colleague.

Patricia and La-Keisha have used the teaching profile as a means of tracking their progress during the school year. Together, they have worked on more student-student interaction, and more meaningful teacher-student interaction, focusing on the indirect categories of the Flanders system for data collection. Recently, in one of the informal discussions, La-Keisha and

EXHIBIT 14-4   TEACHING PROFILE

Classroom Management

1. Learning outcomes		
	Not measurable	Measurable
2. Directions		
	Often needs to repeat. Lack clarity; are not concise	Clear and concise
3. Aware of student activity		
	Does not intervene before the problem escalates	Consistently intervenes
4. Materials ready		
	Materials are never prepared in advance	Materials are ready
5. Lesson planning		
	Strategies do not match outcomes	Strategies are appropriate
6. Engaged learning		
	Students are often off-task	Students are engaged

Classroom Atmosphere

1. Paraphrasing of feelings		
	Rarely employed	Consistently used in an instructional day
2. Paraphrasing of ideas		
	Rarely employed	Consistently used in an instructional day
3. Acknowledgments and door openers		
	Rarely employed	Consistently used in an instructional day
4. Tone of voice		
	Harsh or judgmental	Accepting
5. Equitable response opportunities		
	Response opportunities are limited to a small group of students	Opportunities are equitable

Positive Reinforcement

1. Simple verbal acknowledgments		
	Infrequently employed	Frequently employed

Exhibit 14-4   *(continued)*

2. Differentiated (rewarding part of answer)	Rarely employed	Frequently employed
3. Delayed (rewarding an earlier response)	Rarely employed	Frequently employed
4. Extended reinforcement	Rarely employed	Frequently employed
Cooperative Learning	Rarely employed	Frequently employed

Frequency and Quality of Teacher-Student and Student-Student Interaction

1. Direct/Indirect	Ratio is not matched to students' developmental level	Ratio is matched to students' developmental level
2. Adequate student talk	Student talk is infrequent and perfunctory	Student talk is frequent and meaningful

Questioning

1. Cues and feedback	Little probing occurs	Probing is frequent
2. Wait time 3+ seconds a. After question by teacher	Not employed in a lesson	Consistently employed
b. After question or response by student	Not employed in a lesson	Consistently employed
3. Higher-level questions	Rarely employed	Employed in every lesson

Metacognitive Strategies

1. Encourages use of student learning logs	Yes _____	No _____
2. Prompts student self-questioning	Rarely employed	Employed in every lesson
3. Models metacognition by "talking out loud" about thinking	Rarely employed	Employed in every lesson

EXHIBIT 14-4 *(continued)*

Models of Teaching

Model 1—Knowledge transmission	Needs improvement _____	Strength _____
Model 2—Inquiry	Needs Improvement _____	Strength _____
Model 3—Interpersonal	Needs Improvement _____	Strength _____
Model 4—Teaching for understanding	Needs improvement _____	Strength _____

Patricia talked about the equitable use of response opportunities. La-Keisha submitted that too many teachers interact with only a small group of kids who, typically, always have the right answer. "Teachers love to hear the right answers," La-Keisha argues. "But the end result is that a large number of kids are not being included in the learning process." Patricia and La-Keisha agree to spend at least one month looking at their own teaching to see whether it models equity in response opportunities.

As this example points out, the teaching profile became a guide for charting professional growth in instruction, and it also became a reflective tool, prompting the teachers to ask deeper questions about the teaching/learning process. Naturally, the current cognitive-structural level of these teachers intersects with the teachers' willingness to adapt new innovations. And, as we pointed out in Chapter 8, the Inquiry model and the Interpersonal model place greater cognitive and affective demands on the teacher.

 ## TEACHING AND SUPERVISORY PORTFOLIOS

There has been a growing discussion about how portfolios can contribute to more authentic self-assessment and documentation, and the improvement of instruction and teaching/learning. Articles on the topic range from discussions of how portfolios represent teaching and learning, to specific "how-to's" for developing portfolios (Wolf, 1991). Common to all of the discussions, however, is a definition of the portfolio as a purposeful collection of work that records one's learnings, dispositions, development, and "demonstrated teaching ability" (Darling-Hammond, 1996). And you have been building a supervisory portfolio as you have proceeded through the text and completed the activities at the end of each chapter.

WHY PORTFOLIOS?

The answer lies in its main purpose, which is to document, with purposefulness and from multiple sources, one's own learning and growth. Documentation is conducted by selectively preserving self-reflective statements, collected data (artifacts) on chosen "best teaching practices," work samples of students' learning along with teacher analysis, and related work that represents one's cognitive-structural development and professional growth.

A remarkable learning experience unfolds when you reflect on your teaching and on the learning of your students. Nonetheless, the concept of developing a teaching portfolio may seem confusing and complex to a beginning teacher. The supervisor or mentor can help reduce this confusion. Before we make some recommendations for portfolio development, however, we would like to offer you a number of cautions about portfolios:

1. Keep the focus on instructional growth, students' learning, and personal growth and development.
2. Ask the "value-added" question. Does the addition of a particular artifact qualitatively strengthen the portfolio's portrayal of learning and growth?
3. Avoid overdocumentation or "padding."
4. Highlight the very best teaching or supervision.

With these cautions in mind, let us turn to the development of a portfolio. First, remember the adage that "actions speak louder than words." If, in your role as a supervisor, you are actively maintaining a teaching profile, then it will be far easier to guide and support the portfolio development of a colleague. Also, because our emphasis in this text is developmental instructional supervision, our recommendations favor those aspects of portfolio development that directly relate to the teaching/learning process and cognitive-structural growth.

Perhaps the best beginning for a teaching portfolio would be a narrative account of your thoughts on the goals of schooling, how students learn, and your own role as a teacher. This personal philosophy of teaching can be followed by a section on teaching/learning, a section on students, and a section for your own self-reflections about your growth as a human being. Each section would typically end with goals for instructional improvement or personal growth. In this chapter we have mentioned the teaching profile as an important resource for guiding the supervisory process. Naturally, it also would be an important part of the teaching portfolio. The teaching profile serves as an organizing framework for guiding instructional improvement on selected new teaching methods and models. In Exhibit 14-5 we outline the major components of our proposed teaching portfolio.

Can you visualize how the supervisor's portfolio might need to be altered? After all, the goal of the portfolio is the purposeful collection of work that records one's learnings, dispositions, and development over time. As we have mentioned before, a mentor, peer coach, principal, or program supervisor should be able to model effective teaching practices, self-reflection, and careful analysis of student learning. Thus the supervisor's or coach's portfolio can include all the dimensions that are briefly described in Exhibit 14-5. Still needed, however, are categories to address supervisory skills. In Exhibit 14-6 we outline additional components of a supervisor's portfolio.

Exhibit 14-5 TEACHING PORTFOLIO

Personal Philosophy
1. Goals of schooling
2. How students learn
3. The role of the teacher

Instruction
4. Teaching profile assessment
5. Coaching plans
6. Documents supporting coaching plans (e.g., lesson plans, written self-analysis of the lesson, audiotapes or videotapes of instruction)

Information About Students
7. Student work including teacher's analysis
8. Samples of dialogue journals between the teacher and student
9. Careful analysis of a student's own cognitive development

Personal and Professional Growth
10. Written reflections on an ethical dilemma (value judgment)
11. Summary of benchmark feelings and thoughts from personal journal (personal development)
12. Description of problem solving employed in work with students, teachers, and parents (conceptual development)

 # PUTTING ALL THE PIECES TOGETHER

The challenge for developmental instructional supervision is how to translate the admittedly lofty goals of building instructional repertoire and promoting growth and development into a plan of action for supervision. After

Exhibit 14-6 SUPERVISOR'S PORTFOLIO

Personal Philosophy
1. Mission and goals of supervision
2. How adults learn
3. The role of the supervisor

Supervision
4. Supervisor profile
5. Coaching Plan for Supervision
6. Documents supporting coaching plans (e.g., lesson plans, written self-analysis of the coaching of the colleague, pre-conference, observation, post-conference, and audiotapes or videotapes of supervision)
7. Narrative on effective matching/mismatching strategies

Information About Your Colleague
8. Colleague's work including his or her self-analysis
9. Samples of dialogue journals
10. Careful self-analysis by a colleague of his or her cognitive development

all, some of our own research has shown that even experienced teachers who try out their current methods, master those, and systematically enlarge their repertoire of models and methods of teaching are more effective teachers and show definite evidence of developmental growth (Thies-Sprinthall, 1984). However, such growth does not take place automatically without a plan of action and continuous reflection, both of which are forms of self-assessment and documentation. Indeed, the two processes must go hand in hand. First you try a new approach, then you review the results, analyze, make changes, and try again.

We now present two case studies that are drawn from our work over the past 15 years. Both case studies include self-assessment and documentation. Additionally, the first case study integrates much of what has been discussed in Part III, and the second case study introduces the concept of the miseducative supervisory experience. The Teaching/Learning Framework, as described in Chapter 4, outlines the conditions needed for building a repertoire of teaching models as well as the conditions needed for growth and development. Exhibit 14-7 reviews the framework. As we introduce each of the case studies, we will refer to the Teaching/Learning Framework, as well as to the adapted Flanders system.

Remember that development toward greater flexibility starts when you become aware of the supervisory strategies with which you are most comfortable, and then proceed to refine those strategies and to acquire new models of supervision. Our goal throughout the text is to help supervisors and mentors look at their practice from a variety of perspectives. However, we know that it is tempting to maintain strategies that are comfortable and to be reluctant to modify approaches, particularly if the new approach or model does not fit into the framework one is currently employing. In a Piagetian sense, we would call this part of the process of assimilation. Only through moving to the next level of awareness can a supervisor become more able to ascertain his or her colleague's thoughts and feelings, and begin to reframe his or her supervisory practice to accommodate to the new, disequilibrating information.

Exhibit 14-7   TEACHING/LEARNING FRAMEWORK

INSTRUCTIONAL REPERTOIRE*	**CONDITIONS FOR GROWTH AND DEVELOPMENT†**
1. Theory/rationale	1. Complex new role
2. Demonstrations	2. Guided reflection
3. Practice with feedback	3. Balance between new role and reflection
4. Adapt and generalize through coaching	4. Support and challenge
	5. Continuity

*For instructional repertoire model, see Joyce and Showers (1995).
†For the cognitive-developmental model, see Sprinthall and Thies-Sprinthall (1983).

As you read the case studies, give attention to both the supervisor and the colleague, and how they are reflecting-in-action. Hunt (1978) argued that the theory-to-practice approach to the implementation of developmental programs is flawed without careful consideration of the role played by context and individual differences. He encourages us to think of practitioners as theorists and as persons-in-relation. The message is an important one. Not only should we take into account the intentions, prior knowledge, and competence of the supervisor or teacher, it is also important for the theorist to be reflective and responsive to the lessons of practice. We like to say that *theory should be visible in practice, and practice should be visible in theory*. Developmental behaviors and interactions should be classified by a variety of methods over time (for example, interviews, observations, and unobtrusive measures). And theorists must be willing to apply the theory to themselves. This final observation would seem like good common sense. Remember, however, what happened to Freud and Jung's relationship when Jung attempted to apply Freud's theory to Freud. Jung's boldness led to the ending of their friendship.

Developmental supervision can be employed at all junctures in the supervisory continuum. This continuum includes a number of benchmark activities. Among them are the following initiatives in their proper sequence:

Phase 1. Establishing the teacher-supervisor relationship
Phase 2. Gaining knowledge
Phase 3. Developing and implementing the coaching plan
Phase 4. Planning for the observation
Phase 5. Observing instruction
Phase 6. Analyzing the teaching/learning process
Phase 7. Conducting the post-observation conference
Phase 8. Renewed planning and coaching

The first case study takes you through each of these benchmark activities between a mentor and protegé that includes effective or educative mentoring.

Case Study—Sandy and Don

Don is new to the world of teaching. Both of his parents are educators and Don has always assumed he would become a teacher. He has not been very reflective about his education courses, preferring to "just get by." Although he is relatively unfamiliar with what lies ahead in the teaching journey he is eager to begin. Don's personal maturity, conceptual level, moral judgment, and ego development are at Stage A. Thus, he prefers high structure, leans toward a "single tried-and-true approach to teaching," resolves ethical issues based on what his peers or supervisors think, and rarely reflects on his thoughts and feelings about experiences.

Don's supervising mentor is Sandy, who has had extensive preparation for her role as a mentor, having participated in a two-semester sequence of courses collaboratively conducted by the school system and a nearby university. Sandy enjoys working with beginning teachers and recognizes the importance of effective mentoring. She has worked with three beginning teachers previously and has been a classroom teacher for 12 years. Sandy is at post-conventional conceptual and ego levels. She prefers low structure when she is learning, is autonomous, and enjoys collaborative projects, when she has time. However, when ethical issues emerge, she normally resolves the issue at the conventional level of moral reasoning, using school/university rules and policies as her guide.

PHASE 1—ESTABLISHING THE TEACHER-MENTOR RELATIONSHIP

Don and Sandy conducted a getting acquainted conference, which Sandy tape-recorded, ten days before the first official day of Don's teaching experience. Sandy began the conference by inquiring about Don's hobbies. This was followed by Sandy's sharing her interest in gardening. A series of questions from Sandy followed: "How do you learn best?" "Based on your experiences to date, what do you consider your teaching strengths?" "What areas of instruction would you like to develop further?" "What concerns do you have?" Don mentioned his preference for concrete examples when he discussed his own learning, as well as his interest in taking the lead from Sandy. He also mentioned classroom lecture as his teaching strength. However, he was less forthcoming about concerns, stating that he did not have any concerns. Sandy actively listened to Don, shared her own recollections and apprehensions when she was a beginning teacher, and discussed the importance of confidentiality in the mentoring experience. The conference concluded with Sandy and Don setting a time for a "diagnostic" conference. Sandy also asked Don to begin maintaining a "-dialogue journal" in a three-ring binder that Sandy would read and respond to, and for Don to write some reflections about the getting acquainted conference.

Mentor Assessment. Afterward Sandy listened to the tape recording of the conference. She noted Don's insistence that Sandy always take the lead, a possible indication of Don's dependence on the mentor. It is clear Don would prefer for Sandy to take major responsibility for the content and direction of the mentoring. Don mentioned his preference for concrete examples and the lecture method, possible clues that Don believes there is a single right way to teach. Sandy makes some notes to herself about Don's continued references to the role his parents have played in his decision to become a teacher. Finally, Don's comments on the tape recorder remind Sandy that Don's awareness of both self and others appears quite limited. Don was unable to specify in any detail his teaching strengths and weaknesses, did not mention students in his conversation, and he did not disclose personal feelings.

PHASE 2—GAINING KNOWLEDGE

At the gaining knowledge conference Don and Sandy reviewed Don's work as a student teacher. His cooperating teacher and his college supervisor encouraged him to keep a record of all observations and evaluation data. Don discussed the observations in very general terms. Each week included a variety of activities with observation and assistance dominant in the early part of the semester, and teaching taking precedence in the second half of the semester. Don gave Sandy a packet that summarized specific observations and assistance activities he had completed. Don did not complete the questionnaire which explored instructional strengths. Recognizing its importance, Sandy encouraged Don to complete it as part of their conversation. Sandy concluded the conference by asking for Don's written reflections on the getting acquainted conference, which she promised to respond to and return to Don. She also asked him to write a similar set of reflections about the "gaining knowledge" conference. Don's written reflections were very brief and summarized the main parts of the conference and Don's willingness to meet Sandy's expectations.

As part of this phase of mentoring, Sandy also arranged to observe Don conducting a lesson for the third-grade students while she observed. Don understood that the observation would be diagnostic in nature, and that together, Don and Sandy would develop an initial coaching plan to guide his work on a particular instructional focus. Don planned to teach a lesson he had prepared in one of his method's classes. The topic was conservation. Don began by explaining that the lesson would give the students a better appreciation of the importance of conservation. He then proceeded to lecture for 15 minutes on the importance of conservation, concluding by asking the students if there were any questions. The lesson incorporated up-to-date information on the topic, but it did not engage the students, did not have a measurable learning outcome for the students, and provided no opportunity for guided practice.

In the debriefing session at the end of the day, Sandy asked Don how he was feeling now that the lesson was over. He stated he was fine and that he thought the lesson had gone well. When Sandy probed for the reasons, Don acknowledged that he made it through the entire lecture without "tripping over his own words." When asked what he might want to improve, Don recounted his professor's admonitions that teachers need to teach for higher-order thinking, thus, he stated that he might want to ask more higher-level questions.

Mentor Assessment. Sandy's reflection on the "gaining knowledge" conference confirmed her prediction that Don prefers high structure. The discussion revolved around Don's prior experiences. Sandy noted that Don was so focused on the mechanical aspects of the discussion that he once again did not ask how aspects of the plan might relate to student learning and overall classroom activities. The bulk of Don's questions about the plan were personal (focused on self) in nature: "How will I be evaluated?" "What happens if I do not understand the goal of an observation?" Don's continued focus on self and his written reflections underscore his dependence on Sandy.

PHASE 3—DEVELOPING AND IMPLEMENTING THE COACHING PLAN

Sandy used Don's statement about higher-level questions as an opportunity to discuss the importance of questions to check for student understanding. The coaching plan that they developed identified checking for understanding as Don's initial instructional focus. Sandy also included in Don's coaching plan several opportunities for him to observe Sandy and other teachers employing "checking for understanding," as well as multiple opportunities for practice and self-assessment. Additionally, Sandy added specific dates for follow-up on the progress of the coaching plan. When the coaching phase was implemented, Sandy offered frequent feedback and reinforcement to Don, and related discussions of the teaching skill to specific classroom events. Thus, the coaching plan and the subsequent implementation followed a concise, step-wise format with frequent opportunities for Sandy to monitor Don's progress.

Mentor Assessment. Clearly Sandy is beginning to translate the theory of development into mentoring practice. The coaching plan uses the theory of Joyce and Showers, and the follow-up coaching and assistance conferences have built-in, numerous opportunities for guided reflection and support. Sandy also has employed an important principle related to conceptual level, in which she provides high structure to keep Don's anxiety at a manageable level and to encourage success with the new teaching strategy.

In terms of ego development, Sandy's sustained positive feedback encourages Don to feel greater confidence in his abilities. As his confidence grows, his need for feedback, and his dependence on Sandy for guidance will subside. The frequent follow-up conferences during the coaching phase allow Sandy to monitor how Don is reflecting and making meaning from his experiences. The self-focus, characteristic of less complex ego levels, limits Don's ability to accurately judge his effectiveness with the students.

Finally, Don's preference for moral reasoning at the Conformity level (Kohlberg) helps explain why he defers to Sandy for leadership and advice. However, a goal of Sandy's is to encourage greater risk taking, independence, and decision making based on curriculum guidelines and sound professional judgment. Thus, she often asks Don to explain his rationale for his decisions. Such a supervisory strategy encourages more independent thinking, and prompts Don to rely less on the advice of Sandy.

PHASES 4 TO 7—CLINICAL CYCLE OF ASSISTANCE

A cornerstone of Sandy's mentoring work are the cycles of developmental instructional supervision that she conducts with beginning teachers. The objective is to initiate a cycle (pre-observation conference, observation, analysis, and post-observation conference) after substantive coaching and assistance with the colleague. The assumption is that the cycle represents an opportunity for the teacher to demonstrate some level of "executive control" with the specified teaching behavior focus. Because the second case study goes into detail regarding the clinical cycle, this case study summarizes only the main outcomes of Don and Sandy's cycle, leaving the more in-depth account for later.

In Don's case, the teaching behavior focus is checking for student understanding through questioning. With Sandy's assistance, Don was able to review current research on questioning, observe Sandy and two other teachers employ questioning as a means of checking for student understanding, and practice the questioning skill in his own classroom. The demonstrations and practice sessions took place over a month. Sandy suggested that they conduct a clinical cycle of supervision as a final component of Don's learning. He agreed, stating that his confidence with questioning had grown dramatically during the past two weeks.

Notable aspects of the pre-observation conference were Don's new confidence with questioning, his understanding of its role/rationale for effective instruction, a continued reluctance to share feelings, and his ongoing difficulty in writing measurable learning outcomes. Throughout the pre-observation conference Sandy actively listened, encouraging Don to elaborate on his ideas.

Sandy used the same questioning observation form Don had used when he observed Sandy and the other teachers. The form required Sandy to write verbatim examples of questions. Don used significantly more questions and they were interspersed throughout the lesson to check for student understanding. However, the questions were largely lower-order questions, recall and comprehension, and the lesson did not connect with students' prior knowledge and experiences. Although the students were more involved in the lesson, there were many opportunities for student involvement that were not realized.

During the post-observation conference Sandy and Don reviewed the lesson. Sandy began each component of the post-conference by asking for Don's thoughts, "Were the learning outcomes reached?" "Are there any changes you would make to the outcomes?" Can you describe classroom management?" "Are there any changes you would make in your classroom management?" "Can you discuss your teaching behavior focus—questioning?" "Please summarize the main points we have discussed in the post-conference." As Don responded to each of the questions, Sandy listened carefully, occasionally paraphrasing one of his comments, or probing with a door opener like, "tell me more." Don had some difficulty remembering details about the lesson, but he was confident that a larger number of questions were asked. During Sandy's follow-up remarks she asked Don about the types of questions he asked. He appeared confused, so she read some of the verbatim questions she had recorded during the observation. Don still seemed confused by Sandy's question, so she asked if he was familiar with Bloom's taxonomy of questions. He said he had heard of Bloom but that he could not recall any specifics. As a consequence, Don and Sandy developed a new coaching plan that focused on Don's employment of at least five higher-order questions during a lesson. Throughout the post-conference Sandy also offered her own data and suggestions.

Mentor Assessment. The cycle of assistance had dual purposes: the completion of the coaching plan that Don and Sandy had developed, and Don's introduction to clinical supervision as a valued process for his learning and development. Sandy's challenge as a mentor is significant, to balance Don's input with her own contributions. Recall the discussion of the Flanders system earlier in the chapter. A more directive style of supervision vis-à-vis the adapted Flanders system matches the needs of teachers at pre-conventional levels of development. Thus Sandy provided a more direct style of mentoring. Her actual ratio in the pre-conference was 54 percent direct to 46 percent indirect supervisor responses. The post-observation conference was 64 percent direct to 36 percent indirect supervisor responses. Although Sandy used all categories of indirect supervision in the conferences, accepting feelings, encouragement, accepting ideas, and asking questions, the conferences included a greater percentage of information sharing (data, conference procedures) and direction giving. Thus, her supervision matched Don's current preferred style of problem solving. Note that Sandy's attention is with *how* Don thinks and feels, not *what* Don thinks and feels!

Case Study—Melanie and Ruth: Miseducative Supervision

Melanie is a student teacher, yet her teaching prowess exceeds that of most student teachers. She is equally adept at managing whole group instruction, small group work, and individual learning needs. In fact, Melanie seems to embody Hunt's concept of "reading and flexing." She views the students as participants in learning, and varies the instruction and pace according to the needs of the students.

Melanie is entering the post-conventional levels of conceptual, ego, and value judgment. She prefers low structure, consistently reflects on her experiences as a teacher, accepts both the joys and tribulations of teaching as important parts of her experience, and is committed to social justice issues. In fact, the previous spring she participated in a college of education program that looked at equitable and inequitable instruction according to race, gender, and ethnicity.

In contrast, her cooperating teacher Ruth holds quite strongly to the view that there is a single correct way to teach. She is considered to be a strict teacher who exclusively employs whole group instruction, giving out large amounts of homework with the expectation that the facts be memorized. Some of the students excel in her classroom; however, there also are students who learn very little in her classroom. Ruth sees her cooperating teacher role as that of gatekeeper, assuring that the intern is indoctrinated into the rigorous values and expectations of the school. Ruth also subscribes to the "sink or swim" philosophy for student teachers, believing that good teaching (teaching with the ruler in hand) will be justly rewarded. Ruth, although she has 22 years of teaching experience, is at pre-conventional levels of development. She prefers high structure, is not very self-aware, does not take the perspective of students or colleagues, and relies on reward and punishment to resolve ethical issues.

The following narrative (see Exhibit 14-8 on page 304) summarizes a pre-observation conference between Melanie and Ruth. The elements of the conference are derived from the pioneering work of Cogan with supervisors of intern teachers at Harvard University. The letter C represents cooperating teacher talk. The letter S represents student teacher talk.

The pre-observation conference had a ratio of 80 percent direct to 20 percent indirect supervisor responses. Ruth, the cooperating teacher, dominated the conference discussion. After analysis of the observation data Ruth found that 23 out of 26 students had received response opportunities. Furthermore, the learning outcomes were met as evidenced by student projects. However, Ruth thought there was too much small group work and that, at times, the noise in the classroom was counterproductive.

During the post-observation conference Ruth once again dominated the conference, listened only in a perfunctory way, and recommended changes rather than asking Melanie what she would change.

Supervisor Assessment. As you can see from the selected narrative comments, the pre-observation conference was controlled by the cooperating teacher. Additionally, feelings were not addressed, and listening by Ruth was, at best, perfunctory. Melanie had few opportunities to explore some significant ideas that she raised; among them were equitable instruction and curriculum integration. Furthermore, there were large gaps in the pre-conference format. These outcomes are not surprising given Ruth's current development—low conceptual level, low ego development, and pre-conventional thinking in value judgment. She dominates the conference, is reluctant to pursue feelings, and avoids open-ended questions that might lead to unfamiliar terrain.

Such a supervisory response, particularly from the developmental standpoint, is discouraging. After all, Melanie has a surprisingly deep awareness of herself and she can articulate her own learning and teaching with depth. As we mentioned earlier, she is at the beginning of post-conventional levels of conceptual, ego, and moral reasoning. Thus, Melanie "reads and flexes" her instruction according to the needs of the students, she is flexible and is not easily threatened, she gladly engages in discussions about theory, and she is able to self-evaluate her instruction. She also is probably

EXHIBIT 14-8 PRE-OBSERVATION CONFERENCE—MELANIE AND RUTH

SUPERVISOR'S SELF-EVALUATION FORM

COMPONENT	BEHAVIOR
1. Purpose—select one a. _____ Orientation b. _____ Concern c. __x__ Instruction d. _____ Review progress	*C: "Our purpose for this meeting is to discuss your efforts to improve instruction."
2. Feelings a. _____ Evidence of listening b. _____ Teacher feelings c. _____ Mentor feelings	Left blank.
3. Learning Outcomes a. __x__ Learning outcome b. __x__ Rationale for selection c. _____ Lesson plan for outline d. _____ Evidence of listening	C: "I see from your lesson plan that you have several outcomes. Are they connected to the state curriculum guidelines?" †S: "As a matter of fact they are. In fact, I have been attempting to integrate the curriculum in my classroom. This lesson is one of my first attempts to accomplish this." C: "I see."
4. Teaching Behavior a. __x__ Teaching focus b. __x__ Rationale for selection c. _____ Evidence of listening	C: "What is your teaching focus for this lesson?" S: "Equitable response opportunities." C: "Okay, why did you select that focus?" S: "I want all of the students involved in the lessons. I have worked hard to improve in this area and I know your feedback will be helpful."
5. Information Gathering a. __x__ Observation instrument b. _____ Collect data on three additional questions: • Did you reach outcomes? • Was management supportive? • What else did you do effectively or need to change?	C: "I will write down the names of every student you call on during the lesson." *The mentor did not comment about the other categories.*

EXHIBIT 14-8 *(continued)*

SUPERVISOR'S SELF-EVALUATION FORM

COMPONENT	BEHAVIOR

6. Ground Rules
    a. __x__ Notes will be written
    b. __x__ Share notes
    c. _____ Notes on three items
    d. _____ Logistics—where should I sit?
	C: "I'll sit at the back of your classroom while I collect my data. I will share them with you during the post-conference."
	S: "That will be fine."

7. Follow-up
    a. __x__ Feedback time
    b. __x__ Self-analysis sheet
    c. __x__ Any questions
	C: "I have arranged to discuss the outcomes of the observation at 3:30. I hope that is satisfactory with you. I would also like you to complete this self-evaluation sheet before we meet for the post-conference. Any questions?"
	S: "No. I am ready to get started."

*C: Cooperating teacher
†S: Student teacher

aware of the limitations implicit in the cooperating teacher/student teacher relationship. Melanie probably needs minimal supervisory input, and she probably is able to ask for assistance when she needs it.

In some of our own work (Thies-Sprinthall, 1980), a study was conducted to distinguish the elements of educative from miseducative supervision. The findings indicated that if a low conceptual level supervising teacher is matched with a student teacher at high conceptual levels, it leads to a negative learning environment. The supervising teacher is unable to be responsive and accommodative to the needs of the student teacher.

SUMMARY

In this chapter we turned to the question of how to self-assess and document your use of each teaching model and the instructional strategies within the models. We argued that supervisors or peer coaches need to have a comprehensive understanding of their own skills, aptitudes, and development before they work with others. The adage "action speaks louder than words" says it best. All of us must be willing to model best practices for our colleagues and associates. This is particularly true in the field of developmental instructional supervision. A familiar litany among student teachers is that their college professors never model the practices they verbally espouse. The absence of modeling must be anathema to effective supervisors and mentors in schools and universities.

We believe that instructional improvement and cognitive development require more than just excessive contemplation of the possibilities. Granted, the supervisor must become knowledgeable about self-assessment and documentation tools that can facilitate learning and growth. After all, we described the process of self-assessment, the advantages of a teaching profile for documentation, and the merits of maintaining a teaching portfolio, as contributions to your background knowledge.

However, it is also important to act on this knowledge. In particular, we hope your review of this chapter underscores the importance of modeling behavior. If self-assessment, teaching profiles, and coaching plans are necessary parts of a new teacher's learning and development, then they must be modeled as best practices by the supervisor.

Hopefully, as you read through the chapter, you reflected on your own beginnings as a teacher. How did you document your own teaching? Did you approach the month of May with a teaching portfolio that included "best works" from your year of teaching? If so, what kinds of supervision and/or staff development were most facilitative? If your experience was bereft of careful support, supervision, and purposeful professional growth, do you consider the types of self-assessment and instructional documentation described in this chapter helpful?

As you begin to implement teaching portfolios, remember that too much documentation is as unwise as too little documentation. Beware of "padding." A teaching portfolio should chronicle your learning and development as a supervisor and as a teacher. Use the teaching profile as an organizing framework for the instructional part of your portfolio, and highlight the very best episodes. And don't forget to record the learnings of your colleagues, as well as your ongoing reflections on their learnings.

The adapted Flanders system represents one solution to the thorny problem of trying to understand supervisory style. Specifically, the problem has been the failure to match and mismatch strategies according to the needs of the supervisee. The Flanders instrument can be used as a tool for self-evaluation of the clinical supervision process. It allows for careful analysis of the ratio of indirect to direct supervisor talk, as well as the percentage of supervisor talk to supervisee talk. Additionally, a simple coding system can account for nonverbal interactions. As we mentioned in the chapter, a supervisory goal for work with a teacher at low stages of conceptual, ego, and moral development is 60 percent direct responses to 40 percent indirect responses. In effect, the ratio represents a more structured conference. In contrast, a supervisory goal for work with a teacher at high levels of conceptual, ego, and moral development is 40 percent direct responses to 60 percent indirect responses. As you might suspect, for the teacher at moderate developmental complexity, the ratio would be balanced (50 percent/50 percent).

SUPERVISION FOR TEACHER DEVELOPMENT ACTIVITIES

APPLIED

1. As we mentioned earlier, the work of Ned Flanders (1970) has been a very helpful framework for assisting prospective supervisors in the self-evaluation of their supervision. What follows is a review before you complete the practice activity. Although Flanders and his associates did not look directly at supervision, Blumberg (1980) saw the importance of connecting Flanders' work to the field of supervision. The ten categories he adapted are as follows:

   (1) Accepts feelings
   (2) Praises or encourages
   (3) Accepts or clarifies ideas
   (4) Asks questions
   (5) Provides information
   (6) Gives directions
   (7) Criticizes or justifies authority
   (8) Supervisee talk—response
   (9) Supervisee talk—initiation
   (10) Silence or confusion

      The main point we have tried to make is that the adapted Flanders system permits in-depth analysis of developmental supervision. It can ascertain the following:

   • The percentage of indirect to direct supervision
   • The percentage of supervisor talk to supervisee talk
   • The patterns of supervisory communication
   • The number of supervisor questions
   • The supervisor responses to feelings
   • The presence of facilitative nonverbal communication

      Although we recommend a more direct and structured style of supervision for teachers at lower developmental stages, it is still important for the effective supervisor to ask questions, encourage, accept and clarify ideas, and respond to feelings.
      Data on the adapted Flanders system can be collected primarily in two ways. The first method is to simply place tally marks to the right of a category each time the interaction is observed. Flanders recorded data every 3 seconds. The advantage of this process is its ease of use. The disadvantage of this method is that it does not permit analysis of the

patterns of interaction over the length of the lesson or supervisory conference. The second method, and the one preferred by Flanders, is to record every 3 seconds the numeral that represents the category observed. Thus, a 3 would be noted for an accepting or clarifying response. In our modified system, a 3+ would indicate that the nonverbal message was congruent with the verbal message. Once the lesson or conference had been coded in entirety, a number of analyses could be conducted. Let's examine the following abbreviated set of interactions that were collected on a supervisory conference. Read the interactions from top to bottom and from left to right:

5	5	2	8	4	5	8	8
5	5	4	1	8	5	8	9
5	4+	4	3	8	5	5	2
5	4+	8	3	8	9	3	5
5	8	8	3	8	9	3	5
4	8	8	3	8	9	5	6
8	8	8	3	8	9	5	6
8	8	8	5	8	5	5	6
8	3	8	5	9	5	4	2
8	3	8	5	9	4	8	2
1+	2	8	4	9	4	8	9

Now complete the following directions. Place the total or percentage in the space to the right.

Tally

1. All indirect interactions (Categories 1–4) would be added together. _____

2. All direct interactions (Categories 5–7) would be added together. _____

3. All interactions (Categories 1–7) would be added together. _____

4. All supervisee talk interactions would be added together (Categories 8 and 9). _____

5. The total of the indirect interactions (Categories 1–4) would be divided by the total supervisor interactions (Categories 1–7) to give the percentage of supervisor indirect talk. _____

    Subtracting this percentage from 100 gives you the percentage of *supervisor direct talk.*

6. The supervisor interactions (Categories 1–7) and supervisee interactions (Categories 8 and 9) would be added together. _____

7. Dividing the total interactions (Categories 1–7) by the total interactions (Categories 1–9) gives the percentage of *supervisor talk.* _____

> Subtracting this percentage from 100 gives you the percentage of *supervisee talk*. _____

Evaluating yourself using the Flanders scale provides you with another tool for analysis and self-reflection. After you have completed the analysis look at the end of the Activities section for the answers.

2. Consider "what if?" Pretend that you are a student. Call up all the characteristics of that person—the classroom experiences, the beliefs, the current developmental stage, and the life experiences. Once you have become that student, take a fresh look at how his or her (your) learning and problem solving are assessed and documented. Open your mind to how the student would view this process. Then write a one-page paper summarizing your "what if?" experience. (This idea was developed by Johnston, K. (1995). Preparing the professoriate program. In R. Pritchard (Ed.), *Emphasis: Teaching and Learning*, 4(2), 7–8. Raleigh, NC: North Carolina State University.)

3. Think about the context of schools, then list three or four major obstacles to the implementation of a teaching portfolio.

4. How would a student teacher's coaching plan be different from the coaching plan of a beginning teacher?

5. In Chapter 3 we discussed the concept of supervisory matching (starting where the beginning teacher is). Explain this concept of matching as it relates to the teaching profile discussed in this chapter.

6. One of the continuing debates for policy makers and principals is the one of portfolio assessment for teacher evaluation versus portfolio development for formative growth. Outline your position on the role portfolios should play in the teaching profession.

PORTFOLIO DEVELOPMENT

1. Write reflections according to your own interest. Include them in the portfolio.

2. Write a summary on your present supervisory style. Include the summary in your portfolio.

SUGGESTED READINGS AND RESOURCES

1. Hunt, D. (1981). Teachers' adaptation: "Reading" and "Flexing" to students. In B. Joyce, C. Brown, & L. Peck (Eds.), *Flexibility in teaching* (pp. 59–71). New York: Longman.

   This chapter is the best summary of Hunt's provocative notion of "reading and flexing." The ideas and concepts have direct application to the field of supervision.

2. Barton, J., & Collins, A. (1993). Portfolios in teacher education. *Journal of Teacher Education, 44*(3), 200–209.

   This article is an excellent review of the use of portfolios in pre-service teacher education. Less emphasis is given to the role played by portfolios in the induction phase of teaching.

3. Wolf, K. (1991, October). The schoolteacher's portfolio: Issues in design, implementation, and evaluation. *Phi Delta Kappan, 73*(2) 129–136.

   An excellent summary of the strengths and weaknesses of portfolios. The ideas and the critique are first-rate and based on years of experience in the schools.

4. Ideas on using portfolios in teaching and assessment, from kindergarten through university, are collected in a quarterly *Portfolio News.* Subscriptions are $32 a year. Send to: *Portfolio News:* Subscriptions, University of California, San Diego, Teacher Education Program, 9500 Gilman Drive-0070, La Jolla, CA 92093-0070.

Answer Key 1—26. 2—24. 3—50. 4—34. 5—52%, 48%. 6—84. 7—59%, 41%.

REFERENCES

Blumberg, A. (1980). *Supervisors & teachers: A private cold war,* (2nd ed.). Berkeley, CA: McCutchan.

Darling-Hammond, L. (1996). The quiet revolution: Rethinking teacher development. *Educational Leadership, 53*(6), 4–11.

Flanders, N. A. (1970). *Analyzing teacher behavior.* Reading, MA: Addison-Wesley.

Galloway, C. (1977). Nonverbal. *Theory into practice, 16*(3).

Hunt, D. (1978). Theorists are persons too: On preaching what you practice. In C. A. Parker (Ed.), *Encouraging development in college students.* Minneapolis: University of Minnesota Press.

Joyce, B., & Showers, B. (1995). *Student achievement through staff development.* New York: Longman.

Sprinthall, N. A., & Thies-Sprinthall, L. (1983). The teacher as an adult learner: A cognitive-developmental view. In G. Griffin (Ed.), Staff development: Eighty-second yearbook of the National Society for the Study of Education (pp. 13–35). Chicago: University of Chicago Press.

Thies-Sprinthall, L. (1980). Supervision: An educative or mis-educative process? *Journal of Teacher Education, 31*(4), 17–20.

Thies-Sprinthall, L. (1984). Promoting the developmental growth of supervising teachers: Theory, research programs, and implications. *Journal of Teacher Education, 35*(3), 53–60.

Thies-Sprinthall, L., & Reiman, A. J. (1995). *Supervision of the novice teacher curriculum.* Raleigh: North Carolina State University.

Wolf, K. (1991, October). The schoolteacher's portfolio: Issues in design, implementation, and evaluation. *Phi Delta Kappan, 73*(2), 129–136.

P·A·R·T
IV

CURRENT ISSUES
AND FUTURE TRENDS

. . . .

$\mathcal{T}$he purpose of Part IV is to connect supervision and mentoring to several broad issues facing the field. Chapter 15 examines ethics and supervision and relates the discussion of teacher learning, growth, and development to ethics. A number of propositions are introduced that can frame ethical supervision. In Chapter 16 we look at research and methodological issues related to supervision. We conclude in Chapter 17 with a discussion of emerging trends in supervision, mentoring, and teacher professional development.

C·H·A·P·T·E·R
15

Ethics and Supervision

• • • • • • •

*T*hroughout the text we have described mentors and supervisors as teachers and principals who have had special preparation for their role of providing formative assistance to other teachers. The goal of the assistance is to encourage the building of teachers' instructional repertoire and growth and development. The Teaching/Learning Framework has served as a theoretical template for our discussions.

In this chapter we introduce a number of propositions that can frame ethical supervision. In addition, we return to the Teaching/Learning Framework as we consider ethics and supervision. Specifically, we look at the special role played by mentors and supervisors in "modeling" ethical principles and practice, and the need for supervisors to encourage their supervised colleagues to make educational decisions and commitments based on principles. We also look at a number of ethical concepts that are embedded in the discipline of developmental supervision.

 ## RATIONALE FOR ETHICS IN SUPERVISION

There are three major reasons for an examination of the ethical issues in developmental supervision: (1) developmental supervision and mentoring are intensive interpersonal processes that involve understanding and respecting teachers, their backgrounds, their aspirations, and their developmental needs; (2) developmental supervision and mentoring require a commitment to a primary intervention for promoting new teaching skills and personal growth; and (3) being fully responsive to persons and situations requires ethical decision-making that includes both moral reflection (ethical reasoning and judgment) and moral action that is principled.

We have discussed mentoring and supervision as an interpersonal process in Chapter 7, and developmental supervision as coaching and assistance in Chapters 8 through 14. Still needed, however, is an examination of ethical reasoning and ethical decision-making as it relates to supervision. Therefore we begin by examining definitions of ethical decision-making.

 ## ETHICAL DECISION-MAKING IN A PROFESSION: WHAT IS IT?

As Rest points out (1994), the professions are not so much concerned with issues of rudimentary socialization as they are with issues that involve deciding between conflicting values, each value representing an inherent good (for example, the school supervisor who must decide between giving more attention to one beginning teacher with special needs or to give equal time to the three beginning teachers being supervised). Sergiovanni and Starratt (1993, p. 52) and Strike (1996) also talk about the need to take moral action based on resolution of conflicting values or moral judgments. And Schön (1983) describes the need for professionals to effectively act in "indeterminate zones of practice."

Ethical decision-making occurs at three levels: ground level, in which "deep" structures or stages of moral judgment are predictive of persons' fundamental way of interpreting the social world; an intermediate level, which includes applied concepts and practices like confidentiality, competence, due process, informed consent, dual relationships, and documentation; and the practical level, which encompasses codes of ethics that typically are descriptive (the situation) or prescriptive (the course of action), but limited regarding connecting theory and/or rationale. Although the field of instructional supervision has discussed the possibility of a code of ethics, to date, no code exists. Furthermore, there is little relationship between the presence of a code of ethics and ethical behavior. For example, in a recent study of public administrators (Stewart & Sprinthall, 1993) there was no difference in the level of ethical reasoning and behavior between groups of administrators with versus without a code of ethics.

On the other hand, recent research has shown a consistent and significant relationship between ethical behavior and the levels of moral judgment across a number of professions. Bebeau (1994) has documented the positive relationship in moral judgment and ethical practice in dentistry. Ponemon and Gabhart (1994) have shown a similar connection in a large number of research studies with certified public accountants. Incidentally, in these stud-

JOHN GOODLAD

John Goodlad, noted researcher and educator, was born in North Vancouver, British Columbia in 1920. He received his teaching degree in 1939 and applied for his first teaching position in Georgia. Since he was still legally a Canadian citizen, he was not allowed to complete his application. Undeterred, he was absolutely determined to find a position in his chosen field, eventually landing a one-room K–8 school in rural Canada. By definition such an assignment would require all his skill, imagination, and resourcefulness. He did succeed and soon returned to the United States for his masters and doctorate at the University of Chicago. Somewhat ironically he eventually did return to Georgia, only this time as a professor at Emory University. Later he joined the University of Chicago, and then the University of California, Los Angeles. Most recently, he has served as Director of the Center for Educational Renewal at the University of Washington.

His early experience in a one-room school also planted the seeds for another educational innovation. He realized, full well, the impossibility of the elementary school teaching role even with "just" one class, with multiple responsibilities, for example, the three Rs, plus science, plus music and art, plus recreation, plus physical fitness. Instead he created a model for team teaching with another eminent educator, Robert Anderson. Clusters of elementary teachers crossing specializations would join to offer broader and more comprehensive education. His research with Frances Klein, *Looking Behind Classroom Doors* (1974) had shown the boring and repetitive recitation method as endemic to singular and isolated classrooms. In its place a new model would serve as an alternate method. He found, however, that there was a world of difference between proposing reform and demonstrating its power through pilot examples and having a broad impact on the education of schools and colleges of the country.

More recently, Goodlad has been outspoken about the need for more effective preparation and supervision of prospective teachers. He points out that everybody complains about teacher training and supervision, and many are trying to do something about it, but there has been little effort to get the facts before plunging into various reforms. Consequently, the diagnosis and the recommendations for reforming teacher education have wandered in endless reiterations over the past 100 years. In contrast, Goodlad and his associates have set out to carefully study teacher training. The results of a recent five-year study of university and teacher education programs are reported in *Teachers for Our Nation's Schools* (1990) and *Places Where Teachers Are Taught* (1990). In these studies Goodlad compares good teacher preparation with good preparation of physicians, saying he would like to see the creation of a counterpart to the "teaching hospital" in education. He is quick to point out that physicians in the communities are proud to be designated clinical professors at their local university. Likewise, he would like to see the best teachers and administrators in the schools work closely with university teacher education programs, and be given similar distinction and rewards. Goodlad also agrees that clinical faculty should receive additional university training in coaching and supervision to prepare them for their roles as clinical educators.

Better schools depend on better-trained educators, and exemplary school-based training sites where prospective educators can observe, learn, and practice teaching. Such innovation, in Goodlad's opinion, must anchor future school-university partnerships. Recently, Goodlad has reasserted the importance of moral responsibilities for educators. "If we can educate educators to be thoughtful about their role, aware of their moral responsibilities, and able to use their own best judgment, we can start calling teaching a profession."

REFLECTION QUESTIONS

How have Goodlad's personal and professional experiences shaped his ideas about teacher education and public school reform?

What is the rationale for clinical staff like Goodlad describes?

Exemplary school-university partnerships can bolster teacher education and induction programs. What are the defining properties of successful school-university partnerships?

ies amount of experience was not related to ethical behavior (e.g., the ability to detect fraud in various accounting schemes), while higher levels of moral judgment were the most important predictor. Also studies of physicians (Self, Olivarez, & Baldwin, 1994), have shown the same pattern of ethical/democratic behavior in relation to higher levels of moral/ethical reasoning. Also recall in Chapter 3 that Oser (1994) found a consistent relationship between ethical/democratic approaches to student discipline and higher levels of moral reasoning. Thus professional ethics and behavior is directly connected to the overall concept of moral judgment. Further, some prominent educators (Goodlad, Soder, & Sirotnik, 1990) have persuasively argued that all questions concerning public schooling are actually moral questions requiring not only that educators act ethically, but that they fulfill the complex charge of helping students and the larger community develop the deepest values of our culture. Goodlad (1992) and Strike (1990, 1996) also remind us that widely applicable concepts of ethics and morality do not adequately prepare teachers for the unique context of teaching in public schools. In fact, Goodlad has given considerable attention to institutions and systems of schooling, judging them according to moral criteria. In a recent presentation (Goodlad, 1992) his position is honed to a fine point:

> Preservice and inservice teacher education are virtually silent on issues pertaining to the morality of interventions into school and classroom cultures. Further, there is little or no discourse regarding schools as moral cultures; there is similar omission in regard to preparing teachers to foster such. Teachers are alone and defenceless in regard to penetrations into schools of the pathology in the larger society that schools are called upon to repudiate and remediate. Yet, they are expected to produce moral citizens. It is time for us to recognize that healthy societies have healthy schools. To call upon our schools alone to produce a healthy nation is to engage in fraud. And fraud is immoral. (pp. 96–97)

We will now lay out some of the main propositions for ethical judgment and supervision.

ETHICAL JUDGMENT AND ETHICAL DECISION-MAKING IN SUPERVISION

Although it is beyond the scope of this chapter to engage in a long philosophical discussion on the meaning of moral and ethical considerations and decision-making, the main point is important. Essentially, the content of ethical decision-making and moral judgment in teaching and supervision involves questions of justice and equity (Rawls, 1971, 1985). Thus, we are considering questions that are fundamental to human existence in general, and to teacher education and supervision in particular.

The following six propositions about ethical decision-making in supervision have emerged from conversations between beginning teachers, principals, mentor teachers, and university faculty. Discussion follows the introduction of the six propositions:

1. Ethical decision-making requires an ability to think abstractly, reflectively, and with flexibility about the ethical dilemma.
2. Ethical decision-making requires the ability to see events and ideas from another's perspective.
3. Autocratic leadership and/or supervision and the desire to win or control at any cost is incompatible with ethical decision-making.
4. There will be natural conflicts and concerns between the various roles a supervising principal or "assisting/coaching" teacher must play.

5. Ethical supervisory leadership requires a knowledge of social justice issues and related contemporary professional issues, and a commitment to be a model and change agent when confronted with institutional injustice or individual racism or sexism.
6. Ethical decision-making for supervisors and teacher leaders doesn't mean having all the answers.

The first proposition is that *ethical decision-making requires an ability to think abstractly, reflectively, and with flexibility about the ethical dilemma*. If a teacher, for example, can't think abstractly and with flexibility, anticipating the various causes and effects, it is difficult to fully comprehend the complexity of the moral problem. Obviously, the ability to abstract, and the ability to distinguish between self and other affects the value systems that persons use. Furthermore, without abstract reasoning, it also is difficult for the

---

CONTEMPORARY ISSUES

IS A CODE OF ETHICS FOR SUPERVISORS NEEDED?

Although there have been discussions about the need for a code of ethics for supervisors, to date, none exists in the teacher supervision arena. Yet teacher supervisors are responsible for promoting novice teachers' learning and development, enhancing their understanding of the school culture and student/family life, and advancing the education profession and its ideals.

Granted, there often is little relationship between the presence of a code of ethics and demonstrated ethical behavior. Nonetheless, such a code would advance the essential purposes and responsibilities of supervising professionals. The following list represents some of the possibilities for a code of ethics:

1. Treat supervisees and colleagues as individuals who possess dignity and worth.
2. Practice confidentiality in relationships with supervisees and inform colleagues of the limits of confidentiality.
3. Avoid dual relationships with supervisees.
4. Practice informed consent. Inform colleagues about the purpose and outcomes of the supervision.
5. Prior to observations, review with colleagues the purpose and planned outcome of the observation.
6. Confront colleagues regarding attitudes and behaviors that have ethical implications.
7. Monitor and update professional competencies as needed.

Many other standards could be a part of a code of ethics. For example, what ethical standards should supervisors practice that relate to the larger institution of which they are a part? What responsibilities does an ethical supervisor have to society?

supervisor to symbolize the contemporary educational and ethical issues in ways that are accessible to the supervisee.

Without doubt the most significant and influential theory and research on value development and ethical decision-making springs from the exhaustive theory, longitudinal research, and applications of Lawrence Kohlberg, and the careful study of ethical decision-making by James Rest. Since Kohlberg's work was described in detail in Chapter 3, we review his six stages only briefly.

At Stage 1, the person is most impressed with the power of others. Getting along with others means doing what you are told to do by others who are "superior" to you.

At Stage 2, the person recognizes that everyone has interests, not just those with superior power, and doing good means doing what is personally satisfying. In this token economy, decisions are based on short-term cooperation in order to exchange favors.

The person at Stage 3 becomes interested in establishing more long-term relationships and values loyalty and commitment in the relationship. Decisions are made based on the relationships and on what one's peers think about the particular issue.

At Stage 4, the person recognizes the shortcomings of Stage 3 reasoning. What is missing is a code or scheme of cooperation for society as a whole. Thus, decision-making at this stage draws on the laws and formalized codes of conduct that have been developed for society.

At Stage 5, the person draws on "due process" to resolve conflicts, thus elections, polls, and consensus building are examples of Stage 5 reasoning.

Finally, at Stage 6, the person makes decisions based on visions of how an idealized society balances the burdens and benefits of cooperative living.

Rest's insights have helped spur researchers in a variety of professions to further elaborate on the relationship between moral development and ethical decision-making (Rest & Narvaez, 1994). Having developed and tested the Defining Issues Test (Rest, 1979), which assesses persons' ability to evaluate moral issues, he has gone on to review research in moral development and ethical decision-making across a spectrum of professions including teaching. His extensive review of literally hundreds of studies offers plentiful evidence for developmental trends in moral reasoning. Furthermore, his four-component model of moral development suggests that moral sensitivity (awareness of how our own actions affect others), moral judgment (reasoning), moral motivation (reconciling competing values), and moral character (ego strength), all are powerful predictors of behavior (Rest & Narvaez, 1994, pp. 17–18).

The second proposition is that *ethical decision-making requires the ability to see events and ideas from another's perspective and to consider how one's own actions affect others* (Gibbs, 1992). If you can't empathize and take alternative perspectives, it is difficult to take into account what the consequences of your actions will be for others. Rest calls this moral sensitivity (1994). Such perspective taking is a fundamental part of the supervisory process. In fact, most teachers conclude that supervisors are not helpful and/or collaborative if they are not able to be empathic.

The third proposition, *autocratic leadership and/or supervision and the desire to win or control at any cost is incompatible with ethical decision-making*, relates to school context and styles of supervision. In the case of autocratic supervision, other values ("might makes right" or "what's in it for me") completely compromise the moral values.

The fourth proposition, *there will be natural conflicts and concerns between the various roles a teacher supervisor must play*, relates to the concept of moral motivation. Sometimes other values compromise one's moral values. Take, for example, the mentor teacher who, because of various leadership responsibilities, must occasionally decide between the needs of his or her beginning teacher, and the competing needs of the school-based decision making committee and their restructuring efforts.

When you have concerns or feel conflicts between the desire to meet the needs of self, colleagues, administrators, parents, and students, consider these concerns and conflicts as a natural part of leadership and supervision, and be willing to share these conflicts with those involved.

The fifth proposition, *ethical supervisory leadership requires a knowledge of social justice issues and a commitment to be a model and change agent when confronted with institutional injustice or individual racism or sexism*, is an important one for supervisors. Teaching and supervision are full of ethical issues (Sirotnik, 1990). It is the responsibility of supervisors, individually and collectively, to consider these issues, to have informed opinions and actions related to the issues. Moreover, many of the ethical issues can be reflected on using the principles of "greatest good for the greatest number," and the principle of equity (Strike, 1988; Strike & Soltis, 1992). Our notion of the supervisor as a model of ethical decision-making has parallels in Sergiovanni and Starratt's supervision as moral action (1993).

The sixth proposition is that *ethical decision-making for supervisors and teacher leaders doesn't mean having all the answers*. It is more important to recognize that many of the challenges are best resolved through dialogue with colleagues. Certainly our own research on the role of supervisors, the advantages of guided reflection, the impact of teacher and counselor support groups, and the role of discourse (Habermas, 1979; Strike, 1993) have highlighted both the complexity of supervision and ethical decision-making as well as the cognitive and affective components.

These propositions have been drawn from the work of Rest and his four components as noted as well as the work of Douglas Heath and form a model for the effective and ethical supervisor. Heath documents four dimensions that were derived independently from Rest yet bear striking similarity (see Exhibit 15-1).

Finally from a theoretical standpoint both Heath and Rest present frameworks that are highly consistent with Jurgen Habermas's concept of ideal speech as the critical goal for a democratic society, namely a commitment to the democratic principles of equity and justice.

Exhibit 15-1 COMPARING REST AND HEATH

HEATH (1991)	REST (1994)
1. Symbolize experience: The ability to reflect abstractly.	1. Recognition of ethical reasons.
2. Allocentrism: To understand the other person's perspective intellectually and emotionally.	2. Empathy.
3. Individuation:To be self-directed.	3. Character/Ego strength.
4. An allegiance to and to act on democratic values.	4. Set aside personal interests for democratic ethics.

PROMOTING ETHICAL SUPERVISORY PRACTICE

To date, the means of promoting more ethical decision-making in most professions has involved some version of the dilemma discussion first introduced by Socrates, and pursued in the twentieth century by the likes of Lawrence Kohlberg (1985). As Rest points out, "Preparing professionals to discern the right course of action in problematic work contexts has become an immense enterprise. One estimate of the number of applied ethics courses taught annually in colleges and universities in this country is 10,000" (1994, preface).

Courses tend to be either very abstract excursions offered by a philosophy or theology department as a requirement or elective, or infused into one or more core courses, often so fragmented as to be ineffective. Each approach is problematic. Discrete courses too often are criticized for excessive contemplation of the cosmic possibilities with no connection to practice. On the other hand, infusion means that since ethical decision-making is every instructor's responsibility, it may end up being no one's responsibility.

SITUATIONS THAT REQUIRE ETHICAL DECISION-MAKING

Situations with ethical implications for supervisors fall into three categories. First, there are those situations in which moral principles and caring for the colleague provide a very clear course of action. For example, a supervisor is clearly obligated to alert the colleague to the kinds of supervision and assistance that can be provided.

A second kind of situation is one that a group of supervisors would agree on but that a novice teacher might be confused about because of conflicting loyalties. Take as an example the situation in which a friend and coworker of the novice teacher is arriving at work late and the five-year-old students are left unattended. The novice teacher may not want to confront his or her colleague and jeopardize the friendship, instead looking at other solutions. It is not clear to the novice teacher that the friendship has been placed above the well-being of the young students.

The third type of situation is one that challenges the ethical supervisor. There are two or more ethical principles that are relevant to the dilemma, and each principle has value. Take as an example the student teacher who chooses to exclusively use the lecture method of teaching, even though the supervising teacher views such exclusive reliance on one model as very limiting for students' growth and development. Here student teacher autonomy and supervisor stewardship of the students' well-being compete for precedence.

With the development of instructional supervision as a discipline with a growing body of knowledge on which to base professional practice, supervisors are faced with the need to develop skill in ethical decision-making. The question, however, is how to go about such a preparation.

 # MENTORS, SUPERVISORS, AND ETHICAL ISSUES

As we mentioned, there is an intermediate level of ethics that includes applied concepts and issues that supervisors face. As practitioners, mentors and supervisors need to be aware of the ethical issues that they will face. It is our experience that very few supervisors are well versed in the common issues that may be faced. We limit our discussion to issues that are distinct to mentors and supervisors.

CONFIDENTIALITY

Confidentiality is defined by Siegel (1979) as follows: "Confidentiality involves professional ethics rather than any legalism and indicates an explicit promise or contract to reveal nothing about an individual except under conditions agreed to by the source or subject" (p. 251). Confidentiality is a principle given a significant amount of attention in our preparation programs for supervisors. We submit that confidentiality is at the very heart of effective developmental supervision. Administrators and teachers need to know that the supervisory relationship is based on safety, trust, and regard. As mentors and supervisors, we earn our colleagues' respect when we affirm the principle of confidentiality at the very beginning of the relationship.

Confidentiality includes safeguarding information about the colleague's instructional competence, as well as agreement between the persons in the supervisory relationship that supervision will not be discussed outside of the relationship. When group supervision is employed, all the participants should agree to the norm of confidentiality. If videotapes or audiotapes are used to improve instruction or supervisory skills, the supervisor or instructor must reaffirm the importance of confidentiality. Privacy, the flip side of confidentiality, is the teachers' right not to have information, including information acquired during supervision, divulged without informed consent. In a court of law, however, confidentiality cannot be used as a reason not to testify.

COMPETENCE

Every one of us who entered education through the teaching portal remembers his or her first year of teaching. Likewise, as novice mentors or supervisors, we remember how we doubted our ability to effectively support and assist a colleague for the first time. Such self-doubt is common in complex new helping roles like mentoring and supervision. Typically, with the passage of time, the doubt subsides, replaced by confidence and certainty. However, as Bernard and Goodyear (1992) point out, a supervisor's own competence can be taken for granted, yet the supervisor's competence is one of the most important ethical responsibilities, because it determines the supervisor's ability to support the colleague. Additional recommendations on competence made by Bernard and Goodyear are as follows: (1) restricting one's area of expertise, (2) continuing education to ensure up-to-date competence, and (3) consultation (networking with other supervising colleagues) so as to reduce isolation that can lead to diminished competence (1992, p. 143).

DUE PROCESS

Due process is a legal term that guarantees individual rights. In supervision, a novice or experienced teacher or beginning supervisor also has due process rights. For example, a student teacher's due process rights have been violated when the supervising teacher or supervising faculty member gives a negative final evaluation without prior communication to the student teacher that selected performances are inadequate. A preferred course of action would be to have a mid-term "communication conference" where strengths and weaknesses are reviewed, and where a coaching plan is developed for working on weaknesses. Ideally, the mid-term conference would be recorded in some way and signed by each participant in the conference.

INFORMED CONSENT REGARDING SUPERVISION

Informed consent means that the supervisee understands and agrees to the supervision before its beginning. This agreement would include a review of the types of milestone activities that will occur (e.g., diagnostic conferences, coaching plans, clinical cycles of supervision), preferred kinds of feedback, preferred learning style, role of formative supervision in the overall training program, and how documentation of experiences will occur. Discussion of the terms of the assessment or assistance process should be clear and straightforward rather than ambiguous. For example, if a midterm conference will be a part of the supervision, the supervisor would use language like, "I will be initiating a midterm conference during the sixth week of your internship," rather than "I hope we will have a chance to do a midterm conference." Informed consent can occur during the initial getting acquainted conference that we described in Chapter 7. Our main point is that the teacher or the supervising trainee should enter the supervisory experience knowing the conditions, events, and outcomes of the experience.

DUAL RELATIONSHIP

Dual relationship means that the supervisor and the supervisee are participating in both a supervisory relationship and an intimate or deeply personal relationship. Obviously, dual relationships are incompatible with the goals of ethical supervision. Pope, Keith-Spiegel, and Tabachnick (1986) suggest that training programs for supervisors should do more than simply admonish dual relationships, instead encouraging supervisors to seek out other supervisors, to discuss possible sexual attraction to certain supervisees. Such a strategy encourages openness about the situation, and promotes ethical practice.

PREPARING SUPERVISORS FOR ETHICAL DECISION-MAKING

Although numerous supervisory programs in nursing, counseling, dentistry, public administration, and education have employed the dilemma discussion to promote moral development and ethical reasoning of supervisors, an alternative approach uses George Herbert Mead's theory (1934) of social role taking as a means of promoting greater moral development and ethical decision-making. In this experiential and constructivist context, you learn supervision by doing supervision and you learn ethics by resolving the dilemmas faced in the "line of fire" so to speak. Any complex new human helping role (e.g., mentor, principal, clinical teacher, program supervisor) provides a significant opportunity for development. The other conditions that appear to be most crucial are carefully guided and graduated experiences with reflection (praxis), continuity in the supervision activities, and ongoing support (see Exhibit 15-2).

EXHIBIT 15-2   TEACHING/LEARNING FRAMEWORK

INSTRUCTIONAL REPERTOIRE*	CONDITIONS FOR GROWTH[†]
1. Theory/rationale	1. Complex new role
2. Demonstrations	2. Guided reflection
3. Practice with feedback	3. Balance between role and reflection
4. Adapt and generalize through coaching	4. Support and challenge
	5. Continuity

*Joyce, B., & Showers, B. (1995). *Student achievement through staff development* (2nd ed.). New York: Longman.
†Sprinthall, N. A., Reiman, A. J., & Thies-Sprinthall, L. (1993). Roletaking and reflection: Promoting the conceptual and moral development of teachers. *Learning and Individual Differences* (Special Issue: Wisdom and Expertise in Teaching), 5(4), 283–300.

New models and methods of supervision (e.g., effective communication, helping skills, differentiated supervision strategies, instructional coaching) are learned and applied in school and university settings, and a series of field-based studies with teachers, counselors, and teacher/counselor supervisors (Oja & Sprinthall, 1978; Peace, 1992; Reiman & Thies-Sprinthall, 1994; Reiman & Parramore, 1993; Thies-Sprinthall, 1980; Watson, 1995) have demonstrated that new and experienced teachers, counselors, and administrators can engage in new role-taking experiences, learn new methods and models of teaching and/or supervision, and develop more complex ethical decision-making vis-à-vis moral, ego, and conceptual development. In each researched intervention careful attention was given to building initial trust (Chapter 7), promoting intensive ongoing guided reflection (Chapter 12), and, of course, participating in a new role with concomitant curriculum to be learned and applied. Furthermore, the studies embrace the career spectrum from preservice teacher education, through the induction phase, into inservice teacher and counselor education and staff development.

In addition to assuming a complex new role, there are a number of focused activities that appear to be important to promoting moral development:

1. Initiation of a getting acquainted conference at the onset of the training experience.
2. Implementation of sustained (weekly) guided dialogic reflection that includes differentiated instructor responses according to the current developmental needs of the trainee (Chapter 13) for the duration of the training experience.
3. Providing substantial time for supervising trainees to discuss the ethical dimensions of their supervision.

We have found that both practical and support groups provide a marvelous opportunity to discuss the ethical dimensions of practice.

Case Study in Resolving an Ethical Dilemma

We have discussed moral development and ethical decision-making at two levels: stages of moral reasoning and at the intermediate level of supervisory ethical issues. We now turn to a case study of a teacher supervisor that involves different stages of moral and ethical decision-making and consideration of several ethical issues (e.g., confidentiality and due process). The case study is adapted from research by Head (1994), who developed and tested an instrument called the Teacher Supervisor Development Inventory, and by Fon-Yean Chang (1993, 1994), who explored the moral and ethical aspects of teaching in a teacher-specific moral reasoning test called the Test of

CONTEMPORARY ISSUES

LEADING A DILEMMA DISCUSSION

A major review of dilemma discussions (Rest, 1986) strongly supports the technique as a process for promoting moral maturity. However, several caveats are necessary. First, dilemma discussions that occur over a weekend or a one- or two-week workshop are not effective. Second, the method is most effective with older students and adults. Third, the gains are modest. One should not expect large gains for supervisor trainees or novice teachers. Fourth, dilemma discussions are bolstered by indirect teaching. Recall our discussion of Flanders in Chapters 8 and 9. The main point is that the direct mode of teaching (e.g., lecturing, giving directions, and criticizing or justifying authority) has little impact on moral growth. On the other hand, accepting feelings and ideas, supporting discussion through encouragement, and challenging colleagues with questions, is more effective. Marvin Berkowitz (1984) has explored how different methods of discussion promote or hinder discussion and moral growth.

We recommend that discussion of moral and ethical issues become a part of the preparation of supervisors. If you are interested, we suggest that you tape-record your early efforts with the discussions. Steps in the discussion could include the following:

1. Begin by clarifying the facts of the ethical issue.
   a. Check for understanding by paraphrasing.
   b. Use open-ended questions.
2. Clarify the issue.
   a. Identify feelings.
   b. Encourage colleague-to-colleague talk (dyads).
   c. Perhaps do a role switch to encourage alternative perspective taking.
   d. What are the possible actions?
3. Closure
   a. Ask a colleague to review the issues.
   b. Raise the issue of justice and equity for all questions.

Afterward, you can review your tape to assess your use of indirect instruction. Furthermore, we encourage you to listen to the tape for the structural content of the discussion. What types of reasons do individuals give? And remember that moral growth moves more at the pace of a glacier than that of the incoming tide. Also realize that persons are attracted to one-stage-higher moral reasoning than their modal level of moral reasoning (Turiel & Killen, 1988). Turiel called this the one-plus phenomenon. Implicit is the idea of mismatching reasoning at one level higher. Thus, group discussion provides a natural kind of mismatching for the participants' different modal levels of moral reasoning.

Sources: Berkowitz, M. (1984). *Process analysis and the future of moral education.* Paper presented at the annual meeting of American Education Research Association, New Orleans, April 23. Rest, J. (1986). *Moral development.* New York: Praeger.

Teachers' Moral Reasoning. In each case, the investigator's work was modeled after the Defining Issues Test developed by James Rest. Read the situation and the perspectives of the various faculty and staff.

SITUATION

You have been supervising a student teacher, Beth. It is time for the midterm conference. Dr. Moore, the supervisor representing the University, suggests that a number of instructional areas be addressed before the end of the semester. You agree, and, together with Beth, a coaching plan is developed for the next two to four weeks. You agree to send Dr. Moore a copy of the written coaching plan once it is complete. However, when the principal, Mr. Johnson, who is a friend of Beth's family, hears about the conference outcome, he asks that the coaching plan be revised to more favorably reflect on Beth. Mr. Johnson also asks that a copy of the revised coaching plan be given to him before a copy is sent to the University. Before deciding what you will do, read the following additional information.

University Person (Dr. Moore). Dr. Moore sees Beth as a marginal performer who may lack the maturity to be a classroom teacher. As Beth's academic adviser and instructor for a methods course, he has noted Beth's lack of motivation to try innovative new teaching strategies, and to be an active participant in classroom discussions.

Student Teacher (Beth). Beth has been reluctant to try new teaching models and methods, and tends to turn to you for most of the important decisions about lesson planning. Beth has been quick to negatively judge students' performance, does not see the connection between her own teaching and student motivation, and considers herself an adept classroom manager.

Principal (Mr. Johnson). Mr. Johnson has known Beth's family for 12 years, and he was instrumental in getting Beth assigned to his school. Mr. Johnson has commented on Beth's character and her strong family background, noting that he would be proud to have his daughter in Beth's classroom.

Your View. Although you have been a classroom teacher for 20 years, you have been in the current school system for only three years. Mr. Johnson, a long-time resident of the community and a highly respected principal, will be conducting an end-of-year observation and review of your teaching, as part of the process of recommending or denying tenure for you.

The format shown in Exhibit 15-3 of reading an ethical dilemma, then responding to different issues, and finally rating the most important issues, is one means of identifying one's preference for principled reasoning. Your responses to the situation, questions, and final identification of importance, are suggestive of your preferred ways of solving complex ethical issues.

EXHIBIT 15-3 SHOULD YOU REVISE THE COACHING PLAN ACCORDING TO THE PRINCIPAL'S REQUEST?

(Check one)

__Should alter the coaching plan __ Can't decide __ Should not change the coaching plan

How important are the following issues:	NOT IMPORTANT	SOMEWHAT IMPORTANT	VERY IMPORTANT
1. Don't you owe Mr. Johnson a favor since he was responsible for hiring you into the school system?	____	____	____
2. In the past, you have noticed that Mr. Johnson has reassigned uncooperative teachers to extra duties. Don't you have to look out for yourself?	____	____	____
3. As a supervisor, don't you have a responsibility to the profession to assure that feedback to Beth is honest and comprehensive?	____	____	____
4. School colleagues tell you that you are taking a considerable risk if you do not cooperate with the principal. Isn't it important to be a team player?	____	____	____
5. Isn't the principal, after all, the lead decision-maker in the school?	____	____	____
6. Haven't you always thought about the long-term consequences for the welfare of persons?	____	____	____
7. Don't you need to consider the benefits and burdens for all concerned?	____	____	____

From the list of statements above, select the three most important:

Most important ____

Second most important ____

Third most important ____

For illustrative purposes we now walk through the triangular dilemma of Beth, Mr. Johnson, and you according to the resolutions presented in the scenario. For example, in the first proposition the decision would be based on *Stage 2* reasoning—materialistic concern about employment and favoritism.

The second proposition, fear of reassignment and punishment actually moves close to *Stage 1* and physical consequences. The third statement represents *Stage 4* as a professional duty. It is a professional expectation to provide honest feedback. The fourth statement serves as an example of *Stage 3* and social conformity. It is important to go along and cooperate regardless of the welfare of the students. The fifth statement also represents *Stage 4* since the principal does have legal authority over the school. It is not until we consider the issues in the sixth and seventh statements that the issues from the Rest/Heath model come into play. In those statements it is obviously most important that the welfare of the pupils (present and future) and even the long-term welfare of Beth take precedence. After all would we really want to reward lackadaisical and manipulative behavior even though the consequences to self may be dire? It has often been said that it takes a great storm to find out a sailor's competence. Similarly it is really only in very difficult and personally agonizing situations that we find out our own level of ethical and professional behavior. This also means that it is critical for all of us to have opportunities for discussion and dialogue when confronted with such difficult dilemmas. This is one of the reasons why we have included some further examples in the activity section of this chapter and have listed some additional resources. All the research agrees on one point. Ethical development is the most complex growth issue across all the various domains of development. It requires the abilities to see broadly, choose wisely, and act democratically.

 SUMMARY

We have attempted to not only describe aspects of ethical decision-making, but also to articulate a means of promoting such reasoning and growth. Too often, professional training in supervision, if it exists at all, leaves out the issues of human relationships and moral and ethical reasoning. The role-taking/reflection focus we have described in this chapter and in Chapter 4 requires a significant modification of the conventional approach to teacher education and supervision. The action/reflection studies suggest the possibility of promoting adult development in a variety of supervisory roles, and at a variety of career levels (preservice, induction, inservice).

In this chapter we also introduced a number of ethical concepts that are embedded in the discipline of supervision. Among the concepts are confidentiality, due process, dual relationship, and competence. Our main point is that the ethical mentor or supervisor is aware of these concepts and always considers the welfare of the novice teacher or supervising trainee.

Undoubtedly the most important aspect of the entire chapter is that it confronts supervision with questions about the form of stages of moral maturity and ethical decision-making. Questions of ethics and moral education in supervision have been avoided. We think it is time to consider ethical decision-making and moral development as legitimate areas of inquiry for prospective mentors and supervisors and for the teaching profession, and to investigate those programs and methods that encourage such development.

SUPERVISION FOR TEACHER DEVELOPMENT ACTIVITIES

APPLIED

1. Read the following case study. Afterward, write five questions that might be asked of the supervising mentor. Each question should address a different stage of moral reasoning. Use the summary of the stages of moral development in the chapter as a guide.

   "In his second year as a beginning teacher, Bill had become the adviser to the student staff for the school newspaper. Several students wanted to print a story on racism on the campus. The principal, hearing about the article, suggested that the students' view of the problem was greatly exaggerated, and said to the students, "We can't print this article! Our parents won't stand for such untruths." The students disagreed. In private, the principal asked Jill, in her role as mentor, to make sure the story wasn't printed. Bill decided to share the controversy with his mentor, Jill, who listened, as Bill described the students' concerns, as well as the private conversation with the principal."

2. Read the second case study. Afterward, write a short summary of the ethical concepts and issues that are involved in the case.

   "The principal has hired a beginning teacher in mid-September due to an enrollment increase, to shore up a number of instructional needs. The teacher, Sue, is assigned five different preparations in science as well as several committee assignments including adviser to the yearbook. Additionally, the principal is considering asking Sue to coach the tennis team. Sue is assigned a mentor, Grace, in the second week of October. Grace has been very active on a number of innovative school initiatives including a task force to explore the elimination of interscholastic sports from their school program, the committee on multicultural education, and she is chair of the school-based committee on curriculum integration. Grace has worked hard to lobby for the principal's support on the elimination of interscholastic sports but the principal is undecided. Grace feels like she is walking on eggs. When Grace and Sue have their first getting acquainted conference Grace learns about Sue's teaching and extracurricular assignment. She is very troubled."

3. Write a critique of the chapter. How effective was it in addressing ethical decision-making? Did it bridge theory and practice? What changes would you make to strengthen the chapter?

PORTFOLIO DEVELOPMENT

1. Continue to write reflections according to your own interests.
2. Write a short narrative about an ethical dilemma you have faced as a supervisor. What stage or stages of moral reasoning did you use to interpret and resolve the dilemma? Were there any ethical concepts like confidentiality that were a part of the dilemma? Were you satisfied with the outcome? What would you have done differently if you were faced with the same dilemma tomorrow? Include the narrative in your portfolio.

SUGGESTED READINGS

1. Sprinthall, N. A., Sprinthall, R., & Oja, S. N. (1998). *Educational psychology: A developmental approach* (7th ed., chap. 7). New York: McGraw-Hill.

   This chapter entitled "Value Development," is a comprehensive review of Kohlberg's theory of moral reasoning. Included in the chapter is a discussion of the relationship between moral reasoning and moral action, an extensive summary of Gilligan's critique, and recent research reviews showing no gender differences in moral reasoning.

2. Strike, K. A., & Soltis, J. F. (1985). *The ethics of teaching.* New York: Teachers College Press.

   This work has an excellent review of the philosophical issues that relate to Stage 5 reasoning, utilitarianism and Stage 6 reasoning, the Golden Rule. The authors also include a number of challenging ethical dilemma case studies of teachers that could be incorporated in small group discussions.

3. *Journal of Teacher Education*, 42(3).

   This issue's theme is the ethical responsibilities of teaching, and includes a range of topics and perspectives on how to promote educational experiences that encourage teacher ethical reasoning.

REFERENCES

Bebeau, M. (1994). Dentistry. In J. Rest & D. Narvaez (Eds.), *Moral development in the professions: Psychology and applied ethics.* New York: Erlbaum.

Bernard, J. M., & Goodyear, R. K. (1992). *Fundamentals of clinical supervision.* Boston: Allyn and Bacon.

Chang, F. Y. (1993). *The development of a test of teachers' moral reasoning.* Doctoral dissertation, University of Minnesota.

Chang, F. Y. (1994). School teachers' moral reasoning. In J. Rest & D. Narvaez (Eds.), *Moral development in the professions: Psychology and applied ethics.* New York: Erlbaum.

Gibbs, J. (1992). Moral-cognitive development and the motivation of moral behavior. In W. Kurtines, M. Azmitia, & J. Gewirtz (Eds.), *Role of values in psychology and human development* (pp. 222–238). New York: John Wiley and Sons.

Goodlad, J. I. (1992). The moral dimensions of schooling and teacher education. *Journal of Moral Education*, 21(2), 87–97.

Goodlad, J. I., & Klein, M. F. (1974). *Looking behind the classroom door*. Worthington, Ohio: Press.

Goodlad, J. I., Soder, R., & Sirotnik, K. (Eds.) (1990). *The moral dimensions of teaching*. San Francisco: Jossey-Bass.

Goodlad, J. I., Soder, R., & Sirotnik, K. (1990). *Places where teachers are taught*. San Francisco: Jossey-Bass.

Goodlad, J. I., Soder, R., & Sirotnik, K. (1990). *Teachers for our nation's schools*. San Francisco: Jossey-Bass.

Habermas, J. (1979). *Communication and the evolution of society*. London: Heinemann.

Head, F. A. (1994). *Modifying moral dilemmas for mentors and supervising teachers: An initial validation study of a cognitive developmental assessment model*. Doctoral dissertation, North Carolina State University.

Heath, D. (1991). *Fulfilling lives: Paths to maturity and success*. San Francisco: Jossey-Bass.

Kohlberg, L. (1985). The just community approach to moral education in theory and practice. In M. Berkowitz & F. Oser (Eds.), *Moral education: Theory and application* (pp. 27–87). Hillsdale, NJ: Erlbaum.

Mead, G. H. (1934). *Mind, self, and society*. Chicago: University of Chicago Press.

Oja, S. N., & Sprinthall, N. A. (1978). Psychological and moral development for teachers. In N. A. Sprinthall & R. L. Mosher (Eds.), *Value development as the aim of education* (pp. 117–134). New York: Character Press.

Oser, F. (1994). Moral perspectives on teaching. In L. Darling-Hammond (Ed.), *Review of Research in Education*, 20, 57–128. Washington, D.C.: American Educational Research Association.

Peace, S. (1992). *A study of school counselor induction: A cognitive-developmental model*. Doctoral dissertation, North Carolina State University.

Ponemon, L. A., & Gabhart, D. R. L. (1994). The accounting and auditing profession: An application of ethical reasoning research. In J. Rest & D. Narvaez (Eds.), *Moral development in the professions: Psychology and applied ethics*. New York: Erlbaum.

Pope, K. S., Keith-Spiegel, P., & Tabachnick, B. (1986). Sexual attraction to clients: The human therapist and the (sometimes) inhuman training system. *American Psychologist*, 41, 147–152.

Rawls, J. (1971). *A theory of justice*. Cambridge, MA: Harvard University Press.

Rawls, J. (1985). Justice as fairness: Political not metaphysical. *Philosophy and Public Affairs*, 14(3), 223–251.

Reiman, A. J., & Parramore, B. (1993). Promoting preservice teacher development through extended field experience. In M. O'Hair & S. Odell (Eds.), *Diversity and teaching: Teacher Education Yearbook I* (pp. 111–121). Orlando: Harcourt Brace Jovanovich.

Reiman, A. J., & Thies-Sprinthall, L. (1994). Promoting the development of mentor teachers: Theory and research programs using guided reflection. *Journal of Research and Development*, 26(3), 179–185.

Rest, J. R. (1979). *Development in judging moral isuues*. Minneapolis: University of Minnesota Press.

Rest, J. R. (1994). Background: Theory and research. In J. Rest & D. Narvaez (Eds.), *Moral development in the professions: Psychology and applied ethics*. New York: Erlbaum.

Rest, J. R., & Narvaez, D. F. (Eds.) (1994). *Moral development in the professions: Psychology and applied ethics.* New York: Erlbaum.

Schön, D. (1983). *The reflective practitioner.* New York: Basic Books.

Self, D. J., Olivarez, M., & Baldwin, D. C., Jr. (1994). Ethics and medicine. In J. Rest & D. Narvaez (Eds.), *Moral development in the professions: Psychology and applied ethics.* New York: Erlbaum.

Sergiovanni, T. J., & Starratt, R. J. (1993). *Supervision: A redefinition.* New York: McGraw-Hill.

Siegel, M. (1979). Privacy, ethics, and confidentiality. *Professional Psychology, 10,* 249–258.

Sirotnik, K. A. (1990). Society, schooling, teaching, and preparing to teach. In J. I. Goodlad, R. Soder, & K. A. Sirotnik (Eds.), *The moral dimensions of teaching.* San Francisco: Jossey-Bass.

Strike, K. (1988). The ethics of teaching. *Phi Delta Kappan, 10,* 156–158.

Strike, K. (1990). Ethical discourse and pluralism. In K. Strike & P. Ternasky (Eds.), *Ethics for professionals in education: Perspectives for preparation and practice* (pp. 176–188). New York: Teachers College Press.

Strike, K. (1996). The moral responsibilities of educators. In J. Sikula (Ed.), *Second handbook of research on teacher education* (pp. 869–892). New York: Macmillan.

Strike, K., & Soltis, J. F. (1992). *The ethics of teaching* (2nd ed.). New York: Teachers College Press.

Thies-Sprinthall, L. (1980). Supervision: An educative or miseducative process? *Journal of Teacher Education, 31,* 17–30.

Watson, B. (1995). *Early field experiences in teacher education: A developmental model.* Doctoral dissertation, North Carolina State University.

C·H·A·P·T·E·R
16

Teacher Development Research Issues and Methods

• • • • • • •

*D*uring the 1980s, Joyce and Showers (1980) asserted that

> An emphasis on the effects of "coaching to application" on "problem solving"—with coaching administered by other teachers, principals, supervisors, and so on—should provide useful information not only on coaching as a training strategy but on the relative effectiveness of various training agents as well. If, in fact, coaching by peers proves to boost the magnitude of classroom implementation, an extremely practical and powerful training method can be added to the already tested strategies of theory presentation, modeling, practice, and feedback. (p. 385)

More recently, Glickman and Bey (1990) struck a similar chord, arguing that one remedy for the current lack of research in supervision would be the initiation of a new generation of studies on the outcomes of different models of supervision and coaching. Likewise, in the field of teacher induction Gold, (1996) points out that although many programs are being developed at the local and state levels, to date, little research has been initiated. And Murray (1996) argues that a necessary remedy for the current state of affairs in teacher education would be a new science of teacher development. Oja and Reiman (1997) have drawn similar conclusions for the field of supervision and adult learning.

Nate Gage, a prominent educational psychologist, has raised the same question in his well-known inquiry (1978), "Is there a scientific basis for the art of teaching?" He encourages educational scholars to build a scientifically developed knowledge about the relationships of variables. Noting that systematic theory is needed, Gage argues that such research on teaching must examine relationships between variables, and these relationships do possess order, organization, rationale, and meaning. "They are not mere random collections of correlation coefficients or effect sizes" (Gage, 1985, p. 7). The application of this nomothetic knowledge, that is, generalized across individuals, to particular events or individuals represents artfulness, and is applicable to most professions (Schön, 1983).

Although there have been literally thousands of studies on student learning (Wittrock, 1986), research on teacher learning and development, at best, is emergent (Sprinthall, Reiman, & Thies-Sprinthall, 1996). For example, a science of teacher development might look at the evolution of teacher professional content knowledge or how teacher self-knowledge affects relationships with students. However, to date, little research has been conducted in this area (Murray, 1996). As researchers develop instrumentation (e.g., King & Kitchener, 1994), and models (e.g., Black, 1989) unique to teacher development, there should be significant forward movement in the profession of teaching as well as complementary fields like supervision, staff development, and teacher education.

In this chapter we examine research issues and methods that could advance our understanding of teacher development. We believe that supervision initiatives, coaching programs, induction efforts, and preservice teacher education programs are promoting professional learning and personal and professional development. In the professional learning realm, teachers are being steeped in two distinct realms of knowledge: formal theories and observation that have been confirmed, or are confirmable, by research; and knowledge that has been acquired through experience. In the personal development realm, teachers are provided experiences and interactions that promote psychological growth and development, and that have been confirmed by research also. The placement of this chapter near the end of the book reflects our hope that you will be provoked to investigate and expand the scientific basis for the art of teacher development. Because we recognize that our readers are at different levels of understanding about research in general, and supervision, coaching, and developmental research in particular, we plan to steer a middle course that should provide all readers with some necessary and helpful information.

As you review the chapter, check your comprehension by answering these questions:

- What is the role of questions in research?
- What research strategies can be employed for a study of teacher development?
- If you were to initiate a study, which questions would you find compelling?

THE FIRST STEP: IDENTIFYING THE QUESTIONS

The major reason for doing research in education is to develop new knowledge about teaching, learning, development, and administration (Borg & Gall, 1989). Additionally, the new knowledge should eventually lead to improvement in educational practice. And it is the initial questions (or problem) that frame and bolster the investigation. Therefore, questions are a most important part of the research process. The following questions serve as examples of potential research questions. "What changes can I make in my supervision to increase interest among teachers?" "What conditions in my school promote teacher learning of new instructional skills?" "What misconceptions do students make when solving subtraction problems?" "Why are some children not volunteering ideas during end-of-class activities?"

The ultimate value of your research is determined by initial insight into the current literature, and creativity regarding the selection of a relevant and important question. The difference between a trivial project and a significant project is related to the insight and creativity that is required to select and define a set of questions. Additionally, the identification of questions should be of considerable interest to you. After all, you will be spending valuable time exploring the questions.

THEORETICAL AND METHODOLOGICAL ISSUES

Theory building is one of the most important purposes of educational research. A theory is a logical system that attempts to explain phenomena by outlining constructs and the assumptions that bind these constructs together. For example, Piaget's theory of child development outlined a number of constructs based on his observation of his children. These constructs, inferred from observations, became the basis for a wealth of research during the last four decades. Based on Piaget's theory, variables (quantitative expressions of the construct) have been identified and measured, and each successive generation of studies have led to revisions and refinements in his theory as an explanatory framework for child development. If you are interested in identifying a question or problem for possible exploration, insight can be drawn from exploring theories that are relevant to your question.

In addition to your search for theories (recall Katz and Rath's "Goldilocks principle"), there are methodological considerations. No study is without limitations, and this fact can be illustrated through an example from geometry. When asked, "How long is the coast of Britain?" Beniot Mandelbrot, a prominent geometer of the twentieth century, answered that the coast has no real length separate from one's judgment (Hardison, 1986). If you use a measurement scale of 100 miles to an inch to draw the British coastline, your drawing portrays large expansive bays and capes. If, on the other hand, you use a scale of 10 miles to an inch, new inlets would appear in your drawing. Further, the incoming tide diminishes the length of the coast and the outgoing tide lengthens the coastline. Thus the question can only be resolved by deciding on the purpose of the measurement, the perspective of the measurement, and the unit of measurement.

Likewise, a study with a rigorous research design might have high internal validity but at the expense of external validity (generalization). Changing the design to increase external validity alters (sacrifices) internal validity. The ongoing tension of research is between *rigor and relevance*. However, we are not suggesting that investigators throw up their hands in disgust, foregoing strong methodological design. In fact, there is considerable room for improvement in the state of teacher development research. Glickman and Bey, for example, point out that studies of "direct supervision"—tasks that create one-to-one instructional dialogue and planning (e.g., curriculum development, clinical supervision, peer coaching, staff development, action research, program evaluation) do not seem to cumulate.

> There is no replication of studies using similar models, methods, or populations, nor are there longitudinal studies utilizing the same treatment of samples over several years. What exists in the research of direct supervision is a scattering of isolated, onetime studies that have little coherence among themselves. Generalization across such studies becomes largely speculative. (1990, pp. 549–550)

Regarding teacher development, Kuhn (1991) illustrates that very little is known about how teachers actually think about their teaching, other than that teachers employ a kind of naive psychology in their explanation. Other reviews of teacher learning and development have reached similar conclusions (Furth & Pajak, 1997; Lanier & Little, 1986). In the following section we will address some research strategies in greater depth that could advance the science of teacher development.

 # RESEARCH STRATEGIES FOR A SCIENCE OF TEACHER DEVELOPMENT

PHASE ONE RESEARCH

A scientific basis for the art of teacher development acknowledges the evolutionary nature of the scientific endeavor. Although there are numerous descriptions of the evolutionary process of educational research (see Borg & Gall, 1989), there are three dominant strands or phases that research progresses through in its evolution: Phase 1, in which descriptive observation of a phenomenon is collected in its natural environment; Phase 2, in which specific variables are identified and relationships between them are explicated;

and Phase 3, in which a theory is developed or reframed based on the empirically derived evidence about variables and their interrelationships.

Our discussion of teacher development embraces a number of fields and disciplines (e.g., supervision, staff development, coaching, induction programs, preservice teacher education, and human development). The common denominator, however, is the teacher. As we have pointed out in the text, most of these disciplines have accomplished Phase 1 with multiple descriptive observations of phenomena. A number of research strategies (Borg & Gall, 1989) match the need to acquire rich description of observed phenomena. Naturally there are limitations and strengths with each of the strategies. However, when the strategies are matched to the phase of inquiry for which they are particularly well suited, inquiry is advanced.

Qualitative Research. This type of research tends to be exploratory, may or may not be guided by "grounded theory" (see Woods, 1985), tends not to have hypotheses, uses purposive rather than random sampling, includes guiding questions, and utilizes inductive data analysis. Sometimes referred to as naturalistic or ethnographic inquiry (Lincoln & Guba, 1985), qualitative study emphasizes participant observation and in-depth interviews that allow researchers to learn firsthand about the social world and/or how persons construct meaning (Burgess, 1985). A drawback of this research strategy is that it is much more difficult to do well than quantitative research, and it requires extensive training and practice in the methods. An example of this type of research is the study conducted by Sara Lightfoot (1983), who investigated the social patterns in good high schools. Likewise, a study by Huberman (1993) which examined the career trajectories of 160 experienced teachers was a qualitative study that included extensive use of interviews and participant observation.

Case Study Research. A case study also is an effective strategy to employ in the first phase of building a science for teacher development. The case study approach provides in-depth description of multiple variables that might affect an individual. Kegan's theory of human interpersonal development (1982) is based on clinical case studies he conducted over many years. There also are numerous examples of the case study approach in supervision (Glickman & Bey, 1990), and in preservice teacher education (Houston, 1990).

The rigor of the case study approach can be enhanced by employing multiple measures that include psychometric data, the evaluations of trained raters, the observations of other individuals, and audiotaped or videotaped data. For example, Heath's ongoing investigation (Heath, 1994) of the characteristics of psychologically mature adults employs a case study approach with overlapping measures.

Interactional Research. As we have illustrated throughout the text, supervision and coaching are verbal and nonverbal endeavors that warrant examination. As we have noted, Flanders (1970) developed a system for analyzing verbal interactions between a teacher and students, Galloway (1968) developed a parallel system to Flanders that analyzed nonverbal interactions, Blumberg (1970) developed a system for analyzing supervisory conferences, and Reiman (1988) adapted the Flanders system for analyzing written narrative reflective discourse. Each of these systems has been studied extensively and together they have deepened understanding of teacher development, particularly as it relates to the collegial or supervisory context. See, for example, a study conducted by Pajak and Glickman (1989) of informational and controlling language in simulated supervisory conferences. Using the interactional approach, the researcher tabulates moment-to-moment verbal or nonverbal interactions to attain numeric ratios and patterns that are most useful to research in the first phase—description. A limitation of this type of research, however, is that the correlational data precludes drawing causal inferences.

Phase Two Research

Phase 2 research requires an analysis of relationships between and among teacher development–related variables. We recommend that researchers consider aptitude-treatment interactions (ATI) as a model for teacher development research at this phase. Although space limitations constrain the coverage of this model of research, there are a number of excellent discussions of the model (see Cronbach & Snow, 1969, 1977; McNergney & Carrier, 1981; Sprinthall, Reiman, & Thies-Sprinthall, 1996).

ATI Research

A central idea of ATI research is that an appropriate environment (E) for one person (P) may be inappropriate for another. For example, a study by Domino (1971) examined college teaching. Domino hypothesized an interaction between a student's achievement orientation and the style of teaching to which he or she was exposed in a psychology class. Examining the Achievement via Conformance scale of the California Psychological Inventory (CPI), Domino found that students high on this scale performed better when taught by an approach that stressed discipline, attendance, clearly defined homework, and class lectures as a means of acquiring course material. Students who were high on the Achievement via Independence scale of the CPI, on the other hand, performed better when class discussion was emphasized and attendance and discipline were de-emphasized. Thus ATI research counters the notion that all students or adults constitute a uniform or homogeneous group. Naturally developmental educators are interested in the person-environment matches (and mismatches), examining how the developmental level of a teacher interacts with different professional development, training, or supervisory environments.

The empirical support for person-environment interactions is limited (Sprinthall, Reiman, & Thies-Sprinthall, 1996) and there are numerous conceptual and methodological, as well as practical limitations that inhibit ATI research. Nonetheless, there is sufficient evidence to suggest that person-environment research (ATI) is important, needed, and addresses what educators and psychologists have long suspected, that no professional development context is capable of appropriately meeting the needs of all persons. McNergney and Carrier (1980) have, in fact, submitted that ATI is at the very heart of teacher development research. In their conceptual scheme, the practicing teacher behavior (B) is the result of an interaction between person (P), the environment (E) or context, and various tasks (T). This pluralistic view of the teacher, and of teacher development, requires the researcher to study the process of differentiated professional development (context and tasks) with different teachers.

Ultimately, ATI research must also account for student learning and development. Gage (1978) was on the mark when he stated that the study of teacher development and effectiveness cannot be divorced from student learning. The worth of teacher development must be measured, at least in part, in terms of teachers' effects on students. In summary, then, research on aptitude-treatment interaction provides a compelling means for advancing our understanding of teacher learning and development processes and effects.

PHASE THREE RESEARCH

Theory building is the final phase of our evolutionary scheme for teacher development research and, perhaps, the most important because it subsumes the other two phases of inquiry. If research on the science of teacher development is to explain a set of phenomena, it must describe and predict such phenomena with a high degree of accuracy. Teacher development theories, therefore, must provide constructs for predicting and controlling phenomena involving different persons and settings occurring at different times and with different tasks. Theory can also explain how various factors are causally linked to one another.

If you are interested in a detailed discussion of how theories evolve and how they are related to intellectual paradigms, we recommend Thomas Kuhn's book, *The Structure of Scientific Revolutions* (1962) which describes how theories come into being and how they are replaced by more satisfactory theories over time. Kuhn argued that a scientific discipline progresses cumulatively within an agreed-on paradigm until anomalies unexplained by the paradigm provoke a "revolution" and the creation of a new paradigm.

 ## SELECTED PROCEDURAL ISSUES
IN METHODOLOGY

As we mentioned earlier, there are a number of practical and procedural issues and considerations that must be made irrespective of the phase of inquiry and/or research strategy employed. Once again, space limitations constrain what we can cover; however, many excellent texts exist that focus on research and methodology. We have chosen to address nine issues that we believe are of special importance in teacher development research.

Qualitative Inquiry. As we mentioned earlier, qualitative inquiry is ideally suited to the first phase of a science for teacher development, namely, description. It has been rewarding to witness the emergence of qualitative inquiry as a respected and valuable form of research. The issue, however, is one of training. Qualitative research has established its own set of assumptions and guidelines regarding methodology and ethics (Woods, 1985). Therefore, persons interested in conducting qualitative inquiry should be steeped in these methodologies and ethical principles. Substantial training is needed before conducting qualitative research.

Sample Size. When quantitative research is conducted, sample size becomes a practical issue. How does the researcher obtain a sufficiently large sample when the research involves staff development, supervision, a coaching or training program, or collaborative inquiry? Obviously research in education cannot investigate an entire population. Thus, because the sample will typically be small, researchers must select a sample of subjects who are representative of the population to which they wish to generalize research findings. Volunteer sampling as opposed to random sampling is often used in educational research. In such cases every effort should be made to generalize findings only to highly comparable groups. Borg and Gall (1989) include a process for determining what a statistically significant sample size would be (p. 239). As a word of caution, many educational field studies are biased because the researcher chose experimental and comparison groups from different populations.

Replication and Extension. Glickman and Bey (1990) point out that most of the research in supervision has not been replicated. We therefore recommend replication-and-extension research as a means of gaining confidence in selected hypotheses in teacher development. If inconsistent results are obtained, the researchers can determine whether there was a problem in methodology or theory. It is important to note that replication does not mean duplication (Borg & Gall, 1989). Instead, the replication can duplicate the dominant elements of a study yet extend the inquiry into new domains.

Rater Reliability. When using raters and/or rating procedures, provide enough information about the raters and their training so that interested readers can ascertain the preparation and qualifications of the rater as well as the potential for biases.

Reporting Demographics Information. In studies that are nonrandomized, there should be a full reporting of the demographics of the volunteer participants of the study. Demographic data can include age, gender, level of education, as well as other professional experiences.

Clear Definitions. Although it is a given that any phenomena being investigated should have clear operational definitions, it is our observation that there are not more replication-and-extension studies because working definitions of the variables are not clear. One has only to look at the different meanings of teacher development to realize that the study of developmental processes necessitates clear operational definitions.

Effect Sizes. Too little use is made of the concept of effect size (ES)(Glass, 1982), which describes the magnitude of gains from any educational practice, innovation, or teacher development intervention. Such effect sizes are important because they help us predict the future strength of using such a practice or intervention. A practice that increases learning or development by up to one-half of a standard deviation might be considered a modestly effective practice, whereas an innovation that had an effect size of more than one standard deviation, would be considered a very effective innovation that shows great promise for educational practice (Joyce & Showers, 1995, p. 51).

For example, imagine that a study was conducted on support groups for teachers. The mean score of the experimental group of teachers on a post-test measure of reflective complexity is 56, and the corresponding mean score of the control group is 47. The mean difference between the groups is nine points. Is this difference large enough to have significance for teacher development practice? To answer this question, the investigator would divide the mean difference (nine points) by the standard deviation of the control group on the post-test. If, for example, the standard deviation was 9.0, the ES will be 1.00 (nine point mean score difference divided by the standard deviation of 9.0). The ES score of 1.00 means that the experimental group scored at the 84th percentile of the control group distribution.

Self-Reports. Perhaps for the next 20 years, we should voluntarily support a moratorium on self-reports of teacher satisfaction as an outcome measure for teacher development research. The relationship between reported "satisfaction" and learning, effectiveness, or teacher development is very tenuous at best, and such evidence creates the impression of significant results where none exist.

Ethical Issues. Because of the growth of research there has been increasing concern with the ethics of research. Among the principles that should frame any research initiative are: (1) consider whether participants in the planned study will be at risk or minimal risk; (2) except in minimal risk research, the investigator should establish a clear and fair agreement with research participants before the study which clarifies obligations and responsibilities; (3) after data collection, the investigator should debrief the participants; and (4) confidentiality of individual research participants must be protected.

ISSUES AND TOPICS FOR FUTURE RESEARCH

Throughout the text we have identified the Teaching/Learning Framework as an applied theory for teacher development across the career span (refer to Exhibit 15-1). In this final section, we examine issues and topics for future research that relate to the Teaching/Learning Framework.

TEACHER DEVELOPMENT AND IMPLEMENTATION OF STAFF DEVELOPMENT

There is a need to monitor the implementation of new curricula, staff development, teacher as leader, and other innovations. Recent work by Joyce and Showers (1995) is instructive regarding needed directions in research on coaching and staff development. One area of focus is level of transfer. Joyce and Showers have devised a transfer continuum: Level 1: low use—imitative; Level 2: mechanical use—horizontal transfer; Level 3: moderate use—routine; Level 4: integrated use; and Level 5: executive control. Such a continuum could be used to study teacher implementation of new models of instruction.

Another area to examine is variables that affect variation in implementation. For example, the research studies of McKibbin and Joyce (1980) and Hopkins (1990) have examined how "states of growth" affect implementation of staff development. In both studies the states of growth were found to be more powerful predictors of implementation than was school climate. Continued research is needed on individual teacher characteristics (e.g., developmental levels, phases of concern, career phases, years of experience), small group characteristics, and school variables (e.g, principal leadership, faculty cohesion, system level support) that might affect teachers' rates of implementation of innovations known to have positive effects on student learning and development, and teacher learning and development.

ADMINISTRATIVE SUPPORT AND CHALLENGE

Another set of questions relates to how various styles of principal leadership affect teacher learning and development. Recall our earlier discussion of ATI research. The main point of this line of inquiry is to better understand how support and challenge are differentiated according to the needs of staff. Thus, how do variations in principal support and challenge promote teacher learning and development? A similar question, by the way, was asked by Vygotsky when he hypothesized the "zone of proximal development."

CARROLL MODEL OF SCHOOL LEARNING

Student and teacher learning could be studied using Carroll's model of school learning (1989). In the Carroll model, mastery learning is defined by the equation $ML = f(Ts/Tn)$. Time needed for learning or development (Tn) is a function of the person's ability/competence/current preferred ways of solving complex problems plus (or minus) the teacher's (facilitator, teacher educator, or supervisor) effectiveness. Time spent on learning (Ts) is a function of the learner's perseverance or the time allocated by the teacher for learning the lesson, whichever is less. The Carroll model offers numerous possibilities for investigation.

TEACHERS' THEORETICAL REASONING

Murray (1992) points out that we know very little about how teachers actually think about their teaching. Thus, like Piaget's investigations with children, a needed area of inquiry would be to investigate how teachers reason about their work. Are some reasons better or more mature than others? Murray advocates the development of assessments similar to the Kohlberg scale of moral development. Such an inquiry would systematically pose generic teaching dilemmas or cases that could be stated in such a way that the structure of the teacher's reasoning about teaching and schooling would be revealed. Ammons and Hutcheson (1989) have speculated on a five-level sequence of teacher conceptions about behavior, teaching, and student learning. Further, Head (1993) has field-tested a scale that assesses mentor teachers' reasoning about assistance and supervision. Naturally, the key question in such inquiry would be how well a teacher understands and explains any professional problem or event. Murray (1992) argues that better explanations would represent more integrated and differentiated reasoning that have wider applicability in professional situations. He also thinks that "a true profession of teaching . . . awaits a pedagogy that has formal operation properties" (p. 305).

ROLE TAKING AND REFLECTION

Our vision of teacher development incorporates new professional roles with ongoing reflection, both of which are requisite for learning and development. But many questions remain to be answered. How do new teacher roles affect schoolwide change? How do new professional roles affect collegial peer interaction? How does teacher reflection affect teachers' pedagogical or theoretical knowledge? These are but a few of the questions needing study.

Instructional Supervision

A recent article by Keedy (1994) raised a number of research questions that warrant attention in the field of instructional supervision. Which organizational structures, for example, teacher study groups, peer observation, and beginning teacher support groups, do teachers and principals use to provide intellectual empowerment as a precondition for school renewal? How can supervisors work with teachers to encourage explicit development of tacitly held practical knowledge? Should principals become responsible for administrative functions (as legally responsible for their building) and teachers responsible for the technical core (teaching and learning)?

The last question relates to the ongoing debate about the role that evaluation should play in supervision and teacher professional growth (Hazi, 1994).

Supervisor or Coach as Action Researcher

The idea of supervisors or teachers researching their own practice is a fairly recent one. However, numerous networks, coalitions, and school/university professional development partnerships have committed to the concept of administrators and teachers as site-based scholars in the study of instructional improvement. These activities are often referred to as action research. Typically they involve five basic phases: problem identification; planning (which includes deciding how data will be collected); management (which includes deciding how data will be organized); analysis; and refocusing (which includes modifying goals and strategies based on analysis and interpretation of the data). Thus, a supervisor might decide, for example, to examine his or her conferencing style. The specific focus might be to explore the proportion of colleague talk during conferences. Data would be collected from audiotapes or videotapes, analyzed (using, for example, the Flanders Interaction Analysis System), and practice would be revised based on the data. This is an example of the supervisor or coach engaging in action research, examining his or her own practice.

Another form of action research would require the coach to participate in *collaborative* action research with colleagues. Richard Sagor (1993) wrote, "By turning to collaborative action research . . . we can renew our commitment to thoughtful teaching and also begin developing an active community of professionals" (p. 10). This form of collaborative inquiry increasingly is seen in professional development partnerships between the universities and schools. A form of collaborative inquiry is the coaching plan described in Chapter 12. Both the supervisor or coach and the colleague co-construct a coaching plan which requires self-analysis, practice, and eventual revisions or refinements in instruction. If you are interested in initiating collaborative action research, we encourage you to read an in-depth researched account of the process described by Oja and Smulyan (1989) entitled *Collaborative Action Research: A Developmental Approach.*

THE FOUR-COMPONENT MODEL OF REST

Rest (1994) has called for more comprehensive research on moral reasoning and moral action by proposing a four component model of inquiry. His model has intriguing implications for the broader study of adult and teacher development. The first component is sensitivity. For example, a teacher in a classroom might be unaware that he or she is giving more attention to boys than girls. Conceptual or moral sensitivity, then, is the awareness of how our actions and cognitions affect other people. As Rest points out, sensitivity includes being aware of alternate lines of action and how such courses might affect persons.

Judgment is the second component. In the moral domain, Kohlberg's work advanced this component. How we justify our choices of action represents a continuum of complexity that is less or more adequate. The important point here is that moral judgment and caring, for example, is not the only determinant of moral behavior. The third component is motivation and has to do with the importance a person gives moral values when they are in conflict with other values. Little in the way of research has been conducted on this component. Finally, the fourth component involves ego strength and perseverance. A person may be morally sensitive, make sound moral judgments, and be morally motivated, yet if the person wilts under pressure or is easily discouraged, a moral line of action will not be carried out. Rest acknowledges that there are complex interactions among the four components, and the components do not represent a temporal order. Further, very little is known about how the components interact.

Teacher development researchers will continue to have many provocative hypotheses to test for many years to come. Although the arena of teacher development and the related field of supervision are young, the call for a science of teacher development parallels a recent surge of interest in teacher professional development. In fact, the limited amount of research on coaching, mentoring, adult development, and supervision can be considered as a cause for much excitement. After all, as a profession, educators have much to learn and many innovations to study.

More coordinated research from a network of researchers and program developers might resolve a number of knotty questions including the special case of how aptitude treatment interaction is applied to adult development. Progress may be slow, but it need not be circular. It is our hope that this book will play a small part in contributing to this discovery of a scientific basis for the art of teacher development.

REFERENCES

Ammons, P., & Hutcheson, B. (1989). Promoting the development of teachers' pedagogical conceptions. *Genetic Epistemologist, 17*(4), 23–29.

Black, A. (1989). Developmental teacher education. *Genetic Epistemologist, 17*(4), 5–14.

Blumberg, A. (1970). A system for analyzing supervisor-teacher interaction. In A. Simon & E. Boyer (Eds.), *Mirrors for behavior—III* (pp. 1–15). Philadelphia: Research for Better Schools.

Borg, W. R., & Gall, M. D. (1989). *Educational research: An introduction* (5th ed.). New York: Longman.

Burgess, R. G. (1985). *Field methods in the study of education.* Philadelphia: Falmer Press.

Carroll, J. (1989). The Carroll model: A 25-year retrospective and prospective view. *Educational Research, 18,* 26–31.

Cronbach, L. J., & Snow, R. E. (1969). *Individual difference in learning ability as a function of instructional variables.* (Final Report No. OEC-4-6-061269-1217). Washington DC: U.S. Office of Education.

Cronbach, L. J., & Snow R. E. (1977). *Aptitudes and instructional methods.* New York: Irvington Press.

Domino, G. (1971). Interactive effects of achievement orientation and teaching style on academic achievement. *Journal of Educational Psychology, 62,* 427–431.

Flanders, N. A. (1970). *Analyzing teacher behavior.* Reading, MA: Addison-Wesley.

Furth, J., & Pajak, E. (Eds.) (1997). *Handbook of research on school supervision.* New York: Macmillan.

Gage, N. (1978). *A scientific basis for the art of teaching.* New York: Teachers College Press.

Gage, N. (1985). *Hard gains in the soft sciences: The case of pedagogy.* Bloomington, IN: Phi Delta Kappa.

Galloway, C. (1968). *A description of teacher behavior: Verbal and nonverbal.* Unpublished doctoral dissertation, Ohio State University.

Glass, G. V. (1982). Meta-analysis: An approach to the synthesis of research results. *Journal of Research in Science Teaching, 19*(2), 93–112.

Glickman, C., & Bey, T. (1990). Supervision. In R. Houston (Ed.), *Handbook of research on teacher education.* New York: Macmillan.

Gold, Y. (1996). Beginning teacher support: Attrition, mentoring, and induction. In J. Sikula (Ed.), *Second handbook of research on teacher education* (pp. 548–594). New York: Macmillan.

Hardison, O., Jr. (1986). A tree, a streamlined fish, and a self-squared dragon: Science as a form of culture. *Georgia Review,* 394–403.

Hazi, H. M. (1994). The teacher evaluation-supervision dilemma: A case of entanglements and irreconcilable differences. *Journal of Curriculum and Supervision, 9,* 195–216.

Head, F. (1993). *Modifying moral dilemmas for mentors and supervising teachers: An initial validation study of a cognitive developmental assessment model.* Unpublished dissertation. North Carolina State University, Raleigh, NC.

Heath, D. (1994). *Schools of hope: Developing mind and character in today's youth.* San Francisco: Jossey-Bass.

Hopkins, D. (1990). Integrating staff development and school improvement: A study of teacher personality and school climate. In B. Joyce (Ed.), *Changing school culture through staff development* (pp. 41–70). Alexandria, VA: Association for Supervision and Curriculum Development.

Houston, R. (Ed.) (1990). *Handbook of research on teacher education.* New York: Macmillan.

Huberman, M. (1993). *The lives of teachers*. New York: Teachers College Press.

Joyce, B., & Showers, B. (1980). Improving inservice training: The messages of research. *Educational Leadership, 37*(2), 379–385.

Joyce, B., & Showers, B. (1995). *Student achievement and staff development* (2nd ed.). New York: Addison-Wesley Longman.

Keedy, J. (1994). Ten critical research questions in instructional supervision. *Instructional Supervision—AERA/SIG newsletter, 14*(1), 5–7.

Kegan, R. (1982). *The evolving self*. Cambridge, MA: Harvard University Press.

King, P. M., & Kitchener, K. S. (1994). *Developing reflective judgment*. San Francisco: Jossey-Bass.

Kuhn, D. (1991). *The skills of argument*. New York: Cambridge University Press.

Kuhn, T. (1962). *The structure of scientific revolutions*. Chicago: University of Chicago Press.

Lanier, J., & Little, J. (1986). Research on teacher education. In M. Wittrock (Ed.), *Handbook of Research on Teaching* (pp. 527–569). New York: Macmillan.

Lightfoot, S. (1983). *The good high school*. New York: Basic Books.

Lincoln, Y. S., & Guba, E. G. (1985). *Naturalistic inquiry*. Beverly Hills, CA: Sage.

McKibbin, M., & Joyce, B. (1980). Psychological states and staff development. *Theory into Practice, 19*(4), 248–255.

McNergney, R., & Carrier, C. A. (1981). *Teacher development*. New York: Macmillan.

Murray, F. (1992). Restructuring and constructivism: The development of American educational reform. In H. Beilin & P. Pufall (Eds.), *Piaget's theory: Prospects and possibilities*. Hillsdale, NJ: Erlbaum.

Murray, F. (1996). Educational psychology and the teacher's reasoning. In F. Murray (Ed.), *The teacher educator's handbook* (pp. 419–437). San Francisco: Jossey-Bass.

Oja, S. N., & Reiman, A. J. (1997). Describing and promoting supervision for teacher development across the career span. In G. Firth & E. Pajak (Eds.), *Handbook of research on school supervision*. New York: Macmillan.

Oja, S. N., & Smulyan, L. (1989). *Collaborative action research: A developmental conceptualization*. New York: Falmer Press.

Pajak, E., & Glickman, C. (1989). Informational and controlling language in simulated supervisory conferences. *American Educational Research Journal, 26*(1), 93–106.

Reiman, A. J. (1988). *An intervention study of long-term mentor training: Relationships between cognitive-developmental theory and reflection*. Unpublished doctoral dissertation, North Carolina State University, Raleigh.

Rest, J. (1994). Background: Theory and research. In J. Rest & D. F. Narvaez (Eds.), *Moral development in the professions: Psychology and applied ethics* (pp. 1–25). New York: Erlbaum.

Sagor, R. (1993). *How to conduct collaborative action research*. Alexandria, VA: Association for Supervision and Curriculum Development.

Schön, D. A. (1983). *The reflective practitioner*. New York: Basic Books.

Sprinthall, N. A., Reiman, A. J., & Thies-Sprinthall, L. (1996). Teacher professional development. In J. Sikula (Ed.), *Second handbook of research on teacher education* (pp. 666–703). New York: Macmillan.

Wittrock, M. (1986). *Handbook of research on teaching*. New York: Macmillan.

Woods, P. (1985). Ethnography and theory construction in educational research. In R. G. Burgess (Ed.), *Field methods in the study of education*. Philadelphia: Falmer Press.

C·H·A·P·T·E·R
17

Teacher Development and Revitalization Across the Career Span

• • • • • •

In this chapter we look forward to the next millennium, and how supervision, teacher development, and school, university, and community collaboration intertwine in the service of students and democratic communities.

You may recall that in Chapter 2 we cited a call by Harvard president emeritus James Conant in 1963 for a new model of the teacher professional. Using the medical model, he called for "teaching hospitals" to be developed. Of special interest to Conant were complex new roles for clinical teachers and clinical professors, educators specially prepared to work side by side as they educate future teachers. The idea never caught on in education.

In the early 1980s there had been similar calls for reform and simultaneous restructuring of schools and teacher education programs (Carnegie Forum on Education and the Economy, 1986; Holmes Group, 1986, 1990; Wise & Darling-Hammond, 1987; Commission on Teaching and America's Future, 1996). Other prominent educators have called for the invention and establishment of professional development schools (Darling-Hammond, 1994; Goodlad, 1993; Zimpher, 1990). And Corrigan and Udas (1996) recommend the establishment of interprofessional development schools, and the integration of child- and family-centered education, health, and human service systems. As yet, such reforms are in the preliminary stages and research to support their continuation is limited (Book, 1996). In fact, Book (1996) suggests that caution be taken. The challenges of lack of time, mission uncertainty, and lack of reward systems for K–12 educators, as well as for universities, coupled with the expense and labor intensiveness of engaging in such new and complex relationships, should not be underestimated.

Another innovation of the 1980s has been the creation of collaborative inquiry teams that support action research on student learning and development, as well as teacher learning and development (Oja & Smulyan, 1989). In these models, the school becomes the center of inquiry and teachers, supervisors, faculty, and perhaps even parents, become investigators of school improvement. As Sagor (1993) writes, "By turning to collaborative action research . . . we can renew our commitment to thoughtful teaching and also begin developing an active community of professionals" (p. 10). The main focus of this innovation is the encouragement of teacher-led research in which teachers identify a problem, decide what data to collect and how it will be collected, collect the data, analyze the data, and act based on findings (Calhoun, 1992).

CREATING A NEW CULTURE FOR THE TRANSFORMATION AND RENEWAL OF SCHOOL, UNIVERSITY, AND COMMUNITY THROUGH COLLABORATION

Innovations such as professional development schools, quality induction programs, quality preservice teacher education programs, and collaborative inquiry teams require the creation of a new culture in which school, university, and community work together through collaborative efforts. A large part of the success of such initiatives depends on teachers taking leadership roles (Darling-Hammond, 1994). It also requires that teachers, supervisors, and university faculty collectively develop and implement new approaches for the preparation of cadres of teacher leaders or clinical mentor teachers who acquire a knowledge base in areas such as building trusting relationships, the developing adult learner, preservice teacher education, teacher induction and mentoring skills, instructional coaching, clinical supervision, action research, team building, and reflection. Such a unique preparation program would unfold over many months and needs the support of all educational stakeholders. In our own state we have begun to explore if it is possible to prepare large cadres of clinical professors and clinical teachers who could assume significant responsibility for school-based supervision, coaching, and school improvement. We believe that supervision and mentoring, in its various forms, performed thoughtfully and compassionately by well-

LINDA DARLING-HAMMOND

Linda Darling-Hammond received her B.A. at Yale University in 1973, and her doctorate in urban education from Temple University in 1978. She began her career as a public school teacher and was a co-founder of a preschool and day care center. Before joining Teachers College in 1989, she was Senior Social Scientist and Director of the RAND Corporation's Education and Human Resources Program.

She is an eminent scholar and a prolific writer, having authored or edited six books, including *Professional Development Schools: Schools for Developing a Profession*. In addition, she has authored more than 150 journal articles, book chapters, and monographs on issues of teaching and educational practice. Her energy and enthusiasm are legendary. To some degree the most important aspect of her work may be its implications for educational policy.

Her own career path faced a critical turning point in 1992. As a result of her scholarly eminence she was offered the deanship of the Harvard School of Education. She would now be in a position to influence education policy even more broadly than in her role as a professor of educational policy. Her acceptance of the position, however, created a major conflict within her professional self. As the dissonance grew, and in spite of the official announcements and major headlines in the media, she realized that the fundamental choice was stark. A deanship would mean inevitably giving up one's own research and inquiry, particularly since private graduate schools of education were faced with major financial difficulties in an era of reduced federal grants and a subsequent increase in the pressures on private foundations. The decision wasn't easy, yet she realized that her own career path was at a turning point. As a result she decided to turn down the deanship and return to Teachers College.

Currently Darling-Hammond is William F. Russell Professor in the Foundations of Education at Teachers College, Columbia University where she is also co-director of the National Center for Restructuring Education, Schools, and Teaching. Most recently she was invited to serve as executive director of the National Commission on Teaching and America's Future. Her many recent contributions clearly attest to the wisdom of the choice to remain in the professoriate.

Darling-Hammond has been invited to write on the role supervision and coaching play in teacher development, and she has been a strong advocate for the careful preparation of cadres of school-based teacher educators and teacher leaders who can support the preparation of the nation's teachers. Unlike doctors, architects, and many other professionals, she argues that teachers are often thrown into their field without adequate training, supervision, and support. In her view, this "sink or swim" phenomenon cripples public education by encouraging teacher isolation, and retarding the acquisition of teaching skills. In *A License to Teach: Building a Profession for 21st Century Schools*, which she co-authored with Wise and Klein, she elaborates on some of the problems quality supervision faces. Funds for supervision are meager and the result is a preparation program that is very low budget, with very high supervisory caseloads. She also points out that an additional serious problem for supervision is the lack of training for cooperating teachers.

As we go to press, Darling-Hammond is at work on another book as well as an array of scholarly papers. We look forward to the results of her continued work with educational reform, and we surmise that her ideas will continue to play a significant role in framing national educational policy.

REFLECTION QUESTIONS

Do Darling-Hammond's observations about supervision ring true in your school system?

Why are budgets for supervision and coaching so meager?

Do cooperating teachers in your school system receive substantive preparation for coaching and supervising novice teachers?

---

prepared faculty at both the university and school level, lead to promising outcomes (Edelfelt, 1996).

In this chapter, we describe our efforts with developmental teacher education programs. As with past chapters, the programs are linked to the applied theory that we have referred to as the Teaching/Learning Framework (see Exhibit 17-1). Although all of the conditions cited in the framework drive the programs described in this chapter, we give special emphasis to the role played by the fifth condition—continuity.

 # THE PROBLEM OF DISCONTINUITY IN TEACHER EDUCATION

We made an important point early in the text that effective theory can be judged as somewhere near the midpoint of the continuum between wild fads and excessive reductionism. We used the Goldilocks principle (Katz &

Exhibit 17-1   TEACHING/LEARNING FRAMEWORK

Instructional Repertoire[*]	**Conditions for Growth and Development**[†]
1. Theory/rationale	1. Complex new role
2. Demonstrations	2. Guided reflection
3. Practice with feedback	3. Balance between new role and reflection
4. Adapt and generalize through coaching	4. Support and challenge
	5. Continuity

[*]Adapted from B. Joyce and B. Showers, *Student Achievement Through Staff Development*, 1995, New York: Longman.
[†]N. A. Sprinthall and L. Thies-Sprinthall, Teacher as an adult learner: A cognitive-developmental view. In G. Griffin (Ed.), *Staff Development: Eighty-Second Yearbook of the National Society for the Study of Education*, 1983, pp. 13–35. Chicago: University of Chicago Press.

Raths, 1985) to stress our main point that a framework for teacher development needs a theoretical bed that is not too big (overly abstract and broad), nor too narrow, in which human complexity is reduced to a few simpleminded propositions. Without careful integration of theory, research, and practice, the consequence for Goldilocks, and for educators, is excessive wandering from place to place and fad to fad, as the field attempts to find a better fit. Thus, supervision for teacher development programs must apply the Goldilocks principle, always seeking continuity, parsimony, and balance between a theoretical framework and practical applications. Unfortunately, discontinuity is too often the norm.

A number of decades ago Dewey recognized the problem of discontinuity in teacher preparation and the need for continuity if supervision for teacher development was to be maximally educative. Without continuity in the experience, the growth potential is forfeited. More recently, in a comprehensive overview of educational issues facing countries worldwide, a number of dilemmas related to discontinuity were identified (Leavitt, 1992). The main trends in discontinuity were as follows:

1. There is too little coordination between the college and the schools regarding field experiences.
2. Field experiences for preservice teacher education are as yet unrealized due to insufficient numbers of highly skilled and exemplary teacher educators at both the university and school level.
3. Although an extensive and growing knowledge base exists for how children learn and develop, a comparable knowledge base for clinical teaching and clinical supervisory experiences is, at best, emergent at the

preservice and induction levels for the developing young adult and adult learner.

4. There is little connection between preservice teacher education and the next phases of education, even though preliminary evidence shows that quality teacher induction programs, including year-long internships, represent a cost-effective means of increasing beginning teacher instructional repertoire, beginning teacher self-efficacy and personal development, teacher retention, and experienced teacher (mentor) renewal.

5. Observing exemplary teaching does affect practice, yet prospective teachers take most of their coursework outside of the university or school of education. In many cases, effective teaching practices are not modeled outside of the university. Most prospective teachers identify teacher education faculty within the university as some of their best models of effective instruction.

6. There is rarely a consistent theory guiding preservice teacher education. Instead, educational fads prevail and/or the current popular "ism" is predominant. Thus preservice teachers must try to decipher the rhetoric of the reconstructionists, deconstructionists, and constructivists. Small wonder that the undergraduate throws up his or her hands in frustration and proclaims, "Just give me some real-world practice."

7. Interdisciplinary programs are rare in teacher education and instruction typically is segmented by content specialty.

 ## MISSING LINK: GREATER CONTINUITY THROUGH NEW CLINICAL MENTOR ROLES

One of the discontinuities in teacher education mentioned in the previous summary is the lack of adequate numbers of specially prepared clinical mentor teachers who can guide the development of novice and experienced teachers. In the 1970s, Ralph Mosher and David Purpel (1972, p. 192) explored ways to prepare teachers and counselors for their role as clinical educators, "We have argued previously that there is no quick and easy way to produce master teachers or to develop in-depth supervisory capabilities" (1972, p. 192). Instead, like Conant and Cogan, Mosher and Purpel called for the careful preparation of a cadre of teacher leaders capable of sustaining school-based teacher development and renewal. Similar proposals have been raised by Bolin and Falk (1987) and Sergiovanni and Starratt (1993).

Over the past 10 years Nancy Zimpher and Ken Howey have developed an important synthesis of theory and research on successful teaching practices and supervision (1987, 1996). They described four major types of teaching competence that they believe can be facilitated by supervisory practice and staff development:

NANCY L. ZIMPHER

Without question, Nancy Zimpher's most important contribution to education lies in her steadfast commitment to improving the linkages between schools and colleges of education in universities. One of her many legacies will be the study and implementation of professional development schools that are jointly governed by the school and the university's College of Education.

Completing her B.S. in English Education from Ohio State University in 1968, Zimpher began her work in education as an English teacher in the Ohio and Missouri schools where she taught for four years. After receiving her Ph.D. in Teacher Education and Administration in Higher Education at Ohio State University in 1976 she directed preservice teacher field experiences for the College of Education at Ohio State University. It was here that she cut her teeth on the complexities and limitations of supervision and field experiences for teachers. Zimpher quickly rose to the rank of professor at her alma mater in 1991, and became the Dean of the College of Education in 1993.

A prolific writer, she has published over 60 articles, chapters, and technical reports. An example of her scholarship is a recent book which she co-authored with her spouse, Ken Howey. Called *Profiles of Preservice Teacher Education* (1989), the work presents institutional profiles and data on selected teacher education programs, faculty, and students. From the mountains of data they collected, generalizations are made about the content, structure, and quality of preservice teacher education as well as the supervision that must bolster quality programs.

One of Zimpher's most far-reaching efforts is her work with professional development schools. She is not naive, however, concerning the ability of professional development schools to become a new delivery system for school-based development. The entrenched educational establishment clearly resists what appears to be a radical departure from university centers. She wrote somewhat wryly that working with a faculty committee on such issues could be summed up as an example of "Ready, fire, aim." Nonetheless, as the Dean of the College of Education at Ohio State University, she has demonstrated a high degree of tenacity and commitment to fashioning new partnership agreements with public schools, in which practicing teachers, clinical faculty, and administrators are given a greater role in preparing and supervising new teachers (student teachers and beginning teachers).

Recently she was invited to present a white paper to the first-ever National Congress on Teacher Education that was held in December, 1995. The conference was called *Teachers for the New Millennium: Aligning Teacher Development, National Goals, and High Standards,* the conference and its organizers sought out leaders in teacher education to present their latest thinking. In Zimpher's paper, "Right-Sizing Teacher Education: The Policy Imperative," she passionately called for a number of national values for colleges of education including the recruitment of a more diverse cohort into the teaching profession, the creation of a professional development continuum wherein teacher preparation is extended into the early years of teaching, and the national testing of selected teacher education program prototypes. We can anticipate that Nancy Zimpher will play a leading role in encouraging teacher education reform well into the twenty-first century.

REFLECTION QUESTIONS

What is a professional development school?

What are the challenges to implementing professional development schools?

Howey, K., & Zimpher, N. (1989). *Profiles of preservice teacher education.* Albany, NY: State University of New York Press.

---

1. Technical—focus on mastery of methods of instruction with the supervisor filling the role of translator of research and theory.
2. Clinical—focus on inquiry and models of teaching with the supervisor encouraging reflection.
3. Personal—focus on self-understanding and the supervisor providing a helpful and caring environment for addressing concerns.
4. Critical—focus on moral autonomy and commitment to social justice with the supervisor encouraging dialogue on ethical issues in an educational community.

Their groundbreaking synthesis was framed by a conception of the developing adult learner. However, Zimpher and Howey acknowledged that a missing link has been the careful preparation of a clinical faculty that can bolster development of teachers along the continuum of competencies they described.

A recent symposium that included clinical teachers, administrators, and university teacher educators (Reiman, et al., 1995) drew similar conclusions as they dialogued on the importance of careful selection and preparation of teacher educators and clinical mentor teachers. There was agreement that clinical teachers are a keystone in the immensely complex and important process of preparing teachers for excellence in the classroom. Further, the professional interchange between the clinical mentor teachers and novice teachers can be renewing for the mentor (Thies-Sprinthall & Sprinthall, 1987). The causes for our current challenges in education are complex, beginning with the teachers' preservice program and escalating as teachers enter the "real world" often without adequate support from carefully trained mentor teachers or coaches, and left to cope with some of the most demanding teaching assignments that are available at the school (Huling-Austin, 1990). Cogan observed, "The profound underestimation of the difficulties teachers face in learning how to teach and in improving their teaching on the job is at the root of the major problems in the preservice and inservice education of teachers" (1972, p. 15). Cogan's observation still rings true today.

ELEMENTS FOR EFFECTIVE TEACHER DEVELOPMENT PROGRAMS

The overall problem of implementing new kinds of teacher development programs is difficult. Unfortunately, there is no neat linear equation translating theory into practice, nor vice versa, translating practice into theory. Is theory embedded in practice and is practice visible in theory? Gary Griffin (1987) underscores the importance of attending to both sides of the theory-practice coin when designing and implementing programs. Along with a number of prominent associates such as Virginia Richardson, Willis Copeland, Hilda Borko, Beatrice Ward, and Kenneth Zeichner, he explored clinical teacher education. The central theme of the work is that clinical teacher education is one of the most promising trends for teacher professional development yet is seldom and poorly practiced. Griffin has pointed out that a number of central assumptions about teacher education are seriously compromised once teachers enter the classroom for the first time. *Learning to teach is developmental*, yet beginning teachers are expected to manage full assignments from the onset. *Observation and feedback are crucial*, yet there are a paucity of school settings in which such practices are the norm. *Differentiated supervision is recognized as an important tool*, yet rarely are teachers able to employ the skills with adequate depth and versatility. *Background knowledge of relevant theory and research is vital*, yet most cooperating teachers and many teacher educators have a very limited background.

Faced with these contradictions, Griffin and his associates conducted research with the support of the National Institute of Education. The research team conducted three major studies: a large scale multimethod, multisite descriptive study of student teaching; an analytical study of formal state-mandated teacher induction programs; and an experimental study of inservice teacher education (1986, p. 3).

Analysis of the separate studies led to the identification of elements of an effective teacher development program across the career span. Griffin

(1986) stresses that an effective program must be embedded in a school context (defining property), and be (p. 7):

1. Context-sensitive
2. Purposeful and articulated
3. Participatory and collaborative
4. Knowledge-based
5. Ongoing (continuity)
6. Developmental
7. Analytical and reflective

Another prominent scholar of professional development and teacher change, Fullan (1995) submits that any teacher professional development enterprise must engage: moral purpose, the school culture, and a continuum between preservice-induction-inservice teacher education. Among his guidelines for teachers are the following (p. 265):

- Practice reflection
- Practice collegiality
- Support principals and other administrators to develop interactive professionalism
- Monitor and strengthen the connection between personal development and student development

Guidelines for principals include (Fullan, 1995, p. 265):

- Value teachers
- Promote collaboration
- Make menus, not mandates
- Connect with the wider environment

Guidelines for faculties of education include (Fullan, 1995, p. 266):

- Commit to producing teachers as change agents of educational and societal improvement
- Value and practice exemplary teaching
- Model and develop collaboration
- Form partnerships with schools
- Work collaboratively to build regional, national, and international networks

And Borko and Putnam (1995) point out that professional development across the career span requires a focus on expanding and elaborating teachers' knowledge systems (Resnick, 1985, 1987). See Schiro (1992), for example, for a fascinating examination of the relationship between teacher conceptual level and level of sophistication in thinking about curriculum issues.

What these scholars have in common is a passion for understanding the process and function of teacher professional development in diverse contexts. In many respects, their findings converge. Effective teacher development programs (1) are based on a conception of teacher growth and development (that correlates with student learning and growth); (2) acknowledge the complexities of classroom, school, and community; (3) are grounded in a substantial and verifiable knowledge base; and (4) are sensitive to the ways teachers think, feel, and construct meaning from their experiences.

 ## NEXT STEPS: THE PREPARATION OF CLINICAL TEACHERS

It is our belief that an important part of the delay in realizing school reform, teacher education reform, and reculturing (Fullan, 1991) is attributable to the lack of a "supervision and coaching culture," cadres of prepared clinical educators, mentors, and teacher/administrator/faculty action research teams who can offer direct in-class support to preservice teachers and beginning teachers, and who make school the center of inquiry. Such lead educators (see Walling, 1994) would participate in significant preparation in methods of instruction, clinical supervision, teacher development, collegial reflection, action research, and coaching. Such an endeavor would be costly. However, it is far less expensive than permitting inadequately prepared teachers to work in the classrooms.

For more than a decade we have worked in earnest to realize the goal of preparing clinical educators and action researchers in selected school systems (Oja & Reiman, 1997; Sprinthall, Reiman, & Thies-Sprinthall, 1996). However, we are not sanguine when we consider the enormous scope of the needs. The present corps of clinical educators that numbers almost 1500 is so minuscule in proportion to the needs of our own state that many new teachers are not adequately supported. Further, until policy makers and local school personnel change the teaching and extracurricular assignments given to new teachers, chances are that such a powerful innovation as clinical mentor teachers, school-based teacher educators, or action researchers will be greatly underutilized. It also appears that a "critical mass" of these unique educators is needed at a school site to overcome the pressures of the status quo. Yet another challenge we face is providing for the continuing needs of this new culture of educators. Given these caveats, we still believe that one of the best hopes for education is the development of a new kind of teacher professional (clinical teachers, mentors, school-based teacher educators, or action researchers). These educators ask for and deserve collaboratively developed preparation for their roles and they need to be rewarded for their new responsibilities.

For example, a program was developed to test out the preparation of clinical educators by the second author (Thies-Sprinthall, 1984) as a beginning step. She created a method of using a coaching model from Weil and Joyce (1978) in concert with the developmental conditions displayed in Exhibit 15-1. Specific and focused skills of supervision were taught to a group of experienced teachers in a sequence of rationale, modeling, peer practice, and generalization for each component. The teachers' role-taking behavior was for each to become a teacher supervisor. Journals, audiotaping and videotaping, and readings were added for guided reflection. The program was the equivalent of a two-semester course to provide for continuity. In fact, one of the major goals was to help such teachers apply different models of supervision according to the developmental needs of a student teacher or beginning teachers. This meant mastering the process of systematically varying the amount of structure according to the needs of the neophyte teacher. A reflective practicum provided the opportunity for the teacher supervisors to discuss ideas and emotions in a relaxed mode.

Further refinements in the model are from our more current work (Reiman & Thies-Sprinthall, 1993). Vygotsky's work in particular suggests that there is an optimal focus for developmental growth in his zone of proximal growth. The zone is conceptualized as the area of problem solving and dissonance just beyond the learner's current preferred conceptual stage. By varying assignments and role-taking instruction, the aforementioned studies had involved adjusting the activities to the teachers' current conceptual stage. There was, however, only a loose connection between their zones of proximal growth and the reflective capacity of the teachers.

The first author of this text (Reiman) created a more systematic method of dialoguing in journals. The method, following Friere, included equal attention to the thoughts and emotional themes presented in journals and assignments. The system, though labor-intensive, does show how the learners' level of reflective complexity can be promoted through written dialogue. Other studies by De Angelis Peace (1992), Watson (1995), and Mann (1992) have applied the same framework to a group of in-service school counselors being educated for the new role of counselor mentor, sophomore education students being prepared for their first extended field experience, and to a group of college students being prepared for the new role of tutor to high school students. All three studies showed growth in the experimental group. Further, within-group analysis of journal entries showed that counselors, preservice teachers, and tutors on the "high road" to development wrote entries that included more perspective taking, more personal disclosure of feelings, and more complete diagnosis of the supervisee or tutee learning needs.

 ## ROLE TAKING, REFLECTION, AND TEACHER DEVELOPMENT

The research base for the elements of effective teacher development programs continues to expand and indicates that role taking without reflection does not promote growth. Also the opposite is true. Reflection without role taking does not work. Short-term workshops versus continuous ongoing programs indicates the former does not produce growth. Atmospheres that are either exclusively supportive in a Rogerian sense or exclusively challenging do not produce growth (Sprinthall, Reiman, & Thies-Sprinthall, 1993).

Another important set of findings indicates very clearly that experienced teachers and counselors can perform the functions of a new role as supervisor with a high degree of competence across the domains discussed by Zimpher and Howey (see earlier section on new clinical teacher roles). Even more important may be the findings which indicate that such teachers can also become school-based teacher educators, for example, a cadre of "clinical" faculty. For example, in a select group of North Carolina public schools there is now a network of some 40 interdisciplinary two-person teams of school-based teacher educators in 12 school systems who instruct their colleagues in year-long courses in developmental supervision and coaching. The overall network now consists of 1500 teachers and counselors educated in the new role of mentor.

Furthermore, in a series of quasi-experimental studies results have shown the impact of a developmental curriculum on teachers and counselors who have assumed complex new human helping roles: mentors have become skilled in developmental supervision and grown in conceptual complexity and moral reasoning. Thus, we have found that the conditions described by Griffin and Fullan earlier in this chapter can be successfully applied to developmental supervision programs.

The program is conceptualized as an operational example of Don Davies' triple "T" framework with mentor teachers/clinical teachers as the first "T," experienced school-based teacher educators as the second "T," and the university faculty as the third "T." The mentor teachers/clinical teachers serve to induct both preservice and beginning teachers in their initial assignments. The new teachers gain from careful mentoring. The school-based teacher educators improve their supervision skills as models for the mentors, and the university faculty improve their instructional skills as models for the school-based teacher educators (see Figure 17-1). In summary then, the program prepares educators for three new roles: clinical mentor teacher, school-based teacher educator, and clinical instructor.

Phillips and Glickman (1991) have begun similar work designed to engage teachers as peer coaches while promoting their cognitive development. In the Phillips and Glickman model, teachers are placed in the new role of peer coach. Over a seven-month period the teachers are introduced to supervisory strategies which they learn to apply with their colleagues. As Phillips and Glickman conclude, "The peer coaching program gave teachers the opportunity to come together in collegial groups, assume more complex roles, reflect together in their work, and take an important step toward lasting professional growth" (Phillips & Glickman, 1991, p. 25). Yet another comparable teacher development program is described by Oja and Smulyan (1989). They have examined collegial supervision and action research projects as new roles for teacher leaders. Their results found that a teacher's cognitive-developmental stage perspective defines a meaning system through which the teacher interprets and acts on issues related to teaching, action research, and supervision.

FIGURE 17-1   A COLLABORATIVE PYRAMID MODEL OF CLINICAL TEACHER PREPARATION

Phase 1
- Office of School Services staff, director of Teacher Education, Teacher Education Committee, and director of Model Clinical Teaching Program review applications from school districts.
- Once districts are accepted, university commits personnel, materials, and financial resources to collaborative staff development programs with districts.
- Districts commit personnel and resources to staff development programs for educating clinical teachers, and designate two persons per district to be prepared as school-based teacher educators.
- University and district personnel together review design of plan and clarify expectations of parties.

Phase 2
- University professors begin two-semester program to prepare school-based teacher educators (see box, bottom center). Pairs of teachers from districts enroll in spring seminar and fall practicum.

Phase 3
- Pairs of school-based teacher educators enroll 12–14 teachers per district in local two-semester program to prepare clinical teachers.
- Districts demonstrate commitment in various ways—for example, offering release time for 45 contact hours.
- University professors begin year-long internship for school-based teacher educators. Model is fully implemented, and collaboration achieved, when district's teacher educators are ready independently to continue cycle of preparation and to assist on university faculty as clinical instructors.

Phase 4
- School-based teacher educators are invited back to university to serve as clinical instructors in methods courses for 2–3 years. They are based in academic departments.
- Clinical instructors also assume responsibility for supervising cohorts of student teachers in their districts.
- Office of School Services staff, director of Teacher Education, and director of Model Clinical Teaching Program coordinate implementation of phase 4.
- When clinical instructors return to districts, they assume new instructional leadership roles and continue to serve as school-university teacher education liaisons.

Course Work for Preparation of School-Based Teacher Educators and Clinical Teachers
Seminar: Introduction to Developmental Instructional Supervision (3–5 credits)
Participants (a) learn adult development theory and apply it by planning strategies to match assistance to conceptual level of beginning teacher, student teacher, or colleague; (b) use effective communication skills, clinical supervision, and coaching to assist colleague in course; and (c) develop materials and effective teaching strategies to use when working with student teacher, beginning teacher, or colleague as supportive, knowledgeable, and willing clinical teacher.

Practicum (3–5 credits)
Participants acquire and practice skills in (a) building and maintaining supportive helping relationships; (b) identifying conceptual level and organizing working relationships with appropriate structure; (c) using cycles of clinical supervision (preplanning, observation, and post-observation conference); (d) serving as resource; (e) using constructive feedback and confrontation; (f) evaluating themselves as clinical teachers; (g) maintaining record of strategies; and (h) encouraging teachers to reflect on their practice.

Additional Course Work for School-Based Teacher Educators
Internship (5 credits)
Participants implement the seminar and the practicum with prospective clinical teachers while refining their own skills in (a) building and maintaining supportive helping relationships; (b) applying developmental theory and research to course instruction; (c) critiquing candidates' use of developmental instructional supervision; (d) encouraging colleagues to reflect on their practice; (e) serving as a peer coach; and (f) evaluating themselves as teacher educators.

TECHNOLOGY AND TEACHER DEVELOPMENT

The meteoric rise of technology has outpaced educators' ability to keep up. This is certainly the case for scholars and teachers involved in professional development enterprises. However, we believe that technology can become a compelling tool in the service of teacher development, if it is engaged wisely as a human-centered information technology.

The kinds of assistance, supervision, and coaching described in this book require a human-centered approach characterized by new professional roles, individualized support and challenge, ongoing reflection, and "progressively collaborative teaching" (Tomlinson, 1996). As our use of technology increases, we must not become complacent and allow a computerized response to suffice when what a teacher or student needs is individualized attention. Our goal, therefore, should be for technology to be used in ways that allow us to be more human-centered. Thus, our goal should be to use new technologies to improve our connectedness, rather than to further societal fragmentation. Many questions, however, must be answered.

Can information technologies build better "vertical connections" across different-experience groups of teachers (preservice, induction, experienced)? Can better "horizontal connections" be made across groups of teachers and educators in different roles and ethnicities? How can information technologies facilitate novice teacher understanding of student learning and development? How can information technologies enhance supervisor skills in communication, coaching, and developmental assistance strategies?

Naturally we see in our communities frightening examples of the growing separation of people based on race, gender, age, and wealth. Some scholars suggest that television and other telecommunications technologies may accelerate this trend of isolation and fragmentation (Postman, 1992). The role of the teacher leader or supervisor is to ascertain whether new technologies are "value added" due to their potential to dignify teachers and students and to promote connectedness rather than fragmentation. In a phrase, to be human-centered.

At their heart, various forms of supervision, coaching, and mentoring promote excellence in teaching/learning—passing along to persons and future generations some of the things we have managed to understand. Coaching and mentoring are connected life-enhancing activities. Thus, we need to promote growth-supporting educational communities through horizontal and vertical integration of information technologies. Two examples of such integration follow.

Dr. Bill Blanton, a faculty member at Appalachian State University, in collaboration with colleagues, has developed a course for prospective teachers during their sophomore year. The course requires the sophomore students to visit an after-school enrichment program for elementary school students. The centerpiece of the elementary school students' experience is computer programs that encourage student problem solving. Dr. Blanton's innovation is to have the prospective teachers carefully observe the students as they work at the computers, collecting data on how the kids resolve problems and master learning concepts. In fact, the sophomore students are told they may not interrupt students while they are learning, but they may answer questions the students have. The enrichment class is diverse in student makeup, and the sophomore students engage in an extraordinary learning experience in which the focus is on inquiry into how students are motivated and how they learn. Called the "Fifth Dimension," the program has demonstrated that students' achievement scores go up, while the sophomore students have an opportunity to link theory with practice as they "connect" with students in the act of learning via information technologies. This is an example of vertical connecting, by bridging age groups.

Our second example involves a beginning teacher and a clinical mentor teacher. The mentor and the beginning teacher had been involved in sustained coaching and supervision during the fall semester. One attribute of their relationship was active journal dialoguing. The beginning teacher was not new to education, but had returned after an extended absence to raise her children. In the third month of the school year, the beginning teacher, who we will call Janice, was experiencing many demands and pressures to excel in an innovative magnet program. Unfortunately, the stress of the teaching responsibilities had begun to take its toll and the teacher became ill, needing to be absent from school on a more frequent basis. During this time the beginning teacher chose to maintain an ongoing dialogue with her clinical mentor via the Internet. The dialogue provided an opportunity to explore some questions Janice had about the learning and developmental needs of three of her students.

In the example above we see an information technology that connects rather than fragments. We know of other examples in which supervisors and student teachers, separated by long distances, have interacted via e-mail, or instances in which distance learning technologies allowed isolated rural teaching communities to have access to state-of-the-art professional development experiences. However, we conclude our discussion by encouraging those involved in professional development to weigh the merits of a proposed technology based on whether new technologies are "value added" due to their potential to dignify teachers and students and to promote connectedness rather than fragmentation.

 ## TEACHER DEVELOPMENT AND GROUPS

Instructional problems and/or personal concerns can be ameliorated through groups. Any group of novice teachers and experienced teachers who are committed to collegiality, learning, and growth can benefit from group interaction. In fact, we describe support groups for beginning teachers as a viable and researched strategy for reducing the stress and isolation that is endemic to the teaching profession. Such groups are facilitated by someone with excellent active listening skills, and the groups normally meet in a setting free of evaluation. Confidentiality is a norm and group meetings conclude with each member identifying a main learning from the session. Naturally there are other types of support groups or group supervision arrangements that can promote learning and development.

For example, some undergraduate teacher education programs identify student cohorts that move through their education program as a group. Cohorts range from four to ten students in size. Typically, this cohort is placed in a common school where they coach each other, prepare lessons and units as a team, and are supervised by clusters of cooperating teachers and a university supervisor. During group meetings with the supervisor, videotapes of student teacher instruction might be reviewed and discussed, with the student teacher leading the discussion. Thus the supervisor or clinical mentor systematically structures the small group of peers so that no group member dominates, and all group members participate in the discussion or inquiry. Preliminary research has shown that such approaches to supervision and coaching can promote student teacher learning (Bassett, 1974; Buttery, 1988; Dowling, 1976).

In general, the positive features of small groups as a part of the supervisory or coaching process include:

- Opportunities for peers to observe each other and gain new ideas.
- Supportive and confidential settings for discussing instructional problems.
- Learning to phrase supportive yet objective comments to peers.
- Emphasis on group inquiry.
- Assistance in identifying and developing personal strengths and areas needing further refinement.
- Valuing of group problem solving.

In schools, supervisors are confronted with the problem of promoting learning and development with minimal amounts of time. Group supervision offers one strategy for promoting learning.

 SUMMARY

As we look at the current state of supervision as a field, and the larger teacher development enterprise, we are heartened by the emerging consensus of the teacher as an adult learner. The theoretical work, while incomplete, is attempting to resolve the Goldilocks problem. The age, stage and sequence, and phase theories reviewed in this text provide important insights about the process of adult development. Further, a growing body of evidence confirms that adults at higher stages of conceptual, ego, and moral development perform more adequately in complex human endeavors.

CONTEMPORARY ISSUES

RESTRUCTURING FROM WITHIN A RESTRUCTURED ROLE

In May, 1991 Magdalene Lampert wrote a provocative article for the *Phi Delta Kappan* entitled, "Looking at Restructuring from Within a Restructured Role." The issues of ambiguity and role conflict that she has faced also have been felt by clinical professors and clinical instructors working within our own teacher education program. By way of definition, a clinical professor has a terminal degree and jointly works between a university and a school system. A clinical instructor also works jointly between the university and schools. Such "boundary-blurring" roles, borrowing Lampert's coinage, have been advocated by school reformers, and represent a relatively complex new role for teachers and teacher educators. We have found such roles to foster better communication, and in many cases, to promote highly effective teacher education and supervision. However, such roles require unique kinds of support that are often absent.

Like Lampert, the first author's previous role was that of clinical associate professor. I was expected to teach, to conduct research and scholarship, and to do service, which in my case, included extensive work with a mentoring and teacher induction program in a large urban/suburban school system. I taught graduate courses in supervision. Research, however, meant blending my applied responsibilities with that of qualitative action researcher. The possibilities for "very thick" description were enormous. Yet the responsibilities of developing and implementing a mentoring program with all of its stops and starts, limited the possibilities. My colleagues who are clinical instructors feel less of the pressure to do research, yet struggle, as I did, with the different roles.

For example, each of us has felt that the norms of evaluation inadequately represent our contributions. Like Lampert, we fall outside of the traditional roles of either the theoretical/empirical culture of the university, or the applied culture of the school and classroom. Thus, we end up participating in both evaluation systems. Annual faculty reports are completed for the university, and separate evaluations are conducted by the schools. All of the tensions we face in these restructured roles have forced the institutions to begin to identify new ways to support such efforts, yet work is slow, moving more at the speed of a glacier than that of the incoming tide. We suspect that substantial support systems will need to be embedded into universities and schools if there is to be a chance of expanding new roles in teaching and teacher education that span both cultures.

Source: Lampert, M. (1991, May). Looking at restructuring from within a restructured role. *Phi Delta Kappan*, 670–674.

A second major area of positive change for both supervision and teacher development is toward the creation of theoretically linked applied programs. Although the linkage varies between knowing "about" and knowing "how to," there are emerging supervision programs and teacher development efforts that are grappling with these issues in a substantive manner across the career spectrum. The Lewin dictum that there is "nothing quite as practical as good theory," is dovetailing with Hunt's entreaty "that there is nothing quite as theoretical as good practice."

A third positive trend in supervision is the growing recognition that supervision must match and mismatch supervisory styles to the needs of the adult learner. Matching requires differentiating structure, reflection, and experiences according to the needs of the adult learner. Mismatching requires "stretching" the learner, providing for the "next zone of learning and development."

This said, there are enormous challenges to building developmental supervision and professional development programs, both from theoretical and contextual standpoints. Field-based interactive teacher education and supervision is about as difficult a problem to solve as exists (Murray, 1996). How to create the necessary balance between affective support and relaxed reflection with methods for effective challenge is at the heart of this dilemma. Too much support is as ineffective as too much challenge.

Teachers, teacher education, staff development, and supervision programs face four particularly urgent demands: cultural diversity, a predicted huge increase in children with special needs (Reynolds, 1989), the "sink or swim" socialization of new teachers, and the rise of a plethora of new information technologies. With regard to the first two, these factors will increase the range of individual differences in the classrooms. At the same time, there are greater expectations for teachers to perform a broader range of professional skills to meet these needs. Clearly such conditions and expectations will place extraordinary demands on the profession. With regard to the "sink or swim" phenomenon, teachers, unlike doctors, architects, and many other professionals are often thrown into their field with inadequate preparation, supervision, and support. Darling-Hammond (1994) calls for clinical teachers and school-based teacher educators in a professional development school environment to fill the void.

Finally, the rise of new technologies requires human-centered choices that promote connectedness rather than further societal fragmentation. The hope is that these demands will not outrun our ability to build the requisite programs. Without more collaboration in research and program efforts, progress will be very slow. Granted, collaboration is time-consuming, but the alternative is continued isolation and separation of efforts. We believe that supervision and teacher education are too important to be left either to the university or to the school. There is an African proverb that states, "It takes a whole village to teach a child." We submit that it takes the whole community (schools, communities, and university) to develop teachers. Anything less will fail.

REFERENCES

Bassett, W. J. (1974). A study of the teaching clinic form of supervision and its effects on questioning as a teaching skill. *Dissertation Abstracts International, 35*, 5979A–5980A. (University Microfilms No. 75-5542.)

Bolin, F. S., & Falk, J. M. (Eds.) (1987). *Teacher renewal professional issues, personal choices.* New York: Teachers College Press.

Book, C. (1996). Professional development schools. In J. Sikula (Ed.), *Second handbook of research on teacher education* (pp. 194–212). New York: Macmillan.

Borko, H., & Putnam, R. (1995). Expanding a teacher's knowledge base: A cognitive psychological perspective on professional development. In T. R. Guskey & M. Huberman (Eds.), *Professional development in education: New paradigms and practices.* New York: Teachers College Press.

Buttery, T. (1988). Group clinical supervision as a feedback process. *Journal of Research and Development in Education, 21*(4), 5–12.

Calhoun, E. F. (1992, April). *A status report on action research in the League of Professional Schools.* Paper presented at the annual meeting of the American Educational Research Association, San Francisco.

Carnegie Forum on Education and the Economy. (1986). *A nation prepared: Teachers for the 21st century.* New York: Author.

Cogan, M. (1972). *Clinical supervision.* Boston: Houghton Mifflin.

Corrigan, D., & Udas, K. (1996). Creating collaborative, child- and family-centered education, health, and human service systems. In J. Sikula (Ed.), *Second handbook of research on teacher education* (pp. 869–892). New York: Macmillan.

Darling-Hammond, L. (Ed.) (1994). *Professional development schools: Schools for developing a profession.* New York: Teachers College Press.

De Angelis Peace, S. (1992). *A study of school counselor induction: A cognitive-developmental mentor supervisor training program.* Unpublished doctoral dissertation. Raleigh, NC: North Carolina State University.

Dowling, S. S. (1976). A comparison to determine the effects of two supervisor styles, conventional and teaching clinic in the training of speech pathologists. *Dissertation Abstracts International, 37*, 3889B. (University Microfilms No. 77-1882.)

Edelfelt, R. (1996). *Accomplishments in teacher education in North Carolina schools.* Chapel Hill, NC: The University of North Carolina.

Fullan, M. (1991). *The new meaning of educational change.* New York: Teachers College Press.

Fullan, M. (1995). The limits and the potential of professional development. In T. R. Guskey & M. Huberman (Eds.), *Professional development in education: New paradigms and practices.* New York: Teachers College Press.

Goodlad, J. (1993). School-university partnerships and partner schools. In P. G. Altback, H. G. Petrie, M. J. Shujaa, & L. Weis (Eds.), *Educational policy: Vol. 7, No. 1: Professional development schools* (pp. 24–39). Newbury Park, CA: Corwin Press.

Griffin, G. (1986). Clinical teacher education. In J. Hoffman & S. Edwards (Eds.), *Reality and reform in clinical teacher education* (pp. 1–24). New York: Random House.

Griffin, G. (1987). Clinical teacher education. *Journal of Curriculum and Supervision, 2*(3), 248–274.

Holmes Group. (1986). *Tomorrow's teachers: A report of the Holmes Group.* East Lansing, MI: Author.

Holmes Group. (1990). *Tomorrow's schools.* East Lansing, MI: Author.

Howey, K., & Zimpher, N. (1996). Patterns in prospective teachers: Guides for designing preservice programs. In F. Murray (Ed.), *The teacher educator's handbook* (pp. 465–505). San Francisco: Jossey-Bass.

Huling-Austin, L. (1990). Teacher induction programs and internships. In R. Houston (Ed.), *Handbook of research on teacher education* (pp. 535–548). New York: Macmillan.

Katz, L., & Raths, J. (1985). A framework for research on teacher education programs. *Journal of Teacher Education, 36*, 9–15.

Leavitt, H. B. (Ed.), (1992). *Issues and problems in teacher education: An international handbook.* New York: Greenwood Press.

Mann, A. (1992). *A quantitative and qualitative evaluation of a peer tutoring-training course: A cognitive-developmental model.* Unpublished doctoral dissertation. Raleigh, NC: North Carolina State University.

Mosher, R., & Purpel, D. (1972). *Supervision: The reluctant profession.* New York: Houghton Mifflin.

Murray, F. (1996). Beyond natural teaching: The case for professional education. In F. Murray (Ed.), *The teacher educator's handbook* (pp. 3–13). San Francisco: Jossey-Bass.

National Commission on Teaching and America's Future (1996). *What matters most: Teaching for America's future.* New York: National Commission on Teaching and America's Future.

Oja, S. N., & Reiman, A. J. (1997). Describing and promoting supervision for teacher development across the career span. In J. Firth & E. Pajak (Eds.), *Handbook of research on school supervision.* New York: Macmillan.

Oja, S. N., & Smulyan, L. (1989). *Collaborative action research: A developmental approach.* London: Falmer.

Phillips, M., & Glickman, C. (1991). Peer coaching: Developmental approach to enhancing teacher thinking. *Journal of Staff Development, 12*(2), 20–25.

Postman, N. (1992). *Technology.* New York: Knopf.

Reiman, A., Spooner, M., Alley, C., Beacham, B., Edelfelt, R., Knowlton, T., & Schmidt, P. (1995). Teacher as teacher educator: Model Clinical Teaching Network Report. *North Carolina Journal of Teacher Education, 7*(2), 50–73.

Reiman, A. J., & Thies-Sprinthall, L. (1993). Promoting the development of mentor teachers: Theory and research programs using guided reflection. *Journal of Research and Development, 26*(3), 179–185.

Resnick, L. (1985). Cognition and instruction: Recent theories of human competence. In B. L. Hammonds (Ed.), *Master lecture series Vol. 4: Psychology and learning* (pp. 123–186). Washington, DC: American Psychological Association.

Resnick, L. (1987). Constructing knowledge in school. In L. S. Liben (Ed.), *Development and learning: Conflict or congruence?* (pp. 19–50). Hillsdale, NJ: Erlbaum.

Reynolds, M. (1989). *Knowledge base for the beginning teachers.* Oxford, England: Pergamon.

Sagor, R. (1993). *How to conduct collaborative action research.* Alexandria, VA: Association for Supervision and Curriculum Development.

Schiro, M. (1992). Educators' perceptions of the changes in their curricula belief systems. *Journal of Curriculum and Supervision, 7*(2), 250–287.

Sergiovanni, T., & Starratt, R. (1993). *Supervision: A redefinition.* New York: McGraw Hill.

Sprinthall, N. A., Reiman, A. J., & Thies-Sprinthall, L. (1993). Roletaking and reflection: Promoting the conceptual and moral development of teachers. *Learning and Individual Differences, 5*(4), 283-300.

Sprinthall, N., Reiman, A., & Thies-Sprinthall, L. (1996). Teacher professional development. In J. Sikula (Ed.), *Second handbook of research on teacher education* (pp. 666–703). New York: Macmillan.

Thies-Sprinthall, L. (1984). Promoting the developmental growth of supervising teachers: Theory, research programs, and implications. *Journal of Teacher Education*, *35*(3), 53–60.

Thies-Sprinthall, L., & Sprinthall, N. A. (1987). Experienced teachers: Agents for revitalization and renewal as mentors and teacher educators. *Journal of Education*, *169*(1), 65–79.

Tomlinson, P. (1996). *Understanding mentoring*. Buckingham, England: Open University Press.

Walling, D. R. (1994). *Teachers as leaders: Perspectives on the professional development of teachers*. Bloomington, IN: Phi Delta Kappa Educational Foundation.

Watson, B. (1995). *Early field experiences in teacher education: A developmental model*. Unpublished doctoral dissertation. Raleigh, NC: North Carolina State University.

Weil, M., & Joyce, B. (1978). *Social models of teaching: Expanding your teaching repertoire*. Englewood Cliffs, NJ: Prentice-Hall.

Wise, A., & Darling-Hammond, L. (1987). *Licensing teachers: Design for a teaching profession*. Santa Monica, CA: The RAND Corporation.

Zimpher, N. (1990). Creating professional development school sites. *Theory into Practice*, *29*(1), 42–49.

Zimpher, N., & Howey, K. (1987). Adapting supervisory practice to different orientations of teaching competence. *Journal of Curriculum and Supervision*, *2*(1), 101–127.

PHOTO C·R·E·D·I·T·S

CHAPTER 2
Morris Cogan: Permission of University of Pittsburgh Archives

CHAPTER 4
John Dewey: Permission of University of Chicago News Office

Norman Sprinthall: Permission of Norman Sprinthall

CHAPTER 5
Frances Fuller: Permission of The University of Texas at Austin, Office of Public
    Affairs

CHAPTER 8
James Banks: Permission of University of Washington Office of News and
    Information

CHAPTER 10
Elliot Eisner: Permission of News and Publication Service, Stanford University

Ned Flanders: Permission of Ned Flanders

CHAPTER 12
Beverly Showers: Permission of Beverly Showers

CHAPTER 15
John Goodlad: Permission of Information Services, University of Washington

CHAPTER 17
Linda Darling-Hammond: Permission of Teachers College, Columbia University

Nancy Zimpher: Permission of University Communications, The Ohio State
    University

I·N·D·E·X